S0-AYY-571

THE EASTERN EUROPE COLLECTION

FRENCH INFLUENCE AND THE RISE OF ROUMANIAN NATIONALISM

John C. Campbell

ARNO PRESS & THE NEW YORK TIMES

New York - 1971

Reprint Edition 1971 by Arno Press Inc.

Reprinted by Permission of John C. Campbell

Reprinted from a copy in
The Harvard University Library

LC# 73-135839

ISBN 0-405-02781-8

The Eastern Europe Collection

ISBN for complete set: 0-405-02730-3

Manufactured in the United States of America

FRENCH INFLUENCE AND THE RISE OF ROUMANIAN NATIONALISM

THE GENERATION OF 1848

1830-1857

by

John C. Campbell

A thesis submitted in partial fulfillment of the requirements for the degree of Doctor of Philosophy in the Department of History of Harvard University

April 1, 1940

CONTENTS

FOREWORD

The generation of 1848, to which the Roumanians refer by the single word "Pasoptistii,"[1] had in its ranks a group of men who may justly be called the founders of the modern Roumanian national state. Not all of them were of superior talent; only two can be said to have made a success of statesmanship when, after the many years of struggle, they finally assumed the task of guiding the fortunes of the state which they had created. Yet they all, despite certain differences of outlook, were animated by the same national ideal, and by their activities were able to make that ideal, for better or for worse, the dominating element in the political and cultural life of the Roumanian people. The full attainment of national unity after the World War was in fact the final stanza of a national epic in which they were the prophets and the early heroes.

In this composite biography of over a score of men I have tried to hold to two guiding threads: first, the influence of the West, and particularly of France, in the life and thought of these leaders, as manifested in their education both at home and in Paris, and also in their political activities, as revolutionaries *à la francaise* in 1848, and as exiles in Paris and elsewhere after the failure of their revolution; secondly, the growth of a doctrine of nationalism,

---

1. Forty-eight = *patruzeci si opt* = *pasopt*. Forty-eighter = *pasoptist*; plural, *pasoptisti*; articulated plural, *pasoptistii*.

based partly on theories borrowed from the West, partly on conditions existing in the Roumanian provinces at that time. I conclude with the return of the Pasoptisti to their country in the late 1850's. By that time the national ideal had become crystallized, and it had won a great political victory from which the later victories followed in a natural sequence; and after that time the contact with the West was less direct and much less important.

Because of the sprawling nature of the subject, some of the chapters are given rather summary treatment.

CHAPTER I

WESTERN INFLUENCE AND THE ORIGINS OF ROUMANIAN NATIONALISM

1. Nationalism in Southeastern Europe

Southeastern Europe has ever been the stage for the conflict of civilizations, the channel for the ebb and flow of cultures from East to West and West to East. The Asiatic hordes which swept into Europe in the Middle Ages could not but leave their mark on the Balkan Peninsula, which most of them either traversed or made their permanent home. Likewise that civilization which grew up in the West was destined to push its way eastward, a movement less spectacular but with more permanent effects, for it has been a conquest that is more cultural and economic than military. The history of the middle ground in this conflict, the Balkan Peninsula, has in the last two centuries been a history of a gradual absorption into the political, economic, and cultural framework of the western world.

The rule of the Ottoman Turks in Southeastern Europe represented, until well into the 19th century, the continuation, and perhaps the ultimate phase, of the westward movement of the nomadic peoples of Asia. The Turks had done what none of their predecessors had been able to do, namely establish a lasting system of political domination which could stand the test of centuries. However, the decline of the Ottoman governing system and the simultaneous impact of the West, represented both by the aggressive policies of the great powers of Europe and by the vigorous nationalism of the awakened Balkan peoples, spelled doom for the empire, none the less inevitable in being prolonged far beyond expectations.

For Europe that prolonged death agony involved a struggle among the great powers for trade, for prestige, for world power. For the Balkan peoples it represented revolutionary changes in their life; changes, at first cultural and only afterwards political, which ultimately gave them an occidental culture and a political existence as national states on the western model. Because of its proximity to Asia and because of the remarkable endurance of the Ottoman state, it was long before the Balkan Peninsula fully identified itself with the Occident. That development, however, came rapidly with the growth of nationalism.

Nationalism, as we understand the term today, implies the conscious participation of the masses of a nation in the national life, implies also the loyalty of the masses to the national state as above all other loyalties. From this standpoint it is difficult, especially in the case of Roumania, to concede the existence of nationalism in eastern Europe in the 19th century. Nevertheless, it must be admitted that the whole history of the Roumanian people in that period can be explained only by giving full consideration to the nationalistic feeling which inspired almost the entire articulate portion of the population, albeit a small portion. It is the history of the spread of that doctrine on an ever widening base, coincident with the fairly rapid growth of a native middle class. The line of development has been the same for all the nations of central and eastern Europe: what is at first a cultural and literary movement soon finds itself in possession of a political program with complete national unification as the final goal. The difficulty lies in trying to interpret that development, to discover why and out of what circumstances it arose and why it proceeded in that particular direction.

It is characteristic of the doctrine of nationalism, resting as it does on the existence, or legend, of a "folk spirit" or "national soul," that its spokesmen profess to seek their inspiration in the national traditions and minimize, if they do not altogether deny, the importance of the extensive borrowing process which has taken place everywhere that nationalism has arisen, except in France and England, the only two instances where it may safely be said to have stemmed directly from combinations of particular constitutional and social conditions. In the rest of Europe, and in the rest of the world, the tendency has been for the theory to be adopted by certain groups--notably the intelligentsia and the bourgeoisie, which, by their possession of various instruments of political and social control, their monopoly of education and of the instruments of propaganda, are able to mold opinion and give a direction to political and cultural activity--and then to be gradually accepted by all classes of the population. Such a process could not take place without the presence of potent factors, economic and sentimental, which could be and have been harnessed to the chariot of nationalism. In southeastern Europe the economic factor was of relatively minor importance, for there nationalism preceded industrialism, indeed the measure of industrialization which has taken place is a result, rather than a cause, of political nationalism. The sentimental factor, on the other hand, was of crucial importance. It resulted from the fact that, in contrast to the West, where smaller ethnic and linguistic groups tended to become absorbed by larger units, to form states resting on a common language and eventually on a common civilization, the various racial and language groups in eastern Europe had preserved their identity in spite of centuries of close contact with each other, and the large political units, particularly the Ottoman Empire, had given constitutional recognition to this state of affairs and made no attempt at cultural assimilation of their subject peoples.[1] Social and religious differences, as in Transylvania, sometimes deepened the cleavage between these groups, giving added reinforcement to national antagonisms. This

---

1. See the interesting discussion of this question in C. A. Macartney, National States and National Minorities, (London, 1934), pp. 50-91.

pattern afforded the new nationalists of the 19th century an almost perfect field of operations.

Looking back from the vantage point of one hundred years' subsequent history, we can say without hesitation that many of the forms and concepts adopted from the West never struck deep root. The political and constitutional forms arrived at in England and France after centuries of evolution and revolution could not, after hasty transplanting, flourish on Balkan soil. Quite the contrary was true of the idea of the political and cultural freedom of nations from foreign domination, considered to be but a logical consequence of the principles of political liberalism and popular sovereignty; this was not transplanted but grafted on to the already sturdy tree of national consciousness. Popular sovereignty and the freedom of the individual fell by the wayside long ago in eastern Europe, if indeed it can be said that they were ever seriously tried. Nationalism, on the other hand, became a dynamic and revolutionary force which was destined to wreck the empires whose sovereigns had for so many centuries ruled over this mosaic of peoples. The latent strength of the Balkan nations had always existed, even when it lay dormant and obscured by religious issues and by the tremendous force represented by the Ottoman Empire as a unity. Yet to galvanize that strength into action new forces were necessary. Those forces were the economic changes which affected the whole of Europe, and for the East the all important catalyst was the invigorating breath of western influence.

The vague term "western influence" represents roughly two general currents, that of the 18th century Enlightenment and the French Revolution on the one hand, that of the Romantic Movement on the other. These were not always very congenial bedfellows in the West, but in the simplified form in which they penetrated to the peoples of the Habsburg Empire and European Turkey they combined to create an extraordinarily effective nationalist doctrine. The part played by the influence of the French Revolution has often been exaggerated. It is true that the ideology which was the rationalization of the economic and political program of the French bourgeoisie, namely that the world belongs not to tryannical rulers but to their oppressed peoples, was of enormous potentiality. But its adaptation to local conditions in many cases went no further than a borrowing of revolutionary phraseology, as in the revolt of the Serbs and in the peasant rising led by Tudor Vladimirescu in Oltenia in 1821. To the Balkan peasant, liberty, equality, fraternity if he heard about them at all, meant only one thing: the removal of the immediate oppressor, be he Turkish beg, Phanariot tax-gatherer, Greek priest, or native boyar. Later on in the 19th century, with the growth of a class of Balkan intellectuals, the influence of western liberalism was greater, but even then it suffered inevitable distortions in the process of transportation.

As for the Romantic Movement, it undoubtedly gave a great impetus to the new consciousness of nationality, to the new cult of the national past, to the philological, historical, and literary efforts which laid the foundation of national cultures. The shining example is the unquestioned influence of Herder and the German Romantics upon the awakening of the Slavs. This trend might have represented a repudiation of the Occident, an attempt to draw strength from the native soil rather than from imitation of a foreign civilization, but there was never any doubt that those peoples were becoming more and more a part of that "Europe" to which, by their own admission, they did not previously belong.

2. The Beginnings of French Influence in the Principalities

Because France was the unquestioned fountain-head of intellectual endeavor in the 18th century, the penetration of European ideas into areas which had formerly been wholly in the sphere of Asiatic or Byzantine civilization meant the penetration of French ideas. At Constantinople and throughout the Levant, where direct diplomatic and commercial contacts with France existed, there was a receptivity to the ideas of the Enlightenment extending even to government circles. Westernism found adherents among the Greeks, particularly the prosperous merchants, who had commercial connections with the trading bourgeoisie of France and England, and the Phanariots, many of whom became acquainted with the Occident through their education or their position as administrators and diplomats in the Ottoman Empire. The areas of southeastern Europe which tended to fall within the cultural radius of Vienna were subject to the same influences, for the Austrian court under Maria Theresa and Joseph II lived in an intellectual atmosphere which was largely French.

There were several factors which made the Roumanians more receptive than the nations south of the Danube to the influence of French culture. Their geographical position opened channels to the outside world and exposed them to a contact with intellectual currents such as that of the Renaissance. Poland, and to a less extent Hungary and Transylvania were the countries through which these currents penetrated to Bucharest and to Jassy in the 16th and 17th centuries.[2] Geographically on the outskirts of the Ottoman Empire, the political status of the Roumanian Principalities was correspondingly different from that of Serbia, Bulgaria, or Greece, which were under the direct rule of the Turks. The Principalities, although conquered by Ottoman armies, were never made an integral part of the empire, the conduct of administration being left in the hands of native princes, who were later replaced by Phanariot Greeks sent from

---

2. Ramiro Ortiz, _Per la Storia della Cultura Italiana in Rumania_, (Bucharest, 1916), pp. 1-18; N. Iorga, "La Pénétration des Idées de l'Occident dans le Sud-Est de l'Europe," (_Revue Historique du Sud-Est Européen_, I, 1924, pp. 1-36, 102-38, 250-96), pp. 2-4.

Constantinople. Thus although they had to supply money and grain in large quantities to the Ottoman Government, these provinces never really felt the weight of Turkish rule as did those on the other side of the Danube. The Turks did not settle in the Principalities as landowners, nor was there religious apostasy by any considerable portion of the population. This variety of factors explains why the Roumanians, preserving an aristocracy of their own, were able to maintain an intellectual life, at first Byzantine and largely religious but later tending to become occidental and secular, which set them apart from the Serbs and the Bulgarians. The Greeks, of course, were in a position in many ways more favorable for the reception of French influence, but they never succumbed to it to the same extent as did the Roumanians. This may be partially attributed to the "Latin" character of the Roumanian language and the tendency to look on France and Italy as sister-nations whose cultures were eminently worthy of imitation.

The 18th century in the Principalities, the period of Phanariot rule, has a very unsavory reputation as a time of unparalleled corruption, intellectual stagnation, and of the ruthless exploitation of a naturally rich land by a swarm of foreign and native locusts.[3] Professor Iorga has spent many

---

3. Pompiliu Eliade, De l'influence française sur l'esprit public en Roumanie, (Paris, 1898); following the line laid down by Marc Zallony, Essai sur les Fanariotes, (Marseille, 1824); N. Bălcescu, "Românii și Fanarioții," (Magazin Istoric pentru Dacia, vol. I, 1845); and G. Ionnescu-Gion, Din Istoria Fanarioților, (Bucharest, 1891).

years challenging that interpretation, and although he may be stretching a point when he brings the Phanariot princes into the circle of the enlightened despots, he has succeeded in giving them a more respectable place in Roumanian history.[4] Some of them were, indeed, instrumental in bringing a new reforming spirit to the Principalities. Constantin Mavrocordato, the emancipator of the serfs, and Alexander Ypsilanti were well aware of the theories prevalent in other parts of Europe and showed a desire to import a bit of occidental illumination to light up the darkness of their surroundings.[5] The theory that they represented an alien Greek civilization, which tended to suppress the native Roumanian, is untenable.

---

4. N. Iorga, Cultura română supt Fanarioţi, (Bucharest, 1898); idem., "Au fost Moldova şi Ţara-Românească provincii supuse Fanarioţilor?," (Analele Academiei Române, Memoriile Secţiunii Istorice, hereafter cited as Ac. Rom., Mem Sect. Ist., Ser. III, vol. 18, 1937, pp. 347-56); idem., La Place des Roumains dans l'histoire universelle, vol. II, Epoque Moderne, (Bucharest, 1935), pp. 195-7; idem., Istoria Românilor, vol. VII, (Bucharest, 1938). Cf. Ioan Lupaş, Istoria Unirii Românilor, (Bucharest, 1937), pp. 193-7.

5. "Constitution faite par S. A. le prince Constantin Maurocordato, prince des deux Valachies et de Moldavie," (Mercure de France, July, 1742, pp. 1506-25), probably inserted by the abbé Desfontaines, an admirer of Mavrovordato; I. Minea, "Opere de reforme a lui Constantin Mavrocordato," (Cercetări Istorice, Jassy, 1927, Nos. 2, 3); Iorga, La Place des Roumains dans l'histoire universelle, vol. III, Epoque Contemporaine, (Bucharest, 1936), pp. 1-10; idem., "Le despotisme eclairé dans les pays roumains au XVIIIe. siècle," (Bulletin of the International Committee of Historical Sciences, IX, Part I, No. 34, March 1937, pp. 101-15); idem., Istoria Românilor, vol. VII, pp. 129-42, 321-48. Cf. Nino Cortese, "La Valachia durante il principato di Alessandro Ypsilanti," (Europa Orientale, Rome, II, Mar. 192[illegible] pp. 159-179).

They were in fact representatives of an international civilization, men of cosmopolitan outlook and servants of a non-national empire. They actually encouraged the official use of the Roumanian tongue and contributed not a little to the preparation of the ground for the national renascence.

It is undeniable that the second half of the 18th century saw the appearance of a strong current of French influence in the Principalities. The uncertainty lies in the determination of the methods by which it made it way into countries so distant from France. Diplomatic relations had not existed between France and the Principalities before the French Revolution, but since the Ottoman Empire and Poland represented important links in the French security system, Paris could hardly neglect the diplomatic non-man's land between them, where the princes were wont to pursue policies not wholly in keeping with their status as Ottoman functionaries.[6] French influence made itself felt not so much through representatives of official France as through certain merchants and adventurers, and through the fortuitous fact that in the

---

6. For the role of the Principalities in French policy in the 18th century, see V. A. Urechia, Relaţiunile Franţei cu România, (Bucharest, 1884); I. C. Filitti, Le rôle diplomatique des Fanariotes, (Paris, 1901); A. A. C. Sturdza, La diplomatie européenne et les pays roumains au XVIIIe. siècle, (Paris, 1913); V. Mihordea, "Contribution aux relations franco-roumaines au XVIIIe. siècle," (Mélanges offerts à M. Nicolas Iorga par ses amis de France, (Paris, 1933), pp. 895-924; idem., Politica orientală franceză şi Ţările române în secolul al XVIII-lea, (Bucharest, 1937).

latter half of the century the accepted language of diplomacy in the Near East, as elsewhere, was French. Whether or not they were fluent in it themselves, and they generally were, the Phanariot princes felt the need of surrounding themselves with French secretaries, and the use of French in court circles became common. Frenchmen were engaged by the princes as tutors for their sons, and soon this example was being followed by the boyars.[7] The princes were also instrumental in opening the gates to French literature. Constantin Mavrocordato built up a large library containing many works in French. Members of the high clergy and aristocracy began to read French authors, the Bishop of Râmnic going so far as to order the Encyclopédie for his private library; Voltaire

---

7. Partial lists of these secretaries and tutors are given by Frédéric Damé, Histoire de la Roumanie contemporaine, (Paris, 1900), p. 51, and by P. Eliade, De l'influence française, pp. 146-64. The most notable were J. L. Carra (later an active Jacobin who lost his head in 1794), Comte d'Hauterive, and I. S. Raicevich, a Ragusan. These three wrote books on the Principalities, which, though of dubious value as sources for the period, did make a start in the matter of presenting the Roumanians to the western public. (Carra, Histoire de la Moldavie et de la Valachie, avec une dissertation sur l'état actuel de ces provinces, Jassy, 1777, and later editions at Paris, 1778, and at Neuchatel, 1781; Hauterive, Journal d'un voyage de Constantinople à Jassy dans l'hiver, and La Moldavie en 1785, of which the latest edition is that put out by the Roumanian Academy in 1902; Raicevich, Osservazioni sulla Valacchia e Moldavia, Naples, 1788, and a French translation by J. M. Lejeune, Paris, 1822. Lejeune was also a private tutor to a Phanariot prince. Comments on these works may be found in Eliade, op.cit., pp. 152-60; Iorga, Istoria Românilor prin călători, vol. II, (Bucharest, 1928), pp. 221-7, 139-43; idem., Histoire des relations entre la France et les Roumains, (Paris, 1918), pp. 88-119.

was said by one observer to be very popular, though his works were with difficulty obtainable since the Patriarchate had banned them as dangerous Catholic literature likely to lead the Orthodox astray.[8]

This penchant for the French language and literature was attributed by some observers to the influence of the Russian officers who, during the many military occupations inflicted on the Principalities, brought with them the customs of the society of St. Petersburg, which was French in tone.[9] This may well have been true for the introduction of French dances and card games, but the more solid elements of culture, books, periodicals and newspapers, came by way of Vienna. French journals, principally those published in Holland and Germany, reached Bucharest and Jassy by this route, a traffic which was encouraged by the Phanariot princes.[10]

The increasing acquaintance with the literature of the West stimulated the beginnings of a new literary effort by the Roumanians themselves. The flourishing ecclesiastical

---

8. Carra, _op.cit._, p. 196.

9. Raicevich, _op.cit._, p. 137; A. Langeron, _Journal des campagnes faites au service de la Russie_, (published in _Eudoxiu de Hurmuzaki_, _Documente privitoare la Istoria Românilor_, Supl. I, vol. 3, pp. 70-394), p. 75; P. Eliade, _op.cit._, pp. 172-92, greatly exaggerates this influence, though he admits that the Roumanians adopted only superficially what was already a superficial adoption of French civilization.

10. Iorga, _La Pénétration des Idées de l'Occident_, pp. 14-16.

culture, of which Bucharest and Jassy had been the centers in the 15th and 16th centuries,--for they had been the cultural heirs of Byzantium just as the Ottoman state was its political heir--had long since reached a condition of sterility. Now for the first time attempts were made to translate French works into Roumanian, no easy task in view of the rustic character of the latter language. These few translations, and the efforts made to create a native literature on the new standards, were not works of great literary merit, but they were significant in being the first trickles of what was to become an ever-broadening river carrying the Roumanians away from a static oriental existence into the main stream of western civilization.[11] The process of imitation represented in most cases a superficial taking over of the forms of French manners and ideas without the substance, but that is always true of the first contacts of a backward people with a higher civilization. For all these evidences of change, they were not in themselves sufficient to produce the new pattern to which Roumanian society was to

---

11. It was not the French classics which were translated, but rather the lighter romances and poetry going the rounds of Europe at that time, e.g. those of Florian and Gessner. Iorga, _A History of Anglo-Roumanian Relations_, (Bucharest, 1931), p. 68, points out that a Roumanian poet, Conachi, produced a translation, by way of the French, of Pope's _Essay on Man_. See also Iorga, _Histoire des relations entre la France et les Roumains_, pp. 136-43. The same author's _Istoria literaturei românești în secolul al XVIII-lea_, 2 vols., (Bucharest, 1901), is the fullest account of Roumanian literature in the 18th century.

conform in the next century. The real turning point came with the effects of the upheavals of the revolutionary and Napoleonic era, and with the birth of the Roumanian national movement in Transylvania.

3. The Influence of the French Revolution

The repercussions of the French Revolution, though incidental and not of great importance, are none the less of considerable interest. News of what was happening in France came to the Principalities chiefly through the merchant class whose centers of operations were Vienna, Trieste, Budapest, and the Transylvanian cities of Hermannstadt and Kronstadt. This class, in which the Greeks were a majority, but which included Roumanians and Macedonian Slavs, made positive efforts to propagate the new revolutionary ideas in the urban centers of southeastern Europe, their commercial preserve.[12] They published several newspapers in Vienna, in Greek, for that

---

12. Two Roumanians, who maintained a printing establishment at Vienna, expedited to the Principalities a series of books in French intended to enlighten the reading public as to the events in France. They included the following titles: "Histoire de la convocation et des elections aux Etats généraux," "Histoire politique de la révolution en France," "Lettres du Père Manuel," "Sur la souveraineté du peuple," "Histoire de la Belgique républicaine," and "Essai historique sur la vie de Marie-Antoinette d'Autriche," pure propaganda which must have made some impression on the "advanced thinkers" among the boyars and cafe sitters. (Hurmuzaki, Documente, vol. XIX, Part 1, pp. 815-16). There were also certain openly seditious writings, not printed but passed from hand to hand in manuscript, dealing with the tyranny of princes, the secrets of freemasonry, and other dangerous subjects.

was the lingua franca of the commercial world, and the cultural life of the whole Balkan Peninsula wore at that time a Greek aspect, even in the Principalities where the French influence was so strong.[13] The later Phanariots had founded Greek academies at Bucharest and Jassy. The Greek Philomuse Society had adherents in the Principalities, and the widespread organization of the Orthodox Church, with its Hellenic intelligentsia, served to facilitate this whole process. This explains why Rhigas, who spent much of his life in Bucharest, and the leaders of the Hetairia Philiké, envisaged as their field of operations the whole Christian Near East and not just that territory peopled solidly by Greeks.

This fermentation of ideas might have been put to some use by the various French governments desirous of extending French and revolutionary prestige in the East, had the agents sent to the Principalities been more capable. One of them reported:

> "For the small portion of the boyars who know how to reason, the French Revolution is not wholly without attraction. They like to be told about it and cannot help showing a certain approval and at least admiring its prodigious accomplishments; in time, especially if youth continues the studies

---

13. I. C. Filitti, Frământările politice şi sociale în Principatele Române de la 1821 la 1828, (Bucharest, 1932), pp. 9-18; V. A. Urechia, Istoria Românilor, vol. VII, p. 243; ibid., vol. VIII, pp. 721, 730; Iorga, La Place des Roumains dans l'histoire universelle, vol. III, pp. 14-26; Hurmuzaki, Documente, Supl. I, vol. 2, pp. 359-60; 368, 454; ibid., Supl. I, vol. 3, p. 484; N. Moschopoulos, La Presse dans la Renaissance Balkanique, (Athens, 1931), pp. 129-35.

> which it is beginning to take up, there is no doubt whatever that the French principles will eventually have here, as elsewhere, their agreeable and beneficent influence." 14

It was to be a long time before this "small portion" of the boyars was to be able to initiate political action on the basis of these principles. The new French consuls certainly did very little to promote such action. They were men who had no knowledge of the conditions of the country or of the various languages, other than French, spoken there. In spite of the benevolent attitude of the Phanariot princes, these agents accomplished little or nothing.[15]

While there were few political events in this period of Roumanian history illustrating the new spirit, two which took place in the year 1791 deserve mention. The first was in Transylvania, where the disfranchised Roumanians had had little contact with the French literature with which certain circles in the Principalities had become acquainted, but had had some experience with the enlightened despotism of Emperor

---

14. Hurmuzaki, Documente, vol. XVI, p. 520; see also ibid., vol. XIX, p. 587.

15. Iorga, La Révolution française et le Sud-Est de l'Europe, (Bucharest, 1934), pp. 15-21; A. Oteteа, "Infiinţarea consulatelor franceze în ţărilor româneşti," (Revista Istorică, Bucharest, XVIII, 1932, pp. 322 ff.; idem., "Les consuls de France et l'éveil de la nationalité roumaine," (Résumé des communications présentées au VIIe. Congrès international des Sciences historiques, Warsaw, 1933, pp. 271-2; D. J. Ghika, La France et les Principautés Danubiennes de 1789 à 1815, (Paris, 1896); and the documents on the whole period of the Revolution and Empire in Hurmuzaki, Documente, vols. XVI, XIX, Supl. I, vols, 2, 3.

Joseph II. In 1791 a petition, to be presented to the Emperor Leopold II, was signed by the two chief Roumanian bishops of the Orthodox and Uniate churches, the only acknowledged representatives of the Roumanian population, for here the church played a much more significant part in the national movement than was the case in the Principalities. Behind the bishops was a group of students and professional men, some of whom had studied in Vienna and in Italy, and the petition was drawn up for a former imperial functionary who was imbued with the ideas of the _philosophes_ and of the Revolution. This _Supplex Libellus Valachorum_ was an affirmation of rights in the name of the "Wallach nation," not a nation in the old sense but a nation which drew its justification from natural law as well as from history. Although much was made of the historical rights of the Roumanians as having inhabited Transylvania long before the arrival of the Magyars, more important for the future of Roumanian nationalism than the barren historical controversy were the demands for equal rights for all "citizens" and for a national assembly for Transylvania not dominated by the privileged groups.[16]

A document with similar phraseology was drawn up by a group of boyars in Wallachia in the same year. It was a

---

16. Iorga, _La Révolution française et le Sud-Est de l'Europe_, pp. 25-6; R. W. Seton-Watson, _A History of the Roumanians_, (London, 1934), pp. 188-91.

petition to the powers who were negotiating the treaties of Svishtov and Jassy. Their appeal was mainly for the restoration of historical rights of which they claimed to have been deprived; the right to have a native prince elected by the boyars, their own national militia, and freedom of trade; they demanded that Wallachia be considered as a "nation" and not as a Ottoman province.[17] It is worthy of note that here the word "nation" refers not to the whole body of Orthodox or Roumanian-speaking citizens, as was the case in Transvylania, but rather to a certain state, or territory, and to the boyar class as representing that territory. For the boyars were the only class which had any political existence. The merchant class, which brought in many of the new doctrines, had never been, and for a long time would not be, a political factor, partly because of its cosmopolitan and non-national character. The national regeneration of the Roumanian people was to be carried on by the intellectual youth of the boyar class, and not until much later, when a truly Roumanian bourgeoisie had appeared, can it be called a middle class movement. In this instance it was the boyar class which was making claims to a limited national independence. It had made such claims before, though without using the word "nation,"

---

17. Memoirs of Ioan Cantacuzino, cited by Iorga, La Place des Roumains dans l'histoire universelle, III, pp. 40-42; Letter of the historian von Hammer, cited by Iorga in Revue Historique du Sud-Est Européen, X, 1934, p. 361.

and it was to make them again. As the national movement grew in character and in intensity, the phrasing of such claims changed accordingly, influenced by the ideas which were brought back by youths from the West, or which derived from the new intellectual endeavors of both bourgeois and aristocratic circles in the Principalities.

In the Napoleonic period the rapidly changing map of Europe bore witness to the fact that many old ties were being broken, and a few forward-looking Roumanians attempted to make capital out of the situation. They applied not to their sovereign, the Sultan, nor to the Russian Emperor, their former benefactor, but to the _arbiter mundi_, Napoleon himself. There is evidence to show that at least one delegation made the long trip to Paris armed with claims and requests. We know little of the nature of the requests and nothing of their reception.[18] Napoleon, unlike his nephew, was no enthusiast for nationalities _per se_, and he may not even have known that the Roumanians were a nationality. He considered the Principalities as territories which he could

---

18. It is said that they asked that the Principalities be made into a republic, _i.e._, a boyar oligarchy. For the various appeals to France made by groups of boyars, see A. D. Xenopol, _Istoria Partidelor Politice_, (Bucharest, 1910), vol. I, pp. 42-3; P. Eliade, _De l'influence française_, pp. 231-5; Iorga, "Penseurs revolutionnaires roumains de 1804 a 1830," (_Revue Historique du Sud-Est Européen_, XI, 1934, pp. 81-102), pp. 85-6; _idem._, _Istoria Românilor_, vol. VIII, pp. 180-1; Hurmuzaki, _Documente_, vol. X, pp. 132, 182, 220; Elias Regnault, _Histoire politique et sociale des Principautés danubiennes_, (Paris, 1855), p. 102.

regard as an inalienable part of the Ottoman Empire or assign to Russia, according to the direction of his policy at any given moment.

Napoleon's lack of interest did not prevent the development of a legend about him as the future liberator of all oppressed peoples. His career was followed with interest by all those Roumanians who had any political interests at all. Even those who had given up hope that the conquering hero would ever appear in the Principalities retained the idea that in some way his great influence would bring about a better future for them. News of his exploits came chiefly through pamphlets printed at Budapest, in Roumanian; these, along with manuscript, journals describing the latest events, passed from hand to hand in the Principalities. Among the Roumanians the name of Napoleon came to be known as that of no other foreign hero had ever been, and this fame of the temporal power of France could not but reinforce the influence already gained by French thought and literature.[19]

4. Latinism and Nationalism

The nationalistic movement was a product of the blending of three distinct intellectual currents: the strong influence of French culture, which opened the doors to a knowledge

---

19. P. Eliade, *op.cit.*, pp. 258-61; Iorga, *Histoire des relations entre la France et les Roumains*, p. 132; P. P. Panaitescu, *Corespondenţa lui Constantin Ypsilanti cu Guvernul Rusesc*, (Bucharest, 1933), pp. 7-8.

of the West; the resurrection and glorification of the Roumanian past; and the so-called Latinist movement, which had its origin in Transylvania. It must not be forgotten that these currents were at first confined to small groups of intellectuals. French nationalism had its birth in a mass movement, the Revolution; German nationalism in the war of liberation against Napoleon; Serb and Greek nationalism in holy wars against the Turk. There was no similar struggle in Roumania. There, as in Italy, the evolution of nationalism can be described as a long and successful campaign on the part of the intellectuals to win over to their national ideals other sections of the population. To study Roumanian nationalism in this period, therefore, means to keep one's eye on the schoolroom, the reading club, and the publishing house, rather than on the battlefield or the market place.

One of the most important elements in Roumanian nationalism came, surprisingly enough, from Transylvania, where the Roumanian majority formed the helot class, politically and socially disfranchised. It was among the clergy that the new spirit found expression.

The generation which followed that of Bishop Micu, the first great advocate of the Roumanian cause in Transylvania, produced three men who made an immense contribution to Roumanian nationalism through their propagation of the theory of the Latin origin of the Roumanian people. That theory was not new; it had been held by many previous writers and chroniclers, but it was not until the late 18th and early 19th centuries that this gospel, as preached by George Şincai, Samuil Micu, and Petru Maior, acted as a breath of new life where before there had been stagnation. As at that time the only Roumanians who had any education at all were the priests, those three men started their careers as theological students of the Uniate Church, but their studies soon led them outside the realm of theology to lay the foundations of the secular dogma of nationalism. They studied in Vienna and in Rome, and it was in the Eternal City that they were inspired by the monuments of the Roman Empire, especially by the famous column of Trajan and its connection with ancient Dacia, their own homeland. It was but natural that they, the representatives of a people which had for centuries suffered from an inferiority of status and an inferiority complex, should jump to the conclusion that they were the direct descendants of the noble Romans, rightful owners of a heritage since filched from them by the barbarians. Hence their proclamation of the Roman origin and Latin character of the modern Roumanians, and the uncritical acceptance of the theory by intellectuals and popular leaders in Transylvania and in the Principalities as well. The importance of this for Roumanian nationalism was manifold. It provided an immeasurable stimulus to the consciousness of nationality. The Roumanian would now no longer be willing to be merely the despised "Wallach"; he was of nobler stock than his Magyar and German superiors. The Roumanians were no longer a "geschichtloses Volk" but were the inheritors of a great imperial civilization. With all the nations of Europe, under the influence of the German Romantics, digging into their past in search of forgotten civilizations, certainly none could match these claims. Closely connected with this new pride of "race" and flowing equally from the theory of Latin origins was the idea of being a chosen people with a mission. The modern Roumanians, so went the argument, are the standard bearers of Latin civilization, which during the centuries of barbarian migrations they were able to defend and maintain in the fastnesses of the Carpathians. They are, therefore, pure-blooded Romans, more so than the Romance peoples of the West, who have been corrupted by other strains; they are an island of Latinism in a sea of Slavic and Turanian barbarians, their mission to serve as an eastern outpost of Latin culture.[20]

The most tangible result of the Latinist enthusiasm was the concrete effect on the Roumanian language. The grammar written by Şincai and Micu in 1780 was the first attempt to

---

20. Iorga, Geschichte des rumänischen Volkes, (Gotha, 1905), vol. II, pp. 227ff.; idem., Istoria Românilor, vol. VIII, pp. 155-71; Alex. Lăpedatu, Ioan Lupaş, and Sextil Puşcariu, "La Centenariul Morţii lui Petru Maior," (Anuarul Institutului de Istoria Naţională, Cluj, I, 1921-2, pp. 77-119); A. Papiu Ilarian, "Viaţa, operele şi ideile lui Gheorghe Şincai," (Ac. Rom., Discoursuri de Recepţiune, No. 2, 1869); A Lăpedatu, "Istoriografia română ardeleană în legătura cu desfăşurarea vieţii politice a neamului românesc de peste Carpaţi," (ibid., No. 55, 1923), pp. 8-17.

analyze Roumanian as a Latin tongue, with Latin roots and inflections.[21] In the preface the authors strongly urged the use of the Latin alphabet instead of the Slavonic characters that had long been used in religious books. Thus began the long campaign for the adoption of the Latin alphabet and for the purging of all non-Latin words and forms from the language. The importance of these linguistic reforms cannot be overestimated. In eastern Europe, even more than elsewhere, language is the badge of nationality, and the nationality struggle has tended to centre around language questions. The rise of nationalism among these submerged peoples was in every case predicated upon the conscious effort of the intellectuals to create a uniform national literary language upon which could be based a national culture.

The St. Paul of the new creed was Gheorghe Lazăr, who in 1816 forsook Transylvania for Bucharest, where he took over the school of St. Sava and turned it into a center for the propagation of new national teachings. At that time the Wallachian schools were conducted in Greek; Lazăr boldly broke with that tradition. The native language, which had been considered incapable of expressing other than the most elementary thoughts, became in this school the language of instruction. Under Lazăr and his assistants, courses were

---

21. *Elementa linguae daco-romanae sive valachae.* (Buda, 1780).

given in philosophy, mathematics, the Roumanian language, and several other subjects. In the 1820's, when the school, or college, was under the direction of Lazăr's most illustrious pupil, Ioan Eliade Rădulescu, the emphasis was still national and Latinist, but more attention was given to French, for the first state _boursiers_ who had been sent to study in Italy and in France were now back in Bucharest and on the faculty of the college.[22]

What was the connection between this Latinist trend, originating in Transylvania and continued in the Principalities by the college of St. Sava, and the general stream of French influence which was so great a factor in the rise of nationalism? Those who attribute overwhelming significance to the influence of France are inclined to consider the Latinist phase of the national movement as transitory, and as noteworthy caiefly because in emphasizing the Latinity of the Roumanians it turned them even more decisively to the shining light of the "Latin world" of the time, France. It provided additional historical justification for throwing

---

22. N. Bănescu, "Cei dintâi bursiere români în străinătate," (_Revista Generală a Invățământului_, Bucharest, VI, 1910, pp. 216ff.; P. Eliade, _Histoire de l'Esprit public en Roumanie au XIXe. siècle_, vol. I, _L'Occupation turque et les premiers princes indigènes_, (Paris, 1905), pp. 224-43. Iorga, _Histoire de l'enseignement en pays roumains_, (Bucharest, 1933), pp. 147-53. The best biographies of Lazăr are G. Bogdan-Duică, _Gheorghe Lazăr_, (Bucharest, 1924), and Bogdan-Duică and G. Popa-Lisseanu, _Viața și Opera lui Gheorghe Lazăr_, (Bucharest, 1924).

off the weight of orientalism; a western origin seemed to indicate a western future. The French influence, however, was strong enough to stand on its own feet, and the French themselves, with a few notable exceptions, paid little attention to the claims of this unknown nation to be accepted into the Latin family. Even at home the Latinist movement dissipated much of its prestige by an attempt to fit the developing Roumanian language into the dead mold of classical Latin, thus divorcing it from the language of the people and of folk literature. The Latin idea has nevertheless always remained in the minds of the Roumanians as something fundamental. The very shakiness of its historical foundations adduces in compensation a loud insistence on "Latinism" in history, in philosophy, in literature.[23]

5. Roumanian Constitutionalists, 1821-1828

In the decade of the 1820's these currents were all present but had not merged into any conscious doctrine of nationalism. The Transylvanians at St. Sava, Lazăr and his successors, continued to make headway against the prevailing Greek character of education and literature. But they

---

23. P. Eliade, *De l'influence française*, pp. ix-x, 277ff.; V. A. Urechia, *L'idée latine chez les Roumains*, (Alais, 1900); C. I. Istrati, "La Roumanie dans la latinité," (*Rivista d'Italia*, XVIII, 1915, fasc. 2, pp. 169-89); Iorga, *Le rôle des Roumains dans la latinité*, (Bucharest, 1919); D. Onciul, "Ideea latinității și a unității naționale," (*Revista Istorică*, V, 1919, pp. 141-162); André Tibal, "Le Psychologie du Peuple Roumain," (*Académie des Sciences morales et politiques, Séances et Travaux*, Paris, 1933, vol. 2, pp. 65-94), pp. 70-2.

treated western culture more like a new toy than as a living body of ideas which would contribute to the transformation of Roumanian life.[24] Also, there was a marked emphasis in the literature of this period on the sentiment of patriotism. Although vaguely expressed it did show the influence of foreign models and the existence of a new spirit in the Principalities. On the part of Eliade and several others there was a clear recognition of the necessity of enriching Roumanian culture by taking from France what had proved beneficial there, by extracting that which was univeral and human, and therefore applicable to the Roumanians.[25]

Politically, the nationalism of this decade was also inchoate and rudimentary. The Russians were still looked upon in many circles as benefactors, as in fact they were. The Turks were vaguely disliked as infidels and as robbers of the products of the Roumanian soil, but contact with them

---

24. The rather sterile controversies between the believers in Kant and the followers of Condillac and Destutt de Tracy are interesting only as marking the beginning of the conflict of French and German cultural influence in Roumania. See I. Eliade Rădulescu, "Gheorghe Lazăr," (Curierul Romănesc, 1839, No. 66); Bogdan-Duică, Gheorghe Lazăr, pp. 87-92; G. Adamescu, "Primii profesori de filosofie ai școalei de Sfântul Sava," (Revista Generală a Invățământului, XV, 1927, pp. 19-32), pp. 20-1. Lazăr cannot be called an uncompromising opponent of French influence, either in philosophy or in politics. One of the reasons why he lost his teaching position in Transylvania in 1815 was that he proposed a toast to Napoleon and liberty in the public park of Hermannstadt. (Bogdan-Duică and Popa-Lisseanu, op.cit., p. 190).

25. P. Eliade, Histoire de l'Esprit Public, pp. 284-93, 377-83.

was slight. The Greeks had a double role. While they were hated for their exploitation of the Principalities, they were also a civilizing influence, and their plans to liberate the whole Christian Near East were endorsed by some Roumanians. The events of the year 1821 are a good indication of the confused state of affairs and of the undeveloped nature of Roumanian nationalism. The complete failure of Alexander Ypsilanti demonstrated that the Roumanian masses would never rise in favor of Greek nationalism. The Vladmirescu revolt did not necessarily prove, however, that they would rise in favor of Roumanian nationalism. For that revolt, since become an integral part of the nationalist legend, was primarily social in origin. The peasants revolted against the "ciocoi," against all their oppressors regardless of what language they spoke.[26] It was only later that clever manoeuvring turned it against the Greeks. The fact that the year 1821 saw the end of Greek rule in the Principalities does not warrant ascribing that development to the "national" revolution of Vladmirescu. Tudor himself, as his proclamations show, was inspired by the ideas of liberty, equality and fraternity, just as were the Greek revolutionists whom he at first worked

---

26. The word "ciocoi" has no equivalent in French or English, though "parvenu" is the translation usually given. It implies the existence of many unpleasant characteristics which, in the eyes of the peasants, were typical of the small boyars, the middlemen, and others not of their own class with whom they had to deal.

with and then opposed. Only a couple of months after the revolt started, he himself was murdered and his followers melted away; but the "regenerator of Roumania" did make a contribution to the development of nationalism. He helped to rid the country of the Greeks; and he associated the peasants in his revolt, something which later nationalists lacked either the ability or the desire to do. Less important than the actuality was the legend which grew up about "Domnul Tudor." One of the essential points of modern nationalism is the cult of the national hero. Vladimirescu, the man of the people, provided later generations of Roumanians with an admirable one.[27]

Meanwhile in Moldavia there was in progress a movement which illustrates clearly the penetration of the political

---

27. Until the recent monographs of Mr. Emil Vîrtosu, the revolution of 1821 was studied with far too little detachment; consequently it has been difficult to break through the crust of the national legend. Despite the fact that the bibliography on the subject is enormous, the lines are not yet wholly clear. See especially C. D. Aricescu, Istoria Revoluțiunii romîne de la 1821, 2 vols., (Craiova, 1874); Iorga, Izvoarele contemporane asupra mișcării lui Tudor Vladimirescu, (Bucharest, 1921); Filitti, Frământările Politice și Sociale, pp. 24-72; D. Bodin, "Tudor Vladimirescu," (Figurii Revoluționari Române, Bucharest, 1937, pp. 45-71); Emil Vîrtosu, Tudor Vladimirescu. Glose, fapte și documente noi, (Bucharest, 1927); idem., 1821. Date și fapte noi, (Bucharest, 1932), esp. bibliog. pp. xxxvii-lxi; idem., Tudor Vladimirescu. Pagini de revoltă, (Bucharest, 1936). For the conception of Vladimirescu and his revolt held by the generation of 1848, see N. Bălcescu, "Mersul Revoluției in Istoria Românilor," (România Viitoare, Paris, 1850, pp. 7-15); Cezar Boliac, "Domnul Tudor," (Revue de l'Orient, de l'Algérie, et des Colonies, Nov. 1856), and separately, (Paris, 1857, in French and in Roumanian).

ideas of the liberals in the West. A group of boyars of the second and third class,—the boyar class was legally divided into three groups, most of the wealth and political power being in the hands of the first class boyars,—who had won the support of the new native prince, Ion Sturdza, proposed a new constitution for the principality. From a perusal of its provisions we can see easily enough why these boyars were called "Cărvunarii," the Carbonari. They were indeed another instance of the carbonaro epidemic which appeared in Italy, in France, and in Spain at this same time. They were true "constitutionalists" in that the magic word "constitution" meant as much to them as did the specific reforms which they recommended. Their constitution, apparently modelled on the French Charter of 1814 or the Spanish Constitution of 1820, contained articles guaranteeing individual liberty and equality before the law, and providing for freedom of contract and of trade, a representative assembly, a state-owned printing press to publish books in "our language," and an extensive school system with teaching done in Roumanian. The word "nation" (norod) was used for the first time instead of the word "country" (țara).[28] This "democratic" system was to

28. Xenopol, "Primul proiect de constituțiunea Moldovei din 1822. Originile partidului conservator și ale celui liberal," (Ac. Rom., Mem. Sect. Ist., Ser. II, vol. 20, 1898); idem., Istoria Partidelor Politice, pp. 76-116; D. V. Barnoschi, Originele Democrației Române, (Jassy, 1922); I. C. Filitti, "Originele Democrației Române," (Viața Românească, Jassy, XIV, 1922, pp. 183ff.; XV,

extend only to members of the boyar class. It made no provision whatsoever for artisans and peasants. This was the manner in which liberty and equality were adapted to Moldavian conditions. The radicals wanted an equalization of privilege within the boyar class, nothing more. Nevertheless, their constitution was by its very terms an introduction of dynamite into the stratified society of that day. The logical extension of those terms to the whole of society would mean real democracy. The development of that creed was to be the work of the generation of 1848.

At the same time other projects were being drawn up by groups of boyars who, as a consequence of the disturbances of 1821, had taken up residence outside the Principalities; the Wallachians were for the most part in Brașov (Kronstadt) and the Moldavians in Cernăuți (Czernowitz). Opposition to the newly named native princes was the chief reason which

---

1923, pp. 13-27, 182-09). Filitti shows here and in his larger work (Frământările Politice si Sociale, pp. 95-124) that this project was but one of many being put forward in both principalities. It deserves special notice mainly because of the phraseology lifted bodily from occidental constitutions. Iorga presents the carbonaro movement as a continuation of the activities of a group of lesser boyars who as early as 1804 had made similar constitutional demands and were tracked down by the government because they shared "French ideas of insubordination." (Iorga, Penseurs révolutionnaires roumains de 1804 à 1830, p. 87; cf. V. A. Urechia, Istoria Românilor, vol. IX, p. 27; A. Russo, Scrieri, (Bucharest, 1934, ed. P. V. Haneș), pp. 187-201).

kept them from returning.[29] These voluntary exiles busied themselves with both literary and political matters; although most of them were conservative boyars, bitter opponents of the "subservive carbonari," they were interested in the movement for a national literature and for the purification of the language, though they themselves used French, and they had a certain patriotism which was manifested particularly in anti-Greek sentiment. They were strongly pro-Russian, hoping for the Tsar's aid in gaining full autonomy for the Principalities and positions of influence for themselves. Some favored incorporation in the Russian Empire. Among the Moldavians was Michael Sturdza, author of several memoires to the Tsar, later Prince of Moldavia.[30] Among the Wallachians were Ion Câmpineanu, the future leader of the national party,

---

29. Teodor Bălan, Refugiații Moldoveni în Bucovina după 1821 și 1848, (Bucharest, 1929), pp. 1-15; E. Vîrtosu, 1821. Date și fapte noi, pp. xx-xxxv; C. Erbiceanu, Istoria Metropoliei Moldovei și Sucevei, (Bucharest, 1888), containing the correspondence of the Moldavian emigrés with their friends who remained at Jassy; P. Eliade, Histoire de l'Esprit Public, pp. 67-82, 127-37; Filitti, Frământările Politice și Sociale, pp. 83-91; A. A. Mureșianu, "Știri nouă despre refugiații munteni la Brașov în secolul al XVIII-lea și în rasmerita de la 1821" (Țara Bârsei, Brașov, II, 1930, pp. 3-15).

30. Both conservatives and carbonari found their final justification in an appeal to patriotism. "Patrie! que ce type est grand, sacré, et obligatoire pour tout homme qui l'appartient." (Mémoire of Michael Sturdza to Nesselrode, 1825). "...Ces mesures realisées, nous pouvons organiser un Etat qui soit digne de figurer à côté des autres....Ces changements nous permettront même de redevenir un Etat maître de lui-même." (Mémoire of Carbonari to the Porte, 1824). These mémoires are quoted in P. Eliade, op.cit., pp. 83-6, 91-7).

and Constantin (Dinu) Golescu, who has been called "the first modern Roumanian." The secretary of the Wallachian group was a Frenchman, Claude Coulin, who drew up many of their constitutional projects.[31]

Constantin Golescu was the first who strongly advocated imitation of the West, which he visited on several occasions in order to place his sons in Swiss and German schools. Dazzled by the material and spiritual wonders of the occidental world (the post offices, the libraries, the latest developments in science, and especially the apparent well-being of all classes), he published on his return an account of his travels, which bubbled over with enthusiasm for this superior civilization.[32] The last part of his book strongly recommends that efforts be made to close the gap between the Roumanians and "Europe." It is time that we awoke, said Golescu; let us abandon our luxury and our indifference to public welfare; let us take account of the miserable condition of our peasantry and do what we can to remedy it; let us travel, and send our sons abroad to learn foreign languages

---

31. In a later appeal to the Wallachian Government for payment for his many services, Coulin made a resumé of his career, stressing the importance of the ideas, some of them already realized, set forth in the writings of the emigré group in that period. (Ministère des Affaires Étrangères, Paris, hereafter cited as Aff. Etr., Correspondance Politique des Consuls, Turquie, Bucarest, vol. 2, enclosed in Billecocq to Guizot, Jan. 10, 1844, No. 120).

32. C. Golescu, Insemnare a călătoriei mele, (Buda, 1826), later editions in 1910 (N. Hodoș, ed.) and 1915 (P. V. Haneș, ed.).

and foreign ways of doing things. Golescu's appeal was addressed to his own class, which he hoped would see the error of its ways. He had no carefully worked out program of reform but thought that the peasant problem could be solved by philanthropy and good will on the part of the boyars. This may have been a miscalculation, but it does not detract from his role as patriarch of the school of Westernizers. He was in many ways the spiritual father of the generation of 1848, and more than that, he was in actual fact the father of four of its members.[33]

On his return from his travels Golescu set out to put into practice some of his own recommendations. He secured the collaboration of Eliade Rădulescu, who had just abandoned his chair at St. Sava in order to devote all his time to literary pursuits. They founded a "Society for Progress," the principal purpose of which was to increase the knowledge of Western literature and culture and to try to bring the Roumanians nearer to that level. It was under the auspices of this society that Eliade made the most important of his translations from Molière, Boileau, and Lamartine. The program, concerned principally with the creation of an educational system, proposed the establishment of national

---

33. His four sons were Nicolae, Ştefan, Radu, and Alexandru C. (Albul, "the White") Golescu. His brother Iordache, author of an early Roumanian grammar, had three sons, Dimitrie, Radu, and Alexandru G. (Negrul, "the Black") Golescu. All seven were Forty-eighters.

colleges at Bucharest and Craiova, normal schools in the provincial centers, primary schools in every village; newspapers printed in the national language, a national theatre, and "other useful institutions" were to be created.[34] Golescu, to make a start toward the distant goal of national education, set up a model school on his own estate, to which he imported some teachers from abroad, notably Florian Aaron, a Transylvanian historian and apostle of Latinism.

Constantin Golescu and Eliade seem to have had some plans for political agitation as well, but in the political field the fortunes of the Principalities were determined by the relationships of the great powers. Through no fault of their own, the Roumanians were a part of the Eastern question, the evolution of which put their fate in the hands of the Tsar of Russia, with only such limitations as could be placed on his power by the feeble strength of Turkey and the doubtful attitude of Austria and the more distant powers.

6. Kiselev and the Règlement Organique

The Convention of Akkerman and the treaty of Adrianople set the seal of legality upon the power which Russia had been exercising in the Principalities. Thereafter the Sultan's authority as sovereign (or suzerain, as he was now called)

---

34. Eliade Rădulescu, *Mémoires sur l'histoire de la régénération roumaine*, (Paris, 1851), pp. vi-vii; *idem.*, *Issachar*, (Bucharest, 1859) p. 77; I. Cretu, *Viața lui Eliade*, (Bucharest, 1939), pp. 26-9.

was limited to investing the princes and receiving the annual tribute. The powers assigned to "the suzerain and protecting courts" were exercised, in actual practice, by Russia, for the Sultan was in too weak a position to challenge the Tsar on this question. In the Principalities the power was in the hands of the Russian representatives; during the war of 1828-1829 the military authorities were all-powerful, then General Kiselev was supreme until 1834, when he retired and left Russian consuls in Bucharest and Jassy to carry on.

The years of direct Russian control, 1828 to 1834, brought all the hardships which go with supporting a foreign army of occupation. During the war the Roumanians of all classes were fearfully, even brutally, exploited in order to supply the Russian military needs. But Russian domination also brought compensations, and one of these was General Paul Kiselev, who concealed beneath his Russian officer's uniform the spirit of an 18th century Frenchman. He was sincerely desirous of improving political and social conditions among the Roumanians; he did not consider that to be in the least inconsistent with Russia's interests.[35] He set out to establish "a strong and just government", and his reforms represented an immense advance in the fields of administration,

---

35. Hurmuzaki, Documente, Supl. I, vol. 4, p. 420; T. Codrescu, Uricariul, vol. IX, (Jassy, 1875), pp. 358-9.

the judiciary, sanitation, and internal security.[36] His influence was considerable in the drawing up of the Règlements Organiques, which were to serve as constitutions in the Principalities, with a brief interruption in 1848, until the Crimean War.[37]

The Règlement Organique has been pictured as of French, of Russian, and of a native Roumanian origin, and has been

---

36. Kiselev's career in the Principalities deserves even more thorough study than it has been accorded. The standard biography is A. P. Zablotzki-Desiatovski, Graf P. D. Kiselev i ego Vremia, 4 vols., (St. Petersburg, 1882). Its material on this period is summarized by A. Papadopol-Calimach, "Generalul Pavel Kisseleff în Moldova şi Ţara-Românească, 1829-1834," (Ac.Rom.,Mem. Sect. Ist., Ser. II, vol. 9, pp. 65-148. The following are brochures: A. de Grammont, De l'administration russe en Valachie et de ses résultats, (Bucharest, 1840); Anon., Paul Kisseleff et les principautés de Valachie et de Moldavie, par un habitant de Valachie, (Paris, 1841); Anon., Les Principautés de Moldavie et de Valachie sous le gouvernement de Paul Kisseleff, (Paris, 1841).

37. The Règlement for Moldavia (French text) can be found in British and Foreign State Papers, vol. XXXII, (London, 1846), pp. 586-789. The Roumanian texts are given in Radu Rosetti and Sturdza-Schéianu, Acte si legiuiri privitoare la chestia ţărănească, Ser. I, vol. 1, pp. 90ff., 166ff. Separate editions were published in the 1830's at Bucharest, Jassy, and "New York" (Brussels?), in both languages. A careful analysis of the Règlement in I. C. Filitti, Les Principautés Roumaines sous l'occupation russe, (Bucharest, 1904), pp. 83-262; idem., "Partea boerimii în elaborarea Regulamentului organic," (Cugetul Romănesc, Bucharest, II, 1923, pp. 258-65, 743-53. Their social implications are discussed in David Mitrany, The Land and the Peasant in Roumania, (London, 1930), pp. 28-34; and M. Emerit, Les paysans roumains depuis le traité d'Andrinople jusqu'à la libération des terres, (Paris, 1937), pp. 55-120. There were only slight differences between the two documents; we are therefore justified in referring to the Règlement Organique, in the singular, as the constitution of both principalities.

attacked and defended on each interpretation. Those who defend it as a French importation point to its clauses concerning elections, the majority rule, the executive veto, the control of the assembly over taxation, etc. Although these are no more French than English or American, they certainly came by way of France; some were included through the personal intervention of Kiselev.[38] Although Russia had the deciding voice in the determination of the final provisions, it can hardly be maintained that the Tsarist regime, allowing its own subjects no constitutional rights at all, drew on Russian sources in providing the Principalities with a representative government, which, in view of the time and the place, might be called semi-liberal. The fact is that the Règlement was directly in line with the various programs worked out by Roumanians in the previous decade. The oft-expressed desires for national autonomy, for an elected native prince, for the opening of the Principalities to trade, etc., had made their way into the treaties of Akkerman and Adrianople; in expanded form they appeared in the Règlement Organique, which, especially in its provisions regarding landlord-peasant relations, was made to order for the big boyar class. The few boyars serving on the committees

---

38. P. Eliade, La Roumanie au XIXe. siècle, vol. II: Les Trois Présidents Plenipotentiaires, 1828-1834, (Paris, 1914), pp. 100-6, 121-31, 147-8, quoting the opinions of noted French legal scholars.

of redaction who had liberal and westernizing tendencies made their influence felt on details but not on crucial questions. In putting an end to the influence of Greeks and Turks, in breaking down the barriers to the export of grain and in increasing the burdens of the peasantry, the new constitution made sure that the Principalities would remain in the hands of the big boyars; and the boyars were in the hands of the Russian Emperor and his representatives. These facts made it certain that the younger nationalists, growing in strength in the next fifteen years, would become bitter opponents of the Règlement, for the controlling position which it gave to Russia offended their national pride, and the exclusion of all but the boyars from political power offended their newly acquired doctrines of liberalism and democracy. It was to have a stormy career. Center of a controversy which shook Wallachia in 1837, target of attacks throughout the 1840's, it was symbolically burned in 1848 at a great ceremony presided over by Ion Brătianu, restored in modified form after the defeat of the revolution, and finally, as a result of the Crimean War, was swept away along with the Russian "protectorate" which had presided at its birth.

CHAPTER II

THE FRENCH INFLUENCE IN THE PRINCIPALITIES, 1834-1848

1. Eliade Rădulescu and the Philharmonic Society

Tendencies which before the period of the *Règlement Organique* were halting and without direction became fixed, after 1834, in a pattern which was, in the succeeding decades, to expand but not to lose its original outline. The ourward manifestations which serve as evidence of the crystallization of such a pattern are the creation of a national literary language not too far removed from the language of the people, the rapid increase of French influence, to the virtual exclusion of all others, in the field of literature, and the appearance of still vaguely expressed aspirations pointing in the direction of national autonomy, the union of the Principalities, independence, the unity of all Roumanians in fact all the aims which Roumanian nationalists were, by gradual stages, to attain within the next hundred years.

The dominating figure in this literary generation was Ioan Eliade Rădulescu, who, by the quantity and the diversity of his work rather than by its intrinsic merit, won for himself a pre-eminent position. A professor at St. Sava, later inspector-general of schools, he was the author of one of the first Roumanian grammars,[1] in which he pressed the claims of the Latin alphabet, without which, he held, the

1. *Grammatika Romăneaskă*, (Bucharest, 1828).

Roumanians could not imbibe Latin culture nor escape from Slavism.[2] Eliade was the foremost journalist in Wallachia as well as the leading pedagogue and man of letters. His Curierul Românesc, founded in 1829, continued regularly until 1848 and proved a potent means of assuring the penetration of the new ideas into the lower ranks of the literate public.[3] A year later he purchased the only private printing press in the country. In 1836 he brought out a literary periodical, Curierul de Ambe Sexe, in which he presented his poems, his translations, and his various theories on literature and philology.

To bring the ideal closer to reality, he helped to establish the so-called Philharmonic Society in 1833.[4] Music was

---

2. "The Latin letters (litere), with which our ancestors wrote, are the teats through which our language can suck in the milk of the Latin mother, for literature (literatura) can be born only of Latin letters (litere), while from Slavic leters (slove) can come only words (slovnire). (Comments of Eliade on a sonnet by Iancu Văcărescu, quoted by I. Crețu, Viața lui Eliade, Bucharest, 1939, p. 36).

3. The same service was performed for Moldavia by Gheorghe Asachi, editor and publisher of Albina Românească, also founded in 1829. These papers had only a few hundred subscribers but undoubtedly reached a greater number of readers.

4. Ion Câmpineanu, one of the big boyars and a veteran of the now defunct society of 1827, supplied the money and influence, Eliade and C. Aristia the talent. The government of Prince Alexander Ghica, installed in 1834, was not hostile to the venture. (J. A. Vaillant, La Romanie, Paris, 1844, vol. II, p. 369). For the statutes of the society, lists of subscribers, and its early activities, see Eliade Rădulescu, Echilibru între antiteze, (Bucharest, 1916, ed. P. V. Haneș), vol. I, pp. 140 ff.

but one of its minor preoccupations. The "harmony" which it sought was something wider, comprising every method of pursuing what was moral and good. Not only was the language to be purified and literature encouraged, but the whole moral tone of the society of the time was to be improved. Eliade's ideas were grandiose; they were not limited to any one field of human endeavor, and their scope extended to all humanity.[5] The society was not wholly successful, even for the more restricted aims of providing the Roumanians with a literary language and with an acquaintance with some of the great works in other languages. Perhaps its most signal success lay in the encouragement of translations, which Eliade thought absolutely essential as a first step in bringing the Roumanian people out of the wilderness. They made the native tongue richer, more noble, he maintained, blazing the trail for original compositions.[6] He was himself the most prolific

---

5. His cosmopolitan ideal stamps him as perhaps the least narrowly nationalistic of the generation of 1848, more a product of the 18th than of the 19th century. In 1832 he wrote: "The good patriot is no fanatic, he loves men and he knows that nature does not recognize Germans, English, French, Greeks or Roumanians, but only men." (Curierul Românesc, 1832, No. 87). Literature to him was an instrument which could be made to serve mankind; art had a definite civic and moral purpose. His literary and his political were two sides of the same coin. (See D. Popovici, Ideologia Literară a lui I. Heliade Rădulescu, Bucharest, 1935, pp. 146-7, 159, 197ff., 302; I. Heliade, Mémoires, p. xvii.).

6. Popovici, op.cit., pp. 147ff, 309-10. Popvici lists forty translations by Eliade, most of them done in this period. A contemporary, Félix Colson, who describes in

producer of translations and was ably seconded by some of the younger men whom he had gathered about him, notably C. A. Rosetti and Cesar Boliac, later to become his bitterest enemies. These young poets, whose enthusiasm exceeded their ability, acquired through this work an admiration for Byron and for Lamartine which they were never to lose; it influenced not only their literary efforts but their political ideas and actions as well.

Besides the production of translations, the importance of which should not be over-estimated since the educated class could read French in the original and the others did not bother to read anything, the Philharmonic Society proposed and inaugurated an educational program including classes in music, declamation, moral principles, and the French and Roumanian languages; this was done with the help of the College of St. Sava.[7] In addition, there was a great effort to establish a national theatre. Eliade regarded such a theatre as the most powerful single means of destroying the detestable customs of the past, of inspiring virtue, and of

---

some detail the society's activities, credits its members with a total of eighty translations. (Colson, De l'Etat présent et de l'avenir des Principautés de Moldavie et de Valachie, Paris, 1839, pp. 169-198; Vaillant, op.cit., vol. II, p. 370).

7. T. T. Burada, "Cercetări asupra Şcoalei Filarmonice din Bucureşti, 1833-1837," (Convorbiri Literare, Bucharest, XXIV, 1890, pp. 1-29, 115-144), pp. 10-11; Creţu, op.cit., p. 55.

forming the nation's taste.[8] This was easier said than done, for their were hardly any "national" dramas to present. The repertory was made up largely of translations of the plays of Molière, Voltaire, Alfieri, and others. This was a welcome addition to the life of Bucharest's upper crust, and the court circles, including Prince Alexander Ghica, contributed money to the Philharmonic Society in order to keep the theatre alive. Yet it can scarcely be said to have fulfilled the function required of it by Eliade, and when the society was dissolved in 1838, amid much wrangling among Eliade and his younger lieutenants, the theatre dropped out of sight also. Financial support for it had been insufficient, and it had incurred the displeasure of the Russian Government, which was beginning to frown on all manifestations of nationalism and of the "insubordinate French spirit" as a threat to Russia's hold on the Principalities.[9]

---

8. Burada, op.cit., p. 6; Popovici, op.cit., pp. 118-27, 158-9. For the history of the theatre in Bucharest in this decade, see D. C. Ollănescu, "Teatrul la Românii," (Ac. Rom., Mem. Sect. Lit., Ser. II, vol. 20, 1997-98); M. M. Belador, Istoria Teatrului Român, (Craiova, n.d.); I. Xenofon, Filarmonica dela 1833, (Bucharest, 1934). For Eliade's first "national drama," see C. Gerota, "Cea dintâi piesă teatrală originală în Muntenia," (Convorbiri Literare, LXV, 1932, pp. 483-9".

9. Eliade Rădulescu, Echilibru între antiteze, vol. I, pp. 148-55; Cretu, op.cit., pp. 62-4; Vaillant, op.cit., vol. II, pp. 400-1. A Ubicini, Provinces d'origine roumaine, Paris, 1856, p. 154, says that Prince Ghica suppressed the theatre at the behest of the Russian consul.

The Russian fear was justified. These harmless cultural activities had already undermined the Tsar's "protectorate"; they could have had no other effect. The Roumanians could not go to school in the West and borrow all their forms from the West without becoming a party to the new division of Europe into liberal West and reactionary East. The scales fell from the eyes of those hopeful souls who had expected Russia to guide the Roumanians along the path of civilization.[10] The situation was entirely changed within a few years, and the Tsar, who had become the bugbear of the liberals of the West, was cast in the same role by the Roumanian nationalists. This was partly the effect of Russian policies and methods, of the tightening control of the Russian consuls in Bucharest and Jassy, who arrogated to themselves a power superior to that of prince or assembly. The impression was created that Russia intended to stifle the Roumanians' national existence, rob them of their autonomy, or even annex the Principalities outright.[11] These fears created a fierce

---

10. During the Russian occupation many of the idealistic young men had clustered round Kiselev and applauded his enlightened reforms; the _Règlement_ was hailed as the beginning of a new era. Eliade had written an ode, (which he later regretted), to the greater glory of the Tsar. These sympathies were soon dissipated. "The whole country," he wrote in retrospect, "expected salvation from the Russian campaign of 1828....I sang of its glories amid general applause and satisfaction." (Eliade Rădulescu, _Issachar_, p. 69).

11. Roumanian historians have often stated that annexation was the goal of Russian policy. It is true that the Russians certainly intended to retain full control over

hatred of Russia among the younger boyars. Russian imperialism seemed to be violating their legal rights, Russian reaction to be crushing their newly discovered liberalism, and Slavism to be stifling their national spirit. The national movement now has a clear issue on which to fight, opposition to Russian "protection." The secret political group composed of the leaders of the Philharmonic Society began to

---

the Principalities in order to be in a good strategic position vis-a-vis Turkey and the rest of Europe. But that they ever wanted to add another minority problem by annexation is doubtful, for on several occasions they probably could have done so without a European war, but refrained. Annexation would hardly have been consistent with the policy laid down at Adrianople in 1829, of maintaining an integral, nominally independent, and manageable Turkey. Cf. R. J. Kerner, "Russia's New Policy in the Near East after the Peace of Adrianople," (Cambridge Historical Journal, V. 1937, pp. 279-90). Lord Augustus Loftus, Diplomatic Reminiscences, First Series, vol. I, pp. 342-4, is our only authority for the information that Mahmud II in 1829 offered to cede the Principalities to Russia, but that Orlov rejected this, on the ground that Russia had no desire to annex provinces whose "liberal and democratic tendencies" would be dangerous to the Russian state. Many of the boyars thought that Mahmud secretly conceded sovereignty over the Principalities in 1833. (Hurmuzaki, Documente, vol. XVII, p. 470). Kiselev's letters are commonly cited to prove his annexationist designs, but his opinion shifted several times on this question, and though he once said that he considered the Danube as the frontier of the Russian Empire, he never was able to change the non-annexation policy favored by the Tsar and by Nesselrode. (Zablotzki-Desiatovski, Graf P. D. Kiselev i ego Vremia, vol. IV, pp. 61-2, 64-5, 68, 82-3, 92-8, 109-10; Papadopol-Calimach, Generalul Pavel Kiseleff, pp. 99-102; I. C. Filitti, "Corespondența Consulilor Englezi din Principate, 1828-1836," (Ac. Rom., Mem. Sect. Ist., Ser. II, vol. 38, pp. 839-920), pp. 880-2, 891-2). See the discussions on this point in W. G. East, The Union of Moldavia and Wallachia, (Cambridge, Eng., 1929), p. 11; T. W. Riker, The Making of Roumania, (Oxford, 1931), pp. 12-13; Iorga, Geschichte des rumänischen Volkes, vol. II, pp. 255-6.

organize an anti-Russian "national party," from which the many conservative, pro-Russian boyars who had contributed to the society and to its theatre were of course excluded. This national party secured adherents even in the general assembly, where Câmpineanu led a revolt against an attempt by Russia to secure the acceptance of an additional article to the <u>Règlement Organique</u> which would make constitutional amendment impossible without Russian consent. Russia won a victory in this controversy, but by such strong-arm methods that great indignation was aroused, and the national party had grown in strength to the point where more serious enterprises could be undertaken. Not all the boyars in and outside the assembly who supported Câmpineanu and opposed Russia on certain specific issues were sincerely imbued with Western liberalism. The foreign consuls in their reports did not always distinguish clearly between the large group of boyars who resented Russian interference in domestic affairs, and the smaller group of young men, the future "Forty-eighters," who really wanted to make over the whole fabric of Roumanian society on the occidental model. The older boyars, for positions and political power, wanted the autonomy and even the union of the Principalities. Their economic interests also made them, in a limited sense, nationalistic; the Moldavian-Wallachian customs union, consummated in 1847, was due to them and to the princes, not to the young doctrinaires.[12] Câmpineanu, the link between the two factions, had won great

---

12. Cf. V. J. Puryear, <u>Economics and Diplomacy in the Near East</u>, (Berkeley, 1935), pp. 187, 200.

prestige; he began to dream of putting an end to Russia's control over the Principalities and of the formation of an independent Roumanian state. Such a policy did not concern Wallachia alone. It lifted the Roumanian question onto the international stage and threatened to open up the whole eastern question.

2. The National Party, 1838-1840

The politically-minded members of Eliade's Philharmonic Society set forth as their ultimate aims the following: 1) abolition of the Russian protectorate, and its replacement by a collective guarantee of the European powers; 2) respect for the ancient treaties with Turkey; 3) confederation or union with Moldavia; 4) equality of all Roumanians before the law; 5) the responsibility of ministers; 6) freedom of the press; 7) free education for all; 8) the emancipation of the Gypsies; 9) the emancipation of the dedicated monasteries.[13] This is an astounding program for this early date. Among the boyars there had existed for some years sentiment in favor of ending the Russian protection and uniting the Principalities, and also in favor of scaling down the privileges of the boyars, though this latter point was less

---

13. Crețu, op.cit., p. 58.

widely held.[14] This program of the Philharmonic Society leaders, however, went much further; it might with justice be called the first expression of the ideals of the generation of 1848. The devoted followers of Câmpineanu, the acknowledged leader, included a few of the older boyars (e.g., Grigore Cantacuzino, Ion Filipescu, Ion Rosetti), and another group to which the French consul referred as "a few patriotic men with exalted ideas." These were Nicolae Bălcescu, C. A. Rosetti, Boliac, Ion Voinescu, and others, the future Paşoptişti, now getting their baptism of conspiracy and politics; for most of them, the two were to remain forever synonymous.

There was at this time great dissatisfaction with the rule of Alexander Ghica and with the continued interference of Russia. Resentment reached its height over the claim of Russia to a veto power over all constitutional changes, by virtue of a fraudulently inserted additional article of the Règlement. Seeing the possibilities of the situation, Câmpineanu pressed forward with a national program conceived in the grand manner. His first plan, that of securing the throne of Wallachia for himself, soon gave way to more far-

---

14. Ion Câmpineanu, though not one of the extreme radicals, is perhaps the best example of the group which favored both national freedom and a new deal for the unprivileged at home. He is said to have advocated both universal suffrage and emancipation of the peasants. (F. Colson, De la Pologne et des Slaves, Paris, 1863, p. 214; G. Bogdan-Duică, in Gazeta Transilvaniei, June 22, 1921, cited in M. Emerit, Les Paysans roumains, p. 248).

reaching projects. The union of the two Principalities, an idea which found favor in all circles, was taken up.[15] Union and the abolition of the Russian protectorate were considered by Câmpineanu and his friends to be so desirable that they were even willing to see Michael Sturdza on the throne of the united Principalities. Sturdza was approached in January, 1839, and considered the matter seriously, under the impression that the plan had the support of Lord Palmerston, but later in the same year he finally decided that Russian power was too near and the risk too great.[16] Meanwhile

---

15. This was no new idea. It had been proposed by certain boyars in 1829, and mentioned as desirable in the text of the Règlement. As Russia became unpopular, sentiment grew in favor of union under a foreign prince; it was felt that no native boyar could avoid intrigues or win the confidence of all. Foreign observers on many occasions noted this desire for union and a foreign prince. (Report of Baron de la Rue, 1834, (reproduced in Revue Historique du Sud Est Européen, VIII, 1931, pp. 6-30), p. 23; Hurmuzaki, Documente, vol. X, pp. lxxviii, 647-9; ibid., vol. XVII, pp. 393-4, 472-5, 496-7, 699, 725; Saint-Marc Girardin, Souvenirs de Voyages et d'études, Paris, 1853, vol. I, pp. 301-2; Colquhoun to Palmerston, May 18, July 21, 1839, Public Record Office, London, Foreign Office Reports, 78, Turkey, vol. 363: "These views are now so general that I think it right to mention them to your Lordship."..."This I believe to be the only view on which all parties unite unanimously."

16. Hurmuzaki, Documente, vol. XVII, pp. 724-5, 728-34, 737-41; Felix Colson, De l'Etat présent et de l'avenir des Principautés, pp. 56-9; P. P. Panaitescu, "Planurile lui Ioan Câmpineanu pentru Unitatea Naţională a Românilor," (Anuarul Institutului de Istoria Naţională, Cluj, III, 1924-5, pp. 63-106, and separately, Cluj, 1924), pp. 78-80; M. Handelsman, Czartoryski, Nicolas Ier, et la Question du Proche Orient, (Paris, 1934), pp. 78-84; Mihail Popescu, "Contributiuni la istoria dinaintea unirii Principatelor," (Convorbiri Literare, LXV, 1932, pp. 690-712), pp. 694-701. Sturdza, it appears, was

Câmpineanu was being dazzled by a much brighter vision, that of the union of all Roumanians in a single state. Encouraged by his contacts with the Polish emigration, whose leader in Paris, Prince Adam Czartoryski, was charting out a grandiose anti-Russian confederation of free peoples and hoping to use Roumanian nationalism as a stepping-stone to the liberation of Poland, he drew up, for his followers to sign, a declaration of principles which stated the necessity for "the complete independence of all the scattered members of our nation," and did not hesitate to attack Turkey as well as Russia for trampling upon the rights of the Roumanians. These violations, it said, had put an end to the tie between the Roumanians and the Sublime Porte. Wallachia was to become an independent state, and, if possible, all the Roumanian populations were to be united under the sceptre of an hereditary native or foreign prince.[17] These were brave

---

already intriguing in Bucharest for Ghica's fall before being approached by Câmpineanu and Colson. (Colquhoun to Palmerston, Jan. 19, 1839, F.O. 78, vol. 363; Hurmuzaki, Documente, XVII, pp. 724-5; Filitti, Domniile Române sub Regulamentul Organic, Bucharest, 1915, p.507).

17. Panaitescu, op.cit., pp. 87-9. The text of this declaration, dated Nov. 1, 1838, was communicated to Prince Czartoryski in Paris. Another copy, (reproduced in Hurmuzaki, Documente, vol. XVII, pp. 727-8), with many changes and omissions, was submitted to the French consul at Jassy, who sent it to Paris. The changes have the effect of toning down or skating around the more extreme demands and of making the whole thing more palatable to the western powers' alleged solicitude for the integrity of Turkey. The differences are pointed out in detail by Professor Panaitescu.

words, challenging at one and the same time Russia's preponderant position in the Near East, the integrity of Turkey, and the existence of the Habsburg Empire. It was certainly beyond the powers of a small group of patriotic Roumanians to bring about such changes in the map of Europe. They needed a revolutionary army at home and powerful outside allies.

The forces at Câmpineanu's disposition in Wallachia were, to say the most, limited. According to Colquhoun, the British consul in Bucharest, the national party was numerically stronger than those which took orders from Prince Ghica or from the Russian consul.[18] But these boyars, motivated, "some by a supposed patriotism, some by an unconcealed hatred of Russia, others by ambition and less laudable motives," were far from being revolutionary material.[19] In a crisis Câmpineanu would probably be able to count only on his co-workers of the Philharmonic Society group, to whom the French consul referred as young men blinded by misdirected patriotism and subversive ideas.[20] For a military force they had nothing,

---

18. He described it as "most numerous" and "composed of the wealth and talent in the country," and as "holding patriotic views, but of a nature too extensive to hope to see them realized." (Colquhoun to Palmerston, Apr. 14, 1837, Dec. 19, 1838, F.O. 78, vols. 313, 336).

19. Colquhoun to Palmerston, May 2, 1838, F.O. 78, vol. 336.

20. Châteaugiron to Mole, Sept. 23, 1838, Aff. Etr., Corr. Com., Bucarest, vol. 7. The Russian consul had prepared a list of twenty-two suspects, "mostly young men who

only a few patriotic members of the local militia and a vague hope that "the people" would fight if they got arms and training. Emissaries sent to the surrounding districts reported that among the small boyars and peasantry great discontent prevailed.[21]

In Moldavia also there were hopes but few concrete evidences of strength. Câmpineanu's national party had its Moldavian counterpart, and sentiment in favor of union was widespread.[22] Sturdza was far from popular, and his opponents were divided into pro-Russian and nationalist cliques. There were no capable leaders; no definite plans seem to have been made for common action with the Roumanians of other provinces.[23]

As for the idea that the Roumanians in the Austrian and Russian empires would take part in a great national revolt, that was little more than wishful thinking. The nationalistic

---

have recently returned from their studies in Paris, who it is known entertain liberal opinions and who do not hesitate to avow them"; he wanted the Prince to put them in "protective custody," and a few were thus dealt with. (Colquhoun to Palmerston, Sept. 20, 1838, F.O. 78, vol. 336).

21. Colquhoun to Palmerston, Dec. 19, 1838, F.O. 78, vol. 336. Prince Ghica later accused the Câmpineanu party of "tampering with the lower classes and the inferior orders of the militia." (Colquhoun to Palmerston, Apr. 22, 1839, F.O. 78, vol. 363).

22. Huber to Molé, Apr. 16, 1838, <u>Aff. Etr., Corr. Com., Jassy</u> (<u>Dir. pol., copie</u>), vol. 3.

23. "Je crois devoir signaler l'absence totale de relations suivies entre la Valachie et la Moldavie." (Woronicz to Czartoryski, Dec. 12, 1838, in Panaitescu, <u>op.cit.</u>, p.96).

views of the few Transylvanian intellectuals who had established themselves in Wallachia as teachers led Câmpineanu and others to count heavily on the Transylvanian Roumanians. In his negotiations with the Poles, he predicted a rising in Transylvania as certain if a Polish revolt broke out in Gallicia; he was surer of Transylvania than he was of Moldavia.[24] It appears that he envisaged some sort of co-operation with the Hungarians, for he offered to put Czartoryski's agent in touch with Nicholas Wesselenyi. Events were to prove how woefully mistaken he was in trying to anticipate the course of history; the Roumanians of Transylvania could never at this early date have been raised in revolt against the Russians, with whom they had no quarrel, or the Austrian Emperor, against whom they had few complaints. The idea of a rising in Bessarabia was equally fantastic. The fact was that the conception of the union of all Roumanians had no more than a handful of adherents.

Câmpineanu's revolutionary plans were hatched in intimate collaboration with Czartoryski, the idea being that all Poland would rise simultaneously with the Roumanian provinces. Câmpineanu looked to the Poles to supply the direction and military experience which the Roumanians so obviously

---

24. Panaitescu, op.cit., p. 99; cf. Colson, De l'Etat présent et de l'avenir des Principautés, pp. 260-6; G. Bogdan-Duică, "La Inceputul Unirei," (Cele Trei Crişuri, Oradea Mare, X, 1929, pp. 58-60.

lacked.[25] In 1837 Czartoryski was in close contact with Radu Golescu in Paris. In 1838 he sent a personal agent, Woronicz, to open alliance negotiations with Câmpineanu, and on the latter's visit to Paris in 1839, an agreement was signed.[26]

---

25. For some years the Poles had been aware of the common interests of the two peoples in opposing Russia. During the revolt of 1830-31, their agency in Paris produced several memoranda on this question. (Bibliothèque Polonaise, Paris, Liasse No. 356, vol. VII, 13-14, Mss. Nos. 1039-1042). The Polish revolt had had repercussions in Moldavia where the lesser boyars, sympathetic with Poland and strongly anti-Russian, and certain sections of the peasantry, for reasons of their own, attempted to rebel against the new régime of the Règlement Organique. (Stanislaw Lukasik, Rumania a Polska w XIX wieku, Cracow, 1929, p. 22; idem., Pologne et Roumanie, Paris, 1938, pp. 86-7; Ion Ghica, Scrisori către Vasile Alecsandri, 2nd. ed., Bucharest 1887, pp. 629-30; P. Eliade, La Roumanie au XIXe. siècle, pp. 183-7; Emerit, Les Paysans roumains, pp. 88-92; Hurmuzaki, Documente, X, pp. 452-8; ibid., XVII, pp. 255-7, 262-3, 392). Czartoryski seems to have considered the Roumanians as possible allies as early as 1833. Mr. Duzinchevici has unearthed a letter apparently written in Paris in that year and signed "Ghika"; in this letter is set forth the plan of the liberation of all five provinces peopled by Roumanians and to persuade the Turks to resign their suzerainty. The contents of the letter suggest that its author was Ion Ghica, although Mr. Duzinchevici rules that out on the ground that Ion Ghica did not go to Paris until 1834. (G. H. Duzinchevici, "Documente din archivele polone relative la istoria Românilor," Buletinul Comisiei Istorice a României, Bucharest, XIV, 1935, pp. 4-5, 39-45; cf. Ion Ghica, Scrisori către Vasile Alecsandri, pp. 174-6; N. Petrascu, "Ion Ghica," Literatura şi Arta Română, I, 1896-97, p. 408).

26. Panaitescu, op.cit., pp. 66-71, 77-8, 81, 86-101; Handelsman, op.cit., pp. 74-81; T. Holban, "Emigraţia polonă în anii 1831-1848 şi influenţa ei asupra mişcărilor de independenţă ale Românilor," (Revista Istorică, XX, 1934, pp. 325-44), pp. 331-4.

The connections with the Polish emigrés made Câmpineanu's party even more suspect in the eyes of the Russian Government, whose agents were well aware of what was in the wind. They had found out that "propaganda originating in London and Paris and making clever use of the words '<u>nationality</u>' and '<u>independence</u>' was circulating in the Principalities"; revolutionaries, aided by the Poles, were said to be organizing committees and spreading subversive doctrines which embraced Transylvania, the Banat, and Bessarabia as well as the Principalities. Emperor Nicholas warned Metternich of the danger threatening the Austrian dominions, calling the situation very serious.[27] Câmpineanu's attempt to stir up revolution in Austria naturally meant that the idea of using Austria as a counterweight to Russia, held by some Roumanians and by Lord Palmerston, would have to be counted out. Even without that, Metternich would hardly have become the ally of revolutionaries. He seemed to have resigned himself to Roumanian domination of the Principalities despite Austria's extensive commercial interests there; he was sticking to the policy of conservatism and co-operation with the Tsar laid down at

---

27. M. Popescu, <u>Contribuţiuni la istoria dinaintea unirii Principatelor</u>, pp. 694-701, citing letters of Nesselrode to Tatischev, 1838-9, found in the archives of the Ministry of the Interior, Vienna; cf. N. Kretzulescu, <u>Amintiri Istorice</u>, (Bucharest, 1894), pp. 53-4; Hurmuzaki, <u>Documente</u>, vol. XVII, p. 750.

Münchengrätz in 1833.[28] The redoubled vigilance of the Russian and Austrian governments bore fruit, for Metternich's police were later able to pick up Câmpineanu's trail and arrest him on his way back from London to Wallachia. Their fears were exaggerated, however, for the planned Polish-Roumanian revolt had not secured British and French backing and therefore had no chance of success.

Câmpineanu had counted heavily on England. He felt that whoever desired freedom should seek the support of those nations which had it, France and England. The recent policies of those two powers in support of "constitutionalism" on the Continent aroused hopes that help might be had for the asking; encouragement from Colquhoun in Bucharest had strengthened such hopes. But the much-heralded mission to Paris and London in 1839 ended in total failure. The active help given

---

28. Foreign consuls noted the apparent indifference of their Austrian colleagues to Russian encroachments. (Bois-le-Comte to Rigny, May 18, 1834, Hurmuzaki, XVII, p. 395; Cochelet to Broglie, Aug. 10, 1835, *ibid.*, pp. 502-4; Duclos to Molé, Nov. 20, 1837, *ibid.*, pp. 676-7; Duclos to Molé, Feb. 28, *Aff. Etr., Corr. Com. Jassy*, vol. 3; Filitti, *Corespondența Consulilor Englezi*, pp. 887, 898; cf. A. Beer, *Die orientalische Politik Oesterreichs seit 1774*, (Vienna, 1883), pp. 382-6. Metternich was indeed aware of the dangers of Russian control of the mouth of the Danube, but he went no further than informal protests. (E. Molden, *Die Orientpolitik des Fürsten Metternich, 1929-1833*, Vienna, 1913, p. 89; V. J. Puryear, *England, Russia, and the Straits Question*, Berkeley, 1931, p. 18). He did, however, make an attempt to balance England against Russia in 1834, seeking to get from Palmerston a guarantee of the status quo in the Principalities. (H.W.V. Temperley, *The Crimea*, London, 1936, pp. 80-1).

by Félix Colson, a young secretary of the French consulate in Bucharest, and the sympathy shown by Huber, French consul at Jassy, were but personal attitudes which served to deceive the Roumanian nationalists as to the official policy of the French government.[29] Châteaugiron, consul at Bucharest, more nearly represented that policy than did Colson and Huber; an outspoken opponent of the national party, he sent Colson home for "consorting with the enemies of the prince and publicly professing subversive doctrines," and warned the Foreign Office against Câmpineanu as "a dangerous man."[30]

---

29. Colson went from Bucharest to Jassy to spread propaganda; at that time he broached the union plan to Sturdza in an interview near the end of January, 1839. He later accompanied Câmpineanu to Paris, where, to present the Daco-Roumanian case to the French public, he published many newspaper articles and the following brochures and books: Précis des droits des Valaques, (1838); Précis des droits des Moldaves et des Valaques, fondé sur le droit des gens, (1839); Coup d'oeil rapide sur l'état des populations chrétiennes de la Turquie d'Europe, (1839); De l'État présent et de l'avenir des Principautés de Moldavie et de Valachie, (1839). Colson's lack of tact and political sense, however, compromised both himself and the cause he was trying to promote. Huber, more circumspect but favorable to the nationalists, was their channel of communication with the French Government. He considered the union of Bessarabia, Bucovina, Transylvania, and the Banat to the Principalities to be "a rational idea," for it would create a rampart of real moral and physical strength, which would be useful to Turkey and to the other powers. (Hurmuzaki, Documente, vol. XVII, p. 739).

30. Châteaugiron to Molé, Sept. 23, Nov. 19, 1838, Jan. 24, Feb. 18, 1838, Aff. Etr., Corr. Com., Bucarest, vol. 7. "Le colonel Campiniano est un homme dangereux par son exaltation intempestive et ses projets, peut-être patriotiques, mais mal calculés." (Dispatch of Feb. 18, 1839).

Câmpineanu's interviews with Thiers and other ministers in Paris led to nothing. Their attention was fixed on Mehemet Ali, whose successes were threatening to throw the whole Ottoman Empire into the melting pot. The Roumanians were but an insignificant factor in the eastern question; the fate of the Ottoman Empire would determine their destiny as well. The idea of opening up the Polish question in an attempt to attack Russia with the national and revolutionary forces of eastern Europe apparently made no great appeal to Thiers and Louis Philippe. France's political and commercial interests in the Principalities, the "nullity" of which had caused Paris to abolish the consulate at Jassy in 1830, had not increased sufficiently to warrant a serious attempt to keep them out of Russia's orbit. Commercial contacts had become more numerous, but despite strong recommendations by consuls in favor of stimulating trade, France was left far behind England and Austria in the boom created by the rapid development of the Principalities in the 1830's as a source of grain and as a market for finished goods.

Because of England's trade interests and hostility to Russia, Câmpineanu had counted more on Palmerston than on France. As early as 1836 he had asked Colquhoun whether an appeal to the British Government would have any effect; he was told that if he appealed to anyone, it should be to the Porte; any other move might bring trouble from Russia.[31]

---

31. Colquhoun to Palmerston, Dec. 19, 1836, F.O. 78, vol.288.

Colquhoun, however, made no secret of his sympathy for the national party and was a close personal friend of Câmpineanu. He was anxious to prove to Palmerston that the Principalities were the key to Turkey, the crucial point at which Russian influence could and should be blocked.[32] Naturally he did his best to link up the Roumanian question with the larger aspects of Britain's eastern policy, but the final decision on that point lay with Palmerston, who was not easily convinced. When Câmpineanu had left for the West, Colquhoun prepared his followers for what he knew was coming by telling them that England regarded the Principalities with deep interest, but that they formed but a small part of a great question, upon the settlement of which their fate must also depend.[33] That was the substance of Palmerston's reply to Câmpineanu. It was the preservation of the Ottoman Empire in which he was interested, and at the very time of the Câmpineanu visit, the summer of 1839, he was engaged in a

---

32. Colquhoun to Palmerston,Apr. 14, June 39, 1837, Mar. 23, 1839, F.O. 78, vols. 313, 363. Colquhoun did try to calm the more revolutionary spirits, but admitted that "it was difficult to explain to these people the position of their country; often when I have entreated them to look to Turkey as the means through which I believe our Government can aid them, they are as loud in their outcries against the Suzerain as against the Protecting Court." (Colquhoun to Palmerston, May 2, 1838, and cf. also his dispatch of Nov. 5, 1838, both in F.O. 78, vol. 336).

33. Colquhoun to Palmerston, Mar. 23, 1838, F.O. 78, voll 363.

rapprochement with Russia on that basis.[34] The decision of the four great powers, laid down in the collective note of July 27th, to work together in settling the eastern question, froze the status quo in the Principalities. To provoke Russia by raising the Roumanian or Polish question was the last thing Palmerston wanted to do. The new situation dealt the final blow to Câmpineanu's schemes. The bloc of "constitutional" powers in opposition to the Holy Alliance now no longer existed; neither alone nor in concert would France or England lift a finger in favor of Roumanian nationality. Thrust back upon its own resources, the national party had to abandon its bold plans. Persecuted and disillusioned, Câmpineanu gave up his leadership and went over to the Russian camp.[35]

3. Revolutionary Disturbances, 1840-1843

The evaporation of prospective foreign alliances had its inevitable aftermath in the Principalities. In Moldavia,

---

34. H. W. V. Temperley, The Crimea, pp. 107-8; F. S. Rodkey, The Turco-Egyptian Question in the Relations of England, France and Russia, 1832-1841, (Urbana, Ill., 1923), pp. 101ff. Vicomte de Guichen, La crise orientale de 1839 à 1841 et les grandes puissances, (Paris, 1921, pp. 105ff.

35. The discovery of the magnitude of Câmpineanu's plans in 1837-1840 has made of him quite a national hero, a prophet of national unification. See especially the studies of Panaitescu and Popescu, (cited above), and also Alexandru Lapedatu, "Ioan Câmpineanu," (Figuri Revoluționare Români, Bucharest, 1937, pp. 73-99).

where there had been less preparation and where the whole game was in the hands of the Prince, a conspiracy of minor proportions was discovered and easily quelled.[36] In Wallachia, on the other hand, real preparations had been made, and spirits were raised to the point where they could not automatically cool off.

The direction taken by the eastern question and the shifts of policy on the part of the powers alternately raised and lowered Roumanian hopes. With the establishment of a four-power concert in July 1839, it was thought that there might be a fundamental overhauling of the Ottoman Empire and a possibility that the Principalities would be withdrawn from the sphere of Russia and put under the joint protection of all the great powers.[37] At the time when Thiers was threatening the rest of Europe with war, there was hope in some circles that it might become a war of nationalities, with France fulfilling her mission as _puissance régénératrice_. A few bold spirits prepared to invade and reconquer Bessarabia.[38]

---

36. A. D. Xenopol, _Istoria Partidelor Politice_, vol. I, pp. 193-203; Filitti, _Domniile Române sub Regulamentul Organic_, pp. 507-10.

37. Billecocq to Dalmatie, Sept. 9, 1839, _Aff. Etr., Corr. Com., Bucarest_, vol. 7; for similar views a year later, see Huber to Thiers, Oct. 19, 1840, _Corr. Com., Jassy_, vol.3.

38. Vaillant, _La Romanie_, vol. II, pp. 404-5; Elias Regnault, _Histoire politique et sociale des Principautés Danubiennes_, (Paris, 1855), p. 204; Ubicini, _Provinces d'origine roumaine_, pp. 155-6.

These were but vain illusions. All the powers, in settling the Egyptian question, showed their anxiety to avoid any change of the *status quo* in European Turkey. That situation left the Roumanian national party wholly without means of implementing any strong policy in opposition to Russia. Câmpineanu, their leader, was in jail. The boyars in the party were circumspect enough to remain quiet and to adapt themselves to the new situation. Not so the young men who had put heart and soul into the movement, and the groups of middle and lower class people who were in a fighting mood, thanks to the effects of propaganda and the high price of bread.[39]

Câmpineanu's young followers, scorning caution, plotted to overthrow the Ghica regime by armed revolution in Bucharest and in the provincial cities. In May, 1840, Colquhoun reported:

> "I have strong grounds for suspecting the existence of a party, numerous and well-organized, composed of several men of the highest class, and a greater number of those of the second and third classes, and many officers in the militia....I am led to believe there are over four thousand men in this party....I am much afraid some excesses may be committed..., from what I know to be the character of those said to be the leaders." 40

---

39. Colquhoun to Palmerston, Nov. 14, 1839, F.O. 78, vol. 363; I. C. Filitti, "Turburări Revoluționare în Țara-Românească între anii 1840-1843," (*Ac Rom., Mem. Sect. Ist.*, Ser. II, vol. 34, pp. 201-290), p. 214.

40. Colquhoun to Palmerston, May 17, 1840, F.O. 78, vol. 400.

Totally inadequate preparation made these would-be revolutionaries an easy mark for the Russian agents and Ghica's police. The plot was discovered in October and the leaders arrested, among them Mitica Filipescu, Marin Serghiescu, Cesar Boliac, and the future historian Bălcescu. Filipescu was to die a martyr in prison, the others to become leaders of the revolution of 1848. The "foreign agitators," whom the Prince naturally accused of responsibility for the importation of radicalism, were Eftimiu Murgu, a Roumanian professor from the Banat, and J. A. Vaillant, well-known French pedagogue who conducted a French pensionnat connected with the College of St. Sava and had written several French-Roumanian grammars and dictionaries.[41] Murgu and Vaillant were forced to leave Wallachia; the others were given sentences of from three to ten years in salt mines or in monastery-prisons.[42]

---

41. O. Cudalbu-Slușanschi, "Contributions à la biographie et à l'oeuvre de J. A. Vaillant," (Mélanges de l'Ecole Roumaine en France, Paris, vol. XIV, 1937-8, pp. 1-113), pp. 29-30, 39-41. Other "foreigners" whom Ghica held responsible were Colson and Colquhoun. He tried unsuccessfully, through the Porte and through Metternich and by a personal letter to Palmerston, to have Colquhoun recalled. (Ghica to Metternich, Nov. 5, 1840, in Filitti, op.cit., pp. 202-3; Colquhoun to Palmerston, May 15, 1840, F.O. 78, vol. 400.

42. Filitti, op.cit., pp. 220-2. Bălcescu, Boliac, Kogălniceanu, and others of the men of 1848 acquired more than an academic acquaintance with some of the historic old Roumanian monasteries, for these were favorite places of incarceration for political prisoners. In keeping with this tradition, the famous monastery of Văcărești, near Bucharest, is now a state prison.

While all these men had been partisans of the Câmpineanu party, there is evidence to show that they took a view of the national problems different in some respects from that of their former leader. They had put aside for the time being the utopian aim of national unification, although one of the main points of the Government's case against them was their correspondance with Constantin Negruzzi in Moldavia and Gheorghe Bariţ, the leading Roumanian journalist in Transylvania. Their attention was drawn much more to the necessity of reform in Wallachia and of ending Russian control. The influence of France was discernible in Câmpineanu's program of 1838. It was far more apparent in this movement two years later. Mitica Filipescu had just returned from several years of study in Paris; the others had received their French ideas through reading, and through personal contact with men like Vaillant and Colson. Despite Ghica's censorship, the latter's writings were circulating in the Principalities, as were numbers of Le National, in which he had inserted some strongly anti-Ghica and anti-Russian articles.[43] Inspiration was supplied by a stirring "Marseillaise of the Roumanians," written by Cesar Boliac.[44]

---

43. Billecocq to Guizot, Feb. 10, 1841, Aff. Etr., Correspondance Politique des Consuls, Turquie, Bucarest, vol. 1; Colquhoun to Palmerston, May 25, 1840, F.O. 78, vol. 400; Filitti, op.cit., 280-283.

44. Academia Română, Mss. românești, No. 21, fol. 31.

The plotters of 1840 drew up no draught constitution, but their intentions are revealed in their correspondence found by the police and in Vaillant's later work on Roumania.[45] First of all they wanted a "national and independent" administration, free of the influence of Russia and the creatures of Russia, and of the all-pervasive corruption Willing to attack the fundamental problems of the social system, they were the first to include the lower classes in their claims for liberty and political rights. Bălcescu felt that the peasants would have to be freed of the yoke of their proprietors. In their plotting they had intended to make use of the merchants, artisans, and peasants.[46] All were of the opinion that there should be a representative legislative body; some felt it would be necessary to proclaim a republic. There was a difference of opinion on the amount of blood which would have to be spilled; all agreed that, once in power, they would have to break the big boyars' political monopoly and create a large army to defend the new order from internal and external enemies. Thus the general direction in which these unsuccessful revolutions were traveling was straight toward the bourgeois-agrarian democratic society which they tried to establish, again without

---

45. La Romanie, (3 vols., Paris, 1844). vol. II, pp. 358, 373-6, 379, 381-2, 400-4, 409.

46. Ubicini, op.cit., p. 156; Filitti, op.cit., p. 261.

success, in 1848.[47] The inclusion of the middle and lower classes in both theory and action indicated not merely that these young boyars were more deeply marked by French influences than were the "carbonari" and "constitutionalists" of the preceding two decades. It showed also that bourgeois economics were beginning to catch up to bourgeois ideology. The increasing contact with western capitalism was breaking the bonds of the feudal agrarian system, and while the few big boyars still profited by the existence of virtual serfdom, the small boyars began to discover a solidarity between their own interests and those of the townspeople and peasants, whose support was essential in their own fight for political and economic power.[48]

Ghica's suppression of these bold young men restored a surface calm to Wallachia, but this was a period of unrest and general fermentation of spirits which was not long in manifesting itself in other directions. The eastern crisis of 1839-41 had stirred also the neighboring peoples, the Bulgarians and the Serbs, whose leaders were seeking to make capital of the state of flux into which Mehemet Ali had

---

47. Ion G. Ion, "Adevăratul 1848," (Viața Românească, Bucharest, XXX, Feb., Mar., 1938, pp. 7-19, 34-49), pp. 10-11 (Feb.).

48. Cf. St. Zeletin, Burghezia Română. Origina si rolul ei istoric, (Bucharest, 1925), pp. 54-7.

thrown the whole Near East.[49]

The idea that the Roumanians and the Balkan peoples south of the Danube had interests in common was no novelty. At the time of the Serbian revolution, Constantin Ypsilanti, whose ideas included the liberation of all the Balkan Christians had made an attempt to become ruler of a union of Moldavia, Wallachia and Serbia.[50] Prince Czartoryski, was then, as a Russian minister, proposing a union of Christian Balkan peopěes.[51] Like the idea of the union of the Principalities, that of a Balkan or Lower Danubian confederation under the protection of the great powers was current in Roumanian boyar circles in the 1830's.[52] Czartoryski was in 1840 pursuing a similar scheme of federation, this time witn the purpose of forming an anti-Russian bloc.[53] Even without encouragement

---

49. "Les Romains, les Serviens, les Bulgares, dans la prévision d'un conflit général, songent aux moyens de tirer leur épingle du jeu...[Tous] doivent faire cause commune pour résister à toute invasion de leur territoire, et profiter de la conflagration de l'Europe...pour s'affranchir du joug de l'étranger." (Vaillant, op.cit., pp. 404-5).

50. P. P. Panaitescu, Corespondenţa lui Constantin Ypsilanti cu Guvernul Rusesc, (Bucharest, 1933), pp. 13, 19, 32-6; Iorga, Istoria Românilor, vol. VIII, pp. 177-8, 188.

51. Henryk Batowski, "Un préourseur de l'union balkanique, le prince Czartoryski," (Revue Internationale des Etudes Balkaniques, Belgrade, II, 1936, pp. 149-156).

52. Filitti, Corespondenţa Consulilor Englezi, p. 888; Hurmuzaki, Documente, vol. XVII, p. 398.

53. Handelsman, op.cit., pp. 29-30; H. Batowski, "Le mouvement panbalkanique et les differents aspects des relations interbalkaniques dans le passé," (Rev. Int. des Etudes Balk., III, 1937-8, pp. 320-43), pp. 322-3.

on the part of the Poles, the Roumanians and Serbs were sensitive to each other's fortunes, because of their similar position under Turkish suzerainty and Russian protection; both paid close attention to Bulgaria, where a revolt would threaten a new Russian-Turkish quarrel and a new regulation of the eastern question.[54] Those Wallachians who had evaded Alexander Ghica's repressive measures immediately mixed themselves into a new plot, sponsored by a "Society for the liberation of Slavic peoples on the right and left banks of the Danube," and aimed at simultaneous revolts in Bucharest and in Bulgaria, coupled with an invasion of Ottoman territory by groups of Bulgarians crossing the Danube from Wallachia at several points.[55] The exiled Prince Miloš,

---

54. In 1838 Câmpineanu had felt certain of the co-operation of the Serbs, "for Miloš is not far from playing the role of Stephen Dušan." (Panaitescu, Planurile lui Ioan Câmpineanu, p. 91). In 1839, a conspiracy of boyars and bourgeois against Sturdza and the Russian protectorate in Moldavia had as one of its aims the establishment of a confederation of Danubian states. (Xenopol, Istoria Partidelor Politice, vol. I, p. 195). In the spring of 1840, Colquhoun reported; "There are at this moment emissaries at Bucharest from Bulgaria and Servia, and there is no doubt an union existing among these three provinces [Wallachia, Serbia, Bulgaria] which may be highly dangerous to the peace of these countries." (Colquhoun to Palmerston, May 17, 1840, F.O. 78, vol. 400).

55. Filitti, Turburări revoluţionare, pp. 226-7; Iorga, Etudes Roumaines, vol. II, (Paris, 1924), p. 97; Eliade Rădulescu, Issachar, p. 120. The charge that Eliade himself was mixed up in this affair remains unproved. (Cf. Regnault, Histoire politique et sociale des Principautés Danubiennes, pp. 209-13; F. Damé, Histoire de la Roumanie contemporaine, p. 23; Billecocq to Guizot, Mar. 11, Apr. 17, 1842, Aff. Etr., Corr. Pol. Bucaret , vol. 1).

who was living near Bucharest at the time, may not have been a stranger to these proceedings.[56] The new French consul, Billecocq, a bitter enemy of Russia, who conceived as his duty "the preparation of these countries for constitutional institutions and for the spirit of liberty," was probably counted on for support by certain Roumanian nationalists, though he was party to no plot against Ghica. And the plans of the Bulgarians were without question encouraged by the Russian vice-consul in Galatz. With these varied and contradictory forces pushing in various directions, it was no wonder that the great revolution wound up by being a street fight at Brăila, with Ghica's police and militia massacring a crowd of Bulgarians.[57] Similar outbreaks took place in 1842 and

---

56. One of the Bulgarian leaders, Descho, later testified that he was connected with a scheme sponsored by Miloš to make Bulgaria independent. To this project he attributed the agitations among the Bulgarians resident in Wallachia. Miloš's plan was said to be to offer the throne of Bulgaria to a pro-Russian Wallachian boyar, Constantin Soutzo. (Billecocq to Guizot, Sept. 6, Oct. 30, 1844, Aff. Etr., Corr. Pol., Bucarest, vol. 3.). Billecocq later told of a series of nocturnal interviews with Miloš, at which the old prince revealed plans to lead a great rising of nationalities against the despotisms (Russia, Austria, and Turkey), and begged for French support, which Billecocq was unable to give. (Billecocq, Le Nostre Prigioni, (Paris, 1849), vol. I, pp. 152-64; Regnault, op.cit., pp. 223-7). In trying to get British support to regain his throne, Miloš threatened, if not helped, a rising of the Balkan peoples which would leave the fate of Turkey in Europe hanging in the balance. (Colquhoun to Palmerston, Aug. 10, 1840, F.O. 78,vol.363).

57. Filitti, op.cit., pp. 227-35; Radu Crutzescu, Amintirile Colonelului Lăcusteanu, (Bucharest, 1935), pp. 81-9; Iorga, Istoria Românilor, vol. IX, (Bucharest, 1938), pp. 31-33; Billecocq to Guizot, July 30, Aug. 5, 1841, Aff. Etr., Corr. Pol., Bucarest, vol. 1.

in 1843, with similar lack of success. They seem to have been part of a great Hetairist scheme, supported by Greeks, Serbs, Bulgarians, and a few Roumanians to put an end to Turkish rule on the Balkan Peninsula.[58] Russian help was expected and Russian agents mixed up in the affair, though after failure those agents were always disavowed. The participation of Russia in these plots kept most Roumanian nationalists out of them, for their sympathy with the Southern Slavs could not outweigh the fact that Russia, and not Turkey, was the real oppressor of Roumanian nationality. At this very time, certain of the Wallachian boyars were attempting once more to unite the Principalities under Sturdza and be rid of the Russian protectorate. Ion Ghica, recently returned from Paris, was commissioned by them, in the autumn of 1841, to make such a proposal to Sturdza. It was turned down; Sturdza knew that Russia was still master, and that to defy her would be political suicide.[59] Moldavia felt reverberations of the intense revolutionary activity in the sister principality; indeed some were brought by Vaillant in person, whose connections with a revolutionary society in Jassy resulted in his enforced departure from there

---

58. Billecocq to Guizot, Mar. 9, 1842, loc.cit.

59. Ion Ghica, Scrisori către Vasile Alecsandri, pp. 183-4, 248, 646-7.

as well.[60]

The changes of rulers both in Serbia and in Wallachia, plus the Bulgarian revolts in the Danubian cities of Wallachia, and on Bulgarian soil, kept the Balkan question as a whole before the eyes of nationalists on both sides of the Danube. Roumanians hoped that the triumphs of the Serbian national cause would be repeated in the Principalities, and feared that Russian diplomatic defeats in the Serbian question would lead to military measures and occupation.[61] There was a feeling of solidarity between Serbs and Roumanians which however, did not cut very deep and could hardly be implemented, in view of the impotence of both parties as against Russia or Turkey. But the idea of confederation was in the air. Advocated also by certain circles in France, it was later to become an accepted item in the doctrine of many Balkan nationalists. Besides the Czartoryski group, there was Cyprien Robert, who pleaded for recognition of the "Greco-Slavic races" as the key to the eastern question, and urged French support for a federation under Turkish

---

60. Viollier (consul at Galatz) to Billecocq, Junr 20, 1841, _Aff. Etr._, _Corr. Pol._, _Bucarest_, vol. 1; Huber to Guizot, June 20, 1841, _Corr. Com._, _Jassy_, vol. 3; Cudalbu-Slusanschi, _Contributions à la biographie et à l'oeuvre de J. A. Vaillant_, pp. 37-38; Filitti, _Domniile Române sub Regulamentul Organic_, pp. 512-13.

61. Billecocq to Guizot, July 5, 11, Aug. 4, 17, 1843, _Aff. Etr._, _Corr. Pol._, _Bucarest_, vol. 2; Duclos to Guizot, Sept. 9, 1843, _Corr. Com._, _Jassy_, vol. 5.

suzerainty, "which the leaders of the Balkan peoples think is the best solution."[62] Vaillant, back in Paris after fifteen years in the Principalities, also spoke out strongly for federation:

> "Policy will succeed....I hope, in making the five great powers understand the necessity of realizing the idea of Mr. Urquhart and the desire of the peoples of the lower Danube, by making of them an independent confederation...in which the Roumanians, people of noble origin and the advance guard of Christianity, would take their rightful place as a united nation." 63

4. The high tide of French influence

The July Monarchy, under the cautious guidance of Guizot, made not the slightest effort to respond to demands that it become patron and protector of the unliberated nationalities of Europe. The salutory experience of 1840 had left its mark; in eastern affairs, France became a docile member of the Concert of Europe. The Principalities, as a part of the Ottoman Empire, needed, in Guizot's opinion, no special consideration; certainly he had no desire to engage in a diplomatic battle with Russia over the extent of Russian influence there. He looked benevolently on the efforts of

---

62. C. Robert. Les Slaves de la Turquie, (Paris, 1844) esp. vol. I, pp. 1-8; 19-30.

63. Vaillant, La Romanie, vol. I, pp. 10-12. Strangely enough, Austria, Russia, and Turkey were to be members of this "independent confederation" for the provinces of Transylvania and Bulgaria respectively, without dominating it any more than Prussia dominated Switzerland.

the Roumanians to "enter upon the path of progress and civilization" and even looked forward to the time, very far in the future, when the Balkan peoples would be constituted as independent national states.[64] But he felt no call to speed up this development. Appeals in the name of a Roumanian nation were no concern of French policy;[65] appeals to check the Russian advance were the concern of Europe, not of France alone. France's commercial interests were certainly not great enough to change that line of policy.[66]

Guizot had the misfortune to be represented at Bucharest by the erratic and tempestuous M. Billecocq, who felt himself divinely appointed to save Europe from Russian domination.

---

64. Guizot to de Nion, Dec. 12, 1846, _Aff. Etr._, _Corr. Pol._, _Bucarest_, vol. 4.

65. "Nous ne faisons pas de la politique valaque," wrote Bourqueney to Billecocq (Oct. 18, 1842, _Aff. Etr._, _Corr. Pol. Bucarest_, vol. 1) in one of his many dispatches telling the consul not to meddle in internal affairs.

66. Most of the French goods which reached the Principalities came by way of Leipzig or Vienna. With the opening of the sea route, Brăila and Galatz on the Danube became thriving ports, and a sizeable trade, with grain and wood exchanged for luxury goods, might have been developed. But the Marseille merchants were too timid to act on the repeated suggestions sent by the French consuls. Only a handful of French ships per year called at Brăila and Galatz. Cochelet, one of the ablest of the consuls, insisted on the need for increasing trade as the only way to acquire a strong political influence. (Cochelet to Broglie, Aug. 16, 1835, _Aff. Etr., Corr. Com., Bucarest_, vol. 6, and his long report, "Itinéraire des principautés de Moldavie et de Valachie," _Bulletin de la Société de Géographie de Paris_, XIX, 1843, pp. 249-274).

Judging the Principalities to be the crucial point of the great struggle between civilization and barbarism, he made his dispatches a succession of pleas for an active French policy.[67] In Bucharest he saw the hand of Russia in every intrigue, of which there were many. The deposition of his friend Alexander Ghica and the elevation to the throne of George Bibescu, whom he characterized as a mere puppet of the Tsar, put him in an awkward position which grew even more strained until in 1846 Bibescu appealed directly and successfully to Guizot for Billecocq's recall.[68] Though this whole affair was hardly a stimulus to good Franco-Roumanian relations,

---

67. The following is his own eloquent expression of the direction of his policy: "La haute sagacité de Votre Excellence la portera, j'ose espérer, à en apprécier un jour l'accomplissement, si, dans les grands conflits qui peuvent tout.à.coup s'engager, ce berceau d'une civilisation naissante,...venant à être menacé encore par quelques flots venus du Nord ou de l'Orient, peut, grâce à la politique bienveillante que je représente ici, demeurer sain et sauf et donner quelque jour l'essor à un peuple qui sache enfin se montrer digne de la plus noble et de la plus illustre des origines." (Billecocq to Guizot, June 28, 1842, Aff. Etr., Corr. Pol., Bucarest, vol. 1).

68. Adolphe Billecocq, Le nostre prigioni!, (2 vols., Paris, 1849), is a hysterical diatribe against "the ministry of the 29th of October." The whole Billecocq affair is treated at length in G. Bibesco, Règne de Bibesco, (Paris, 1893-4), vol. I, pp. 224-8, 245-300, from Bibescu's viewpoint, and in Regnault, Histoire politique et sociale, pp. 195-229, 246-7, from Billecocq's viewpoint; and more briefly in Anonymous [Billecocq], Coup d'oeil sur les Provinces Danubiennes, (Saumur, 1856), pp. 19-23; Iorga, Histoire des Relations entre la France et les Roumains, pp. 161-9; Vasile V. Hanes, Formarea Opiniunii franceze asupra României în secolul al XIX-lea, (Bucharest, 1929), vol. II, pp. 160-73. Billecocq always maintained that his recall was brought about by the Tsar, working through Mme. Lieven's influence on Guizot.

Billecocq's six year stay in Bucharest was not without significance. He became a sincere Roumanophil, encouraged anti-Russian feeling and faith in France, and acquired a knowledge of the country and people which he put to advantage later in pleading their cause in Paris.

One thing which Billecocq and many of his Roumanian friends could not understand, was why French foreign policy was so reluctant to take advantage of the overwhelming influence exerted upon the upper ranks of society by everything that was French. Revolutionary ideas were not the only importation from Paris; more tangible articles were books, newspapers, clothes, wines, and quantities of _articles de luxe_, which had become necessities to the ladies of society. French merchants did not need to worry about suiting the tastes of the Roumanian consumers; it was sufficient that an article be made in France. It was the same in the theatre, where despite efforts in both capitals to create a national theatre, a French company generally held forth, and in the salons, where only French was spoken. Foreign visitors to Bucharest and Jassy were amazed at finding these bits of France in an out-of-the-way corner of Europe; nearly every travel book comments on the Roumanians' proficiency in the French language and their taste for French literature.[69]

---

69. Bois-le-Comte to Rigny, May 10, 14, 1834, Hurmuzaki, _Documente_, vol. XVII, pp. 352-3, 371; A. Rally, "Le voyage de Cochelet dans les principautés danubiennes,"

Actually, this coat of French varnish on the upper class in Bucharest and Jassy was neither thick enough to cover up what was still an essentially oriental society, nor did it extend much beyond the city limits of the two capitals. Far more significant was the profound effect of French literary influence; having first contributed to bringing the Roumanians in contact with "Europe" and to arousing, or creating, a consciousness of nationality, it had now so pervaded the whole of intellectual life in the Principalities that it threatened to overwhelm and stifle the still unformed national culture.

Until 1830 the contacts with France were mostly indirect and hard to assess; the period after that date saw a manifold increase in those contacts. Roumanian political life, despite the straight-jacket of the Règlement and the bullying of Russia, shook off much of its orientalism; the new educational system gave westernism a more solid foundation; and, most important of all, Roumanian boyars began to send their

---

(Revue Historique du Sud-Est Européen, VIII, 1931, pp. 276-94), pp. 280-290-1; Saint-Marc Girardin, Souvenirs, vol. I, pp. 280-2; Edouard Thouvenel, La Hongrie et la Valachie, (Paris, 1840), pp. 173-5; Stanislas Bellanger, Le Keroutza, (Paris, 1846), vol. I, pp. 310-11; William Rey, Autriche, Hongrie et Turquie, (Paris, 1849), p. 208; and also the following dispatches: Huber to Molé, Feb. 19, Mar. 15, May 23, 1838, Aff. Etr., Corr. Com. (Dir. pol., copie), Jassy, vol. 3, and Hurmuzaki, Documente, XVII, pp. 693-4; Duclos to Guizot, May 20, 1843, Jan. 30, 1846, Corr. Com., Jassy, vol. 4; Codrika to Guizot, Dec. 28, 1846, ibid.

sons to Paris in ever-increasing numbers. In respect to literature, suffice it to say that for almost every example of poetry or prose in this period there existed a French model, classic or romantic, of which it was a copy. The poetry of Lamartine and Béranger, the plays of Scribe, the novels of Dumas underwent but slight change by being decked out in Dacian costume. Only a few Roumanians, Alexandrescu for example, were able to profit by French models without sacrificing originality.[70] Translations, also, continued in an unending stream,[71] and the importation of French books increased every year. Reading clubs and lending libraries were established in the two capitals.[72] The official records of the entrance of books into Moldavia in the years 1837 and 1838, as sample years, show that 3% of the books imported were English and Italian, 17% German, and 80% French. Most

---

70. The following are the most important studies on phases of this question of comparative literature: G. Bogdan-Duică, _Istoria literaturei române moderne. Intâii poeți munteni_, (Cluj, 1923); N. I. Apostolescu, _L'influence des romantiques français sur la poésie roumaine_, (Paris, 1909); Charles Drouhet, _Vasile Alecsandri și Scriitori Francese_, (Bucharest, 1924); _idem._, _Modelele franceze ale teatrului lui Alecsandri_, (Jassy, 1913-14); _idem._, "Grigore Alexandrescu și Voltaire," (_Omagiu lui Ion Bianu_, Bucharest, 1927, pp. 175-92); E. Lovinescu, _Grigore Alexandrescu_, (Bucharest, 1928); P. Eliade, _La Roumanie au XIXe. siècle_, pp. 330ff.

71. A list of translations, not complete, in A.Demetrescu, _L'influence de la langue et de la litterature françaises en Roumanie_, (Lausanne, 1888), p. 45.

72. Nicolae Kretzulescu, _Amintiri Istorice_, pp. 33-4; C. A. Kuch, _Moldauische-Wallachische Zustände in de Jahren 1828 bis 1843_, (Leipzig, 1844), p. 207.

frequent among the French were the works of Molière, Madame de Sevigné, Boileau, Voltaire, J. J.Rousseau, Hugo, Châteaubriand, Lamartine, Thiers, and host of novels. Rotteck's world history, in French translation, was very popular, and Karamzin, also in translation, is listed. Herder, Goethe, and Schiller were among the German works imported.[73] In Wallachia, the proportion of French books was probably even higher.

5. Reaction against the French influence

In the neighborhood of the year 1840 there was a strong reaction, centering around a group of young Moldavians, who had themselves been schooled in the West and molded by French influences, but who now wanted to turn sharply away from the excesses of imitation and seek inspiration in the "soul" of their own people. Mihail Kogălniceanu, returning from Berlin, Vasile Alecsandri from Paris, Alexandru Russo from Geneva, were the three leading spirits, and Dacia Literară their mouthpiece.[74]

---

73. I. Minea. Ce cetise Generatiunea Unirii din Moldova, (Bucharest, 1919), pp. 6, 17-8. There are no statistics on the actual quantity of books received from France. The censorship records give only incomplete lists of books passing the frontier and books kept in stock by booksellers. Among the banned works were Vaillant's La Romanie and Urquhart's Turkey and its Resources. Radu Rosetti, "Despre Censura in Moldova," Parts I-III, (Ac. Rom., Mem. Sect. Ist., Ser. II, vol. 29, 1907, pp. 297-531), p. 415.

74. Ion Ghica, back from Paris, came to Jassy to work with them. In Wallachia, Grigore Alexandrescu, and later

This movement was directed not so much against the fundamental postulates of westernism as against the lamentable effects which a superficial knowledge of the West was having on so many members of a nation not sufficiently mature to exercise selection in submitting to a higher culture. It seemed to Kogălniceanu and his friends that a whole generation of _déracinés_ was coming into being, losing all ties with its native soil in a vain attempt to become part of another world to which it could never belong.[75] Such enthusiastic Francophils, _bonjouristes_ as they were called, speaking and writing a language which included enough French words to be socially acceptable but literarily impossible, were to be

---

Bălcescu, represented the same "historical-popular" current. See Radu Dragnea, _Mihail Kogălniceanu_, (2nd ed., Bucharest, 1927), pp. 95-135; G. Adamescu, _Istoria Literaturii Române_, (3rd ed., Bucharest, pp. 279, 289; Lovinescu, _Grigore Alexandrescu_, pp. 203ff.

75. Iorga, "Le Romantisme dans le Sud-Est de l'Europe," (_Revue Historique du Sud-Est_, I, 1924, pp. 301-401), pp. 354-5; Iorga, _Istoria literaturei româneşti în secolul al XIX-lea_, vol. II, (Bucharest, 1908), p. 34. Cf. Hans Kohn, speaking of the Near East in general: "At the outset some of the native leaders are fascinated by the glamour, the freedom and beauty of European civilization, not only by its external wealth, but also by the internal power of its life-giving, adventurous fullness; they are in danger of losing themselves in Europe, of becoming semi-Europeans with no roots to them; but many realize that the inevitable Europeanization has to be led into safe paths, taken in hand instead of being passively and helplessly submitted to." (_Western Civilization in the Near East_, New York, 1936, p. 90).

found everywhere in Bucharest and Jassy. They had become a favorite subject for comedy and satire.[76] It was, after all, a good subject for comedy, an upper class whose assimilative qualities were such that it was becoming not Roumanian at all but pseudo-European. What was not so comic, to these young Moldavians at any rate, was the fact that literature was undergoing the same evolution. Translation and imitation had gone too far. The worst French novels were translated, for no other reason than that they were French. "Translations are not literature," proclaimed *Dacia Literară* in its opening blast against Eliade and his school.[77] It was the same with the national language; Latinists were trying to take it back to ancient Rome, Eliade to modern Italy, and the aristocrats to France.[78] The answer to all this was plain: there must be a return to the true source of national

---

76. Iorga, *La Romantisme dans le Sud-Est*, pp. 35-7; *idem.*, *Histoire des relations entre la France et les Roumains*, p. 157; P. Eliade, "Les premiers bonjouristes," (*Bulletin du Congrès pour l'extension de la langue francaise, Brussels*, 1904).

77. Dragnea, *op.cit.*, pp. 57ff.; Iorga, *Mihail Kogălniceanu*, (Bucharest, n. d.), pp. 56-69; D. Popovici, *op.cit.*, pp. 194-6; E. Lovinescu, *Gheorghe Asachi*, (Bucharest, 1927), pp. 127-31. The charge that Eliade and Asachi were pure imitators was not justified. Some of their work can be described as "of national inspiration."

78. P. V. Haneş, *Desvoltarea Limbii Literare Române in prima jumatate a secolului al XIX-lea*, (2nd ed., Bucharest, 1927), pp. 58-85, 112-29; Carlo Tagliavini, *Un frammento di storia della lingua rumena nel secolo XIX*, (Rome, 1926); Popovici, *op.cit.*, pp. 279-288.

strength, the people. Roumanians, these men argued, could not buy a civilization ready-made in Paris. Like the Russian Slavophils, they felt that their source of life and strength lay in the homeland and in the peasant and his spirit of "Roumanism" preserved intact through the centuries. This was a return to the past, not to ancient Rome, but to the heroic days of Stephen the Great and Michael the Brave, when the Roumanians were a strong and respected nation. Kogălniceanu dug out and published old and forgotten chronicles.[79] Alecsandri and Russo traveled through the countryside collecting folk songs and folklore handed down from generation to generation.[80]

Among the Roumanians of the Principalities the German influence was negligible, although Kogălniceanu had studied at Berlin under Savigny and was certainly no stranger to the organic approach to intellectual and historical problems. Roumanians like to think of this turning back to the national past as a self-initiated reawakening not attributable to any outside influence, a pleasing theory which overlooks the neighboring peoples and the rest of the European scene.

---

79. His periodical Arhiva Românească, (Jassy, 1841, 1845), published most of these chronicles.

80. N. Petrașcu, Vasile Alecsandri, (2nd ed., Bucharest, n.d.), pp. 88-100; Paul Zarifopol, "Alecsandri," (Revista Fundatilor Regale, Bucharest, II, 1935, pp. 19-28), pp. 19-20; P. V. Haneș, Alexandru Russo, (2nd ed., Bucharest, 1930), pp. 108-16; Jean Boutière, La vie et l'oeuvre de Ion Creanga, (Paris, 1930),pp. 61-9.

It so happened that the inspiration for the philological and historical studies of the Slavs and Hungarians came largely from Germany, while the Roumanians, knowing Hugo and Lamartine well and the Germans but little, drew heavily upon France. In all cases the common denominator was the spirit of the Romantic movement.

Ironically, these opponents of the French influence were, like their entire generation, not sufficiently free of it themselves to make a success of combating it. Like Eliade, who for all his translations was no Francophil and had since 1837 been trying to turn to Italy for inspiration, they could deny France in theory but not in practice.[81] Much of Alecsandri's folk poetry was embroidered or invented by himself, after French models. Russo never learned to handle Roumanian as well as French. Even Kogălniceanu, acquainted as he was with Herder's Stimmen der Völker and other German works, never ceased to represent French thought. At this very time Alecsandri, Kogălniceanu, and Constantin Negruzzi were given the management of the theatre in Jassy, and were reduced to putting on one French play after another. Alecsandri's original plays were closely patterned on what he knew of French drama, and his poems, published in a French-Roumanian periodical, strikingly resembled the

---

81. G. Oprescu, "Eliade Rădulescu și Franța," (Dacoromania, Cluj, III, 1923, pp. 1-128), pp. 34-5, 44-48, 122-3.

Méditations of Lamartine.[82]

Whether or not they proved their case, they at least stated it, and they added to the developing doctrine of nationalism a consciousness of tradition and a pride in the Roumanian past. In the language question they were on solid ground, and even in literature they laid the basis for a more truly national culture than that which Eliade and Asachi, with their encyclopedistic activity, had succeeded in creating.

The problems raised by this controversy have, in one form or another, rocked the Roumanian intellectual world ever since. Is modern Roumanian culture a product of contact with France, or must its roots be sought in the traditions, the folk spirit, the soul of the Roumanian people? That is the central point on which traditionalists have fought with westernizers and so it will probably continue.[83]

---

82. Iorga, Le Romantisme dans le Sud-Est de l'Europe, pp. 350-1, 361; idem., La société roumaine du XIXe. siècle dans le theâtre roumain, pp. 24-35; C. Drouhet, Modelele franceze ale teatrului lui Alecsandri; P. V. Haneș, Studii de Literatura Română, (Bucharest, 1910), p. 50; idem., Alexandru Russo, p. 32; Dragnea, op.cit., p. 50, 103-4; M. Fotino, L'influence française sur les grands orateurs roumains de la seconde moitié du XIXe. siecle, (Bucharest, 1928), pp. 38-47. Alecsandri's poems appeared in Spicuitorul Moldo-Român (Le Glaneur Moldo-Valaque) edited by Asachi and a Frenchman, A. Gallice. It supported westernization and "progress"; its purpose, wrote the editors, was to raise the level of civilization of the people of "Dacia" Moldavia, Wallachia, Transylvania, Bucovina to that of the most enlightened peoples. (No. of Jan.-Feb., 1841, prospectus, pp. 1-39).

83. See especially the studies of French influence by Pompiliu Eliade, product of the Ecole Normale Supérieure,

The terms employed defy exact definition and permit much plausible over-generalization. We can remain on more solid ground by limiting the perspective to those phenomena which appeared in the 19th century, namely an intellectual movement directed toward resurrection of the past glories, real or imaginary, of the Roumanian people; and a political movement which had as its avowed aim the unification of all Roumanian-speaking populations into a single national state. Both were part of a general European trend, which reached the Roumanians through French channels.

6. Links with Transylvania

Another factor which tempered the French influence was the presence in the Principalities of several Transylvanians, who, following in the footsteps of Lazăr, had crossed the mountains in response to the need for teachers in the new national school systems. This group of professors included Ioan Maiorescu, A. T. Laurian, Florian Aaron, Vasile Popp, Aron Pumnul, Eftimiu Murgu of the Banat, and later Axente

---

listed in the bibliography. E Lovinescu, Istoria Civilizației Române, (3 vols., Bucharest, 1926), follows the same line. At the head of the traditionalists stands Iorga, whose innumerable works are tabulated in Barbu Teodorescu, Bibliografia Iorga, (Bucharest, 1937). The following shorter studies show interesting points of view: Sextil Pușcariu, "Renaşterea Noastră Națională," (Omagiu lui Ramiro Ortiz, Bucharest, 1929, pp. 147-51); C. Rădulescu-Motru, Românismul, (2nd ed., Bucharest, 1929); idem., "Rumänien und die deutsche Kultur," (Europäische Revue, Berlin, vol. X(2), Aug. 1934, Sonderheft, pp. 542-8); N. Rosu, Dialectica Naționalismului, (Bucharest, 1935); V. Zaborovschi, "Intre trecut și viitor," (Gândirea, Bucharest, IV, 1925, pp. 307-8.

Sever and Constantin Romanul.[84] They taught in public and private schools, some even shifting from one principality to the other in the course of their careers. Although most of them had been educated in Vienna or Budapest, they were not bearers of any strong outside influence, unless it was that of the occidentalized intelligentsia of Transylvania. Above all they were exponents of Latinism and of the cultivation of the Roumanian language. Popp, on a trip through the Principalities, noted the existence of many large private libraries, furnished mainly with French works; "but what I was looking for, namely Roumanian books, I did not find, but that was not strange,. . .since nobody then spoke Roumanian except the people. . . .The name of Roumanian was synomynous with slave."[85] It was this subordination of the national language, first to Greek and later to French, which the Transylvanians zealously combated. Their weapons were Latinism, sometimes carried to absurd lengths, and a strong national consciousness, born of the historical struggles of the

---

84. Iorga, Istoria literaturei românești în secolul al XIX-lea, vol. I, (Bucharest, 1907), pp. 286ff.; idem., Histoire de l'Enseignement en Pays Roumains, (Bucharest, 1933), pp. 245-51.

85. Ion Mușlea, "Viața și opera Doctorului Vasilie Popp," (Anuarul Institutului de Istoria Națională, V, 1928-30, pp. 86-157), p. 106; cf. Valeriu Branişce, "O convorbire la 1830 despre stările din Muntenia și Moldova," (Convorbiri Literare, LV, 1923, pp. 711-9).

Transylvanian Roumanians.[86]

Their difference in background made it difficult for some of them to fit into or accept the social life of the Principalities. Their reaction to the caste system, with its artificially educated, immoral aristocracy, and inert peasantry, was much the same as that of western observers, with the difference that the latter attributed these things to the Roumanian character, the Transylvanians to "orientalism" and also to the influence of France. Maiorescu wrote in a fiery open letter to a Braşov newspaper: "Where is there any warmth here, any fire? Where is that nationality and patriotism which the Transylvanian Roumanians have? A gross materialism has descended like a thick cloud on Wallachia. Whence came it? From Gaul. . . .This business of putting on a civilization like a new suit, with no originality, is deplorable.

These Transylvanians, with few exceptions, scouted the idea of the early realization of Roumanian political unity as preached by Colson and Vaillant. They knew full well the immense distances yet to be covered before the Roumanians

---

86. "I did not come to this country for my own purposes. You know that well. I came here to work for the rebirth of the nation." (Ioan Maiorescu to F. Aaron, 1838, quoted in N. Bănescu, "Gheorghe Bariţ. Legăturile sale cu Românii din celelalte părţi," (Convorbiri Literare, XLII, 1908, pp. 6-20), pp. 7-8.

87. Foaie Literară, (ed. G. Bariţ), Braşov, Feb. 11, 1838, No. 16, quoted in N. Bănescu and V. Mihăilescu, Ioan Maiorescu, (Bucharest, 1912), pp. 358-9).

would have established the necessary moral and cultural unity. They could feel the differences between themselves and the "oriental" or superficially westernized Roumanians of the Principalities. It was, says Professor Iorga, one of the aspects of the fatal antagonism between a Roumanian society based on inherited name and wealth, tending towards the assimilation of international cultural and social forms, and another and more original Roumanian civilization, developing a moral and national sentiment out of its own social and spiritual struggles.[88]

The task which the Transylvanians set themselves was to knit together the different Roumanian provinces with moral and intellectual ties. Roumanian weakness was real, they felt, not fictitious or a product of misfortune or Russian intrigues; Roumania was a long way from being able to take its place in the European family.[89] Eliade Rădulescu was in fundamental agreement with them on this point, and though pursuing different methods, he agreed on the necessity of common action by the intellectuals of all the provinces.[90]

---

88. Iorga, "Partea Românilor din Ardeal și Ungaria în Cultura Românească. Influența și Conflicte," (Ac. Rom., Mem. Sect. Ist., Ser. II, vol. 33, 1911, pp. 767-86), p. 770. Cf. Wolfgang Höpker, Die Nationalwerdung des rumänischen Volkes, (Munich, 1936), emphasizing the cultural gap between the two branches of the Roumanian people as a prime factor in their history and the central problem of today.

89. Iorga, Ist. lit. rom., vol. I, pp. 290-4.

90. Eliade to Bariț, Nov. 29, 1838, in E. Vîrtosu, I. Heliade Rădulescu. Acte și Scrisori adnotate și publicate, (Bucharest, 1928), pp. 36-41; Eliade to Negruzzi, quoted in A.A.C. Sturdza, Règne de Michel Sturdza, (Paris, 1907), p. 90.

He felt the need of being able to show Europe that the Roumanians were not a "peuplade" but a nation.

This ten-year period, 1838 to 1848, saw the creation of a sort of brotherhood of the intellectuals of all the Roumanian provinces. All were working, not always in the greatest harmony, to create a national literature and spirit. Political boundaries, except in so far as the various censorships were effective, were no real obstacle. Maiorescu hoped to speed up the process by founding "a secret national society, whose members would work unceasingly. . . .Articles should be written on subjects. . .which are wholly national, or foreign subjects which are applicable to our conditions." These articles would be published by Bariţ in a new "National Organ."[91] This society seems not to have been established, but its recommendations were carried out by Bariţ at Braşov, whose journals, Gazeta Transilvaniei and Foaie pentru minte, became, so to speak, national organs publishing the best of what was sent in from other Roumanian lands, and circulating, despite Russian attempts to stop it, in both principalities. It was a gigantic attempt at national education, the effects of which were great but not easily measured. Florian congratulated his countryman for having put the national movement forward fifty years.[92]

---

91. Maiorescu to Bariţ, Aug. 27, 1838, in Bănescu & Mihăilescu, op.cit., pp. 428-30.

92. Bănescu, Gheorghe Bariţ. Legăturile sale, p. 10; Iorga, Ist. lit rom., vol. II, pp. 5-6, 227-53.

7. The Educational System and the French Schools

In the field of education many of these currents came into open conflict; radicalism against conservatism, the French language against the national language, Latinism against Roumanism. The battle to win the coming generation was of crucial importance, especially since education in the Principalities was starting virtually from scratch.

The uniform national school system, established by the Règlement Organique, was both western and national in character. Until then there had been no guiding principle, most schools being under the aegis of the Orthodox Church; the Greek schools, however, had already given way to two large national schools in Craiova and Bucharest and a few smaller ones elsewhere. Barbu Stirbei, author of the new education law for Wallachia, took directly from France the conception that education was the primary need of the nation and a primary obligation of the state. He planned a complete system with four series of schools, from kindergarten to college.[93] With the establishment at Jassy of the Academia Mihăileană in 1835, Moldavia provided itself with its own St. Sava; Michael Sturdza, in his speech of dedication, spoke of the necessity of an easily accessible public education in harmony with

---

93. P. Eliade, La Roumanie au XIXe. siècle, pp. 241-9; Iorga, Histoire de l'enseignement en pays roumains, pp. 175ff.; Almanach de la Cour et de l'Etat de Valachie pour 1838, (Bucharest, 1838), pp. 239-45; Filitti, Les Principautés Roumaines sous l'Occupation Russe, p. 207.

European civilization and with the needs of the country.[94]

The Règlements gave the two principalities similar systems, with Roumanian as the language of instruction and French as the principal foreign language taught. The problem thereafter was to transfer the plans from paper to reality. Despite great efforts this problem was not solved. The official statistics tell great things about the number of schools and of pupils, but these also for the most part remained on paper and were contradicted by other evidence and by the reports of impartial foreigners.[95] Learning certainly did not spread so fast as was claimed by its sponsors and by the two governments, which liked to vote a large school budget, much of which went into governmental pockets. It

---

94. V. A. Urechia, Istoria Şcoalelor, 1800-1864, (Bucharest, 1892-4), vol. II, p. 287.

95. The official figures for Wallachia gave from about 2,000 to 2300 public schools with 30,000 to 50,000 pupils, with the slight fluctuations and a steady increase from 1834 to 1848. (Urechia, op.cit., vol. II, pp. 104,213, 315). Eliade says that normal schools were established in every important town, and primary schools in every village, 4,000 of them. (Mémoires, p. xiv). The separate reports of the different districts told a different story, (Filitti, Domniile Române sub Regulamentul Organic, pp.232-3), as did foreign observers. Kuch, a Prussian consul, reported that there were three elementary schools in Bucharest and seventeen in the rest of the country. (C. A. Kuch, Moldauische-Wallachische Zustände, pp. 205-7). Colson called the official reports a joke, saying (in 1839) that there were but twenty-four schools in Wallachia, with teachers scarce and incompetent. (De l'Etat présent et de l'avenir des principautés, pp. 189-95). In Moldavia the statistics give about 2000 public school pupils. Moldavia had no village school system, as Sturdza thought that might spread "ruinous ideas" among the peasants. (Hurmuzaki, Documente, Supl. I, vol.5, p. 614).

was not in the nature of things that a country-wide secular system of public instruction could be set up overnight, given the almost universal illiteracy, the lack of teachers, texts, and equipment. But the direction had been chosen, and it has been followed ever since.

The cultivation of the national language and of the "humanities," on the example of France, had been begun at Bucharest and at Craiova even before the Kiselev-Ştirbei reform; French began to be taught instead of Greek.[96] Much less progress had been made in Moldavia, but after the foundation of the academy, French professors were installed at Jassy as at Bucharest, and the advanced students in both principalities acquired a good command of French and more than a passing acquaintance with French literature.[97] So rapid was its progress that there was soon talk of making French the language of instruction for the superior schools, on the ground that Roumanian teachers, books, and even the language itself,

---

96. Iorga, Histoire de l'enseignement, p. 173; Urechia, op. cit., vol. II, pp. 137, 208-10, 234; N. Bănescu, "Un dascăl uitat," (Ac. Rom. Mem. Secţ. Ist., Ser. II, vol. 37, 1914-5, pp. 337-83), p. 369; idem., "Inceputurile Şcolii Centrale a Craiovei," (Convorbiri Literare, XLIV, 1910, pp. 885-93, 989-1001), pp. 887-8, 990, 993-1000; G. Adamescu, "Centenarul Invătămânţului Limbii franceze in Şcoalele româneşti," (ibid., LXIV, 1931, pp. 198-207).

97. M. E. Holban, "Un raport frances despre Moldova, 1828," (Buletinul Comisiei Istorice a României, IX, 1930, pp. 147-184), p. 178; Iorga, Histoire de l'enseignement, p. 171.

were inadequate for advanced subjects. This campaign was the work of some of the big boyars, of the French professors, and of the princes.[98] The boyars, whose sons generally did not go to public school at all but studied with private tutors, at French <u>pensionnats</u>, or abroad, were disdainful of the Roumanian language and of the people who spoke it; somehow they felt that its use in higher education gave too many opportunities to the sons of the middle class, threatened their social position and their monopoly of government jobs. The princes, Bibescu and Sturdza, supported the arguments of these boyars, partly to provide a substitute for Paris that would keep young Roumanians at home, partly because they were convinced that the Roumanian language requirement really was an obstacle to the proper teaching of higher subjects.[99] On the other side were the sincere nationalists, (Eliade, and Asachi, the Paris-educated youths, and above all the Transylvanians), all of whom knew that the elimination of the national language from higher education would be a mortal blow to nationalism. To them, "the nation and the national tongue were identical."[100] Their protests

---

98. Filitti, <u>Domniile Române sub Regulamentul Organic</u>, pp. 393-5, 606-16; Lovinescu, <u>Gheorghe Asachi</u>, pp. 81-88; Iorga, <u>op.cit.</u>, pp. 218-241, passim; A.A.C. Sturdza, <u>Règne de Michel Sturdza</u>, p. 92.

99. Bibescu to Kiselev, Aug. 16, 1847, in G. Bibesco, <u>Régne de Bibesco</u>, vol. I, pp. 310-11; Filitti, <u>op.cit.</u>, p.606.

100. Asachi, in the report of the Academic Committee, Jassy, Nov. 29, 1836, quoted in Urechia, <u>op.cit.</u>, vol. I, p.329.

were effective in warding it off until 1847, when reforms in both Moldavia and Wallachia put French in its place as the language of instruction. Bibescu's plan involved setting up in Bucharest a model French *lycée*, and he negotiated with Guizot for the services of *Université de France* professors, but the revolutionary disturbances of 1848 swept away the *lycée* along with Bibescu and settled the controversy once and for all in favor of the national language.[101]

The Russian Government was not very happy about the way in which the seeds planted by Kiselev had sprouted. The whole educational system seemed to have become a breeding ground for anti-Russian sentiments; the French current, spreading the revolutionary virus and building up a French political influence, and the national current, with its dreams of the sacred rights of peoples, were both of a nature to undermine the hold of Russia on the Principalities. The Tsar had indeed lost the game. He had lost the intellectuals for good and all, and his authority rested solely on force. He could never annex the Principalities now without creating another Poland.

Russian efforts to combat these pernicious influences

---

101. Letters between Bibescu, Guizot, and Salvandy, Oct. 8-Nov. 30, 1847, *Aff. Etr., Corr. Pol., Bucarest*, vol. 4; de Nion to Guizot, Jan. 16, 1848, *Corr. Com. Bucarest*, vol. 8; Bibesco, *Règne de Bibesco*, vol. I, pp. 335-47, vol. II, pp. 203-12; Damé, *Histoire de la Roumanie contemporaine*, pp. 43-45.

were unavailing. The Russian consuls tried to keep the boyars from sending their sons to France, offering instead scholarships in Russian schools. They protested against the emphasis on French in the schools, having some courses abolished and insisting that Russian also be taught. They supported Sturdza's abortive plan of having the Moldavian schools reorganized by a German, and when he failed and was replaced by a Frenchman, they secured the latter's dismissal. They forced Sturdza to abolish the two upper classes at the Jassy academy in 1847, and they supported Bibescu's _lycée_ as the lesser of two evils. Yet all this proved nothing.[102] It inflamed nationalistic spirits still more against Russia. Subversive ideas, when they are the doctrines of nationalism and are held by the entire intelligentsia of a nation, are not so easily stamped out, particularly not by such mild and indirect methods as these.

Russia had less to fear from the public schools than from the private French boarding schools or _pensionnats_. These were the schools in which the men of 1848 got their early training and learned to speak French as well as their

---

102. A. D. Xenopol, _Istoria Românilor_, vol. XI, pp. 247-60; Kuch, _Moldauisch-Wallachische Zustände_, p. 108; Duclos to Molé, Feb. 19, 1838, _Aff. Etr., Corr. Com., Jassy_, vol. 3; Billecocq to Guizot, Feb. 25, 1843, _Corr. Pol., Bucarest_, vol. 2; de Nion to Guizot, Sept. 10, 1847, _Corr. Pol., Bucarest_, vol. 4; Filitti, _Domniile Române sub Regulamentul Organic_, pp. 599, 612; Ion Ghica, _Scrisori către Vasile Alecsandri_, p. 253.

own language. In the late 1820's and early 1830's many of these institutions sprung up, especially in Moldavia, and although almost all were beset with financial difficulties, they maintained a comparatively high standard of instruction. The fact that they were outdistancing the public schools was one of the reasons for the strength of the movement to replace Roumanian with French in the latter. The two were not really comparable, however, for the French private schools served a particular purpose, that of preparing the sons of wealthy boyars for the French colleges and universities, which, because of this training, they were able to enter with a minimum of difficulty, whereas the public schools aimed at a combination of general education and practical training which would produce competent government servants, professional men, and technical experts.

The notable pensionnats in Moldavia were those of Mouton, of Cuénim, and of Lincourt. Kogălniceanu speaks of Mouton as teaching "the principles of the French language, enabling his students to read modern and useful books. . .and to gain some idea of geography, history, literature and modern poetry, of which in the Greek schools there was no mention."[103] Kogălniceanu and his brother attended Cuénim's school; their course notes, preserved in the Roumanian Academy, show with

---

103. M. Kogălniceanu, Poezii lui A. Chrisoverghi, Introducere, p. xvi.

what meticulous care French was taught. Guénim wrote that they "had completely mastered the French language and its spirit."[104] The school had a six-year program, ending up with literature, logic, philology, general history, geography, and the theory of rural economy. The program for the earlier years showed the same tendencies which characterized French education in the latter half of the 18th century, with much attention given to the natural sciences. The main emphasis, of course, was always on French. The same was true of the school of Lincourt, Chefneux, and Bagarre, which became the fashionable school for the best families; Vasile Alecsandri, Panaioti Radu, and the sons of Michael Sturdza studied there. At Galatz a Frenchman from Dijon established a school where he announced teaching "according to the methods of Pestalozzi, Lancaster, and Jacotot": and his school immediately secured twenty-five students, some of them from Bessarabia. There were other French pensionnats in Galatz, and also in other provincial cities such as Botoşani, Roman, and Băcău.[105]

---

104. N. Cartojan, "Pensionatele franceze din Moldova în prima jumătate a veacului al XIX-lea," (Omagiu lui Ramiro Ortiz, Bucharest, 1929, pp. 67-75), pp. 73-4.

105. Ibid., pp. 70-75; Iorga, Mihail Kogălniceanu, pp. 159-65; Urechia, op.cit., vol. II, pp. 122-4; Iorga, Histoire de l'enseignement, pp. 215-17. M. Gallice, former editor of the Glaneur Moldo-Valaque, intended to establish an Institut d'éducation classique at Jassy in 1846, but was prevented by the Russian consul. His prospectus said his purpose was to give Moldavia the equivalent of the institutions of higher learning in other countries. (T. Codrescu, Uricarul, vol. X, 1888, pp. 418-28).

There were almost as many schools for girls, highly important for the spread of the French language and customs, less important for the growth of nationalism.

In Wallachia there were fewer French schools. This was perhaps because more French was taught at the college of St. Sava and at Craiova than in the public schools of Jassy. The only notable *pensionnat* was that set up by Vaillant in 1830.[106] It soon put many of its contemporary French and Greek schools out of business, attracting the best minds of the Wallachian youth. Ion Ghica, Nicolae Bălcescu, Alexandrescu, C. A. Rosetti, and Grigore Grădişteanu were among his students. Two years later the official school board, under the direction of Poenaru, set up a unit for resident students as a part of the college of St. Sava. Vaillant was engaged to take charge of it. From the very first he was at odds with the board over his conduct of the school. Going beyond his stipulated functions as teacher of a few French courses and master of the residence unit, he began giving his courses in French and keeping his students away from their other classes in St. Sava altogether, in order to ensure a modern and complete education for these promising youths which he did not think the Roumanian professors at St. Sava could give them. This business of turning his official *pensionnat* into a rival to

---

106. Iorga, *Histoire de l'enseignement*, pp. 217-9, 225-6; Urechia, *op.cit.*, vol. II, p. 31; *Almanach de la Cour et de l'Etat de la Principauté de Valachie pour 1838*, pp. 197, 255; P. Eliade, *La Roumanie au XIXe. siecle*, p. 306.

the national school stirred up a long quarrel, in which Vaillant was supported by many of the boyars, who wanted their sons to have a French education, and the school board by the national language enthusiasts, and also, it seems, by the Russian consul, who feared Vaillant as a revolutionary with dangerous ideas. In 1835 Vaillant was removed from his post, went back to teaching in his own private school, but later regained his job and taught until 1840 when his revolutionary activities resulted in his having to depart in haste never to return.[107]

In these private schools in both principalities was educated a whole generation of intellectual and civic leaders. They imbibed a knowledge of French and an affection for France which was never to leave them. Thanks to Vaillant, the Wallachians probably imbibed also a bit of the revolutionary spirit which characterized his pedagogic and his political activity.

---

107. P. Eliade, op.cit., pp. 308-312; Urechia, op.cit., vol. I, pp. 165-8, 215, 347, 362; ibid., vol. II, p. 110; Cudalbu-Şlusanschi, Contribution à la biographie et à l'oeuvre de J. A. Vaillant, pp. 12-19, 24-26.

CHAPTER III

THE GENERATION OF 1848. YEARS OF APPRENTICESHIP.

1. The attraction of Paris for the Roumanians

Paris has been a focal point in the history of Roumanian nationalism, equal or superior in importance to Bucharest or Jassy, Blaj or Brasov. It trained successive generations of Roumanian leaders and stamped them with its spirit. As the capital of a great power, it has been the source of moral and material support, without which Roumania might not have won independence and unity. For the men of 1848, Paris was a second home; more than that, it was a source of perpetual inspiration, particularly to those who spent the better part of a lifetime there as students, as visitors, and as political exiles.

The prestige which Paris had won in the preceding centuries did not disappear with the reduction of France to impotence as a great power in 1815. The great Revolution had established the reputation of France as the defender of the rights of man and the rights of nations, and in spite of Napoleon's violation of both, that reputation remained. For the whole of unliberated Europe, France, whether Bourbon or Orleanist, Republican or Caesarian, remained a white light of hope. Revolutions in Paris sent a thrill through all the capitals of Europe. Its intellectual primacy made it a Mecca for Balkan students eager to come for inspiration to the very source of the life-giving powers of western civilization. The July Revolution of 1830 gave France a constitutional government which stood out as the most liberal and advanced in Europe. The Balkan nations, groping toward the light of westernism, began to hasten the process by sending their youth to absorb the direct rays of the western sun and sometimes to be blinded by them. The Roumanians came in larger numbers than the Slavs or Greeks, and, perhaps because of their greater facility with the French language, they fitted more easily into the grooves of French life, and they were much more profoundly influenced by French ideas. That is why the political history of the Roumanians in the 19th century is a parallel to their intellectual history; both tell the story of the wholehearted adoption of French forms, even when scarcely applicable to local circumstances.

The magnetic attraction which Paris had for Roumanians was proverbial. All felt the same craving for Paris; boyars on pleasure trips, serious-minded students, and even the more humble persons, like a certain Ion Drăgășanu, courier for one of the Ghica families, whose memoirs tell us that "it is not Paris, it is paradise, it is the city of cities. . . . One must admit that no other people in the world has a capital such as Paris."[1]

---

1. N. Iorga, Les Voyageurs orientaux en France, (Paris, 1927), p. 56. Mihail Anagnosti, a Roumanian student, wrote: "These young men rush right across learned Germany

The dazzling wonder of it all was the principal reason why the first Roumanian students in Paris made no great success of their studies. Insufficiently prepared and more inclined to dabble than to discipline themselves with hard work, they tended to concentrate on the theatre, on manners, and on social life in general. Some returned home with little except a changed exterior; others, like the first Moldavian student in Paris, Gheorghe Bogdan, adopted France as their home and forgot about their native land.[2] Two notable Roumanian students in Paris in the Restoration period were the brothers George Bibescu and Barbu Ştirbei, both future princes of Wallachia. While their stay of several years did not make them liberals, they learned much about how a modern state is governed, as evidenced by their subsequent attempts to establish an efficient and enlightened bureaucratic system in Wallachia.

2. The first boursiers

In 1820 the Government of Wallachia sent four chosen

---

to get to Paris, where life is more costly but exercises on them a far more powerful seduction." ("La Valachie et la Moldavie," Revue des Deux Mondes, Jan. 15, 1837, pp. 129-170, p. 138).

2. Iorga, "Vicisitudinile celui dintâiu student moldovean la Paris, Gheorghe Bogdan," (Ac Rom., Mem. Sect. Ist., Ser. III, vol. 14, 1933, Mem. 2), p. 2; P. Eliadé, De l'influence francaise sur l'esprit publique en Roumanie, pp. 373-4; Iorga, Etudes Roumaines, vol. I, (Paris, 1923), pp. 89-90.

scholars to study in Italy and in France.[3] In this group were Eufrosin Poteca and Simeon Marcovici, later leading professors at St. Sava. They studied first at Pisa, where their surroundings were as much Greek as Italian, and where they were in contact with those elements which were preparing to liberate the whole Balkan peninsula from the Turks.[4] The events of 1821 cut off their source of funds, but certain boyars sent them enough to finish at Pisa and get to Paris for a while. Eager for learning, they took courses in everything at Paris, acquiring a smattering of knowledge on a host of subjects. Naturally they were struck by the contrast between France and Wallachia, and began to think about ways in which the Roumanians could be brought out of their backwardness and ignorance. In a letter of 1824, Poteca recommended a three-point program: education for the priests (he was a churchman himself), so that they would be able to educate the people; the establishment of a system of proportional taxation; emancipation of the Gypsy slaves.[5] These were not unlike the proposals of Dinicu Golescu, who at this very time

---

3. I. Bianu, "Intâii bursieri români în străinătate," (Revista Nouă, Bucharest, I, 1888, pp. 420-431); N. Bănescu, "Cei dintâi bursieri români în străinătate," (Revista Generală a Invățământului, VI, 1910, pp. 216ff).

4. A. Marcu, "Un student român la Pisa si Paris, către 1820: Simeon Marcovici," (Revista Istorică, XV, Jan.-Mar., 1929, and separately, Valenii-de-Munte, 1929).

5. P. Eliade, Histoire de l'esprit publique en Roumanie, pp. 236-7.

was making his journey to the West.

When one of the original four students committed suicide in Paris, his scholarship was given to Petru Poenaru, who had already been studying two years at Vienna. Subsequent study in Paris under Adolphe Blanqui and at the Ecole polytechnique, and a visit to England where he visited mines and factories, took a trip by railway, and picked up much technical knowledge, gave him advantages over his colleagues. From England he wrote back to a friend in Sibiu:

> "I know that in my country no bed or roses awaits me, but the hardest work in trying to serve the country. . . .I do not gloss over the numerous difficulties which I shall meet in introducing there some things which I have seen here are useful to soceity, manufactures, for example....Unless the property of the peasant is protected...unless all classes are obliged to pay taxes in proportion to their wealth, so that the state can make roads, canals, and spread instruction,...unless these are introduced, we shall never be able to establish any industries. We must hope that, little by little, the rights and duties of man in society will be recognized, and that everyone will do his best in contributing to the amelioration of the state of our unfortunate country. As for me, I shall make every effort to serve as best I can...." 6

On his return he succeeded Eliade as head of the school system, and his country profited greatly from his knowledge

---

6. Poenaru to Gheorghe Popp, Oct. 27, 1831, quoted in P. Eliade, La Roumanie au XIXe. siècle, pp. 253-7. See also Iorga, A History of Anglo-Roumanian Relations, pp. 70-9; idem., Istoria literaturei românești in secolul al XIX-lea, vol. I, p. 136. Cf. the letter of Dimitrie Golescu to Eliade Rădulescu, Oct. 3, 1829, concerning the great promise shown by Poenaru, in Urechia, Istoria Școalelor, vol. I, p. 127.

of the material and spiritual aspects of western civilization.

After 1830 the governments of the Principalities sent students to Paris on scholarships only on very rare occasions, and then purely for technical training.[7] Paris was a revolutionary city frowned upon as a bad influence for inexperienced youths; it was considered safer to send them to Berlin or to Vienna.[8] Tsar Nicholas of Russia and Princes Sturdza and Bibescu, alarmed by the conduct and "radical declamations" of youths returned from Paris, tried to discourage the boyars from sending their sons to study there, and after 1840 they were able to divert some of this traffic to Germany and even to Russia.[9] Bibescu and Sturdza both sent their own

---

7. Urechia, Istoria Scoalelor, vol. II, pp. 318, 325; Analele Parlamentare ale României, vol. XIII, p. 177; Filitti, Domniile Române sub Regulamentul Organic, pp. 601-2; Iorga, Histoire de l'enseignement, pp. 208-211.

8. In 1835 Moldavia had seven government students abroad, all of them at Vienna. (Reçueil des Communications Princières à l'Assemblée Générale de Moldavie, p. 63. The Wallachian Government, according to the budget for 1841, sent students only to Berlin, Vienna, and Heidelberg. (Analele Parlamentare, vol. XIII, pp. 185, 188, 197, 224). For information on the few sent to Paris in other years, see references in preceding note.

9. Nesselrode to Titov, Jan. 2, 1840, Hurmuzaki, Documente, Supl. I, vol. 6, p. 175; Sturdza to Titov, Feb. 2, 1840, ibid., p. 189, Iorga, Etudes Roumaines, vol. I, p. 89; T. Schiemann, Geschichte Russlands, vol. IV, (Berlin, 1919), pp. 173-4; de Nion to Guizot, Jan. 25, May 13, 1847, Aff. Etr., Corr. Pol., Bucarest, vol. 4; Colquhoun to Palmerston, Mar. 12, 1847, F.O. 78, vol. 696.

sons to Paris, apparently on the theory that they were less susceptible to subversive ideas. Sturdza, giving advice to his sons, told them to avoid all relations with Polish refugees, and if Félix Colson came to see them, politely to show him the door; as for the other young Moldavians in Paris, they could be received, but "your social relations will be confined solely to the Russian embassy...."[10] In Bibescu's opinion it was not French education which had such harmful effects on Roumanian youth, but rather the reefs and shoals which life in Paris presented for immature spirits.[11] Official pressure was not sufficient to keep the cream of the younger generation away from Paris and from those dangerous ideas which were to undermine the princes' thrones and the Tsar's protectorate.

3. A new generation of students, 1830-1840

In the late 1820's Roumanian students began to go to the West in greater numbers. One of the first groups comprised

---

10. Michael Sturdza to his sons, May 21, 1843, in A. A. C. Sturdza, Règne de Michel Sturdza, (Paris, 1907), p. 366.

11. Bibescu to Kiselev, Aug. 16, 1847, in Bibesco, Règne de Bibesco, vol. I, pp. 310-11; Iorga, Histoire de l'enseignement, p. 242. Colquhoun, though a friend of many of the young nationalists, agreed substantially with Bibescu. "...Left almost to themselves from the age of 18 to 25, they plunge into the vices of the West of Europe and return here totally unfitted for the serious business of life. This is the case with but very few exceptions." (Colquhoun to Palmerston, Feb. 5, 1848, F.O. 78, vol. 742).

the three sons of the Wallachian boyar Lens, soon followed by two sons of Iordache Golescu. They went to Paris on the advice of the French consul, who congratulated himself on starting a trend of the greatest importance.[12] By 1830 the number of Roumanian students in Paris was between ten and twenty. Eight of them, thrilled by the establishment of the new national newspapers of Eliade and Asachi in 1829, wrote congratulatory letters to the editors for their great patriotism.[13] By 1830, thirteen students from Wallachia had passed their baccalaurate, and besides them there were others who took no regular courses and no examinations.[14] Most of these young aristocrats absorbed more than the manners of the French drawing rooms; they began to take up fashionable theories to which they gave universal application, but thus far there was no real effort to organize with the purpose of

---

12. Hugot to Damas, May 25, 1825, Hurmuzaki, Documente, vol. XVII, pp. 17-18; G. Bengescu, Les Golesco, une famille de boyards lettrés au XIXe. siecle, (Paris, 1921), p. 63.

13. "It is unnecessary to describe to you all the joy we have felt in learning of the first newspaper for our country. Know that in our veins flows Roumanian blood, and that our hearts cannot help leaping for joy when we hear that a start is being made in establishing salutary institutions in our country." (Urechia, op. cit. vol. I, p. 126).

14. P. Eliade, "Din Arhivele Sorbonei," (Viaţa Nouă, I, 1905, pp. 223-32), p. 226; idem., Histoire de l'esprit publique, pp. 249-53; cf. Hurmuzaki, Documente, Vol. XVII, p. 247, note 3.

putting such theories into effect in the Principalities.[15] They were vaguely liberal, humanitarian, and anti-slavery, though their families at home continued to retain large numbers of Gypsy slaves. One of the advanced spirits, Constantin Filipescu, was one of the first of a long list of professed traitors to their class; in his letters from Paris he ridiculed the boyar class, crediting them with no brains and still less public spirit. He agreed with Dinicu Golescu in insisting on the boyars' duty to make a sharp break with the past and really devote themselves to the public welfare. He proposed, as necessary remedies, universal education, fixed principles of administration, and complete independence for Roumania under a hereditary monarchy.[16] Even in the 1820's these students were becoming "Moldo-Wallachians" to

---

15. Dimitrie Golescu, in Paris from 1825 to 1830, got his bachelor's at the Sorbonne and at the Faculty of Law. He attended the lectures of Cousin, Guizot, Royer-Collard, and Villemain. (Bengescu, Les Golesco, pp. 154-6; G. Maxim-Burdajenu, "Demètre G. Golesco," (Mélanges de l'Ecole Roumaine en France, 1930, pp. 1-85), pp. 10-14; P. Eliade, Din Arhivele Sorbonei, p. 226; idem., "Din Arhivele Şcoalei de Drept dela Paris," (Viata Noua, I, 1905, pp. 365-80), p. 370.

16. P. Eliade, Histoire de l'esprit publique, pp. 272 ff.; idem., La Roumanie au XIXe. siècle, pp. 263-5, 267-8. Note the similar letter of Constantin Brailoiu to his father, from Geneva, June 17, 1828, which speaks of "this virtuous Switzerland," in comparison to which the imperfections and vices of the social system in Wallachia are clearly evident; what the latter needs most are patriotic sentiment, an improved administration based on equity and justice, and a comprehensive system of education. (Hurmuzaki, Documente, vol. X, pp. 621-2).

foreigners, "Roumanians" to themselves, regardless of which principality they came from.

After 1830 a new set of students appeared in Paris; among them were Ion Ghica, the Golescus, Nicolae Kretzulescu, Vasile Alecsandri, Alexander Cuza and Dumitru Brătianu. The Paris which they experienced was the Paris of Louis Philippe and of the victorious bourgeoisie. They might have been expected to become apologists for this liberal and constitutional régime as a model for their own people. Their general reaction was otherwise. Just as they condemned the semi-constitutional régime of the Règlement Organique at home, so did they oppose the pseudo-liberalism of the July Monarchy. The aristocrats' sons turned radical did not stop at half-way measures. We find them adherents of St. Simon, of Fourier, of Louis Blanc, and especially of the idealistic democratic-republicans like Michelet, Quinet, and Lamartine. This phenomenon may be partially attributed to the fact that at the time of the arrival of these young Roumanians, popular feeling in Paris against the régime was running high; it was obvious enough that this was no "people's government." Also, the stolid, colorless character of the July Monarchy naturally did not appeal to the impressionable Roumanians as did the romantic and idealistic tradition of the Great Revolution as represented by the Left opposition and the illegal republican movement. Thirdly, the foreign policy of France left everything to be desired; Louis Philippe had backed away from the role of savior of liberty in Europe thrust upon him in 1830; it was only the unofficial France of the Left that showed sympathy with the cause of Italy, Poland, and the other nationalities.

The espousal of utopian socialism by some of the students was probably nothing more than conformism and parlor radicalism.[17] Ion Ghica, who arrived in Paris in 1834, wrote in his memoirs that most of his compatriots at that time were "more or less adepts of Saint-Simonism," because they were bored with their studies and were seeking an outlet for their enthusiastic temperaments.[18] Fourier and Considérant found a faithful follower in the Roumanian Diamant, who went regularly to their lectures, spoke on street corners in favor of the new society of harmony, and wrote a propaganda pamphlet. After the death of Fourier, Diamant returned to the Principalities to found phalanstères. The Moldavian government paid no attention to his proposals.[19] In Wallachia he won

---

17. D. Popovici, Românii in presa saint-simonianã, (Jassy, 1934), p. 3, says that the influence of Saint-Simonian thought on certain Roumanians, particularly N. Bălcescu, was considerable. On the latter point, see G. Zane, Marx şi Bălcescu, (Jassy, 1927), pp. 11-15.

18. Those whom he named as Saint-Simonians (Vladoianu, Brăiloiu, Barbu Catargiu, Niculae and Stavrache Niculescu), he lists elsewhere as reactionary and pro-Russian. (Ion Ghica, Scrisori către Vasile Alecsandri, pp. 175-6, 318). Catargiu subsequently became leader of the party opposed to all property reform.

19. N. Cartojan, "Un proiect de falanster în Moldova la 1840," (Convorbiri Literare, LII, 1919, pp. 722-9).

over a young boyar, Manolache Bălăceanu, who gave him free rein to set up a Fourierist colony on his estate, but this "communistic" experiment was far from successful and was soon dissolved by the Wallachian Government and its sponsors sent into exile.[20]

The other Roumanians in Paris weathered the socialistic storm, and for a period of several years they remained comparatively aloof from the eddies of French domestic affairs, devoting themselves to their studies and to dreaming of a future Roumania. Between 1830 and 1837, twenty of them passed their baccalaureate at the Sorbonne. Those who tried the law were less successful, though five of them had progressed as far as the licence.[21] Some, like Ion Ghica, who went directly from the Sorbonne to the Ecoles des mines, and A. G. Golescu, who attended the Ecole polytechnique, knew exactly what they wanted to study. Others, like Dumitru Brătianu, wanting only a general education, generally drifted into law. Brătianu was in Paris for thirteen years, twice

---

20. D. Popovici, Santa Cetate, (Jassy, 1935). The information in Ghica, Scrisori, pp. 326-335, is not strictly accurate.

21. P. Eliade, Din Arhivele Sorbonei, pp. 226-8; idem., Din Arhivile Şcoalei de Drept, p. 371. The marks of some of the future poets and statesmen are of interest. Vasile Alecsandri, Alexander Cuza, Ion Ghica, and D. Brătianu, who took their bachelor's degrees in 1835 and 1836, were all "faiblě" in history and geography, "passable" in most other subjects, though Alecsandri was "faible" in philosophy and "tres faible" in rhetoric.

tried the exam for the doctorate in law, and twice failed.[22] Alecsandri, pushed by his family into medicine, changed to law, then engineering, and wound up reading Lamartine and writing poetry.[23]

As the diligence from Strasbourg continued to deposit more and more Roumanian students in Paris, their contacts with each other increased, first in informal meetings and discussions, and finally in a students' society.[24] Those of them who stuck together in groups, instead of scattering and thus losing themselves in the great city, were the most active. From 1834 to 1836 Ion Ghica lived in a pension on the rue St. Hyacinthe with several compatriots, including Nicolas Kretzulescu, Panait Radu, M. Anagnosti, and more than one Golescu.[25] About a dozen of them lived there, and other

---

22. P. Eliade, Din Arhivele Scoalei de Drept, p. 372. Before taking up law, he toyed with medicine and teaching, but the Ecole Normale would not take foreigners, so he dropped the teaching idea. (A. Cretzianu, Din Arhiva lui Dumitru Brătianu, (Bucharest, 1933), vol. I, p. 9.

23. G. Bengescu, "Vasile Alecsandri," (Convorbiri Literare, XX, 1886, pp. 150-69), pp 159-67; N. Petrascu, Vasile Alecsandri, pp. 15-17.

24. Bois-le-Comte, in 1834, reported that "about fourteen" Roumanians were then studying in Paris, and that the same number had studied there and already returned home. (Hurmuzaki, Documente, vol. XVII, p. 353. Nicolae Kretzulescu gives twenty-four as the number in Paris in that year. (Amintiri istorice, Bucharest, 1895, p. 11). Ion Ghica (Scrisori, p. 173), gives the same number for the autumn of 1837.

25. There were in 1834 four Golescus studying in Paris: Radu and Alexandru C. (sons of Dinicu), and Radu and Alexandru G. (sons of Iordache).

Roumanians came in for meals. After dinner, Kretzulescu tells us, they would sit in the garden and talk about European politics and the situation of the Principalities. Some of the discussions were quite heated; the bonds of friendship were sometimes strained and broken by arguments over principle, as when Anagnosti offended his more radical friends, who swore by the principle of equality, by upholding the necessity of maintaining a distinction between the aristocracy and the bourgeoisie. Later, however, Anagnosti "made more of a compromise with modern ideas" and often discussed politics with an old professor who dated from the Revolution and was a strong republican.[26]

Another group, including Alecsandri and Cuza, Moldavians, who arrived in 1834, lived at 21 rue Notre-Dame-des-Champs under the watchful eye of a professor whom Prince Sturdza had sent to accompany them. Sundays the two groups were in the habit of meeting for walks or for conversation These meetings, says Ion Ghica, taught them to become neither Moldavians nor Wallachians, but Roumanians.[27] Sometimes they met at the Café Corneille or at the Café Procope, where they listened to the inspiring talk of a young French student, Jules Simon. There also they exchanged news they had received from home, discussed and commented upon it. Letters from

---

26. Kretzulescu, Amintiri istorice, pp. 46-50.

27. Ghica, Scrisori, pp. 149-50.

Bălcescu, Alexandrescu, and Ion Voinescu were the most appreciated.[28]

The appearance of Ion Câmpineanu, the national hero, in Paris in 1839 did more than anything else to bring the students together and to stimulate their national feeling.[29] Until that time only Anagnosti and Ion Ghica had done anything more than discuss politics. The former had written an article for the Revue des Deux Mondes, in which he introduced the Principalities to the West, describing their resources, their political and strategic importance, and the desire of their inhabitants for independence under a foreign prince, "who knows Europe and its civilization."[30] Ghica, a personable youth with social connections, was the most active of the students in society and in political circles. He was a personal friend of David Urquhart, of Jules Bastide, of Prince Czartoryski, and of Armand Carrel, who opened to

---

28. Ibid., p. 173; Petrașcu, Vasile Alecsandri, pp. 14-15, 18.

29. Kretzulescu, op.cit., p. 53.

30. M. A... de Bucarest, "La Valachie et la Moldavie," (Revue des Deux Mondes, Jan. 15, 1837, pp. 129-170). Four years later he produced a book, Les Idées de la Révolution et les affaires d'Orient, (Paris, 1841), in which he tried to be pro-French but not anti-Russian, since he considered Russia a civilizing influence in the East, thus stamping himself as a reactionary in the eyes of his student friends. In agreement with him was Alexander Suțu, law student, who wrote, in the same year, a brochure entitled De la probabilité d'une alliance future entre la France et la Russie pour terminer la question d'Orient, (Paris, 1841).

him the columns of Le National, where a long series of articles, labelled correspondence from Bucharest but actually written by Ghica in Paris, appeared in the years 1836 to 1840. Ghica used Le National to plead for a better understanding of the Roumanian problem on the part of the British and French governments, depicting the Principalities as a potential barrier to Russia which would solve the whole eastern question if only action were taken to prevent their falling into the lap of the Tsar.[31] In 1835 he wrote, with the help of his professor and notes sent by Câmpineanu, an anonymous pamphlet, in which he announced the desire of Roumania to enter the family of free, constitutional states, "for the population, the progress of civilization and the rights of the Wallachians destine them for a fate other than to be swallowed by Russia; they should be taken under the protection of all the powers of Europe.[32]

---

31. Ghica, Scrisori, pp. 164-5. V.V. Haneş, Formarea Opiniunii franceze asupra României in secolul al XIX-lea, (Bucharest, 1929), vol. I, pp. 100-106, gives excerpts from many of these articles which appeared in 1838 and 1839. One article of July 23, 1838, mentioned "the eight million Roumanians who must be constituted into a single, powerful and independent state, to hold the balance between Russia and Turkey (p. 104).

32. M. de L***, Coup d'oeil sur l'état actuel de la Valachie, et de la conduite de la Russie relativement à cette province, (Paris, 1835). Another brochure, M. O***. Poids de la Moldo-Valachie dans la question d'Orient; coup d'oeil sur la dernière occupation militaire russe de ces provinces, (Paris, 1838, is generally attributed to him, and he claims to have published an extract of one of Colson's works under the title Précis des droits des Moldaves et des Valaques fondé sur le droit de gens

The Czartoryski-Câmpineanu scheme to free the Poles and the Roumanians gave Ghica and the other students an opportunity to substitute action for their patriotic talk, and they seized it with great zeal. Ghica, who had been introduced to Czartoryski by Mihail (Czaika) Czaikowski, was able to give the Prince much information on the Roumanian question, from the viewpoint of the national party, and Radu Golescu also had many interviews with him.[33] These contacts probably had something to do with Czartoryski's decision to send an agent to the Principalities and to open negotiations with Câmpineanu.[34] According to the secret reports of Russian agents, several Roumanian students, among others two Golescu brothers, were in correspondence with "French and foreign heads of the demagogic fractions, particularly with the Poles Ryzijski and Czaikowski"; their letters, written in invisible

---

(Paris, 1839). Cf. Ghica, Scrisori, pp. 174-7; V. V. Haneş, op.cit., vol. I, pp. 119-121, 135-7, 180: Iorga, Ist. lit rom., vol. II, p. 101.

33. Ghica, Scrisori, p. 176; P. P. Panaitescu, Planurile lui Ioan Câmpineanu, pp. 66-7. Polish emigrés of both aristocratic and democratic factions often came to the pension in the rue St. Hyacinthe, among them Zamoyski, Czartoryski's nephew, Czaika, and Lelewel. (Kretzulescu, op.cit., p. 48). In December 1839, Ghica, through Czartoryski, sent a mémoire to the French minister of war. (Ghica to Woronicz, Dec. 4, 1839, Panaitescu, op. cit., p. 103). We do not have the text, but it is likely that it pointed out the ways in which the Roumanians could help France in a war against Russia.

34. Ion Ghica and Nicolae Kretzulescu were both nephews of Câmpineanu.

ink, were said to be going through Vienna.[35]

When Câmpineanu arrived in Paris, the students forsook their books and their pledges to range themselves under his banner, and Ion Ghica took a hand in the intensive publicity campaign which Colson was conducting. At this time it was decided that the students should meet more regularly; they began the practice of coming together each Sunday, at the rooms of Dumitru Brătianu, Mavrocordato, or occasionally of one of the other students. At these meetings, wrote Ion Ghica many years later, "we discussed the interests and future of our country, we took a vow to remain always united in defense of its rights to autonomy; we agreed that on our return we would found a journal for the propagation of liberal and patriotic ideas; we decided that some of the Moldavians should establish themselves at Bucharest and some of the Wallachians should go to Jassy, in order to spread the idea of union."[36]

Essential to the regeneration of the nation, in the eyes of these young men, was the creation of others like themselves. Enlightenment should reach every Roumanian

---

35. M. Popescu, Contributiuni la istoria dinaintea unirii Principatelor Române, p. 695. It is not clear from this report which Golescus are meant, apparently Stefan and Nicolae in Bucharest. Probably they were involved in the affair as well as Radu, A. C., and A. G. Golescu in Paris.

36. Ghica, Scrisori, p. 177.

village, in order that a whole generation might be allowed to see the new dawn and to hasten its arrival. In 1839 Ion Ghica, D. Brătianu, and A. G. Golescu got together to form a "Society for the education of the Roumanian people," whose members, in Paris and at home, were to pledge themselves to pay regular dues for five years. In the Principalities central reading rooms were to be established, to which the secretary of the Paris group would send the chief Paris journals and brochures.[37] The Paris newspapers to be sent were Le National, Le Moniteur, Le Peuple, La Revue de progrès, La France industrielle, Le Commerce, L'Artiste, and Charivari. That many of them were sent is evident from the alarm of the authorities in the Principalities at the suddenly increased circulation of French journals. News of the machinations of the students in Paris reached the ears of Nesselrode, who complained to Sturdza of certain Moldavian students, notably Mavrocordato, who had relations with "Wallachian demagogues...who profess principles of the purist democracy." Sturdza saw Mavrocordato's father, who agreed to transfer his son to Berlin.[38]

---

37. One copy of the statutes of this society was kept in Paris, another given to Câmpineanu to take back to Bucharest. The text is reproduced in Anul 1848 în Principatele Române, Vol. I, (Bucharest, 1902, p. 11.

38. Hurmuzaki, Documente, Supl. I, vol. 6, pp. 175, 189. The "demagogues" seem to have been D. Brătianu and Ion Ghica. (Cretzianu, op.cit., vol. I, p. 105).

4. Lunéville, Berlin, Munich, Geneva

In a few isolated cases members of the generation of 1848 were educated not at Paris but elsewhere, but since the influences to which they were subjected were of the same sort, liberal and romantic, some mention of them should be included.

Mihail Kogălniceanu, the future leader of the national movement in Moldavia, was in 1834 sent by Prince Sturdza to Lunéville, in the company of the Prince's two sons and several other students. There they were lodged with a safe old abbé, the former tutor of Sturdza himself. Kogălniceanu was kept immune from contact with revolutionaries, whose presence at Paris had caused Sturdza to choose the quiet town of Lunéville for his sons and proteges, but he could not be innoculated against modernism, liberalism, romanticism, and the other currents to which he was, by his voracious appetite for reading, exposed.[39] He spent his whole allowance and more, buying books and magazines, and amassed about five hundred volumes of the French classics, including Racine, Corneille, Voltaire, Buffon, La Harpe, and Châteaubriand. He could not help being surprised and

39. He read the Revue des Deux Mondes, Revue de Paris, Gazette de France, Mercure de France, l'Estafette, Protée, Le Voleur, Caricature, and others. (See M. Kogalniceanu, Scrisori, 1834-1849, (Bucharest, 1913 ed. P. V. Haneș), pp. 24, 29, 32-3; N. Cartojan, "M. Kogălniceanu la Lunéville," (Convorbiri Literare, XLVII, 1913, pp. 713-27), p. 717.

pleased at the liberty with which the opposition press attacked the government. "Here," he wrote to his father, "every man is a king and can say and write whatever he pleases, without being prevented."[40]

In 1835, the Moldavian students at Lunéville were all removed to Berlin by order of Prince Sturdza, whom wild rumors and the Russian consul had convinced that the revolutionary contagion in France was sure to infect them unless they were moved.[41] Kogălniceanu was intensely disappointed, as he desired to finish his three-year course at Lunéville and then go on to study law in Paris, "the wonder of the world."[42] Arriving in Berlin in the summer of 1835, he wrote home:

> "In Germany it is quieter; the instruction more profound the customs more innocent and more patriarchal; nevertheless I should have preferred to stay in France....I was sorry to leave Lunéville, because that also meant leaving France....I would a hundred times rather have stayed in France....[In Berlin] there is a phlegmatic and ceremonial tone, enough to make one die of boredom." 43

In Berlin Kogălniceanu made many contacts with the

---

40. Kogălniceanu to his father, Oct. 22, 1934, Scrisori, p. 45.

41. Cartojan, op.cit., p. 721.

42. While at Lunéville he was in touch with the students in Paris, writing to Alecsandri and greeting Roumanians who passed through Lunéville on their way to and from the capital. (Kogălniceanu, Scrisori, p. 24).

43. Ibid., pp. 141-4; Radu Dragnea, Mihail Kogălniceanu, p. 7.

French colony and intellectual and social circles which were cosmopolitan rather than German; he tried to keep up his French, going regularly to the French theatre. He became acquainted with several of the aristocratic and bourgeois families, and was a special friend of Count Schwerin, whose country estate he often visited. From these people he absorbed something of the Stein-Hardenberg tradition of enlightened reform, and he became a determined opponent of slavery, which still existed in his own country. Their striving for national ideals and for social reform had a tremendous influence on him, he later confessed.[44] Controversy has raged over whether Kogălniceanu represents a French or German influence in Roumania. The answer, as might be expected, is both. He drew from France an attachment to the ideals of the Enlightenment, to the principle of equality, and to French literature; from Germany, his historical approach, his traditionalism, his nationalism.[45]

---

44. M. Kogălniceanu, "Desrobirea Ţiganilor; Oborirea Pronomielor şi Privilegielor de nascere şi de castă; Emanciparea Ţăranilor," (Ac. Rom., Analele, Disc., Ser. II, vol. 13, 1890-91, pp. 255-300), pp. 258-9.

45. Cf. Kogălniceanu, loc.cit.; P. V. Haneş, Introduction to Kogălniceanu, Scrisori, pp. ix-xvi; idem., "Dragostea lui M. Kogălniceanu de Paris şi de Franţa," (Convorbiri Literare, LXVIII, 1935, pp. 486-91; M. Fotino, L'influence française sur les grands orateurs roumains de la seconde moitié du XIXe. siècle, pp. 46 ff.; A. D. Xenopol, "Mihail Kogălniceanu," (Ac. Rom., Disc. de Recept., 1895), p. 8; Iorga, Ist. lit. rom., vol. II, p. 41.

Nationalism, or rather patriotism, was evident, however, before he even went to Germany. From Lunéville he wrote: "France is a beautiful country, rich, ordered, powerful; but since I am not a Frenchman, I prefer my own country.... I was born a Moldavian and want to die a Moldavian."[46] Moldavian patriotism soon changed to Roumanian nationalism, as he conceived the project of writing a history of his people, beginning with the story of "the whole of ancient Dacia" and continuing with the histories of Wallachia and Moldavia.[47] Kogălniceanu wanted to return to Moldavia, but wanted first to be "rich in knowledge";[48] that was what his contact with the West gave him, no inflexible dogmas, no romantic enthusiasm for "the revolution," but a large fund of useful knowledge, a flexible liberalism, and a desire to bring about equality by a thoroughgoing solution of the questions of slavery and serfdom.[49]

---

46. Kogălniceanu, Scrisori, p. 38.

47. Ibid., p. 70. The first volume, entitled Histoire de la Dacie, des Valaques Transdanubiens et de la Valachie, appeared in Berlin in 1837. The second, intended to cover the history of Moldavia to 1834, never appeared, because of lack of material and because Sturdza, fearing it might offend Russia, would not give his permission. (Kogălniceanu to Sturdza, Feb. 22, 1837, Scrisori, pp. 69-71, and also pp. 106-7, 173, 183.

48. Ibid., pp. 147, 164.

49. "True civilization consists in love of the fatherland and of one's nearest, in respect for the laws, in the abolition of slavery, which still exists in our country, to our shame, in the equality of all persons, without distinction of rank or of birth." (Kogălniceanu to his sisters, Feb. 13, 1837, Scrisori, pp. 170-1).

Munich was another center for Roumanian students, some of them with Moldavian and Wallachian government scholarships, others sent by their families. The two younger sons of Dinicu Golescu studied at Munich for three or four years before going to Geneva and then to Paris. In 1834, there were several Moldavians there who were later involved in the revolution of 1848.[50] There were always from five to ten young Roumanians studying there, but they formed no important group such as existed in Paris. Relations with the German students were none too friendly, and after many quarrels and duels, the Roumanians left, one after another.[51]

Geneva was more important. It was within the orbit of French civilization and its associations with J.J. Rousseau gave it an added attraction. Ştefan and Nicolae, the two eldest sons of Dinicu Golescu, attended the University of Geneva from 1825 to 1829, then returned to Bucharest to serve in the militia. Constantin Brăiloiu, future jurist, studied there before going to Paris. After 1830, Roumanians were sent in considerable numbers to a boarding school run by a certain Töpffer. Radu and Alexandru C. Golescu were there from 1830 to 1833, at the same time as five other Roumanians, including Nicolae Niculescu and one of the

---

50. Kretzulescu, _Amintiri istorice_, p. 45; Petraşcu, _Vasile Alecsandri_, p. 159.

51. Ion Ghica, _Scrisori_, p. 327.

Ghicas. Later Nicolae Suţu, a high Moldavian official sent his two sons, and there was also a certain Ioan Suţu who had to be punished for conduct not corresponding to the moral purposes of the school: "...Deception, drink, pipe, debts, classes cut, books sold, promenades and dancing, etc....."[52]

At Geneva from 1829 to 1839 was the Bessarabian, Alexandru Russo, who, though scarcely as important a figure as Kogălniceanu, was a typical member of the generation of 1848, his career following the familiar line of education in the West, adoption of liberalism, return to the Principalities to take part in the campaign for a "national" literature and theatre, and finally revolutionary agitation and exile. He was in Switzerland at the time of the revolution of 1830 which thrilled him as a "year of glory."[53] Associating with exiled Polish and Italian revolutionaries, he took from them his political creed of republicanism, and from Lamennais and Mickiewicz his literary creed of religious, romantic nationalism. His Cântarea României, "Song of Roumania," an important contribution to the lore of Roumanian nationalism, was directly inspired by the Paroles d'un

---

52. Iorga,"Goleştii şi alţi elevi ai lui Töpffer în Geneva," (Ac. Rom., Mem. Sect. Ist., Ser. III, vol. 6, 1925, Mem. 4); Nicolas Soutzo, Mémoires, (Vienna, 1899),pp. 129, 137.

53. Radu Dragnea, "Viaţa lui Alexandru Russo," (Neamul Românesc Literar, IV, 1912, pp. 675-91), p. 678.

Croyant of Lamennais and the Livre des pèlerins polonais of Mickiewicz.[54] Russo does not seem to have been in communication with the students in Paris, and in 1839, the year of Câmpineanu's trip, he returned to Jassy, being arrested en route in Vienna for the possession of revolutionary literature.[55]

5. The Inspiration of the Collège de France

In 1839 and 1840 many of the students in Paris, having remained from five to six years, considered themselves educated and went home. Dumitru Brătianu, alone of the leaders, was left to hold the fort. He had been in Paris as a student since he arrived in 1835 at the age of sixteen and was destined to remain, with slight interruptions, until 1848; he liked Paris too well to exchange his student life for anything which Wallachia could offer him at that time. He leisurely pursued his studies, trying vainly for a doctorate at the Faculty of Law and reveling in the more congenial atmosphere of the Collège de France, where there were no examinations, only inspiring lectures.

---

54. G. Bogdan-Duică, "Alecsandru Russo," (Convorbiri Literare, XXXV, 1901, pp. 631-70), pp. 659-70. Others of the Forty-eighters, notably Bălcescu, C. A. Rosetti, D. Brătianu, Ion Voinescu, and Cesar Boliac, were ardent admirers of both Lamennais and the Polish poet.

55. P. V. Haneș, Alexandru Russo, p. 8; Dragnea, op.cit., p. 680.

After a few years there were important new arrivals and some of his former colleagues began to come back. In 1843 came C. A. Rosetti, who had made a reputation as a poet, and at about the same time came a young officer of the militia, given leave and special dispensation to study in Paris, Ion C. Brătianu.[56] A. G. Golescu returned in 1844;[57] Dimitrie Bolintineanu, the poet, arrived in the same year, sent by Ştefan Golescu and other patriotic boyars.[58] Ion Ghica, seeking a respite from the obstruction, persecution, and censorship which had met his efforts to work for nationalism at home, came back to Paris in 1845.[59] In addition, in 1846, there arrived for the first time the two historians, Kogălniceanu and Bălcescu. After twelve years

---

56. There is uncertainty about the year of arrival of Ion Brătianu and of C. A. Rosetti. It is sometimes placed as late as 1845. On this point, see S. Cantacuzino, Din Viaţa Familiei I. C. Brătianu, 1821-1891, (Bucharest, 1933), p. 18; O. Boitoş, Biografiile româneşte ale lui Ubicini, (Cluj, 1932), p. 54; I. Breazu, "Edgar Quinet et les Roumains," (Mélanges de l'Ecole Roumaine en France, pp. 213-401), p. 310; A. Ştefanescu-Galaţi, "C. A. Rosetti, o biografie critică." (Lui C. A. Rossetti, Bucharest, 1916, pp. 1-61), p. 3; C. A. Rosetti, Note intime, scrise zilnic, vol. I, (Bucharest, 1902, ed. Vintilă Rosetti), p. 83.

57. Bengescu, Les Golesco, p. 243.

58. N. Petraşcu, Dimitrie Bolintineanu, (Bucharest, 1932), p. 15; cf. I. G. Valentineanu, Biografia oamenilor mari, skrisă de un om micu, (Paris, 1859), p. 37; Boitoş, Biografiile româneşte, p. 53.

59. Iorga, Ist. lit. rom., vol. II, p. 163.

of waiting and hoping, Kogălniceanu had at last reached the "center of civilization";[60] Bălcescu, not wealthy like the others, had waited for years to save the money to go to Paris.

These newcomers did not need to come to Paris to become idealists, nationalists, and revolutionaries. Their whole previous training, in which the French influence was strong, had been along those lines. Most of them had studied with Vaillant and at St. Sava; they had been in the militia with Câmpineanu;[61] they had had a hand in the revolutionary plots of 1839 and 1840. They were in Paris for various reasons: to put the finishing touches on their education, to seek out historical material, or to experience the thrill of participating in the life of the cultural center of the world.[62]

---

60. In 1844 he had set out for Paris, but in Vienna the police tipped off by the Russian embassy, confiscated his passport and sent him home. He wrote bitterly to his father: "You know very well that for seven years, ever since my return from Berlin, I have always wanted to go to France, for I consider that journey to be indispensable for any youth who desires to acquire ideas and knowledge, to complete his education by contemplation of all the discoveries and progress realized by the human soul in that happy country; and, finally, one should not remain behind one's century." (May 13, 1844, Scrisori, 1834-1849, p. 189).

61. The militia in the early 1830's attracted many of these patriotic youths. In its ranks were Nicolae and Ştefan Golescu and their cousin Radu, Alexandrescu, Boliac, Ion Voinescu, Constantin Filipescu, Constantin and Scarlat Kretzulescu, C.A. Rosetti, and Ion C. Brătianu.

62. C. A. Rosetti, before going to Paris, noted in his diary how he "built castles in Spain, dreamed of being in Paris, taking courses, and meeting friends, all of us learned in the arts and in the sciences." (Rosetti, Note intime, vol. I, p. 15).

If these young Roumanians were counting on inspiration, they certainly were not disappointed. For these were the great years of the Collège de France, when the immortal trio of Michelet, Quinet, and Mickiewicz stirred all France with their oratory. In France it was the intrepid attack upon the Jesuits which had the greatest reverberations. But to the large group of foreigners in Paris, many of them political exiles, anticlericalism made less appeal than the impassioned speeches of Mickiewicz on Poland's mission to liberate the Slavs and free Europe, of Michelet on the philosophy of history, on the Revolution, on nationality, or of Quinet on the revolutions in Italy. It is almost impossible to recapture the atmosphere of those years, the unlimited emotional enthusiasm, generated by the romantic literature, by the new cult of the Revolution, and by sheer boredom and disgust with the foreign and domestic policies of the bourgeois regime, enthusiasm which lifted the three professors to the status of prophets and sent their listeners out of the lecture hall transfigured, inspired with a love for humanity, for the eternal spirit of the revolution and of the people, and for Poland and the other enslaved nationalities of Europe; men wept with emotion at the inspired message, women sometimes fainted, and after the lectures crowds of admirers would gather around the great men.[63] Foreign students were among the most ardent disciples; Poles, Italians, Roumanians, and many others gloried in the vision of a new world of free and friendly peoples created by the miraculous principle of nationalities, connected organically with the instinct of the people.[64]

This resurrection of peoples was intimately linked, in the minds of both speakers and auditors, with the moral regenerative power of France, the France of 1789. The triumph of the

---

63. On this whole subject, see Ladislas Mickiewicz, La Triologie du Collège de France, (Paris, 1924); Paul Hazard, "Michelet, Quinet, Mickiewicz et la vie interieure du Collège de France de 1838 a 1852," (Livre Jubilaire composé à l'occasion du Quatrième Centennaire du Collège de France, Paris, 1932, pp. 263-276); I. Breazu, Edgar Quinet et les Roumains, pp. 213-35, 264-306.

64. "La nationalité d'un peuple est pour lui ce qu'est pour l'homme sa conscience"...."Mépriser les nationalités, ce n'est pas autre chose que mépriser la vie en sa source la plus profonde."...."Dans cette réunion consacrée au génie des peuples étrangers, il y a naturellement des hommes de race différente ou ennemie. Souvent, j'ai vu ici à côté les uns des autres des Polonais, des Russes, des Italiens, des Hongrois, des Espagnols, des Roumains, des Portugais, des Américains, et même des Noirs...Puisse l'union de ces hommes de races diverses être pour nous l'emblème de l'union, de l'alliance, de la renaissance future de leurs patries, dans un esprit nouveau de justice et de solidarité!" (Quinet, Les Jésuites, l'Ultramontanisme, Paris, 1844, pp. 367, 408-9). Cf. similar ideas in Michelet, Le Peuple, (Paris, 1846, English translation, London, 1846), pp. 163-4. Michelet's lectures on nationality were never published. See also I. Breazu, Edgar Quinet et les Roumains, pp. 290-1, 295-6; idem., Michelet si Românii, (Cluj, 1935), pp. 19-26; Z. L. Zaleski, "Michelet, Mickiewicz et la Pologne," (Revue de litterature comparée, Paris, VIII, 1928, pp. 433-487); G. Monod, La vie et la pensée de Jules Michelet, (Paris, 1923), vol. II, pp. 211ff.; Henri Mignot, Michelet éducateur, (Paris, 1930), pp. 79, 117-8.

spirit in Paris would, it was firmly believed, be the signal for the triumph of the sacred cause of Poland, of Italy, and of the other nationalities.

The mystic, ultra-democratic, revolutionary idealism of the Collège de France lectures made a special appeal to Dumitru Brătianu and to C. A. Rosetti. Both were of a romantic, emotional nature, the type that could easily be reduced to tears when discussing or contemplating either the sorrowful present or the happy future. With these two the younger Brătianu could generally be found, though his was a tougher mind less given to rhapsody. Other Roumanians went to the Collège de France, but these three were the ones most profoundly affected; they became close personal friends and "spiritual children" of Michelet, Quinet, and Mickiewicz.[65]

Dumitru Brătianu was the first Roumanian to put himself

---

65. Breazu, opera cit.; Iorga, Quatre Figures Françaises en Lumière Roumaine, (Bucharest, 1925), pp. 26-34, 46-52; Marya Kasterska, "Mickiewicz şi Românii," (Propilee Literare, Bucharest, IV, 1929, No. 2-3, pp. 20-23); Hélène Vacaresco, "La mystique nationale roumaine aux environs de 1848," (Revue d'histoire diplomatique, Paris, XLII, 1929, pp. 6-19). To the end of his life, Rosetti never ceased to pay tribute to this influence. "Young men, on the benches of your free schools, we received from you the word of life....We owe to you and to M. Quinet more than what is vulgarly known as life." (Rosetti to Michelet, Nov. 2, 1863, Bibliothèque de la Ville de Paris, Papiers Michelet, Dossier K. 2. 11, Roumanie). "My generation owes all its virtues to the electric sparks by which Michelet inspired us and showed us the way....I have done too little for my country, but that little I owe entirely to the teachings of the Collège de France. (Rosetti to Mme Michelet, 1884, in Louis Ulbach, C. A. Rosetti, Paris, 1885, pp. 12-13).

in direct communication with Michelet.[66] He wrote the master a letter from Dijon, in 1846, an outpouring of his feeling for France, for his own country, for humanity and for the ideas of M. Michelet.[67] It was in fact an echo of what he had been hearing from Michelet himself at the Collège de France. Of France he wrote: "What power of attraction!... With the eyes of my soul I see thy hand draw me to thee, and bless thy name...God [is] on the soil of France....Ah, now I know that where France ends, there nothingness begins....France is a religion, she is God." Paris he called "a wonder,...the city of God." Speaking of his own country, without mentioning it by name, he expressed the desire to cover with his tears every bit of that dear land, but that his spirits were revived when he thought again of France. He mentioned being thrilled by Michelet's Le Peuple, which he had just read, especially by the part dealing with the sentiments of foreigners toward France. An interesting

---

66. From Michelet's papers comes evidence that he may have known Ion Ghica, or some other Ghica, in 1845. (Breazu, Michelet şi Românii, p. 33). Ion Ghica (Scrisori către Vasile Alecsandri, p. xix) quotes Michelet as saying: "You Roumanian youths are fortunate; in your country everything is to be done; each of you can distinguish himself by great and patriotic deeds." If Michelet ever said this, it was probably later, after he had met Rosetti and the Brătianus.

67. Bibliothèque de la Ville de Paris, Papiers Michelet, K. 2. 11. The letter is dated Mar. 1, 1846. It has been published and commented upon by Ion Breazu, "Un éloge roumain de la France," (Revue de Transylvanie, Cluj, I, 1934, pp. 276-286).

light is thrown on the Roumanians' tendency to place France on a different plane from England by his reference to the latter, with its industrial and commercial civilization, as having no soul. In contrast to the practical-minded students who saw progress in industrialization, D. Brătianu condemned industry, "which makes the few rich and the many miserable, as the greatest plague of modern times." His radicalism, indeed, was purely idealistic and utopian, based upon a determinism which was moral and religious (in an anti-clerical sense) and not even one percent economic.

This letter impressed Michelet enough to cause him to mention it at his next lecture, but the signature (D. Bratiano) had led him to believe the writer was an Italian, so to Italy went the praise.[68] Rosetti was anxious to have the Roumanians get credit and publicity where they were due. The Italians and Poles certainly had more than their share. He therefore called on Michelet, identified Brătianu as the letter-writer, and unburdened his soul about Roumania. The great historian,

---

68. Michelet's remarks, probably in rough approximation, were given in the Bucharest newspaper Românul, June 28, 1892, and reprinted in A. Cretzianu, Din Arhiva lui Dumitru Brătianu, vol. I, p. 119, note 2. Michelet, after the first applause, said that the letter was written with such flame and sincerity that if he should read it in full, "the walls of this college would fall down." This is confirmed by a letter from Rosetti to D. Brătianu, Apr. 3, 1846, ibid., pp. 119-22. Rosetti admitted not having attended the lecture. He got his information from hearsay.

much impressed, said: "Your friend is a fine writer, you must get him to do more writing."[69]

Brătianu had, in fact, already written again to Michelet, whose reply brought tears of joy to his eyes. He wrote again, giving permission to make use of his first letter, of his name, and of himself, and stating that he would always be proud to march under Michelet's banner.[70] When he returned to Paris a few months later, he became one of the intimate friends of Michelet, with whose daughter and son-in-law, Alfred Dumesnil, he was already acquainted.

In June of the same year Michelet received a letter from another young Roumanian student who preferred to remain anonymous. The letter was signed A. B., initials which do not seem to correspond with those of any Roumanian whom we know to have been in Paris at the time. The sentiments are much the same as those of Brătianu's letter. The Collège de France was "a glorious temple, where faith is strengthened by love," where the crowd gathers to express its love for Michelet and for France. He spoke of his own unfortunate people on the banks of the Danube, and begged encouragement,

---

69. Rosetti to D. Brătianu, Apr. 13, 1846, ibid., vol. I, pp. 122-6. Rosetti noted in his diary: "Today for the first time I spoke with a Christ, I spoke with Michelet. He told me, 'Encourage your friend to write, for he writes to perfection.'" (Note intime, vol. I, p. 110).

70. D. Brătianu to Michelet, Mar. 24, 1846, Bibl. Ville de Paris, Papiers Michelet, K. 2. 11.

that the Roumanians might persevere in their resolution and become worthy of the interest of France.[71]

Rosetti and the Brătianu brothers were eager to do more than just listen to lectures. They wanted action. To serve the cause of liberty they joined the editorial board of a journal known as Les Ecoles, the organ of the students at the Collège de France.[72] On the board also was Paul Bataillard, an intimate friend and warm defender of their cause, and the nominal president was Louis Blanc.[73] The tone of the journal was strongly democratic, and its office was used as an organizing center for the many demonstrations held in favor of the professors and in protest against the frequent governmental action taken against them.[74]

Another example of their participation in the opposition movement in France was their joining a masonic lodge, the Rose du Parfait Silence of which Brătianu became "P∴ F∴" and Rosetti, "Secr∴ Adj∴." Also members were the seventeen-year-old Gheorghe Creţeanu (who lived in the same house as

---

71. A. B. to Michelet, June 11, 1846, in Ion Breazu, Michelet şi Românii, pp. 128-30.

72. C. A. Rosetti, Note intime, vol. I, p. 97.

73. O. Boitoş, "Paul Bataillard et la Révolution Roumaine de 1848," (Mélanges de l'Ecole Roumaine en France, 1929, 2e. partie, pp. 1-158), pp. 22-3; Ştefanescu-Galaţi, C. A. Rosetti, p. 5. The journal appeared as Les Ecoles in 1845, and as Le Journal des Ecoles in the following years.

74. Louis Ulbach, C. A. Rosetti, p. 14.

Rosetti and D. Brătianu). Caracaş (another young Roumanian, a close friend of Ion Brătianu), Paul Bataillard and D. Pilette, who were both editors of Les Ecoles.[75] Pilette wrote to D. Brătianu in March, 1846: "The authorities are excited about our socialistic meetings."[76]

The other Roumanian students did not enter so boldly into the dangerous paths of opposition to the French Government. But they were eager and willing to join in a new society of Roumanian students, the aims of which were patriotic and only revolutionary in so far as they applied to Roumania. The soceity, founded in December 1845,[77] was the Paris counterpart of the "Literary Association" and the secret "Brotherhood" society which were established in Bucharest about two years before; Rosetti, Ghica, and others were members of both. The end, the development of national feeling and the winning of freedom from Russia and from the big boyar clique, was in both cases the same; the means were necessarily different. The Paris society had to confine

75. Cretzianu, op.cit., vol. I, p. 115, note 3. Gheorghe Creteanu was taken into the lodge on Dec. 24, 1846. (C. A. Rosetti, Note intime, vol. I, p. 182). I. G. Bibicescu, 1848 în Romania, (Bucharest, 1898), p. 44, and Lui Ion C. Brătianu, (Bucharest, 1921, p. 10, say that Rosetti and the Brătianus were in the lodge Athenée des Etrangers, noted for its republicanism.

76. Cretzianu, op.cit., vol. I, p. 116.

77. Anul 1848 în Principatele Române, vol. I, p. 80; C.A. Rosetti, Note intime, vol. I, pp. 41-42.

itself to promoting unity of sentiment among the Roumanians in Paris, to preventing them from forgetting about the fatherland, and to preparing them for the task of regenerating the nation. It was concerned chiefly with the problem of education, most of its energy going into the creation of a permanent library at No. 3 Place de la Sorbonne; and since they thought the nation needed nothing more than young men like themselves, they set forth as the main purpose of the society the raising of funds to enable students financially less fortunate than they to come to Paris. The surplus was to be used to buy Roumanian books for the library.[78]

The moving spirits in this new venture seem to have been Ion Ghica, Rosetti, and Scarlat Vârnav, a Moldavian who became respectively president, secretary, and treasurer.[79] There was a great dissimilarity between the Moldavians, who remained fairly close to earth, speaking of the need for

---

78. Dare de séma de lucrările Comitetului Societății Studentilor Români din Paris pe anii 1845-6 și 1847. Piața Sorbona No. 3. Subt patronajul cetățanului Lamartin, (Paris, 1848), a 22-page brochure, reproduced in Anul 1848, vol. I, pp. 73-88.

As a sort of independent venture, within the framework of the society, a group of twenty-four students decided to take up again the project of 1839, that of giving money to be sent to the Principalities to found Roumanian schools there. Each promised to sacrifice to this end a twentieth part of his yearly income. Among the twenty-four were the Brătianus, Rosetti, Bălcescu, Vârnav, N. Ionescu, and A. Kogălniceanu. (Cretzianu, op.cit., vol. I, pp. 132-3).

79. Rosetti to Brătianu, Apr. 13, 1846, Cretzianu, op.cit., vol. I, p. 123.

holding firmly to the national language and feeling, and for working with the enlightened members of the older generation,—Vârnav was author of the above-mentioned brochure—and the romantic spirits like Rosetti and D. Brătianu, whose speeches and writings exuded more Collège de France sentiment than the Moldavians were in the habit of expressing.[80]

The "Society of Roumanian Students," as it was called, put itself under the "patronage" of Lamartine, whose poetry had been such an inspiration to the literary efforts of the whole generation, and whose career in politics was applauded by the students in Paris.[81] Lamartine seems to have accepted with pleasure the honorary post of patron. Unfortunately we do not have his letter of acceptance.

The society set about its work of collecting money. Rosetti was commissioned to gather contributions from the various titled and monied Roumanians in Paris at the time, and though his diary records that he considered them far from

---

80. Iorga, "Rolul fraţilor Vârnav în Renaşterea românească," (Revista Istorică, V, 1919, pp. 170-87), pp. 175-9.

81. Societatea Studenţilor Români sub patronajul domnului de Lamartine, (Paris, July, 1846), a 15-page brochure, reproduced in Anul 1848, I, pp. 17-23. At the head of this document, stating the aims and the rules of the society, was the following verse of Lamartine:

"Viens reprendre ton rang dans ta splendeur première,
Parmi les purs enfants de gloire et de lumière,
Que d'un souffle choisi Dieu voulut animer,
Et qu'il fit pour chanter, pour croire et pour aimer."

agreeable and lacking in patriotism, the society's records show that they pledged or paid substantial sums.[82] He touched them on the average for a monthly payment of fifteen to twenty francs. He himself and the Brătianus each pledged ten, Ghica, twenty, and Vârnav twenty-five. Vârnav also made an outright gift of 3100 francs, and the Brătianus 1190 francs each. Altogether, in the first two years, they raised over eighteen thousand francs, with thirty-three thousand pledged but not paid. Of the grand total, about fifteen per-cent came from "the Roumanian lands," raised by the society's agents there, the rest from Paris, much of it from the legacy of twenty-two thousand francs from one wealthy supporter, Mihai Casimir.[83]

---

82. Rosetti, Note intime, vol. I, pp. 105-7. There was in Paris a considerable number of Roumanian aristocrats who had had little to do with the students. With the founding of this students' society, contacts between the two groups were greatly extended. (Cf. N. Kretzulescu, Amintire istorice, p. 48; Iorga, Les Voyageurs orientaux en France, p. 78; Stanislas Bellanger, "Les Moldo-Valaques," (L. Desnoyers, Les Etrangers à Paris, Paris, 1844, pp. 57-82).

83. Anul 1848, vol. I, pp. 80-88. The lists of subscribers do not tell us the exact number of Roumanian students in Paris at this time, since students, residents, tourists, and contributors from the Principalities are all listed together. Painstaking research might result in showing that of the 150-odd subscribers and donors, nearly 100 were students. That is the figure given by Bataillard at the time. (Anul 1848, I, p. 37). For the comparatively small number obtaining degrees at the Sorbonne and at the Faculty of Law in this period, see P. Eliade's articles in Viața Nouă, I, 1905, pp. 228-9, 372-4.

Early in 1846, before much of this money had been collected, the society set out to fulfil its purpose of "maintaining in Paris youths from all Roumanian lands" by calling two promising students, one from Moldavia, one from Wallachia.[84] The most successful venture was the library, carefully tended by Vârnav at 3 Place de la Sorbonne. He collected many books both French and Roumanian and supplied the library with all the latest magazines and newspapers.[85] The reading room was

---

84. Alexandru Zane, from Bucharest, who later took part in the revolution of 1848 and was exiled; N. Ionescu, from Jassy, a revolutionary in 1848, later a professor and a Foreign Minister of united Roumania. By December, 1847, only Ionescu had arrived. (Iorga, "Păreri vechi asupra Francomaniei," Floarea Darurilor, Bucharest, I, 1907), p. 343.

85. S. Vârnav, Biblioteka Roméné fundaté în anul 1846, (Paris, 1846), a 13-page brochure, reproduced in Anul 1848, I, pp. 23-27. I. G. Bibicescu, 1848 în România, p. 42, says that the Roumanians previously possessed a small reading room at No. 7 Cours de Commerce. This was the address of the Librairie Blosse, which had connections with Cyprien Robert, Mickiewicz's successor as Professor of Slavic literature at the Collège de France.

Many of the books from the library of the Society of Students are preserved today at the Ecole Roumaine at Fontenay-aux-Roses. They include Michelet, Histoire de la Révolution francaise, vol. II, (Paris, 1847); anon., La Voix de la France, (Paris, 1840); L'Echo de la France, (Paris, 1840?); E. de Calonne, Aux Démocrates, (Paris, 1845); Pertusier, La Valachie et la Moldavie et l'influence politique des Grecs du Fanal, (Paris, 1822); anon., Paul Kisseleff et les Principautés, (Paris, 1840); T. Robertson, Nouveau cours de la langue anglaise, (Paris, 1842); anon., Gramatica românească, (Bucharest, 1841); Eliade, Vocabularu, (Bucharest, n.d.); C. Boliac, Poezia, (Bucharest, 1843); Moliere, Les Précieuses ridicules, translated into Roumanian by Ion Ghica, (Bucharest, 1835); Lamartine, Moartea lui Sokrat, Roumanian translation by G. Sion, (Jassy, 1847); P.

"open to every Roumanian daily from the beginning of the day until ten-thirty in the evening," as a place for "meditation, taking notes, and waiting between classes."[86] Next to the library they rented a large room in which to hold their regular Saturday evening meetings and banquets, on the model of the "reform banquets" of the French opposition. In the library and at meetings it was laid down as a rule that among themselves only Roumanian should be spoken and written, an indication that for many of them a special effort was necessary to speak in their own tongue instead of in French. Citing this as "the most wonderful thing that young men could do for the future good of their country," Kogălniceanu's younger brother wrote: "[We] did not come just to learn to speak French like Frenchmen, but to take the ideas and the good things of a nation so enlightened and free." He mentioned also the very bad impression produced on the Paris students by the recent educational reforms in both principalities tending to obliterate the Roumanian language in the schools.[87]

Bataillard, De l'apparence des Bohémiens en Europe, (Paris, 1844). The majority of the books still preserved date from the period of exile, 1848-1857, and not from the student period.

86. Anul 1848, vol. I, p. 25.

87. A. Kogălniceanu to his father, Dec. 20, 1847, in Iorga, Păreri vechi asupra Francomaniei, p. 327. Cf. N. Bălcescu to V. Alecsandri, Nov. 29, 1847, in I. Bianu, "Bălcescu către Alecsandri," (Convorbiri Literare, L, 1916, pp. 19-30), pp. 25-8.

While Vârnav did most of the work for the society, Dumitru Brătianu, though not a founder nor an officer, became its accepted spokesman. It was he who gave impassioned orations at its meetings,[88] he who wrote the letters to noted men like Montalembert, to whom the society presented a copy of Vaillant's La Romanie and later requested that he bring up the Roumanian question in the Chamber of Peers;[89] and he who brought the society into close relations with Quinet. In January, 1847, he organized a deputation of Roumanian students to go to Quinet's residence.[90] Their

---

88. E.g., his speech given in Nov., 1847, published for propaganda purposes by Rosetti as "a speech inspired by God" in his newspaper Pruncul Român, Bucharest, No. 15, July 17 (O.S.), 1848, after the successful revolution in Wallachia. Text also in Anul 1848, I, pp. 61-73.

89. Montalembert to D. Brătianu, Mar. 10, 23, 1847 (Cretzianu, op.cit., pp. 126-8), and Feb. 8, 1848 (Anul 1848, I, pp. 136-7). Montalembert spoke of his "profound sympathy for the cause of the Moldo-Wallachians, for the independence and dignity of those beautiful lands, so intimately connected with the dignity and independence of civilized Europe." Cf. the similar letter of Béranger to Ion Brătianu, acknowledging receipt from the two Brătianus of an article (probably that of H. Desprez) on the Roumanians: "Some day, I hope we shall hold out our hand to the nations which will have grown up during our apparent sleep, and it will not be by conquest, but by fraternity, that we will be able to be useful to them. Advanced sentinel against barbarism, the brave Roumanian people will then regain...a loftier place in the world...." (Jan. 29, 1848, Anul 1848, I, pp. 132-3).

90. C. A. Rosetti's diary notes a previous occasion (Dec. 6, 1846) when "all the students" (probably mainly French students) went in a crowd to Quinet's house. Rosetti wanted to go to class instead, but Golescu grabbed his arm and made him follow the crowd. (Note intime, vol. I, p. 45).

purpose was to show solidarity with a beloved professor deprived of his chair by the government, and to thank him publicly for the sincere and encouraging reply he had made to a letter they had sent to him and to other prominent Frenchmen (probably Michelet, Lamartine, and Montalembert) "who best represented their sentiments."[91] Brătianu was the spokesman, and his speech a tribute to the inspiration of Michelet and Quinet:

> "Ah! how many times we have felt clasped in a divine embrace on hearing the tones of that prophetic voice, which, each day, brought to us new truths; how many times, our eyes bathed in tears, we have leaped up on our benches, when, like two grand priests, sole depositaries of the secrets of Providence, you and your illustrious friend tore away the shroud which covers heroic Poland, and let us see her full of life and strength....O Monsieur, how you have made us suffer! But you do not regret it: it was not the anguish of death which tortured our souls; our sorrow was that of the child which receives life; we were suffering, for we felt ourselves being reborn....Your doctrines have penetrated so far that they cannot any longer be confined within the walls of the temple, even though it be the Collège de France. You needed the world

---

91. Quinet had written: "...It is my duty to occupy myself with this nationality, so menaced today, and to defend its rights as best I can. I am happy to promise you I will do so, whether my chair at the Collège de France be returned, or whether I be reduced to continuing my teaching by other means." The text of this note, of Brătianu's speech, and an account of the whole affair were kept by Paul Bataillard, who was present at the demonstration. The documents are at the Brătianu Foundation in Bucharest, and have been published in Anul 1848, I, pp. 37-44. The incident is also fully described in Breazu, Edgar Quinet et les Roumains, pp. 715-20, and in T. G. Juvara, Edgar Quinet, Philo-Roumain, (Paris, 1906).

> for your temple, and for an altar the heart of each one of us. You have them!"

Quinet, "his eyes moist with tears," protested that he had done nothing to merit such words, then went on:

> "I accept these sacred words as a certain presage of the resurrection of the Moldo-Wallachian populations....Although apparently weak, it is perhaps on you that the great question of this century, the eastern question, will turn....May these words reach Moldavia and Wallachia. They will prove... to your compatriots that France is not for you nor for them a foreign land,...and that the alliance of the French and the Moldo-Wallachians is consummated in our spirits."

At Brătianu's words all the Roumanians had wept. While Quinet spoke, and when he had finished, they cheered and applauded vigorously, and when he told them to be ready to sacrifice even their lives to defend their nationality and country, they cried out "Yes!" Then Vârnav made the final speech, exalting the unity of the Young Roumanians, closing with a loud plea, "Let us all swear to die for our country!" They did so enthusiastically and the meeting broke up.

In 1847, a year and a half after the founding of the society, Dumitru Brătianu wrote to the patron, Lamartine, on its behalf, asking him to present the constitution to the Minister of the Interior, for authorisation to hold meetings "to confer on our national language and literature."[92]

---

92. Cretzianu, op.cit., vol. I, pp. 128-32. Brătianu took the opportunity to speak of the bonds between the Roumanians and France, and spoke of the future when disinherited Roumania might come into her own, with French support. He spoke of how the French soul had, by their

The Prefect of Police referred the matter to Guizot as perhaps of significance to questions of foreign policy and asked for instructions.[93] Guizot replied that he had no objection "in principle" to authorizing this society so long as its aims were purely literary and its conduct in conformity with the law. But he foresaw possible trouble from the governments in the Principalities, and referred the question to Bucharest; meanwhile he perused the statutes of this "association projected by a certain number of Moldo-Wallachians residing in Paris, under the title of Société des Etudiants Roumans."[94] Guizot was inclined to be benevolent: "We can view only with pleasure, in the interest of our moral influence and in that of the future of the Principalities, a great number of young Wallachians and Moldavians coming to study in France and take back to their countries the ideas and examples of our civilization." The consul talked with Prince

---

efforts, been transplated into Roumanian soil, and concluded: "France, France, be always strong, always great! In our darkest days, it is you who appear in the eyes of our soul as...a ray of consolation and hope."

That Lamartine knew some of the Roumanians personally in this period seems evident from a letter of recommendation he wrote in April, 1848. (Sever Zotta, "O scrisoare de recomandație a lui Lamartine pentru un boier din Moldova," (Revista Istorică, XII, 1926, pp. 205-6).

93. June 26, 1847, Aff. Etr., Corr. Pol., Bucarest, vol. 4.

94. Letters between Guizot and the Prefect of Police, July 5, 9, 1847, and from Guizot to de Nion, July 28, 1847, loc.cit.

Bibescu, who informed him that he had known for a long time about the society, its statutes, and its personnel; that he thought it would do more evil than good, and that he had forbidden his sons to join it. Bibescu predicted that daily contact, the spirit of propaganda, perfidious instigations, and individual passions would soon turn it into a dangerous political club, which might set up shop on Wallachian territory and bring on a crisis with Russia. DeNion advised Guizot to adjourn his decision.[95] Nothing further seems to have been done about the matter, and, with or without authorization, the society continued to exist, much to the eventual discomfiture of Prince Bibescu.

The Society of Roumanian Students was not a revolutionary body, but its leading members were certainly coquetting with revolutionary ideas in Paris and dreaming of something not far removed from revolution for their own country. Vârnav and most of the Moldavians tended pretty strictly to their own business. Kogălniceanu devoted himself more to scholarship than to politics, becoming known to many members of the Académie des Inscriptions, and of the Société Orientale de France, of which Lamartine, Montalembert, Cochelet, were honorary members, Drouyn de Lhuys, Vaillant, Colson and

---

95. de Nion to Guizot, Sept. 16, 1847, loc.cit.

Billecocq active members.[96] He supplied to the Academy some material on ancient Dacia, to the Revue de l'Orient some fragments of his collected chronicles, and he was himself elected to membership. He hoped to insert a large number of articles in the newspapers and reviews of Paris.[97]

Although by no means so ultra-French in spirit as Dumitru Brătianu, Kogălniceanu felt that France, as the strongest nation of Latin origin, was the national protector of the smaller sister nations, her mission to prevent their annihilation by Germans and Slavs.[98] Bălcescu, who conferred on historical matters with Kogălniceanu at this time and planned to put out a large-scale dictionary of Roumanian biography with him, also contributed to the Revue de

---

96. N. Cartojan, Mihail Kogălniceanu la Paris în 1846, (Craiova, 1925), p. 10; M. Kogălniceanu, Scrisori, 1834-1849, pp. 196-7; Revue de l'Orient, Paris, vol. I, 1843, pp. 124-7; ibid., II, 1843, p. 95; ibid., XI, 1846, p. 237. The review's regular writer on the eastern question was strongly pro-Roumanian and anti-Russian. Vaillant published several articles on the Roumanians, most important of which was "Tendances politiques des Moldo-Valaques manifestées par leur littérature," showing that the main tendency was toward a union of the provinces of ancient Dacia. (Vol. V, 1844, pp. 213-22. Cf. Cudalbu-Şlusanschi, Contributions à la biografie et à l'ouevre de J. A. Vaillant, pp. 71-2.

97. Cartojan, op.cit., p. 11, lists the articles he planned to write. A careful search in the Paris press of 1846 might reveal whether any of them were written and published. Even after he left for Spain, in the autumn of 1846, he kept in communication with French journals. (Cartojan, Călătoria lui M. Kogălniceanu în Spania, Bucharest, 1919, p. 4).

98. Cartojan, Mihail Kogălniceanu la Paris în 1846, p. 9.

l'Orient.[99] Bălcescu was much more willing than was Kogălniceanu to mix with French republicans and to think seriously of the question of revolution. He was a bold idealist, a Roumanian Mazzini, and one of the most attractive figures of all the Pașoptiști. He lacked the dripping sentimentality of D. Brătianu, having a strong desire to win fame as a man of action.

At this time Bălcescu and Brătianu were in substantial agreement and their contacts were with the same French circles Michelet, Quinet, Armand Lévy, Alfred Dumesnil, etc.[100] Bălcescu was a particular friend of Paul Bataillard, whom he supplied with documentary material for his research on the question of the Gypsies.[101]

The French friends of the students were meanwhile trying

---

99. He contributed unwittingly when Vaillant published, under his own name, a French version of Bălcescu's Puterea armată in vol. X, 1846, of the review, pp. 81-108. In a tone of some indignation Bălcescu corrected the error in a letter to the editor, dated Sept. 2, 1846 (Revue de l'Orient, vol. X, p. 342).

100. Bălcescu's connections with this group are evident from two letters of Ion Alecsandri (brother of Vasile) to Antonin Dessus, Sept. 15, Oct. 7, 1847, (Musée Adam Mickiewicz, Paris, Mss. Dossier 1036, fol. Alexandry), and from the presence of his name on a subscription list to a fund run by Les Ecoles group, two Moldavians also being on the list alongside the names of Michelet, Quinet, George Sand, Lévy, Dessus, Dumesnil, and Bataillard. (Ibid., Dossier 1036).

101. P. P. Panaitescu, Contribuții la o biografie a lui N. Bălcescu, (Bucharest, 1924), pp. 62-3.

to inform the French public of the aspirations of the Roumanian nation. In 1843 there appeared in the Revue Indépendante an article on the Principalities, probably written by Elias Régnault, an editor of Le National and later the author of a lengthy history of the Principalities.[102] In 1847 and 1848 two more articles appeared in the same review, with very similar arguments.[103] In general these articles insist on the legal status of the Principalities as autonomous states, dwell on their ties with France, mention the students in Paris, and point out that it is to the interest of France and England to support "democracy" against despotism on that particular battlefield. If these articles were not written by one of the Roumanian students, they were probably directly inspired, as the information they reveal was certainly not that of the average French journalist.[104]

---

102. Regnauld, "Les Principautés Danubiennes: Romanie ou Moldo-Valaquie," (Revue Indépendante, VIII, June 1843, pp. 520-53. This article has sometimes been attributed to D. Bratianu, because of Ubicini's statement that Bratianu wrote many articles for Le National and La Revue Indépendante under the pseudonym of "Regneult." Cf. O. Boitos, Bibliografiile româneşte ale lui Ubicini, p. 54; A. Petroaie, "L'activité philo-roumaine d'Elias Regnault," (Mélanges de l'Ecole Roumaine en France, XI, 1933, pp. 1-45), pp. 6-8.

103. Saint-Martin, "La Romanie ou Moldo-Valaquie, Rapports des peuples romans avec les Turcs," (Revue Indépendante, XII, Dec. 1847, pp. 291 ff., and Jan. 1848, the second part also published separately as a brochure.

104. "Saint-Martin" is obviously a pseudonym. See the long resume and discussion of these articles in V. V. Hanes, Formarea Opiniunii franceze asupra României, vol. II, pp. 131-141.

Another friend of the Roumanian students was the prominent journalist Hippolyte Desprez, one of the editors of the _Revue des Deux Mondes_ and a former editor of the _Annuaire historique_. In the _Revue des Deux Mondes_ he published a long article entitled "La Moldo-Valachie et le mouvement roumain."[105] Desprez categorically stated the most advanced aims of the Roumanians:

> "The Dniester, the Carpathians, the Theiss, the Danube, and the Black Sea form a national frontier around these diverse provinces [Bessarabia, Moldavia, Wallachia, Bucovina, Transylvania, Eastern Hungary], partitioned among three great empires, and this vast territory seems thus to be disposed to contain a single nation."

He then goes on to prove that this nation exists, made up of the descendants of Roman colonists, now fully aware of their national individuality and their Latin character. He describes this "ideal Roumania," its people, their language, their customs, and their love of France. He demolishes the "old Wallachian" clique of pro-Russian boyars and blows the horn of the "young Roumanians," whose national movement in the direction of unity will become one of the greatest moral and political forces in Eastern Europe. Many copies of this brochure of Desprez were taken back to Bucharest by Balcescu for distribution.[106]

---

105. _Revue des Deux Mondes_, Jan. 1, 1848, pp. 105-33, and separately.

106. S. Dragomir, "Un Precursor al Unității naționale, Profesorul ardelean Constantin Romanul Vivu," (_Ac Rom., Disc. de Recept._, vol. LXII, 1929), p. 14.

Desprez was a link between the Roumanian students and the Polish emigration, for his extensive trips in central and eastern Europe had been facilitated by Czartoryski.[107] Ion Ghica had remained in touch with Czaika in spite of the 1839 fiasco and a temporary disillusionment with the Roumanians on the part of Czartoryski.[108] In 1847 Czartoryski was again making great plans for the creation of a greater Serbia and a greater Roumania within the Ottoman Empire.[109] Late in 1847 there was a meeting at the Hotel Lambert in which A. C. and A. G. Golescu and one of the Crețulescus presented a note to Czartoryski with political and strategic plans in case of a war for the independence of Poland and for the union of all Roumanians.[110] The record of this

---

107. M. Handelsman, Czartoryski, Nicolas Ier, et la Question du Proche Orient, p. 96.

108. Ghica to Czaika, May 30, 1843, Panaitescu, Planurile lui Ioan Câmpineanu pentru Unitatea Natională a Românilor, pp. 105-6; Handelsman, op.cit., pp. 85-6. D. Brătianu seems to have been closer to the left wing of the Polish emigration than to Czartoryski. While at Dijon in 1846 he agitated and collected money for the Polish cause. (Cretzianu, op.cit., vol. I, pp. 116-8). Rosetti was on a Polish committee to raise money for the Poles, and he also collected Roumanian passports to give to them. (Note intime, I, pp. 97-99, 107).

109. Handelsman, op.cit., p. 92.

110. Handelsman, op.cit., pp. 95-6; Stanislaw Lukasik, Rumunia a Polska w XIX wieku, pp. 28-9; idem., Pologne et Roumanie, p. 88. This information from Polish sources does not tell us whether the Golescus were acting in the name of the Society of Roumanian Students, nor do we know the exact date of this meeting. The "Cratzulesco" referred to in the Polish report was probably Dimitrie Crețulescu, younger brother of Nicolae, who was not in Paris at the time.

meeting is proof enough that neither the revolution in Paris nor of central and eastern Europe took the Roumanians in Paris by surprise.[111]

When revolution broke out in Paris on the 22nd of February, the ardent disciples of Michelet and Quinet knew which side they were on. The students were one of the strongest and most spirited of those elements which joined hands to tear down the régime of Guizot and of Louis Philippe; Quinet himself participated in the fighting and led a great crowd to the Tuileries. An interesting question is how many Roumanians fought side by side with the people of Paris on the barricades. The answer given is generally "many," but we have very little evidence.[112] It seems likely that only the Brătianu brothers, and their small group of intimate friends (e.g., Creţeanu and Caracaş), Bălcescu, and perhaps A. G. Golescu, did any actual fighting.

---

111. Cf. Panaitescu, Contribuţii la o biografie lui N. Bălcescu, p. 68.

112. Cf. Breazu, Edgar Quinet et les Roumains, pp. 307, 320; V. V. Haneş, Formarea Opiniunii franceze, vol. II, p. 121; Cretzianu, Din Arhiva lui Dumitru Brătianu, vol. I, p. 21; G. Chainoi, Dernière occupation des Principautés Danubiennes par la Russie, (Paris, 1853), p. 79; Ubicini, in Vapereau, Nouvelle Biographie des Contemporains, 6th ed., p. 223; and an article in Le National, July 15, 1848, Anul 1848, II, p. 275. Ion Brătianu and Rosetti wrote to Quinet, July 8, 1848: "Recall to France that we are her sons, that we fought for her on the barricades." (Anul 1848, II, p. 135). Buchez, mayor of Paris, in a public speech, thanked the Roumanians "for being with us on the barricades." (Ibid., I, p. 140).

Bălcescu's mood in February is shown in his letter to Alecsandri, dated as follows: "FIRST DAY OF THE REPUBLIC, February 24, 1848." He explains that he has been on the streets for three days and has not had much time to write. "The great nation has risen, and the liberty of the world has been saved." He enclosed a souvenir, a piece of velvet which he had torn from the throne of Louis Philippe in the Tuileries on that very day at 1:30 P.M., "the greatest and most solemn moment of my life." He closed with "Long live the Republic!"[113]

Another account which we have, that of Alexandru Kogălniceanu, shows that not all the Roumanian students were out on the streets risking their lives for the republic. He describes the events of the three days of fighting, then tells his father not to be worried, "for I stay at home, and if I see that things are getting worse, I shall be the first to come back [to Moldavia]." Kogălniceanu reported that other Moldavians were also thinking about returning home.[114]

A minor crisis arose over the question of sending a delegation to congratulate the provisional government of the new French Republic, and though a majority decided in the affirmative, there was a minority including Constantin Vârnav,

113. I. Bianu, "Bălcescu catre Alecsandri," (Convorbiri Literare, L, 1916, pp. 19-30), p. 28.

114. A. Kogălniceanu to his father, Feb. 25, 1848, Iorga, Les Voyageurs orientaux en France, p. 81.

Ion Alecsandri, and Costache Negri, who did not want to take part in any action which might provoke Russia and bring on an invasion of Moldavia.[115] The ceremony took place on February 24th at the <u>Hôtel de Ville</u>, where groups representing several nations presented their flags and their congratulations to representatives of the French Republic and of the city of Paris. D. Brătianu was probably spokesman for the Roumanians, who had made a tricolor flag, a combination of the colors of the two principalities.[116] The flag of Roumania floated from the <u>Hôtel de Ville</u> beside those of Poland, Italy, and the tricolor of France, symbols of the union of the peoples of Europe.[117] Buchez, the new mayor of Paris, thanked them in a warm speech in which he called the revolution not only French but European: "In France the principle of the brotherhood of nations had been proclaimed:" As for the Roumanians, "advance guard of Europe in the East," they had reason to hope for eventual liberty and the support of Europe. No definite promises were made. To the Belgian

---

115. Iorga, <u>op.cit.</u>, p. 82, based on A. Kogălniceanu's letters.

116. The red, gold, blue tricolor, which is the flag of Roumania today.

117. <u>Anul 1848</u>, I, pp. 140-1, the information coming from the Paris journal, <u>Le Constitutionnel</u>, quoted in the <u>Gazeta Transilvaniei</u>, Apr. 26, 1848. Cf. P. Quentin-Bauchart, <u>Lamartine et la politique etrangère de la Révolution de février</u>, (Paris, 1913), pp. 22-23.

delegation Buchez said, "France must be ready to give aid to all nations who claim it....It is France's duty to the other nations."[118]

It is no wonder that the Roumanian students thought that the millennium had arrived. The dreams of the Collège de France were coming true. The feverish excitement among the Poles, Germans, and Italians in Paris, the formation of legions to fight for liberty in various parts of Europe, all must have had a great effect on their spirits.[119] The agitation in the clubs, the restoration of Michelet and Quinet to their chairs at the Collège de France, the speeches of members of the new government, the famous manifesto of Lamartine contributed to the conviction that the hour of deliverance had sounded. Bălcescu, A. G. Golescu, and the Bratianu brothers felt that their place was no longer in Paris but in Bucharest. The Moldavians, for their part, began to pack up and leave for Jassy. By the middle of April there was scarcely a Roumanian student left in Paris.

---

118. Quentin-Bauchart, op.cit., pp. 32-3.

119. Cf. Felix Ponteil, 1848, (Paris, 1937), pp. 81-88. "No sooner were the barricades of February down than the Roumanian colony in Paris, in its turn, dreamed of insurrection and progress," wrote Desprez in the Revue des Deux Mondes, Dec. 15, 1848, p. 899.

CHAPTER IV

1848. THE IMPORTED REVOLUTION

1. Background and preparation

The Wallachian revolution of 1848, which turned that principality into a democratic republic for a period of three months, aroused but slight interest in Europe at the time, but in Roumanian history it was an event of great significance, for it represented the first opportunity of the new generation to wield actual political power, to try to give practical effect to those doctrines of which its members had become the most eloquent spokesmen and the most fervent disciples. It is significant also in that it throws light on the question, important for all southeastern Europe, of the degree of success with which political systems and institutions originating in western society can be applied to a social milieu having little in common with that in which those institutions have arisen.

As we have seen the preparation of the revolution took place partly in Paris. In the Principalities also there was a combination of intellectual fermentation and political conspiracy which set the stage for 1848. The impetus came from the new literary group of the early 1840's, which included Ion Ghica, Bălcescu, Kogălniceanu, Russo, Alecsandri, and Costache Negri, most of them fresh from Paris. While Eliade in Bucharest and Asachi in Jassy fitfully dispersed their energies in a hundred different directions, these younger men banded together into a cohesive unit, and in the course of their activities they thrashed out a national and political program which became the platform of 1848.

The three centers of this movement were Bucharest, Jassy, and Mânjina, Negri's estate in Moldavia. At Mânjina they were accustomed to gather and to exchange ideas.[1] Here the emphasis was more national than liberal, thus more Moldavian than Wallachian or French. Insults were hurled at the Milcov, the little river which formed the boundary between the Principalities, "between two little peoples who should form but one," rather than at the boyar oligarchy. "That [separation] is the hydra we must destroy," wrote Negri, "that is the prime source of our common weakness."[2]

At Jassy, which in this period took the literary spotlight away from Bucharest, Ion Ghica and Kogălniceanu were professors at the Academia Mihăileană. Ghica's chair was in political economy and Kogălniceanu's in history; what they taught was liberalism, progress, and nationalism.[3] Kogălniceanu

---

1. G. Bogdan Duică, Vasile Alecsandri, Povestirea unei vieti, (Bucharest, 1926), pp. 16-7, 22; Bengescu, "Vasile Alecsandri," (Convoribiri Literare, XXII, 1888, pp. 27-39), pp. 27-8; G. Adamescu, "Alexandri la 1848," (ibid., LXIII, 1930, pp. 881-9); p. 882; Panaitescu, Contribuţii la o biografie a lui N. Bălcescu, pp. 52-3; Dragnea, Viaţa lui Alexandru Russo, p. 686.

2. Negri to Constantin Filipescu, no date, (Convorbiri Literare, XXXVI, 1902, p. 278).

3. Ghica, Scrisori către Vasile Alecsandri, pp. 254-5; N. Georgescu-Tistu, Ion Ghica, Scriitorul, (Bucharest, 1935), pp. 25-9; Iorga, Ist. lit. rom., vol. II, pp. 101-3.

made this a little too obvious and consequently was relieved of his position because of Russian displeasure, but not before he had sounded a clarion call to all Roumanians for national unity. In Ion Ghica's lectures the same theme recurred. On one occasion he said that "perhaps our generation will see the states of Germany united, as is necessary for a people who speak the same tongue and have the same origin," and it was necessary for Roumanians as well as for Germans.[4]

In order to spread these ideas beyond the limits of the classroom, Ghica and Kogălniceanu, in collaboration with the poet, Vasile Alecsandri, founded a review which they called Propășirea, "Progress." When this revolutionary title ran afoul of the censorship, they brought out the paper with a blank space across the top, and below this the subtitle, "Journal of science and literature."[5] Despite a short career this publication had a considerable influence in the crystallization of a Roumanian national culture, not only through its propagation of the national ideal and the idea of progress, but also because its contributors included Roumanians of the other provinces. Through his connections

---

4. Georgescu-Tistu, op.cit., p. 27.

5. N. Cartojan, "Soarta unei reviste literare în 1844, 'Propășirea,'" (Convorbiri Literare, XLI, 1907, pp. 197-204, 416-29). It lasted only from Jan 6th to Oct. 29th, 1844.

in both principalities Ion Ghica opened the columns of Propăşirea to his friends Bălcescu, Boliac, and Voinescu, whose efforts in national history and poetry might otherwise have remained unknown to Moldavian circles.[6] The melting process by which in Paris the students from the two principalities came to feel themselves as members of the same Roumanian nation was paralleled by this development at home.

In Bucharest the men of the younger generation were participating in a similar idealistic national literary movement, conceding nothing to their Moldavian friends in enthusiasm, even if inferior to them in literary talent. Following the Wallachian practice of organizing, they formed, in 1845, a "Literary Association," which was in fact the successor to the political-literary society of Dinicu Golescu and Eliade in the 1820's and the Philharmonic Society of the 1830's.[7] Its aim was "the advancement of Roumanian literature," and as a means it envisaged "the extension of the association to all Roumanian provinces, since this aim is not local but is intended to initiate literary progress

---

6. Ghica, Scrisori, pp. 681-2; Iorga, Ist. lit. rom. vol. II, p. 103.

7. The first informal meeting was held in 1843, with not only Bălcescu, the Golescus, Voinescu, Boliac, and Laurian participating, but Tell and Eliade also, thus both right and left wings of the new national party. (Panaitescu, Contribuţii la o biografie a lui Balcescu, pp. 27-8, citing a note in Propăşirea, Jan. 1844).

in all Roumania."[8] The leading lights of the society, and members of its steering committee, when they happened, for one reason or another, to be home from Paris, were Bălcescu, Voinescu, Boliac, Bolintineanu, A. G. Golescu, D. Brătianu, C. A. Rosetti and Ion C. Brătianu. Iancu Văcărescu was president, many conservative and wealthy boyars subscribed, and also Prince Bibescu, who was certainly no enemy of romantic nationalism and liked on occasions to don the national costume of Michael the Brave.[9]

Plans for "useful scientific articles," "good translations," and a huge biographical dictionary by Bălcescu and Kogălniceanu came to nothing and a "scientific and literary album," after two issues, was snuffed out by the Government, because of its "political varieties." However, this did not prevent the individual members from publishing their own works, mainly through the printing establishment of C. A. Rosetti, who had shocked the whole boyar class by deserting the traditional life of leisure to become a publisher and

---

8. Vintilă Rosetti, "Societatea Literară din 1845," (Românul Literar, 1893, pp. 15-22, 55-8, 76-8, 106-8, 139-42, 170-4); Iorga, Ist. lit. rom., vol. II, pp. 159-60.

9. The statutes, reports of committees, budget, and list of subscribers were published in brochure in 1847, reprinted in Anul 1848, I, pp. 44-61. The minutes of a meeting in 1845 register the decision to write to the Moldavians Alecsandri, Negri, and Negruzzi, and to the Transylvanians Bariţ, Vasici, and Cipariu, urging them to find subscribers and to send in material worthy of publication.

bookseller. He was instrumental in bringing before the reading public many of the histories, grammars, texts, and poems of his patriotic friends.[10]

The work of the historians, Kogălniceanu and Bălcescu, was perhaps the greatest of the contributions of the new intelligentsia to the growth of nationalism. Uncritical, a mixture of history and propaganda, it accomplished its purpose of giving the Roumanians a new appreciation of themselves. Following the models of contemporary French historiography, they read into the past much that never took place, using it to support their ideals and their opinions on practical issues. They made of their history not only the glorification of a people, but also a paean to liberty to progress, or even to God. To Kogălniceanu, who had studied under von Ranke, as to Bălcescu, a romantic idealist strongly influenced by Vico, Cantù, and Michelet, the concept of liberty meant much, especially after their experiences with prisons and censorship. Both had the conviction that there could be no civilization worthy of the name without a recognition of the rights of man and the citizen.[11]

---

10. C. V. Obedeanu, "C. A. Rosetti, librar," (Arhivele Olteniei, IV, 1925, pp. 483-5); C. V. Rosetti, "Enric Winterhalder," (Adevărul Literar si Artistic, IV, 1923, Mar. 25, p. 6); Ulbach, C. A. Rosetti, pp. 14-15.

11. Iorga, Ist. lit. rom., vol. II, pp. 22, 113-27; idem., Mihail Kogălniceanu, pp. 69-80; Dragnea, Mihail Kogălniceanu, pp. 35-56; Ioan Lupas, "Leopold von Ranke şi Mihail Kogălniceanu," (Ac. Rom., Mem. Sect. Ist., Ser.

Nationalism was the key to their history, and history the key to their program of spreading nationalism. Kogălniceanu propounded his creed in the opening lecture of his history course at Jassy in 1843:

> "My heart beats when I hear the names of Alexander the Good, of Stephen the Great, of Michael the Brave. And I am not ashamed to tell you that these men are for me more important than Alexander the Great, Hannibal, and Caesar....Their battles have a greater interest, because they were won by Roumanians....I regard as my fatherland all that territory where Roumanian is spoken, and as national history the history of all Moldavia, before its partitition, that of Wallachia and that of the brothers in Transylvania....Especially will I not forget the Wallachians, our brothers in blood, in language, in laws, and in the Cross....National history is absolutely necessary to us for the defence of our rights against foreign nations.... They have denied our origin and our name, partitioned our land, trampled upon our rights, only because we have not had the consciousness of our nationality, only because we have not been able to establish and defend our rights." 12

Bălcescu's nationalism was blended with the ideal of human liberty. Like Michelet and Mazzini, he held that

---

III, vol. XVIII, 1936, Mem. 10). Kogălniceanu's work in this period appeared chiefly in periodicals edited by himself, *Dacia Literară* (1840), *Arhiva Românească* (1841, 1845), and *Propăşirea* (1844).

12. M. Kogălniceanu, *Opere*, (Craiova, n. d., ed. Cartojan) pp. 79-81. The lecture was first published in *Propăşirea*, Sept. 24, 1844. Cf. A. Lapedatu, "Nouă Imprejurări de Desvoltare ale Istoriografiei Naţionale," (*Anuarul Institutului de Istorie Naţională*, Cluj, I, 1921-22, pp. 1-18), pp. 2-5. This lecture was in fact an almost word for word translation of the preface to Karamzin's *History of the Russian Empire*, which Kogălniceanu knew in its French edition. (P.V. Haneş, *Studii de Literatura Română*, pp. 44-49).

every nation had a mission to perform, the diversity of nations, each following its own divine light, producing a harmonious whole. The mission of the Roumanians was to stand as a Roman sentinel at the gates of the civilized world and hold off the barbarians.[13]

As was not uncommon elsewhere in Europe in this era, the intellectuals were men of action, or if not they thought they were. Nothing in the world could have induced these poets and historians to confine themselves to poetry and history. For them there was no separating intellectual endeavor from the idea of political revolution, peaceful or violent, which would end foreign domination and clear away the corruption, the injustice, and all the dead wood of the feudal regime. There could be no liberated Roumanian nation without a breaking of the monopoly of political power held by the big boyars, without a bold defiance of Europe's champion of reaction, Tsar Nicholas I, without a revision of the unequal tax system, and, in the opinion of a handful of "radicals,"

---

13. Panaitescu, *Contribuţii la o biografie a lui N. Bălcescu*, pp. 31ff.; *idem*., Introduction to Nicolae Bălcescu, *Patru Studii Istorice*, (Bucharest, 1928), pp. 13-15; Marin Stefanescu, *Filosofia Româneăsca*, (Bucharest, 1922), pp. 143-4; Edgar Papu, "Vico în Cultura Românească," (*Studii Italiene*, Bucharest, II, 1935, pp. 161-85), pp. 164-7; Apostolescu, *L'influence des romantiques français*, pp. 170 ff. Most of Bălcescu's historical work was published in the *Magazin Istoric pentru Dacia*, (5 vols., 1845-47), which he edited in collaboration with a Transylvanian, A. T. Laurian.

without an agrarian reform.

The inevitable counterpart of the Literary Association in Bucharest was the secret revolutionary society, to which was given the name of Frăţie, "Fraternity." The founders of this society were Ion Ghica, Bălcescu, and Christian Tell, an army officer, and the year was 1843.[14] True to its intentions, the society remained secret, and from its inception late one night on the deserted streets of Bucharest until the outbreak of revolution in 1848, it kept few records which might have been of profit to Prince Bibescu's police or to future historians. The statutes of the society were kept by Ghica until he left Bucharest in 1848, and later they were destroyed by fire. He himself tells us that they provided for an organization like that of the Carbonari, with groups of ten working together, each member knowing only his own immediate chief. The motto was Dreptate-Frăţie, Justice-Brotherhood.[15] It is reasonable to assume that the membership included the same men who composed the Literary Association, minus Bibescu and the big boyars.

Even without the society's declaration of ends and

---

14. Ghica, Scrisori, p. 687; N. Bălcescu, Scrisori către Ion Ghica, (Bucharest, 1911), pp. 2, 252; N. Georgescu-Tistu, Ion Ghica, Scriitorul, pp. 25-6; Ubicini, Provinces d'origine roumaine, p. 172, which gives 1844 as the date of the founding of the society.

15. Ghica, op.cit., pp. 687-9.

means, we know the program for which it stood. For it was but the underground continuation of the abortive revolutionary movements of 1839 and 1840 in which Bălcescu had participated and for which he had suffered imprisonment. On the political side, they used the Roumanian past to justify the necessity of introducing the institutions of liberal democracy with which their contact with the West had made them acquainted. As for the extent of their national aspirations, they were those of Câmpineanu in 1839. But in view of political realities, they saw the advisability of not biting off too much in one mouthful, and their revolutionary plans were aimed first and foremost at "regenerating" the Principalities, especially Wallachia.

2. The revolution in Moldavia

Had they not happened in the year 1848, the events of the 8th to the 11th of April in the capital of Moldavia would never have been called a revolution. They need concern us only as a subject for comparison with what happened in Wallachia, and for their relation to the general currents of the year of revolution.

The general dissatisfaction with Prince Sturdza and his clique, plus the electrification of spirits" produced by the news from Paris, provoked a great meeting of boyars and middle class people on April 8, 1848, in the Hotel Petersburg in Jassy, its purpose to draw up a petition to the Prince asking for certain reforms.[16] The petition requested, among other things, strict adhesion to the Règlement Organique, certain economic and judicial reforms, responsibility of officials for their acts, abolition of the censorship, the "improvement" of the condition of the peasants, and a national guard.[17] The few sops thrown to the bourgeoisie and to the peasantry were wholly disproportionate to their real claims. The entire petition, in fact, amounted to little more than a condemnation of governmental corruption, a laudable effort no doubt, but nothing more than the chronic complaints of the "outs" against the "ins" on charges that have been made against every Roumanian régime over a period of three centuries. It was the tragedy of the young nationalists they they either misjudged the situation or were too fearful of bloodshed and Russian intervention, thus passing up the chance to make a real bourgeois-democratic revolution, in which they might have had the support of the population of Jassy and of the peasants, who were undoubtedly influenced by the new developments in the peasant question in the neighboring Habsburg dominions.[18]

---

16. Gheorghe Sion, Suvenire Contimpurane, (Bucharest, 1888), pp. 167ff. On the committee of redaction were V. Alecsandri, Cuza, V. Ghica, Rolla, and others.

17. Anul 1848, I, pp. 176-9.

18. Ibid., pp. 166, 173, 230.

In contrast to the Wallachian "Reds" of the type of C. A. Rosetti, whose ideals they shared, the Moldavians had no revolutionary organization, and they were not convinced of the possibility of establishing a democracy overnight.[19] They paid dearly for their hesitation, for the limitation of the demands to those of the boyars made them little more than palace revolutionaries, and when Sturdza broke up the movement and took a ferocious revenge, they had no popular support on which to fall back. The prince saw that the real danger of the situation was social revolution; he therefore smashed the opposition forcibly before it could develop. The leaders were arrested, some tortured and imprisoned, others chased out of the country. A strict watch was kept on the frontiers to catch Scarlat Vârnav, N. Ionescu, V. Mălinescu, and other students returning from Paris.[20] No resistance was possible. Those who had arms did not use them, and a last minute attempt to raise the mob in Jassy failed utterly. The shopkeepers and peasants were not going to take up arms for the boyars, their class enemies, against the Prince.[21] The young

---

19. Kogălniceanu is reported to have said to Nicolas Soutzo: "Nous sommes des agneaux en comparison, nos frères de Valachie poussent les allures revolutionaires jusqu'à nous faire frémir." (Soutzo, _Mémoires_, Vienna, 1899, p. 366).

20. _Anul 1848_, I, pp. 182, 351; Iorga, "Despre Revoluţia dela 1848 în Moldova," (_Ac. Rom., Mem. Sect. Ist._, Ser. III, vol. 20, 1938, Mem. 2), pp. 14-15; Sion, _op.cit._, pp. 234-6, 287-8, 293ff.

21. _Anul 1848_, I, pp. 219-20, 233; Ghica, Scrisori, p. 703; Petraşcu, _Vasile Alecsandri_, pp. 27-8; Soutzo, _Mémoires_, p. 150; Iorga, _Istoria Românilor_, vol. IX, p. 123.

"national" revolutionaries were not clear-sighted enough to see that that gap could not be so easily bridged. Sturdza's victory had the greatest significance, for it immobilized liberalism in Moldavia and turned the country into a definite stronghold of reaction, soon to be a base from which Russian troops could go forth to stifle revolutions in Wallachia and in Hungary; Moldavia remained immune to the revolutionary waves which rolled over the neighboring provinces later in the year. After the dispersion of the Moldavian nationalists, the chances that the Roumanians would in 1848 achieve national unity, or even the union of the Principalities, were very slim indeed.[22]

The brutal suppression of the attempt to force reforms on Sturdza convinced the national party of the need of making a complete break with the past. They turned to the left and thereafter actually lived up to their hitherto undeserved reputation as revolutionaries. Although their chance for success was lost, it is in their activity after April that

---

22. On the events of April 8-10 in Moldavia, the following contain documents, factual accounts, and interpretations: Anul 1848, I, pp. 176-92; ibid., VI, pp. xxxix-xlii; C. Colescu-Vartic, 1848, Zile Revoluţionare, (Bucharest, 1898), pp. 111-26; Filitti, Domniile Române sub Regulamentul Organic, pp. 635-63; Ion C. Ion, "Adevăratul 1848," (Viaţa Romînească, XXX, Feb. 1938, pp. 12-19; Carol Göllner, Revoluţia anului 1848 şi ecoul ei în presa săsească, (Ms. Diss., Univ. of Cluj, 1933, placed at my disposal through the kindness of Professor Ioan Lupaş), pp. 78ff.

we find expressed the real spirit and aims of the Moldavian Pașoptiști. Their secretly circulated brochures reveal them as propagators of the idea of national unity, and especially of union with Wallachia. Their political and social program is seen to be no less drastic than that of the revolutionary government in Bucharest.

Political agitation in Moldavia was almost impossible in 1848. Most of the young leaders had been deported to Turkey; others had escaped to Transylvania and to Cernăuți (Czernowitz), where they were treated as honored guests by the Hurmuzachi family, the leading Roumanian patriots in Bucovina and editors of a newspaper, Bucovina, which represented the interests of the Roumanians in all provinces.[23] There they spent many hours, whiling away the summer of 1848, discussing the problems facing the nation. It is not clear to what extent they used Cernăuți as a base for intrigues and agitation in Moldavia. They did plan to invade Moldavia with an army recruited in the Banat, in Transylvania, and in Bucovina, thus giving real military aid to a popular rising against Sturdza.[24] They were accused by the Russians of

---

23. Ion I. Nistor, "Un capitol din viața culturală a Românilor din Bucovina, 1774-1857," (Ac. Rom., Disc. de Recept., vol. 44, 1916), pp. 44-51; T. Bălan, Frații George și Alexandru Hurmuzachi și ziarul "Bucovina," (Cernăuți, 1924).

24. Sion, op.cit., pp. 322-3, 354; T. Bălan, Refugiații moldoveni în Bucovina, 1821 și 1848, (Bucharest, 1932)

planning to march on Jassy, depose Sturdza, and declare union with Wallachia in an independent state, and the frontier guards kept a sharp lookout for them and their agents.[25] Those of the comrades who had remained in Moldavia did their share by printing and disseminating propaganda through pamphlets and small books produced by a secret printing press, for the only tolerated non-ecclesiastical press was that of Asachi who, despite his great literary contribution to the growth of nationalism, was a reactionary and a protegé of Sturdza.[26]

The Moldavian Forty-Eighters did not have the experience of political power, which generally tempers the sharpness of radicalism, but on the basis of the political and national aims which they expressed with great clarity, we can attempt an analysis and an explanation of their ideology, and assess their contribution to the development of Roumanian nationalism. Their revolutionary manifestoes began to appear in May, some

---

p. 18; N. Cartojan, <u>Pribegia lui M. Kogălniceanu în Bucovina</u>, (Bucharest, n. d.), p. 12. C. A. Rosetti, in <u>Pruncul Român</u>, Aug. 3, 1848 (o.s.), referred to "the revolutionary committee of Cernăuţi." Alecsandri was secretary of this committee, which had an agent in Paris, probably V. Mălinescu. (G. Bogdan-Duică, <u>Vasile Alecsandri</u>, p. 26).

25. Hurmuzaki, <u>Documente</u>, Supl. I, vol. 6, pp. 582-4; <u>Anul 1848</u>, II, pp. 609-10; Iorga, <u>Despre Revoluţia dela 1848 în Moldova</u>, pp. 11ff.

26. N. A. Bogdan, "Pamflete politice împotriva lui Mihail Sturza-Vodă," (<u>Revista Arhivelor</u>, Bucharest, I, 1924, pp. 31-38), pp. 31-4.

stressing the agrarian question, some nationality, and others were merely diatribes against "Prince Michael the Cruel," "the only ruler in all the Daco-Roman lands who remains deaf to the voice of the people,...today when all peoples are constituting themselves on a basis of freedom." All these pamphlets, printed in a manner that permitted widespread undetected circulation, were calculated both to stir the emotions and to appeal to the material interests of the Moldavian population. Many were anonymous, others bore the signatures of Negri, Alecxandri, Russo, and others who were at the time in Transylvania or Bucovina.[27]

Between some of the declarations of principles there are glaring contradictions which can be explained only when one remembers that the liberalism and democracy of men like Alecsandri was of the most fluid sort. Members of the ruling class, they hardly envisaged the transfer of power to any other class. Romantics, they loved "the people" without comprehending their problems. In April they were adherents of the mild petition to Sturdza, and Cuza was ready to go out on the streets and die gloriously for it.[28] Later

---

27. Most of the brochures are undated, but their contents indicate that they belong to the year 1848. Acad. Rom. Mss. rom. No.5, fol. 166-9; Anul 1848, I, pp. 414ff., 447-479; Bogdan, loc.cit. Analyses of some of them in Xenopol, "Partidele politice în Revoluţia din 1848 în Principatele Române," (Ac. Rom., Mem. Sect. Ist., Ser. II, vol. 32, 1909, pp. 403-57), pp. 413-17.

28. Sion to Barit, Apr. 14, 1848, Anul 1848, I, pp. 223-7.

Alecsandri wrote a pamphlet defending the petition as the program of the national party.[29] Then, after going to Transylvania and being at Blaj for the mass meeting of Roumanians on the 15th of May, these same young men met at Brașov and signed an ultra-radical declaration of policy, which listed as their aims union with Wallachia, the abolition of all privileges, the establishment of a government based on liberty, equality, and fraternity, developed to their fullest extent, and the abolition of all feudal dues and obligations, with land given to the peasants without any payment on their part.[30] In June, at Cernăuți, they put out another declaration which went back to their earlier conservatism.[31] The fact was that, beyond being for "liberty" and against Sturdza and Russia, they were not sure what they wanted. They were not fanatic believers in French ideas, nor were they profound students of what was politically and economically possible in Moldavia. What they favored was "progress," "civilization," and in that

---

29. Anul 1848, I, pp. 414-30.

30. Principiile noastre pentru reforma Patriei, first published in Tribuna Română, Jassy, May 10, 1859, and copied from there by Dragnea, Mihail Kogălniceanu, p. 175. It has been twice published from a privately owned manuscript, each time without knowledge of any previous publication. See Bogdan-Duică, Viața și opera întâiului țărănist român, Ion Ionescu dela Brad, (Craiova, 1922), p. 121; "O învoila de reforme din 1848," (Revista Istorică, XVIII, 1932, pp. 43-4).

31. Anul 1848, I, pp. 457-9.

they represented, willy-nilly, western influence and those economic changes which were breaking down the antiquated feudal structure of Roumanian society. But they could not put their views into action, or even , with any clarity or consistency, on paper, and it was not until the arrival in Cernăuţi of Kogălniceanu, who had had no part in the attempted palace revolution of April, but had finally followed his colleagues into exile in order to escape arrest, that the necessary guiding hand was present. From his pen came the definitive statement of the principles of the Moldavian national party. His two brochures, "Project of a Constitution" and "Desires of the National Party in Moldavia, became the platform on which all the leading men of the party agreed.[32] With a historian's thoroughness, he made a detailed inquiry into all aspects of the domestic and international situation of Moldavia, rejecting with decision both the Règlement Organique and the Russian protectorate and proclaiming union with Wallachia to be the most essential reform of all, "failing which the whole national edifice would crumble."

That Kogălniceanu should make the union of the

32. M. Kogălniceanu, Proiect de Constituţie pentru Moldova, (Cernăuţi, 1848), and Dorinţele partidei naţionale în Moldova, (Cernăuţi, 1848), reproduced in Anul 1848, vol. III, pp. 131-42, and vol. IV, pp. 89-137; Kogălniceanu, Desrobirea Ţiganilor, etc., p. 282; Dragnea, op.cit., p. 175.

Principalities the most important point in his declaration of national aims was quite natural, although union had not yet become the touchstone of the whole liberal and national movement. This shows that the Moldavian Forty-eighters were following closely the course of the Wallachian revolution, waiting for the chance to extend it to their own principality. In May, Moldavian exiles and Wallachian revolutionaries had met in Transylvania and agreed to work together for the overthrow of Bibescu and Sturdza, the union of the Principalities, the emancipation of the peasants and Gypsies, and other reforms.[33] After the revolution of June 23 in Bucharest, the Moldavians were in communication with Wallachian officials and agents, although Ion Ionescu was the only one to take part in the conduct of affairs in Wallachia. The international situation did not permit their flocking to Bucharest as they flocked to Cernăuţi. But contacts were maintained, and Kogălniceanu, writing in August, had before him the Wallachian revolutionary proclamation of June 21st as well as the program signed by the Moldavian exiles when under the influence of the events in Transylvania, at Braşov in May.[34] Every one

33. Sion, op.cit., p. 322. At the time of the disturbances at Jassy in April, the French consul reported that it was "quite apparent that the Moldavian plotters were linked with Wallachian youths." (de Nion to Lamartine, Apr. 20, 1848, Aff. Etr., Corr. Pol., Bucarest, vol. 5).

34. Dragnea, op.cit., pp. 174-7. "The true program of the national party in Moldavia was made in Braşov, and then communicated to the refugees at Cernăuţi, where it was signed." (Kogălniceanu in the Chamber of Deputies, 1883, Monitorul Official, Feb. 11, 1883, cit. Dragnea, p. 174).

of the twenty-two points in the Wallachian proclamation was taken over and expanded by Kogălniceanu. In both principalities the principles professed were substantially the same.[35]

3. The revolution in Wallachia

The Bucharest revolution was one of the last in the chain of successive risings which swept across Europe in the annus mirabilis. What might be called a revolutionary situation existed in Wallachia from the start of the year. The economic misery of the masses had brought them to the point where their wants could easily be exploited by capable leaders. The peasants, influenced by the emancipation of the serfs in Transylvania, were said to be restless and on the point of a jacquerie.[36] The intellectuals, who had never been partisans of the old order, were solidly in favor of change; the boyar class was divided and unable to meet the situation

---

35. Kogălniceanu's constitutional provisions need not be discussed in detail, since the same ground will be covered in dealing with the constitutional question in Wallachia. They fall roughly into three groups, dealing respectively with broad and indestructible principles, application of them to the specific situation in Moldavia, and finally the clearing away of obstacles to commercial and general economic prosperity. It is in the first category that we find the expression of the bourgeois-democratic doctrine taken over bag and baggage from the West.

36. Colquhoun to Palmerston, Apr. 5, 1848, F.O. 78, vol. 742; G. Chainoi, Dernière Occupation des Principautés Danubiennes, (Paris, 1853), pp. 85-6.

with all the means at its command . Bibescu's régime needed the support of Russia and of a united _boyarie_. It was sure of neither.[37] Many of the boyars, particularly those referred to as the "Phanariot party," contributed funds to the revolutionaries and were intriguing against the prince with the hope of supplanting him with a candidate of their own.[38] The belief was widespread that Russian intrigues were also working to undermine Bibescu's position, so as to provoke disturbances and a pretext for a military occupation

---

37. Georges Bibesco (son of the Prince) presents his father as a reformer genuinely desirous of eliminating abuses and gradually modernizing the state, but thwarted by the ambitious young men from Paris who seduced the youth of the country with wild talk of reconstituting ancient Dacia, etc. (_Trois Ripostes_, Geneva, 1901, pp. 8-13, 44-5). This opinion was held by de Nion, whose reports picture the prince as caught between the unyielding stand taken by Russia and the impossible dreams of the radicals. (de Nion to Guizot, Jan. 7, 16, Feb. 7, 1848, _Aff. Etr., Corr. Pol., Bucarest_, vol. 5). But by May the Prince was "coming more and more to rely on Russia and the Porte against the youthful boyars who want a revolution." (de Nion to Lamartine, May 16, 1848, _loc. cit._).

38. C. D.Aricescu, _Capii revoluţiunii române dela 1848_, (Bucharest, 1866), pp. 22-3; Radu Crutzescu, _Amintirile Colonelului Lăcusteanu_, p. 109; Ion Ghica, _Scrisori_, p. 708. This group had just published in Brussels an anonymous brochure, _La Principauté de Valachie sous le hospodar Bibesko_, (1847, and a 2nd edition, 1848), almost universally and incorrectly attributed to Billecocq, former French consul in Bucharest. It violently attacked Bibescu and ridiculed the national party. The latter replied, through Desprez, in the _Revue des Deux Mondes_. (See Ubicini, _Provinces d'origine roumaine_, p. 171).

of the Principalities.[39]

The success of a revolution in Wallachia depended less on the attitude of the army, which was a negligible militia of some ten thousand men, than on the temper of the rural population, without whose support no movement could take hold in the provinces, and of the population of Bucharest, which supplied the mobs which actually made the revolution on the 11th of June and twice saved it. This city population, not noted for its effervescence, displayed in 1848 a remarkable propensity for rising in arms against the representatives of the old order. This can be partially explained by the fact that for some years there had been general indignation against the corruption of the Bibescu administration, and by the fact that the changes made by the government in the educational system, establishing a tuition fee that most of the students could not meet and replacing Roumanian as the language of instruction, threw

---

39. There has been much controversy on this point. Contemporaries, both reactionary and radical, say that Russia had a share in provoking the revolution. Cf. the opinions of Aupick, French ambassador at Constantinople and of the French press (Anul 1848, II, pp. 30, 43, 260), also Crutzescu, op.cit., p. 108; Chainoi, Dernière Occupation des Principautés Danubiennes, pp. 82-3; Bibesco, Règne de Bibesco, vol. I, p. 322; vol. II, pp. 354-7, and the many works cited in Xenopol, Istoria Românilor, vol. XII, p. 53, note. No real evidence has ever been adduced to prove the claim. Russia was working to support the princes against revolution, not to overthrow them. (See T. Schiemann, Geschichte Russlands, vol. IV, p. 174).

some two hundred turbulent students on to the streets in a rebellious mood. "Youth," wrote Ion Ghica, "hunted by the police, insulted at every turn,...was pushed by these humiliations into having a unity and an _esprit de corps_, with the result that it became a force at the disposition of whoever wanted to act against the government of Prince Bibescu."[40] Among those who wanted to act was Eliade, whose long career at St. Sava and in the field of literature had made him an idol of the students of Bucharest, particularly those of the middle classes whose families could not afford to send them to Paris, but he was not the man to organize and direct a revolution. The real leadership was supplied by those just returned from Paris. Some of them had stopped in Vienna, to make themselves acquainted with the new situation brought about by the revolution there. Back in Bucharest, they began immediately to prepare for a revolution.[41]

"Every day one or two youths from Paris arrive," wrote a Transylvanian teacher in Bucharest: "How fine it would be if they bring the principles, of liberty, of love of the Fatherland, and of Roman (sic) nationality, and if these would be made manifest in the acts of the French!! ...Some imagine that perhaps Lamartine will say: 'Now, young Romans, the time has come to make yourselves free and independent!"

---

40. Chainoi, _op.cit._, pp. 71, 80.

41. Ghica, _Scrisori_, pp. 701-4.

The same letter told of the recent arrival of Nicolae Bălcescu, who had brought with him many copies of the Revue des Deux Mondes, with its article on the natural unity of Dacia, and was distributing them everywhere.[42]

The foreign consular representatives took note of the new revolutionary situation brought about by the news from Paris, Vienna, Hungary and Transylvania, and by the return of the students. The French consul reported agitation "by a certain number of young men, mostly from the privileged families....Carried away by generous instincts, rather than guided by a studied conviction, still palpitating with the emotions inspired in them by an education in our schools or drawn from our books, they demand nothing less than the whole of the political liberties so laboriously conquered by France....Various placards, demanding a general abolition of the privileges of the boyars, freedom of the press, the formation of a national guard, etc., have been posted throughout the city."[43] The British consul, who had for years been sympathetic toward the national party, mentioned the arrival, in great numbers, of "young Wallachians, pupils of Michelet and Quinet, and friends of Lamartine," and predicted a revolution.[44]

---

42. S. Dragomir, "Din corespondenţa dăscălilor ardeleni în anul 1848," (Omagiu lui I. Bianu, Bucharest, 1927, pp. 155-70), pp. 164-5.

43. de Nion to Lamartine, Mar. 26, 1848, Aff. Etr., Corr. Pol., Bucarest, vol. 5.

44. Colquhoun to Cowley, Mar. 24, and to Palmerston, Mar. 28, 1848, F.O. 78, vol. 742.

In March the Frăţie society, in whose ranks many representatives of the military and the bourgeoisie had been drawn, began to marshal its forces for action. A committee was formed to organize and direct the approaching revolution. Members of this committee were A. G. Golescu, Ion Ghica, and Nicolae Bălcescu.[45]

At Rosetti's bookstore and the Golescus' house meetings were held and a revolutionary proclamation drawn up.[46] Rosetti by giving readings and making distributions of copies of Collège de France lectures sent to him by Michelet, and by supervising the purchase, storage, and distribution of arms, was a leading figure in both spiritual and material preparation.[47] Everything was ready for the revolution to

---

45. Ghica, Scrisori, pp. 705-6; Eliade Rădulescu, Mémoires, pp. 54-5, 59; F. Damé, Histoire de la Roumanie contemporaine, pp. 59-60. Aricescu, Capii revoluţiunii române dela 1848, p. 23, gives a much longer list including all the Golescu brothers, the Brătianu brothers, and Rosetti.

46. Ghica, Scrisori, pp. 702, 705, 713. Ghica attributes the document, which became the constitutional proclamation of June 21st, to Bălcescu and says it was adopted by the others at this time. This is contradicted by supporters of Eliade. The biblical style and references point to Eliade as the author. (N. B. Locusteanu, "Ion Heliade şi detractorii săi," Dupa Exil, vol. II, Craiova, 1900, pp. 391-440, p. 421). Cf. Eliade Rădulescu, Scrisori din Exil, (Bucharest, 1891), pp. 712ff.; Ubicini Provinces d'origine roumaine, p. 174; Iorga, Istoria Românilor, vol. IX, p. 151.

47. Rosetti, Note intime, vol. II, pp. 8-12; Ion Breazu, Michelet şi Românii, p. 74; Ghica, Scrisori, pp. 707-8.

break out on Easter Day, but the various factors caused its postponement, and in the succeeding interval an agreement was made with Eliade, whose support was a guarantee that the revolution would have on its side the shopkeepers and artisans of the capital.[48]

Several petitions presented to Bibescu in March and April indicate the kind of revolution they intended to make. Some were milder than others, but all spoke of certain reforms, such as the abolition of privileges, equal taxation for all, and theemancipation of the peasantry, as abolutely necessary. On the question of policy toward the suzerain and protecting powers, there was no general agreement. The extremists wanted to denounce the Russian protectorate, and buy independence from the Porte.[49]

Nothing would induce Bibescu to make concessions. The Russian consul had let it be known that if there were the slightest disturbance or any attempt to change the

---

48. Eliade and his disciples say the postponement was due to the fact that no movement could succeed without him, and that Tell refused to act without Eliade. (Locusteanu, op.cit., vol. II, p. 418; Eliade, Mémoires, p. 38; Elias Regnault, Histoire politique et sociale des Principautés Danubiennes, p. 401). Rosetti and Ghica attribute it to disunion among the leaders and to the receipt of a message from Lamartine. (Rosetti, Scrieri din Junete si din Esiliu, 2nd. ed., vol. II, Bucharest, 1885, p. 41; Ghica, Scrisori, pp. 709-10; idem., Amintiri din Pribegia dupa 1848, Bucharest, 1889, p. 835).

49. Anul 1848, I, pp. 376-8; Göllner, Revoluţia anului 1848, pp. 93-5.

constitutional regime then in force Russian troops would be in Bucharest within four days.[50] C.A. Rosetti had several stormy interviews with Bibescu, in which the prince expressed his agreement with the broad principles of the national party but considered the proposed reforms far in advance of the time and absolutely out of the question at the moment; he then warned Rosetti to stop holding seditious meetings.[51]

The necessity of defying both Bibescu and Russia led the reformers to modify their attitude toward Turkey, which some had been wont to blame almost as much as Russia for the oppressed condition in which the Roumanian nation found itself A mémoire presented to Talaat Effendi, the Ottoman commissioner sent to inquire into conditions in the Principalities, illustrates this change in direction and the adoption by the nationalists of a new attitude which was to become the official policy of the provisional government after the success of the revolution. This was less a matter of principle than of tactics. They were faced with the bald fact that the Roumanian nation was in real danger of being swallowed up by Russia. Their whole national movement had been built up on the basis of opposition to the crushing influence of

---

50. de Nion to Lamartine, Mar. 26, Apr. 8, 11, 1848, Aff. Etr., Corr. Pol., Bucarest, vol. 5.

51. Colquhoun to Canning, Apr. 6, 1848, F.O. 78, vol. 742; E. Winterhalder, "Desrobirea Româníei," (Pruncul Român, No. 2, June 17, 1848 (o.s.), pp. 5-6).

Russia. The Turks, on the other hand, despite the oppression and bad faith of which they had been guilty, were very much the lesser of the two evils. They had not extinguished the Roumanian nation in the past; they were not likely to be able to do so in the future. There was no immediate prospect of a break-up of the Ottoman Empire so long as the powers of Europe stood committed to its integrity. Therefore it was only reasonable that the Roumanian nationalists should attempt to conciliate both Turkey and the powers, natural enemies of their own enemy, Russia. The Turkish suzerainty, which in practice meant little more than paying annual tribute and enduring the humiliation of a subordinate position, would not be a serious obstacle to independence if only the heavy hand of Russia could be removed. The young Roumanians had no illusions about the permanence of the Ottoman Empire. The doctrine of nationalism could lead them only to the conclusion that the peoples of the Balkan peninsula would eventually emancipate themselves from Ottoman rule. There was, however, a very widely held notion that, under the liberal influence of the West, the Near East could somehow be turned into a federation of free nations, all independent but nevertheless owing nominal allegiance to a liberal Sultan. Part of the credit for swinging the leaders of the revolutionary committee in the spring of 1848 to an attitude of loyalty to the Sultan should go to the representatives of France and

Britain. Colquhoun, the British consul, continually preached moderation and made unceasing efforts to persuade his impulsive friends that nothing should be done except with the consent of the Porte and in consonance with the Porte's interests. He said he had brought Ion Ghica, with whom he had many conversations, "to view his country in a light which I know to be unpopular here, but which I consider the only one which will be recognized by Her Majesty's Government, namely as forming a part of the Ottoman Empire." With C. A. Rosetti, "a man of ardent mind but not very sound ideas," he had less success.[52]

The arrival of Talaat Effendi, and his apparent sympathy for the national party, clinched the victory for those who had advocated a strictly pro-Turkish policy. They did their best to correct the impression which Bibescu's reports had made at Constantinople, namely that the young liberals were imbued with republican ideas and eager to throw off allegiance to the Porte and unite with Transylvania.[53] From what we know of the activities of Bălcescu and his friends, this impression was not entirely unjustified, but for the present they were anxious to make only those demands which could be defended as legal and legitimate, on the basis of the oft-cited capitulations.between the Roumanian princes and the

---

52. Colquhoun to Canning, Apr. 6, 1848, loc.cit.

53. Colquhoun to Palmerston, June 20, 1848, F.O. 78, vol. 742.

Sultans in the 15th and 16th centuries. The mémoire presented to Talaat, therefore, spoke of a regret for the mistakes of the past, announced that the Wallachians wanted only a sincere rapprochement with the Sublime Porte, and stressed the necessity for Wallachia and Turkey to stand together against the pretensions and the encroachments of Russia.[54] The theory that the national party favored the break-up of the Ottoman Empire they denounced as a Russian lie. Then followed the list of reforms necessary to Wallachia's well-being: a more just national representation in the legislature, liberty of the press, a national guard, distribution of taxation among all classes, the responsibility of ministers, the abolition of boyars' titles and privileges, the reduction of the civil list of the prince, abolition of the slavery of the Gypsies, and the giving of property to the peasants, with compensation for the boyars.

These measures, it was said, would assure the prosperity of Wallachia and draw even closer the ties to the Porte through the elimination of all foreign influence. "The salvation of Wallachia and Moldavia," concluded the mémoire, "resides in the integrity of the Ottoman Empire, just as the security of the Ottoman Empire resides in the progress and... in the power of these Principalities. By their geographical situation, by the homogeneity of their populations and by

---

54. Anul 1848, I, pp. 436-442.

their tendencies to coalesce into one state, these two Principalities form the rampart of the Ottoman Empire and the most natural barrier against the repeated invasions of Pan-Slavism."

These various proposals, intended to achieve a peaceful reform, were followed by the proclamation of Islaz, on June 21st, the opening salute of the revolution. When peaceful change was shown to be impossible, the revolutionary party was no longer inclined to pull its punches, except in maintaining its friendly attitude toward Turkey. Since the proposed constituent assembly never met, this proclamation remains as the fundamental document, the intended palladium of Roumanian liberties, of which the Pașoptiști intended that further constitutions be but an elaboration.

The day to day events of the revolution need not be recounted in detail. On the 21st of June, Eliade, Tell, Ștefan Golescu and others gathered at the town of Islaz, on the Danube, proclaimed a revolutionary government and began to march on Craiova. Aided by George Magheru at Caracal and Ioan Maiorescu at Craiova, they succeeded in gaining control of most of Oltenia and prepared to march on Bucharest. Meanwhile, in the capital, the other leaders had not been idle. On June 23rd, after several days of excitement caused by Bibescu's attempt to nip the revolt in the bud by arresting C. A. Rosetti and other turbulent spirits, impressive street demonstrations caused the prince to capitulate, and he signed the proclamation, which was a duplicate of that issued at Islaz by Eliade. C. A. Rosetti, Bălcescu, and Nicolae Golescu became members of a new reform ministry. Two days later Bibescu abdicated, and the reform ministry became a provisional government. Though a republic was never proclaimed, Wallachia became in effect a republic.

From the very first the new régime was beset with difficulties. It was able to crush two attempts at counter-revolution only through the ability of Ion Brătianu to raise the Bucharest mob in its favor. Every day it was expected that Russian troops would cross the frontier, and on one occasion so sure were the leaders that the Russians were coming that the whole provisional government fled the capital and took refuge in the mountains. Nor did all go well in regard to the Turks, who seemed at first not entirely convinced that the Ottoman Empire had so greatly benefited by the change. Suleiman Pasha, sent to look into the matter, seemed well disposed and granted recognition to the new order after insisting on certain constitutional modifications and the replacement of the Provisional Government by a <u>Lieutenance Princière</u> of three members. As a guarantee against radicalism, this was made up of the conservatives: Eliade, Tell, and Nicolae Golescu. Even this compromise did not endure. Russian pressure at Constantinople brought the Sultan to heel, and as a consequence he refused to receive the delegation sent to get his approval of the new constitution, denounced the whole movement as illegal and the work of communists and "some self-styled Wallachs coming from Paris," and sent Fuad Pasha with troops to cooperate with the Russians in giving the revolution its death blow.

The revolutionary régime melted away to nothingness with but a faint display of resistance. The firemen of Bucharest tried without success to prevent the entrance of the Ottoman soldiers into the capital, but all the leaders had already been captured and the army was not in evidence. In Oltenia, traditionally the home of the sturdiest and most warlike of the Roumanian populations, Magheru gathered about him an army of peasants and the remants of the militia, to defend the revolution. But this too was a hopeless gesture. Colquhoun strongly advised him to disband his army; the advice was taken, the army dissolved, and Magheru and his companions crossed the frontier into Transylvania, on October 10, 1848.[55] Thus ended the glorious revolution.

---

55. Colquhoun to Magheru, Oct. 8, 1848, F.O. 78, vol. 743; Colquhoun to Palmerston, Oct. 10, 1848, ibid.; Hory to French Foreign Ministry, Oct. 10, 1848, Aff. Etr., Corr. Pol., Bucarest, vol. 6; Eliade Rădulescu, Mémoires, p. 354; N. B. Locusteanu, Amintiri din Trecut, (Craiova, 1896), pp. 73-4, 91-2.

4. The constitutional ideal, Democracy

On almost every list of desiderata, including that of Kogălniceanu, and the proclamation of Islaz, were abolition of the boyars' privileges, liability of all to taxation, and equality of civil and political rights. These were the principles on which the Forty-eighters intended to build their constitution and their political régime.[56] Since they never got around electing a constituent assembly, these matters had to be dealt with in makeshift fashion by the decrees of the Provisional Government, which functioned as a dictatorship subject to no popular control but could claim to represent the people by portraying the revolution as the unanimous expression of the popular will.

There was no frontal attack on the boyar class, probably because the new rulers were boyars themselves. Even the fighting which accompanied the abortive counter-revolutions in Bucharest had a comic opera touch, illustrated by the conduct of Ion Brătianu, the most effective rabble-rouser, who saw to it that the opposition leaders, his personal friends of former years, always got away safely.[57] The

---

56. The text of the proclamation of Islaz is given in Anul 1848, I, pp. 490-501. French translation in Eliade Rădulescu, Mémoires, pp. 65-73.

57. Crutzescu, Amintirile Colonelului Lăcusteanu, p. 283; N. C. Bejenaru, "Rolul lui Ion C. Brătianu în Revoluţia de la 1848," (Arhiva, Jassy, 1926, pp. 121-9, 214-20), p. 129.

boyars could not be rooted out of the administration because of the insufficiency of trained men of any other class to put in their place, although jobs were found for the subordinate officials (boyar and bourgeois) who had supported the revolution for the very reason of getting better posts.

Brought up on the French Revolution, the young men waited for a night of August 4th, when privileges would be renounced and the classes melt into a nation in a spirit of brotherhood, but they waited in vain.[58] The question of the boyars' privileges was tied up with their status as landed proprietors, and depended on the solution of the agrarian question, and the Provisional Government was content to stand on its declaration of principles until both could be settled by negotiation. They collected taxes where they could and rested on their oars.[59] The only alternative would have

---

58. Note the phrases of the Islaz proclamation: "Every Roumanian is an atom of the whole sovereignty of the people; peasant, artisan, merchant, priest, soldier, student, boyar, prince, each is a son of the fatherland... Boyars,...extend your hand and welcome all classes of society into a single body, which we can call, without shame, the Nation." (Anul 1848, I, pp. 490, 498). Cf. Pruncul Romān, No. 12, July 12, 1848, (o.s.), p. 45.

59. Reorganization of the finances and tax system was admittedly beyond their powers. They had to appeal to the French Government for experts to come and set up a bureau of statistics, a tax system, and a national bank. The experts never came. (Anul 1848, IV, pp. 7, 199-200, and the instructions of A. G. Golescu, Wallachian envoy, dated Aug. 13, 1848, in Aff. Etr., Corr. Pol., Bucarest, vol. 5).

been to establish equality by terror and civil war, a course which would have brought certain foreign intervention and for which they were unfitted by temperament and by their belief in fraternity. Bălcescu and A. G. Golescu were the only ones willing to be really hard-boiled.[60]

To the constituent and legislative assemblies was left the formulation of the laws establishing the regime of democracy and equality. The manner of electing those assemblies best illustrates the problem of putting into practice principles absorbed in Paris, especially that of equality of political rights. The nationalism of the Forty-eighters was not purely racial, as was that of the Transylvanians, but inclined toward the concept of the nation as an association of free and equal citizens. The proclamation of Islaz was addressed to "Roumanian brothers," but also to "citizens in general, in of whatever class, nation, or religion,...Greeks, Serbs, Bulgars, Germans, Armenians, Jews,....The fatherland is ours and it is yours....From now on we all have the same

---

60. "In truth, a revolution without a terror is impossible in our country; enough of these romantic anachronisms, these policies of sentiment." (A. G. Golescu to Ştefan Golescu, July 21, 1848, Anul 1848, II, p. 371). Note Bălcescu's opinion of Rosetti: "Seduced by the generous inspirations of his heart, he wanted to make of the revolution a sentimental epic and believed that with a few speeches and proclamations all the opposition and hate of the vanquished party would be drowned in a vast fraternal kiss." (Ion Ghica, Amintiri din Pribegia, pp. 481-4).

rights."[61] The accepted way in which to put this into effect, was, on the example of the French Republic, universal suffrage.

The question of elections resolved itself into the same tug of war between right and left that took place on all other crucial issues. The Provisional Government was from the start roughly divided into two factions: those who were officially "members" (Eliade, Tell, and the conservatives), and those holding posts as "secretaries" (Bălcescu, A. G. Golescu, Ion Brătianu, Rosetti), with Nicolae and Ştefan Golescu in the role of peacemakers. The radicals were the Paris-trained younger men, who deplored the compromises into which they were forced by Eliade.

The Islaz proclamation, the work of Eliade, announced the immediate convocation of a constituent assembly "representing all the interests and occupations of the nation," which suggested a system of estates or corporations. Further history of the question revolved around the attempts of the radicals,led by Bălcescu, to interpret this in terms of universal equal and direct suffrage,and of Eliade and others to maintain a class system of voting.[62]The conservatives were

---

61. <u>Anul 1848</u>, I, pp. 498-9.

62. P. P. Panaitescu, <u>Contribuţii la o biografie a lui N. Bălcescu</u>, p. 74. Eliade was supported on this issue by N. Golescu, Voinescu, Câmpineanu, and Rosetti; Bălcescu was later able to win over Ion Brătianu, S. Golescu, Magheru, and others and to secure the reversal of the policy first adopted. (Ghica, <u>Amintiri</u>, p. 485).

behind the document issued by the Government early in July, dividing the population, for election purposes, into three "interests" (1) property, 2) commerce, liberal professions, intelligentsia, 3) peasantry), each of which was to elect one hundred deputies.[63]

While uncertainty abroad and attempted counter-revolution at home kept the election in the background, the radicals did their best to put their own view into law. "The constitution," explained one of their organs, "is a social contract, freely made, between the whole people and each of its members," with "all power...in the hands of the people, which consequently is sovereign." The election might be by three classes, said the writer, but each class should be represented according to its proportion of the population.[64] A draught decree drawn up by Bălcescu providing for universal manhood suffrage for all citizens twenty-one or over failed to get the consent of the Government. It was amended by the introduction of an system of indirect voting, which was far from satisfactory to the radicals.[65] The duty of the Provisional Government, said an inspired article in the

---

63. "Bazurile constituante," (Poporul Suveran, Bucharest, No. 3, June 28, 1848 (o.s.), pp. 9-10).

64. Konstitutionalul, Bucharest, No. 1, July 8, 1848, (o.s.).

65. Anul 1848, II, pp. 495-500. Discussion of the project and comparison with its predecessors in C. T. Axente, Essai sur le régime représentatif en Roumanie, (Paris, 1937), pp. 173-6.

Poporul Suveran, was to give the people the opportunity to express its sovereign will:

> "We urge the Government to adopt the method which is most right in principle, not an unequal system which will allow reactionary intriguers to get the upper hand....When the whole country has the suffrage, then the work of the representatives will have the hearty support of all....All we ask each citizen to do is to vote, and that he can do, for the voice of the people is the voice of God." 66

The voice of God never got a chance to speak, for the elections were postponed, then came the compromise with Suleiman Pasha, Turkish emissary, who recognized the revolution but insisted on the abandonment of its ideological basis, republicanism and popular sovereignty. The prince, or president, to be elected by the people for a five-year term, mentioned in the Islaz proclamation and in Kogălniceanu' hypothetical constitution, never came any nearer to reality than did the constituent assembly. Perhaps it was just as well for the men of principle who set such store by the people's God-given ability to choose proper representatives or even to know what an election or a constitution was. They had brushed aside the argument that some of the citizens might not be equipped with sufficient knowledge to vote. But reports which came in from the provinces urging delay,--

---

66. Poporul Suveran, No. 11, July 23, 1848 (o.s.), p. 43. This paper was run by Bălcescu, Bolintineanu, and Zane (former boursier of the Society of Students). Its device was "Liberty, Equality, Fraternity," considered more expressive and stronger than "Justice-Brotherhood." (See No. of July 21, p. 18).

for it was no easy matter to make the sovereign people see that by the revolution they had entered the circle of civilized nations and should act accordingly,--might have shown them that the wonderful metamorphosis had been confined to their own narrow circle.[67] Ion Bălăceanu, one of those assigned to carry the revolution's benefits to the provinces, wrote to Rosetti of the impossibility of finding men to carry out the new policies:

> "Trustworthy and disinterested men are scarce in our fine country. I came, like Diogenes, looking not for a man but for men, and though our streets are well lighted in this enlightened century, I fear the pains I have taken are useless. You can't imagine how much I regret private life....Today I am unfortunately in a position better to judge men and things, and to acquire the conviction that you and I and many others have been the victims of a mirage, of an optical illusion. What great citizens, what heroes proximity has reduced to sad proportions." 68

The introduction of the outward forms of liberalism was a much easier matter than holding elections or organizing an administration. While the promised economic liberalism (banks, credit, free trade, etc.) was allowed to wait, decrees immediately declared the abolition of ranks and established freedom of speech, of the press, and of assembly.

---

67. See the instructions and reports of Bălcescu's commissars of propaganda, "priests of liberty and the constitution," sent to the provinces, in Anul 1848, II, pp. 201-3, 397, 428, 588-90, 667, 729-38, 744, 774; ibid., III, pp. 97, 105-9, 165, 230, 645, 733.

68. Bălăceanu to Rosetti, Sept. 15, 1848, Ac. Rom., Mss. C. A. Rosetti.

Clubs were organized to spread the principles of the constitution and to act as a moral force behind the Government.[69] A national guard was formed. Everything was done to make Bucharest as much like republican Paris as possible. Mass meetings were organized in the streets and on the "Field of Liberty," while the free press expressed itself freely on Roumania's great future and set out to create a public opinion "which could be formed only through general reading of journals and gathering in clubs."[70] In all this the influence of the years spent in Paris is plain enough. Yet these were but surface matters, beside those of the land and of foreign policy, upon which the fate of the revolution rested.

5. The social ideal, Peasant Proprietors

The question of foreign intervention aside, the Wallachian revolution must stand or fall on its policy toward the peasantry. Every mass movement in Roumanian history has inevitably been agrarian in character, from the very nature of the economic order. The revolution of 1848 is sometimes singled out as the only exception, as an essentially bourgeois revolution; it tried to attack the agrarian problem

---

69. E.g., the "Club of Regeneration," of which Rosetti, Ion Brătianu, Boliac, Bolintineanu, Zane, Radu Golescu, and Constantin Creţulescu were members. (Poporul Suveran, No. 15, Aug. 2, 1848 (o.s.), p. 59).

70. Pruncul Român, No. 12, July 10, 1848 (o.s.), p. 45.

from the point of view of a ready-made bourgeois ideology. The Forty-eighters were sympathetic toward the peasantry for humanitarian reasons and also because the "nation" which they intended to bring to life had to be made up of free men, exercising civic rights and fulfilling civic duties. Hence their freeing of the Gypsy slaves, one of the few really timely reforms they accomplished, and their ostensible willingness to see the peasants wholly freed from feudal dues and given land in full ownership.

The Provisional Government refused to give full recognition to the primacy of this question over all others. Some of the members did not want to touch it all; Eliade, dreading "anarchy" as much as a Russian invasion, was all for conciliating the boyars by leaving the feudal régime intact. Brătianu and Rosetti were obsessed by their idea of the middle class as the backbone of the nation. Where they could find no such class, they invented it. Thus they could hardly have been less fitted to undertake a fundamental solution of the agrarian problem. Only two leaders were really acquainted with the question and realized its significance, Bălcescu and Ion Ionescu.

All over Europe in 1848 bourgeois revolutionaries lifted themselves into power with the help of the proletariat, then proceeded to discard their allies. The same thing took place in Wallachia, though the victorious liberals would have vigorously denied having betrayed the peasants. The proclamation of Islaz, with its praise of the peasants as "brothers of Christ" and its appeal for their support, was couched in a language they could not understand, but there was one point which was clear enough, the famous Article 13, which promised them emancipation from the <u>corvée</u> and free ownership of land, on payment of compensation.[71] That promise was largely responsible for the co-operation which the peasants gave to the revolution. In Oltenia, in the Prahova district and elsewhere they flocked to its banners, and as Eliade and Tell approached Bucharest they had with them a sizeable volunteer army of peasants. Then came the first concrete indication that the peasants' usefulness was over. The revolution had already succeeded in the capital, and the victors did not relish the thought of seeing the city in the hands of a peasant army. Eliade was persuaded, without much difficulty, to disband the army and send its members home.[72]

That did not terminate the revolution in the countryside, for the peasants had been on the point of revolt for some time and were not going to be put off with words. Revolution, constitution and national rights to them meant

---

71. <u>Anul 1848</u>, I, pp. 496-9.

72. Colquhoun to Palmerston, June 6, 1848, F.O. 78, vol. 742.

only one thing, land. While waiting for the Government to fulfill its promise they stopped work. Peasant unrest, which continued throughout the whole summer, disrupted the country's economy and left the boyars without means of getting in the harvest.[73]

The Provisional Government had made a promise which it was not over-anxious to keep. From the first it became clear that the boyars would do anything to avoid a land reform. Even the moderates who had welcomed the revolution were adamant on that point. The Government temporized. Unwilling to risk the alienation of the whole boyar class, it told the peasants to go back to work, "because the nation could not afford to be weakened by the loss of its harvest." Land was promised, but only after the season's labor due to the boyars was done. "Your enemies are not the boyars," it said, "but the evil policies and mistakes of the princes."[74] It was impossible to make the peasants believe that. Continued unrest brought more official exhortations to go back to work. The humanitarian idealists, the lovers of "the

---

73. The records of inquiries, made in the next year on claims of boyars for compensation for the peasants' neglect of their duties, show in detail that the exaltation of spirits was not confined to Bucharest. But the peasant unrest was spontaneous and without direction. (Arhivele Statului, Bucharest, Min. din Lăuntru, 1848, Dos. 976).

74. Proclamation of June 28th, Anul 1848, I, pp. 615-6; cf. ibid., II, pp. 17, 314; D. G. Golescu to A. G. Golescu, July 9, 1848, ibid., II, p. 148.

people," told the peasants to stay serfs for a while longer, and thus they knocked the props out from under their "democratic" revolution.

The Government was more bewildered than lacking in sincerity and good will. It was face to face with a class conflict in which it tried not to take sides and thus lost the respect and collaboration of both classes.[75] The fraternal dissolution of class barriers had not occurred. "Respect for persons, respect for property!" the opening words of the proclamation of Islaz, had brought no solution; property had received most of the respect.[76] Yet they knew of no other formula, so a commission was called, to be composed half of boyars, half of peasant delegates. This commission which only eight boyars deigned to attend, was to thrash out the whole problem and reach a solution satisfactory to all concerned. Its president was Alexandru Racoviţa, and its vice-president Ion Ionescu, one of the most interesting figures of the generation of 1848.

Ion Ionescu's ideas represented an unique combination of French philosophy and a technical knowledge of agriculture.

---

75. Colquhoun considered it "unfortunate" that the national party had held out to the peasants promises which could never be realized. (Colquhoun to Palmerston, Aug. 28, 1848, F.O. 78, vol. 742).

76. For the very conservative interpretation which Eliade put on his proclamation, see his letter to F. Aaron, July 2, 1848, in Vîrtosu, <u>I. Heliade Rădulescu, Acte şi Scrisori</u>, p. 21, note 4.

Sent to France by Michael Sturdza in 1838 he had studied on a model farm at Roville with the most celebrated French agronomists of the time, then under Blanqui and Rossi at Paris. Returned to Moldavia, he managed some of Sturdza's estates for a while, then taught agriculture at the Academy in Jassy. At Mânjina he met Bălcescu, who won him over to the cause of the emancipation of the peasantry.[77] He seemed to be admirably suited to guide the debates of boyars and peasants on the question of settlement, but strangely enough even this warm defender of the peasant cause was unable to rise above the contradictions of the position in which the Government found itself. Promises had been made to both sides, and beautiful theories had been fashioned, but the promises were conflicting and the theories could be translated only into proposals which were unacceptable to the boyars. In his speeches to the commission and in his articles in the press, Ionescu showed that he understood the economic basis of the Roumanian revolution to be the conflict between boyar and peasant, contrasting it with the situation of capitalists against workers in France, but stressing the similarity on one point, namely that in both cases revolution was caused by the fact that labor did not get a fair share of the wealth it produced. He recognized

---

77. G. Bogdan-Duică, Viața și Opera întâiului țărănist român, Ion Ionescu dela Brad, pp. 9-20.

an organic connection between nationality and social reform. Without the latter, he wrote, there can be no future, there can be no nationality. The solution lay in the establishment of harmony, which in France found expression in the organization of labor, in Roumania in the abolition of feudal dues and the creation of a balance between property and labor, with a citizenry of peasant proprietors. "The boyars swear to the constitution," he said, "except for the article on property, that is, they want liberty only for themselves." All this talk about leaving the matter to the good will of the proprietors and peasants and glossing it over with words about the _juste milieu_ just won't work, he argued. "Seventeen years of that in France make us ashamed to recall it."[78] Alternating between bullying and cajoling the boyars, Ionescu and his backers, Bălcescu and A. G. Golescu, were unable to intimidate or to persuade.[79] From the other leaders they

---

78. Ion Ionescu, "Cauza revoluţiilor," (_Poporul Suveran_, No. 15, Aug. 2, 1848 (o.s.), pp. 58-9); _idem._, "Socialistii adversării proprietăţii," (_Pruncul Român_, No. 24, Aug. 7, 1848 (o.s.), pp. 97-8. In "Românii nu sunt communisti," (a defence of his policy later published in _Foaie pentru minte_, Braşov, and apparently distributed in manuscript form, copy in _Ac. Rom. Mss. rom._ 82, fol. 455-61, and reproduced in _Anul 1848_, V, pp. 625-36), he put it this way: "The boyars accepted the political revolution and used it to their own advantage, then gathered their forces to crush the social revolution." See also his letter [to Bălcescu?] in C.D. Aricescu, _Corespondenţa secretă şi acte inedite ale capilor revoluţiunii române de la 1848_, vol. II, (Bucharest, 1874), pp. 48-53.

79. Articles in _Poporul Suveran_, Aug. 6, 9, 13, 23-Sept. 3, 1848, (o.s.), and in _Pruncul Român_, Aug. 10, 19, Sept. 4, 1848, (o.s.).

got no support. In this matter French training was a positive handicap. Ion Brătianu and Rosetti were frankly not interested in the peasant question, the Golescu brothers wanted to leave it to the conscience of the boyars, while Eliade and the military men had only the most childish notions of the problems to be faced.[80]

C. A. Rosetti opened the meetings of the property commission on August 22nd with a speech inviting all to sit down together as brothers with the spirit of Christ in their midst.[81] This was followed by a series of bitter debates between peasants, who dilated upon past sufferings and were not agreed on what they wanted, except land, and the boyars, only one of whom offered to sacrifice his property on the altar of patriotism.[82] Ionescu was able to do little except display his pedantry and secure unanimous approval of principles such as the sacredness of property and of labor, the freedom of work and of contract, etc.[83] The sessions became

---

80. Marcel Emerit, Les paysans roumains, 1829-1864, p. 306.

81. Anul 1848, III, p. 293-4.

82. Records of the debates in C. D. Aricescu, Chestiunea proprietătii desbătută de proprietari si plugari la 1848, (Bucharest, 1862), and in Anul 1848, III, pp. 321-542, passim, taken from the Monitorul Român, Nos. 11-13, Aug. 18-23, 1848 (o.s.). Critical resumé in Emerit, op.cit., pp. 309-20.

83. Note Eliade's comment on Ionescu's speeches, which nobody could understand, as being full of "philosophy, political economy, socialism, communism, Fourierism,

so tumultuous that the Government, yielding to pressure from the boyars, dissolved the commission, which, said the decree, "instead of being penetrated with the spirit of justice, fraternity, and peace, had departed from that role...."[84] The agrarian reform was buried, and the whole revolutionary regime soon followed it to the grave.

The Pasoptisti, in their handling of the agrarian question, left a record of total failure.[85] In view of their character, training, and position, and the division among themselves on the matter, it could hardly have been otherwise. Their democratic theories were applicable only if they were willing to give them social content by drastic

---

Proudhon, Louis Blanc, Babeuf, phalanstères, organization of labor, property is theft, Adam Smith, J. B. Say, routine, utopia, work, free arbiter, capital, salary, privilege, competition, and monopoly." (Eliade Rădulescu, Mémoires, p. 272). This comment is more a reflection on Eliade than on Ionescu.

84. Anul 1848, III, p. 541, and Ionescu's report, in Poporul Suveran, No. 25, Sept. 7, 1848 (o.s.), pp. 98-100, repeating his arguments in favor of expropriation with compensation as necessary in the public interest, for economic, national, and moral reasons. A concise statement of Ionescu's theories in Bogdan-Duică, op. cit., p. 27.

85. Bălcescu, through special commissars and a newspaper, engaged in an intensive campaign in the countryside, which was probably responsible for the periodic peasant gatherings in the capital to cheer for the constitution. But propaganda was not enough. (P. P. Panaitescu, Contribuții la o biografie a lui N. Bălcescu, pp. 74-9; Ion Ghica, Amintiri din Pribegia, pp. 485-6; and the citations in note 67.

action, once love and the fraternal spirit had failed. Only in that way could they have consolidated their revolution and given it a popular base that could withstand attacks from within and from without. For this they lacked not only the will,--most of them preferring to rely on the patriotism of the boyars and of the infinitessimal middle class,--but also the knowledge of the very complex system which could not have been remade overnight, even by the application of the magic formula, "expropriation with compensation."[86] But three months in power hardly provided a fair test, and their record does not suffer greatly by comparison with those of the men of 1848 elsewhere in Europe. Shortcomings as realists and practical politicians were no monopoly of the Roumanian leaders.

6. The national ideal, Unity

The liberal-national revolutions of 1848 in central and eastern Europe were alike in the intensity of their nationalism as in the superficiality of their liberalism. In Bucharest, where the two forces were not in conflict, that was not always evident; Russia, the oppressor of the Roumanian nation, was also the enemy of European democracy

---

86. Bălcescu seems to have been the only leader in favor of giving the peasants the land immediately, without indemnity. (Bălcescu, Manualul bunului Român, Bucharest, 1902, ed. P. V. Haneş, p. 63).

and freedom. By force of circumstances, the Wallachian revolution had to concentrate on political freedom at home. History has tended to obscure the fact that nationalism was none the less deeply ingrained in the Roumanian revolutionaries for having been bound up with the political philosophy of the 19th century bourgeoisie.[87] The Collège de France had taught them democracy and republicanism, but it also had taught them romantic nationalism. Throughout the course of their revolution they never gave up hope of extending to other Roumanian provinces the blessings of national freedom.

They did not have to invent a national ideal. Most of them had been associated with Câmpineanu's plans for creating a "Dacia," and with the works of Colson, Vaillant, Desprez, and others who presented to the world the claims of the Roumanian nation to constitute an independent state. Proof that the Forty-eighters hoped to realize that ideal may be found in their negotiations with Czartoryski. Before

---

87. There has been a tendency to call 1848 a liberal and bourgeois revolution, as contrasted with the "national" movements of 1821, 1839, etc. Cf. Iorga, "Generaţia dela 1840 şi dela 1848 faţă de concepţia unităţii politice a poporului românesc," (Neamul Românesc, XVII, Nos. 115-120, May 23-June 3, 1922); idem., "Solidaritatea românească la începutul secolului al XIX-lea," (Cugetul Românesc, Bucharest, I, 1922, pp. 97-113), p. 113. Bălcescu, for example, did think that the character of the revolution had to be "democratic and social"; that done, they could in the future turn to two other revolutions still to be made, that of national unity and that of national independence. (Ghica, Amintiri, p. 475).

leaving Paris, A. G. and A. C. Golescu had submitted to the venerable prince their proposal to "create a movement embracing Moldavia, Wallachia, Transylvania, Bessarabia, and Bucovina, and to recover an independent Dacia." All during 1848 the Poles worked to stimulate the Roumanian movement for unity at the expense of Austria and Russia.[88]

The resources at the disposal of the Roumanian revolutionaries were not such as to enable them to embark on a crusade to free their brothers in the Austrian and Russian empires. After the failure of the Moldavian rising, the horizon became still more restricted, and the Wallachian revolution, though successful, lived and died within its own borders. From its records, however, we discover that the thoughts of the leaders were constantly on the Roumanians in other provinces; somehow they hoped to be able to join forces and create the bloc of ten million Roumanians, about which they liked to talk. It hardly seemed feasible, in view of the absence of Roumanian armed forces in all provinces, but 1848 was a strange year. Empires were falling, nations were winning freedom, and certainly it would not do to be pessimistic about what "the people" could do, after Paris, Vienna, and Milan.[89] The revolutionary press had a

---

88. M. Handelsman, Czartoryski, Nicolas Ier, etc., pp. 95-103.

89. "This idea [a kingdom of Dacia], which would have been a pure utopia last year, today seems to me so reasonable that one could almost bet that it come true." (D.G. Golescu to Ion Ghica, Aug. 19, 1848, Ghica, Amintiri, pp. 21-3).

perfect field day in explaining to the Roumanian public the meaning of the new words like constitution, democracy, etc. No point was labored more than nationality, and there is perhaps no better illustration of the diffusion of nationalism than the articles in the Bucharest newspapers in 1848. "Homeland" (Patria) and "Nationality" were explained in a simplified version of Michelet and Mazzini on the same subject. The Patria was the land of birth, and also the whole territory inhabited by fellow-citizens speaking the same language, having the same laws, religion, and sentiments. This union of sentiments was called nationality, and "without it there can be no nation, no Roumania." The distinction between a nation and a state was pointed out, also the fact that no true society or state could be made up of several nations, for it was against nature to tie nations together against their will. "All this shows," concluded an article in the Konstitutționalul, that all lands inhabited by Roumanians should be called Roumania and form one state, because all are the homeland of the Roumanians, and because all Roumanian patriots inhabiting them form the Roumanian nation, which demands that it be one and indivisible."[90]

---

90. Konstitutționalul, No. 1, July 8, 1848 (o.s.), p. 3. See also the articles in Poporul Suveran, Nos. 1, 3, 19. This paper "will have as it goal the union of the Roumanian provinces....God and ten million Roumanians stand behind our rights." (No. 1, June 28). Another paper, România, announced that it would use all its powers for the growth and greatness of the Roumanians in all the provinces, propagating the democratic principle and the idea of the union of all Roumanians. (No. 1, Aug. 6, p. 1).

If Dacian plans were utopian, there was always the more limited objective of the union of the Principalities, which could be brought about simply by securing the Porte's consent. It depended on cooperation between the Turks and the Roumanians against Russia, and it required the rebirth of the revolution in Moldavia, no simple matter, as that principality was occupied by Russian troops in June, 1848. Eliade and the conservatives were willing to back water on all larger national hopes and concentrate on securing the autonomy of Wallachia and authority for themselves. No so the radicals, whose newspapers shouted to the Moldavians that liberation was at hand and called the game but half-won so long as Moldavia remained in chains. The first number of Rosetti's paper contained a spirited address to "our brothers in Moldavia":

> "The hour of liberty has struck for every Roumanian... Unite with us, brothers from across the Milcov, over which we stretch to you our arms ardently desiring to give you the embrace of fraternity and of liberty. The Wallachian and the Moldavian are both Roumanians, they are brothers, a single nation... United we will be strong; united we will stand against every enemy of our liberty....Long live liberty! Long live Roumania." 91

wrote the Poporul Suveran:

> "Wallachia is free or on the road to freedom; Moldavia still groans in chains and slavery. Moldavia is enslaved, and you, Roumanian citizens, wear the cockade of liberty? Do not say yet that Roumania is free, when Moldavia is enslaved. The

---

91. Pruncul Român, No. 1, June 12, 1848 (o.s.), pp. 1-2. Similar articles in nos. of June 16, July 13, 19, Aug. 3.

> Revolution of the 11th of June has freed one province of Roumania, but not all Roumania....Tear off your cockades, and do not wear them again until all Roumania is free, great and united! Go over into Moldavia where your brothers are shedding tears and blood, help them to break the chains of slavery...." 92

Union was to be question number one on the agenda of the national assembly. Brothers should and could not be kept apart by artificial frontiers in a day and age when all nations were putting into effect the principle of union.[93]

These were fine words, but the action could be but feeble. Ion Ghica, who had been sent by the revolutionary committee to Constantinople in May and became the Provisional Government's official agent there, had hopes of persuading the Porte to proclaim the union of the Principalities simultaneously with a recognition of the new régime, but all he got was sympathy from a few of the Ottoman ministers.[94] As for direct action, the sending of agents to stir up revolution in Moldavia, we have no proof of the Russian accusation that incendiaries swarmed over the border into the sister principality.[95] Dimitrie Golescu, administrator of

92. Poporul Suveran, No. 1, June 19, 1848 (o.s.), p. 3.

93. Ibid., No. 9, July 19, pp. 33-4.

94. Anul 1848, II, pp. 99-101, 686-7; Ibid., III, pp. 101-3, 121-30; Ghica, Amintiri, pp. 18-19.

95. Nesselrode to Russian representatives abroad, July 31, 1848, Anul 1848, II, pp. 609-14; cf. C. L. Lesur, Annuaire Historique Universelle, (Paris, 1848), p.504;

the district of Brăila, reported that "the fine idea of the union of the two Principalities unfortunately takes root in very few Moldavian heads."[96]

The idea of Roumanian unity was expressed, in 1848, in pious hopes and in contacts between nationalists in the different provinces, rather than in concerted action, for the Transylvanians were absorbed in their own struggle against the Magyars, and the Bessarabians had no leaders and no policy. The idea was fostered by the Moldavian exiles, by the radical wing of the Wallachian revolutionary régime, and by a few Transylvanians. The Moldavians, who wandered about in Wallachia and Transylvania after the failure of their own revolution, saw the Roumanian problem in its larger setting.[97] In co-operation with leaders from

---

Vicomte de Guichen, Les Grandes Questions européennes et la diplomatie des puissances sous la seconde république francaise, vol. I, (Paris, 1925), p. 188.
The Wallachian Government did send a certain Chandrich, a Jew, on a secret mission to Moldavia late in July, to get Poles to desert from the army of occupation and to stir up revolt against Sturdza. He apparently had some success with the first aim, none with the second. (Iorga, Rev. Hist. du Sud-Est Eur., XI, 1934, p. 254).

96. Golescu to Ion Ghica, Aug. 19, 1848, Ghica, Amintiri, p. 22.

97. When they were at Blaj for the great meeting in May, 1848, Alecsandri wrote a revolutionary poem which ended thus:

    Rise, brothers of the same blood,
    This is the hour of brotherhood,
    Stretch out your arms in great pride
    Across the Monita, the Milcov, across the Carpathians."

other provinces, they drew up in August 1848, at Cernăuţi, a petition, taken by a deputation to Vienna, asking Austria to help free the Principalities from Ottoman suzerainty, then unite them to Transylvania and Bucovina in a national state under a Habsburg archduke.[98] Dimitrie Rallet, still in Moldavia, told one of Czartoryski's agents that committees were working for Roumanian unity under Austrian protection, "since Austria had become a constitutional state."[99] A. G. Golescu, official representative of Wallachia, was in Vienna in August making a similar proposal, "Roumanian unity within an Austrian confederation."[100] This was in complete contradiction to the pro-Turkish policy of the Wallachian Government, but then there was no coordination of policy, each Roumanian nationalist pursuing the ultimate goal in his own way.

See Iorga, Ist. lit. rom., II, pp. 259-63; n.b. also Alecsandri's "Deşteptarea României," which became known in all the Roumanian provinces (Bogdan-Duică, Vasile Alecsandri, p. 25).
Even in the affair of April at Jassy, some Moldavians had "greater Roumanian" hopes and plans. (Sion, Suvenire contimpurane, p. 174; Regnault, op.cit., p. 387)

98. I. Nistor, Un capitol din viaţa culturală a Românilor din Bucovina, p. 50.

99. P. P. Panaitescu, Emigraţia Polonă şi Revoluţia Română dela 1848, (Bucharest, 1929), p. 38.

100. A. G. Golescu, to A. T. Laurian and Ioan Maiorescu, Aug. 5, 1848, Dragomir, Din corespondenţa dăscălilor ardeleni, p. 167; A. G. Golescu to Bălcescu, Aug. 6, 1848, Anul 1848, II, pp. 732-5.

Not many of the Transylvanian leaders were interested in vague plans for Roumanian political unity. They had on their hands a three-cornerd struggle for existence with the Magyars and the Saxons, and were taken up with finding for their nationality a framework of political and military organization. Their insistence on national rights, however, brought inevitably to the fore the concept of a Daco-Roumanian state. It was a spectre disquieting to the Magyars and to many of the Saxons, who voiced fears of "a new Decebalus," though one Saxon leader, Stefan Ludwig Roth, welcomed the prospect as the only way to escape from the Magyars.[101] The Daco-Roumanian idea was strongest among those Transylvanians who had been professors in Wallachia and were now leaders of the Roumanian movement in Transylvania. Among these was Ioan Maiorescu, who traveled to Vienna and Frankfort to propose to the Austrian Government and to the Frankfurt Parliament that a united Roumania be given to a Habsburg prince "under the protectorate of Germany."[102] Another was Constantin Romanul, who brought

---

101. Roth, Von der Union und nebenbei ein Wort über eine mögliche dakoromanische Monarchie unter Osterreichs Krone, (Hermannstadt, 1848); I. Lupas, "Un martyre transylvain, le pasteur Ştefan L. Roth," (Revue de Transylvanie, V, 1939, pp. 224-30); Göllner, Revoluţia anului 1848, pp. 39-45, 385-94.

102. Maiorescu to A. G. Golescu, Sept. 9, 19, 28, 1848, (ed. Titu Maiorescu, Convorbiri Literare, XXXII, 1898, pp. 6-18, 155-70); Maiorescu's memorandum to the Frankfurt Parliament, Sept. 27, 1848, Anul 1848, IV, pp. 414-20.

copies of Desprez's article with him when he came from Bucharest. To A. G. Golescu he wrote that the news of the Wallachian revolution had stirred Transylvania.[103] Romanul frankly favored the Dacian idea. The tendency of the times, he held, was for nations to unify themselves, witness the Germans, Italians, and Slavs. Why should not the Roumanians do the same, instead of denying it, as the Wallachian Government did, to hide behind a claim of "legality"? "All cry out that we want to form a Dacia;[104] why keep the cat in the bag any longer? Europe must be awakened to the fact that only the resurrection of Dacia will stop Panslavism....

---

103. S. Dragomir, Un precursor al unităţii naţionale; Profesorul Constantin Romanul Vivu, p. 20. Cf. the letter of Murgu to Bălcescu, speaking of the joy in Transylvania over the news of the liberation of Wallachia, cited by Dragomir, "N. Bălcescu în Ardeal," (Anuarul Institutului de Istorie Naţională, V, 1928-30, pp. 1-34), p. 4.

104. A reference to Hungarian and Russian accusations that the Roumanians were working for a Daco-Roumanian kingdom, indignantly denied by most of the Roumanian leaders. See Anul 1848, II, p. 609-14; ibid., IV, pp. 127-8; Anon., Bemerkungen über die russische Note vom 19/31 Juli d. J. in Betreff der Intervention in den romanischen Donaufürstenthümern, (Vienna, 1848), pp. 10-11; J. H. Schwicker, "Der Dako-romanismus," (Osterreichisch-Ungarische Revue, XVI, 1894, pp. 151-64, 221-46), pp. 224-5; A. Muresianu, "Planul 'Regatul Daciei,' refugiaţii politici din Principate şi Românii braşoveni la 1848," (Casina Română, Braşov, 1935, pp. 114-25); I. Mateiu, "Ideia românismului integral în revoluţia din 1848," (Viitorul, Bucharest, May 15, 1925); [D. Bolintineanu], L'Autriche la Turquie et les Moldo-Valaques, (Paris, 1856), pp. 29-30.

Our device should be the creation of Dacia." Among the Wallachian revolutionaries, there was always a lingering hope that some connection could be established with the Transylvanians, who seemed to possess the cadres and fighting qualities the former lacked. The events of May in Transylvania caused a stir in Bucharest, and it was thought that the young patriots might seek support from the other side of the Carpathians.[105] Bariţ's Gazeta Transilvanei, with a series of articles urging that all Roumanians make common cause, alarmed Bibescu and his Russian mentors, who tried to keep the newspapers out of the country and the young nationalists in.[106]

Bălcescu always kept in mind the possibility of armed help from Transylvania. At the time when rumors of a Russian invasion put the Provisional Government to flight, they went to the mountains, where, concentrating their "army" and with the aid, already promised, of Roumanian

---

105. de Nion to Lamartine, Apr. 20, 27, 1848, Aff. Etr., Corr. Pol., Bucarest, vol. 5. de Nion spoke of the union of all the Roumanian provinces as "one of the utopias of which Wallachian patriotism most likes to dream."

106. Colquhoun to Palmerston, May 27, 29, June 6, 1848, F.O. 78, vol. 742; Göllner, op.cit., pp. 85-6; Anul 1848, I, pp. 480-2. For the panic which the Gazeta's articles caused in Moldavia, and Sturdza's attempts to keep this and other Roumanian language papers out of his country, see Radu Rosetti, "Despre Censura în Moldova," part III, (Ac. Rom., Mem. Sect. Ist., Ser. II, vol. 29, 1907, pp. 473-531), pp. 451-71.

border regiments from Transylvania, they could begin a fight to save their revolution. Our only hope of defence, wrote Bălcescu, "is in an army from Transylvania, and that hope is far from strong."[107] A. G. Golescu was another who had visions of revolutionary Roumanian armies marching from one province of "Dacia" to another. When on his way to Vienna and Paris he met Murgu, leader of Roumanians in the Banat, who claimed to have at his command an army of 10,000 Roumanians ready to invade Moldavia or Oltenia.[108] Golescu urged Laurian to propagate "Roumanism" among the military frontier regiments, following Murgu's example.[109] This plan was about as ephemeral as that of the Moldavian exiles, who were preparing to march on Jassy with an army of Roumanians recruited in Transylvania and Bucovina. All of this was just talk, with nothing behind it but the faith and credulity of these few leaders. There was enough talk, however, to bring "Daco-Roumanism" into the discussions of diplomats and the columns of newspapers, and it is by talking, loud and long, that nationalists often achieve their ends. They may not have convinced many, but at least

---

107. Bălcescu to Ghica, July 28, 1848, N. Bălcescu, Scrisori catre Ion Ghica, pp. 4-7.

108. A. G. Golescu to Bălcescu, July 31, 1848, Anul 1848, II, pp. 614-22.

109. A. G. Golescu to Laurian and Maiorescu, Aug. 5, 1848, Dragomir, Din corespondenţa dăscălilor ardeleni, p. 166.

they convinced themselves, and since they later became the nation's permanent political as well as intellectual leaders, the "Daco-Roumanism" of 1848 was not without significance.

7. The Roumanian revolution and European diplomacy

The easy success of the revolution of June had an indescribably exhilarating effect on the spirits of its leaders. Bălcescu described it as "the most beautiful revolution that has ever taken place among any people."[110] The "most wonderful days of his life," in Paris in February, had been repeated and surpassed. The revolution, which had been delayed a few days so that it might coincide with the entry of Mazzini into Rome and of Ledru Rollin into Paris, was regarded not as a local phenomenon, but as organically connected with the victorious march of liberty everywhere in Europe. Situated as they were in the vestibule of the house of Europe's champion of autocracy and reaction, they naturally looked for support to the democratic forces of the liberated nations, particularly to Paris, which had schooled them in their new creed and which was now the nerve-center of the international revolution. France could not betray Roumania, they felt, without betraying her own soul.

---

110. Bălcescu to Ghica, July 28, 1848, Bălcescu, Scrisori, p. 1.

This sentiment and hope were of course strongest among the exalted spirits. Dumitru Brătianu, like Bălcescu, also found the revolution to be beautiful.[111] He wrote to his friend Paul Bataillard:

> "The glory of the beautiful Roumanian revolution belongs to them [Michelet and Quinet]...Let them popularize our cause among the French, for it is sacred....Our new constitution is based on your republican constitution....We lack only the beautiful name of republic." 112

In the same vein Ion Brătianu and C. A. Rosetti wrote a letter of thanks to Quinet, the spiritual father of their revolution:

> "Our revolution belongs to you, it is your work. It is your spirit that inspired us, your ideas that we have tried to translate....After God, it is you and M. Michelet in who have made our epoch what it is....
>
> "France rose, and all Europe rose at her voice. Liberty sprang forth from the breast of France.... She set foot on our soil, on this Roumanian soil ..., the earth trembled,...and in a moment...the powers of darkness retreated, light and life were born: Lux fiat et lux facta est...
>
> "It is France which raised us and taught us. The spark which has kindled our country we took from her hearth...." 113

---

111. Perhaps "beautiful" is not the proper equivalent of the French "beau" and the Roumanian "frumos" used in such a context. "Wonderful" or "splendid" might be a better translation. But the idea is the same.

112. July 11, 1848, Anul 1848, II, pp. 187-9.

113. July 8, 1848, Anul 1848, II, pp. 134-6. Quinet gave this letter to the Courrier Francais, which published it on July 30, 1848. This, according to Vasile Mălinescu, Moldavian then in Paris, did the cause more harm than good. (Mălinescu to A. G. Golescu, Aug. 4, 1848, Convorbiri Literare, XXXII, 1898, pp. 3-5).

It would be difficult to believe that all this was just high-flown verbiage intended merely to increase the chances of assistance from France by extolling the French influence on the Roumanian revolution and flattering those who might serve as its defenders. The connection with the Collège de France was more than a fortunate circumstance which might be put to account. The will of God and the spirit of France were integral factors in the equation. France would help Roumania because of the very nature of things. How could it be otherwise? Were not Michelet and Quinet the patron saints of both revolutions? Was not Lamartine, honorary head of their student society, Foreign Minister of the French Republic? His manifesto of March 8th had made French policy clear enough to them: "...If the hour of the reconstruction of certain oppressed nationalities seems to us to have struck,...the French Republic will consider itself justified in arming to protect these legitimate movements of the growth and the nationality of peoples."[114]

The Roumanians did not expect the French army to come marching across Europe to save them from Russia. They did expect more than mere expressions of sympathy. The obvious point at which France could give diplomatic support was

---

114. P. Quentin-Bauchart, Lamartine et la politique étrangère de la Révolution de février, pp. 58-9.

Constantinople, and that was one reason for the Roumanians' loud professions of loyalty to the Sultan and disavowal of desires for complete independence. "Liberal" Turkey, the most vulnerable of all states to national movements, was not touched by the revolutions of 1848; thanks to its position as a bulwark against Russia and to the patronage of England, it was placed in the role of protector of those nationalities which wished to obtain both Turkish and French or British support to realize their ambitions at the expense of Russia or Austria.

Before leaving Paris in the spring of 1848, the Roumanian youths were already looking into the question of French support for a possible revolution. Through Czartoryski they secured the nomination of an ambassador to Constantinople, General Aupick, who was favorable to them.[115] Lamartine had been informed of what was going to happen, and in April, when all the preparations for revolution in Bucharest were made, plans were held up because of receipt of news that Lamartine was sending a special agent, Dr. Louis Mandl, to the Principalities and that nothing should be done until he arrived.[116] Mandl, on his arrival, fell

---

115. Handelsman, op.cit., p. 96.

116. Ion Ghica, Scrisori către Vasile Alecsandri, pp. 709-10. Ghica says that de Nion communicated the message to C. A. Rosetti. Cf. Panaitescou, Contribuţii la o biografie a lui N. Bălcescu, p. 68, citing the memoirs of Alex. Cristofi, who says that Bălcescu and A. G. Golescu arrived with definite instructions from Lamartine to start a revolution.

in with the ideas of the revolutionaries, but warned nothing could be undertaken without a previous understanding with the Porte and with Aupick; he promised "moral support" at Constantinople, where they sent Ion Ghica to represent them.[117] Aupick was friendly to Ghica, adopted fully his point of view, and gave what moral support he could, but the two were not able to do much with the Ottoman Government, which had not yet recognized the revolutionary governments in Paris and Bucharest.[118]

The crucial decision lay with the Turks. They had their choice of co-operation with Russia to put the provinces back under Russian control, with perhaps a certain increase in Turkish authority, or co-operation with the Roumanians in defiance of Russia, which would mean war. The argument which Ghica put to them was this: the Roumanians, if granted their autonomy, guaranteed to them by the ancient treaties, would remain as loyal subjects and allies of the Sultan, protecting the Empire from Russian attacks. To some Turks it seemed reasonable, and there were times, such as early in August when Suleiman Pasha came to terms with the Roumanians, when the Porte appeared to be willing to

---

117. Mandl to Aupick, June 14, 1848, Ghica, op.cit., pp. 722-3; report of Zablocki, Dec. 1848, in Panaitescu, Emigratia Polonă și Revoluția Română dela 1848, pp. 103-4.

118. Anul 1848, I, pp. 593-5, 601-10, 681-3; ibid., II, pp. 43-5, 99-101, 195-201, 480-1, 686-8, 719-24; ibid., III, pp. 101-3, 118-31, 157-8, 375-77.

take the risk. When it came to a showdown, however, the Turks disavowed Suleiman and sent troops to stifle the revolution.[119] They "betrayed" the Roumanians for two reasons: first, they could not stand up to Russia without securing from France and England a promise of definite military aid, and when Russia put on the pressure, no such promise was given; second, they were not enthusiastic about the "demagogic" principles of the Roumanian leaders, whom they suspected of working for complete independence, a very bad example for the other provinces of European Turkey. Liberalism, democracy, and the nationality principle, which the Roumanians considered as entitling them to outside support, were the very factors which helped to block the only channel by which support could come.

The Turks, the French, and the English looked at the Roumanian revolution from the point of view of the balance of power in the East. Russia had been in virtual control

---

119. Fuad Pasha, who replaced Suleiman, said that the Turks were given a virtual ultimatum from Russia. (Hory to Bastide, Sept. 8, 1848, Aff. Etr., Corr. Pol. Bucarest, vol. 5). This is confirmed by Aupick to Bastide, Sept. 5, 1848, Anul 1848, III, 656-9; and by Ghica's report, Aug. 29, 1848, ibid., III, pp. 5-1-4. Ghica reported that Russia insisted that the Sultan refuse to receive the delegation (which included Bălcescu, D. Brătianu, S. Golescu) sent to get approval for a new constitution, and consider them not as representatives of Wallachia but as "students from Paris." The change in Turkish policy coincided with the coming intooffice of Reshid Pasha as Grand Vizir.

of the Principalities for some years, without annexing them and without cutting them off from world trade.[120] That situation was accepted by Europe, and until it could be definitely proved that the Russians intended to remain forever in the Principalities or to attack Turkey, no power was willing to back the Roumanians as to the point of war. A strong diplomatic front would be sufficient to call the Tsar's bluff, argued the Roumanians, but that argument was never put to the test.

As always when France and England act as partners in diplomacy, it was at London that the real decisions were made. France would not have moved in the Near East without England, and Palmerston was not at this time in a mood to go out of his way to beard the Tsar. Stratford at Constantinople, advising the Porte to watch and wait, gave no encouragement to Ghica.[121] Brunnov reported from London to Nesselrode that the English position was "quite clear and wholly favorable."[122] Russia had only to secure the

---

120. British trade with the Principalities had increased by leaps and bounds since the commercial treaty with Turkey in 1838 and especially since the repeal of the Corn Laws in 1846, but not enough to change the course of British policy. (V. J. Puryear, Economics and Diplomacy in the Near East, p. 185).

121. Ghica, Amintiri, p. 29; W. G. East, The Union of Moldavia and Wallachia, p. 21.

122. July 28, 1848, cited by R. Averbukh, Tsarskaia interventsia v borbe s vengerskoi revolutsiei, 1848-1849, (Moscow, 1935), p. 61. Palmerston was worried about

compliance of the Porte, which chose to act with Russia. Throughout the whole affair Palmerston showed no sympathy with the Roumanians. He accepted at face value the Russian arguments that the revolution was the work of wild radicals and Polish agents and admitted Russia's treaty right to occupy the provinces and restore order. When the Wallachian Government appealed for his mediation, Palmerston declined.[123]

Despite the importance of England as Russia's rival in the Near East, the Wallachian Government sent no delegate to London, probably because none of the young men had been to school there.[124] Naturally they sent one to Paris; A. G. Golescu's return to the Quartier Latin as Minister Plenipotentiary of the Government of Wallachia forms an interesting

---

reports that Russia was forcing a new Unkiar Skelessi on Turkey, but when satisfied on that point, he was willing to condone the occupation of the Principalities. Cf. de Guichen, Les Grands Questions européennes, vol. I, pp. 250-1; Schiemann, Geschichte Russlands, IV, p. 176; Puryear, England, Russia, and the Straits Question, pp. 149-50.

123. For his general line of policy, see his instructions to Colquhoun, May 21, 1848, F.O. 78, vol. 741. His response to Voinescu, July 17, ibid. On the whole question of British policy, Averbukh, op.cit., pp. 59-62, using the Russian archives; East, op.cit., pp. 20-1, using the British archives.

124. Maiorescu and A. G. Golescu pointed out the urgent need for an envoy at London, but nothing was done about it. (Maiorescu to Golescu, Sept. 21, 1848, Convorbiri Literare, XXXII, 1898, p. 155; Golescu to the Wallachian Government, Sept. 21, 1848, Aricescu, Corespondenta, vol. II, p. 44; Golescu to Ghica, Sept. 25, 1848, Anul 1848, IV, p. 325).

chapter in the story of the men of 1848. Lamartine, on whom the Roumanians had counted, went out of power at about the same time they came in, and all he could send was a message of sympathy. His successor was Jules Bastide, who had been associated with those circles advocating the cause of nationalities and was a friend of Ion Ghica. The situation looked no worse from the Roumanian viewpoint.

The appeal made to France in June for "firm and decided support" had brought no results.[125] A second appeal in July explained the work of regeneration being effected, pointed out that if Wallachia went down, Russia would dominate the whole of central and eastern Europe and march to Constantinople. All this could be prevented if France would merely take Wallachia "under her protection" and declare herself ready to repulse any intervention by force of arms. A confidential postscript asked for munitions and "some experienced officers to organize our army."[126]

Bastide and Aupick were inclined to play with the idea of supporting a Roumanian-Turkish front against Russia. The latter sent two French officers to the Principalities to look over the terrain and report on the possibilities for

---

125. Voinescu to French Foreign Minister, June 26, 1848, Aff. Etr., Corr. Pol., Bucarest, vol. 5.

126. Ibid., July 8, 1848; also the appeal of N. Golescu, July 20, enclosed in Hory to Foreign Ministry, Aug. 1, 1848, ibid.

defense against Russian invasion. They arrived at Brăila on the 19th of August, spent a fortnight traveling through both principalities, then returned to Constantinople. The visit aroused great hopes among the Roumanians. Their conclusions were that the "unfortunate population" possessed no means of defense, "nothing, absolutely nothing," but that they could aid the Turks by retreating to the mountains, whence, supported and supplied by their Transylvanian brothers, they could harass the Russian lines of communication. The Roumanian liberals gave the French officers an earful of propaganda,[127] for the report spoke favorably of their national resurrection, of the future possibility of erecting a "Dacian" barrier of eight millions to break the unity of the Slavs, or, failing that, a barrier of the united Principalities, plus Bessarabia, with a foreign prince. France, the report concluded, was the star on which Roumanian eyes were fixed, and it was to be hoped that France and the other powers would help them to reconstitute their nation, institute salutary reforms, and build up an army.[128]

---

127. Hory, French charge at Bucharest, put them in touch with Suleiman Pasha, with the Wallachian Government, with the leading boyars, and with the British and Austrian consuls. (Hory to Foreign Minister, Aug. 26, 1848, Aff. Etr., Corr. Pol., Bucarest, vol. 5).

128. Aff. Etr., Mémoires et Documents, Turquie, vol. 48, published by Elvire Georgescu in Rev. Hist. du Sud-Est, XIV, 1937, pp. 125-50.

Bastide, in Paris, was taken up with Italy and other pressing matters, but he could not be utterly deaf to certain voices being raised in favor of the Roumanians. Billecocq campaigned for election to the Assembly on anti-Russian platform; his speeches and articles were filled with the Roumanian question.[129] At the Société Orientale that question was debated several times, with Desprez, Vaillant, and Billecocq quoting Bastide to the effect that the French Republic could never permit democratic ideas to be sacrificed and urging that the fleet be sent into the Black Sea, though Drouyn de Lhuys, politically the most influential member, could not see any practical way in which France could help.[130] In the press, Bataillard and Desprez were advocating French promotion of Turkish recognition of the Roumanian nationality and the necessary reforms.[131]

---

129. A. Billecocq, Le nostre prigioni, vol. II, pp. 256-394. He also published an "Album moldo-valaque" in L'Illustration (Sept., 1848), and bombarded the Foreign Ministry with appeals for the Roumanians.

130. Revue de l'Orient, de l'Algérie et des Colonies, III, 1848, pp. 412-7; ibid., IV, 1848, pp. 37-8, 52-5, 104, 117-22.

131. Desprez in the Revue des Deux Mondes and La Pologne, Bataillard in Le National. (See O. Boitos, Paul Bataillard et la révolution roumaine de 1848, pp. 24-28; P. Constantinescu-Iaşi, "Un colaborator francez la Istoria Românilor," Arhiva, XXXII, 1925, pp. 47-57; Anul 1848, III, pp. 43-5, 155-7). At the same time Bataillard was helping Mălinescu with a translation of the Islaz proclamation, which the latter distributed to the deputies. (Boitoş, op.cit., p. 28; Mălinescu to A. G. Golescu, Aug. 8, 20, 1848, Convorbiri

In the National Assembly Bastide was interpellated by a deputy who stressed the vital force of the new nationalities tending to form a Danubian confederation of free peoples; at the head of this great movement were the Roumanians, to whom France should fulfil her mission and give support.[132] Mandl kept after Bastide and took upon himself the functions of Wallachian representative, until one should be sent.[133]

Golescu arrived in Paris early in September, secured an interview with Bastide, and reported that the latter promised to support the right of nationalities in a great confederation, which should exist within Austria and Turkey, to send 5,000 rifles,[134] and to instruct Aupick to support the demands of the Roumanian deputation at Constantinople,

---

<u>Literare</u>, XXXII, 1898, pp. 3-5, 8-9). Golescu planned to have printed 2000 copies of a book, never finished, by Bataillard; it was to be given to all politicians, etc., and to be translated into German and English. (A. G. Golescu to Voinescu, Sept. 16, 1848, <u>Anul 1848</u>, IV, p. 197).

132. <u>Compte Rendu des Séances de l'Assemblée Nationale</u> (Paris, 1849), vol. II, pp. 509-10, Session of July 17, 1848.

133. Mandl to Bălcescu, July 18, 1848, <u>Anul 1848</u>, II, pp. 320-2; Mandl to A. G. Golescu, Aug. 8, <u>Anul 1848</u>, VI, p. 26.

134. To obtain arms was one of his most difficult problems. He had tried to make contracts with firms in Vienna, but they wanted cash, which he did not have, and the Magyars would not let the arms go through Hungary. (A. G. Golescu to Maiorescu and Laurian, Aug. 5, 1848, Dragomir, <u>Corespondenta dăscălilor ardeleni</u>, p. 167; Maiorescu to Golescu, Aug. 15, 1848, <u>Convorbiri Literare</u>, XXXII, 1898, pp. 2-3; Golescu to the Wallachian Government, [Aug.], <u>Anul 1848</u>, III, pp. 150-3).

particularly on the questions of uniting the Principalities and confirming the new constitution. This sounded encouraging, but Golescu noted also that the bourgeois republic was timid and would never take a risk unless pushed by public opinion.[135] In a later letter:

> "I feel there is nothing to expect from a bourgeois republic....I consider myself as one of her[France's] children, and that is why I suffer from her fall. I know that France has material interests to safeguard, but I know also that there is no virtue without sacrifice....If France takes the credit of declaring herself...protector of all weak nations, she should also pay the freight...." 136

Bastide's promises were indeed far from sincere. He and Cavaignac had enough to worry about without raising up trouble in the East, and he was not over-sympathetic toward the Roumanian revolutionaries. He thought their movement too premature and did nothing to carry out his promises.[137]

---

135 A. G. Golescu to Voinescu, Sept. 16, 1848, Anul 1848, IV, pp. 197-200; Golescu to the Wallachian Government, Sept. 21, Aricescu, op.cit., vol. II, pp. 41-4, announcing that the guns had been sent; Golescu to Ghica, Sept. 25, 1848, Anul 1848, IV, p. 325.

136. A. G. Golescu to Bataillard, Sept. 28, 1848, Anul 1848, IV, pp. 395-7.

137. Pencilled in the margin of a dispatch from Bucharest is the comment: "These young men have good intentions but they go too fast." (Hory to Foreign Ministry, June 22, 1848, Aff. Etr., Corr. Pol., Bucarest, vol. 5). Also Bastide to Aupick, July 7, Aug. 6, 1848, Aff. Etr., Turquie, vol. 295; Anul 1848, V, pp. 533-4. Cf. de Guichen, op.cit., vol. I, p. 189, which concludes, from Normanby's dispatches, that Palmerston and Bastide were so alarmed over the Russian occupation of Moldavia that they resolved to act together to defend their mutual interests. But when the Porte asked Aupick about military support in case of war, he had to confess that he had no instructions on that point. (Anul 1848, IV, p. 396).

Golescu made a plea for their early realization and begged for 5,000 more rifles, which would be paid for in Bucharest. It was already too late. Bucharest newspapers were making last desperate pleas for help, especially to France, "the cradle of civilization, the palace of liberty, the protector of the rights of all peoples," but no help came. Meanwhile, to forestall a Russian occupation, the Turks sent their own troops to Bucharest. Brushing aside an unarmed mob, they entered and pillaged the city.

The Sublime Porte and the great powers had proved broken reeds. So also were the other "peoples in revolution," who might have extended a fraternal hand. Dumitru Brătianu, who had been sent to Budapest in June to treat with Kossuth, had no success and was soon back in Bucharest. We know little of the negotiations, only Brătianu's report that "with the Hungarians there is nothing to be done."[138] Kossuth later tried to draw the two revolutions closer together by sending a consul to Bucharest, and Bălcescu hoped for cooperation, but an alliance was never offered.[139]

---

138. Anul 1848, II, p. 646; cf. N. Kretzulescu to A. G. Golescu, Aug. 5-12, 1848, Anul 1848, VI, pp. 24-5, reporting on a visit to Budapest; E. Horvath, Transylvania and the History of the Roumanians, (Budapest, 1935), pp. 66, 70.

139. Panaitescu, Emigraţia Polonă, p. 11; idem., Contribuţii la o biografie a lui N. Bălcescu, pp. 81-2. For the opinions of several of the Roumanian leaders on the Hungarian alliance question, see Anul 1848, I, p. 610;

A. G. Golescu was convinced that with the Hungarians it was not possible or desirable to come to an understanding.[140] With the Poles relations were closer. Czaika at Constantinople took Ghica under his wing and introduced him to Ottoman ministers, but attempts to win Turkey to support a Polish-Roumanian front were fruitless.[141] Agents of Czartoryski were continually present in Bucharest, and Colonel Zablocki did what he could with the Wallachian militia.[142] In Bucharest also was an accredited representative of the democratic Polish faction.[143] Polish solicitude was appreciated, but so long as no serious revolution broke out in Poland, the Poles could be of little real assistance.

In the final analysis, the Roumanians had to depend on themselves, as the less romantic of them realized at an

---

ibid., III, pp. 76-7; Dragomir, Corespondența dascălilor ardeleni, p. 167; Bănescu and Mihăilescu, Ioan Maiorescu, pp. 167-8; P. V. Haneș, Alexandru Russo, pp. 174-6. Most of them were of the opinion that an agreement with the Hungarians was impossible, and predicted the inevitable partition of Hungary.

140. Golescu to Bălcescu, July 19, 1848, Anul 1848, II, p. 614.

141. Anul 1848, I, pp. 604, 645-6; S. Lukasik, "Relațiunile lui Mihail Czaykowski-Sadyk Pasa cu Românii," (Revista Istorică Română, II, 1932, pp. 232-61), p. 245; Ghica, Amintiri, p. 10.

142. Panaitescu, Emigrația Polonă, pp. 7-15, 31-73; Handelsman, op.cit., pp. 96-103, 106-7.

143. Central Polish Committee, Lemberg to Wallachian Provisional Government, July 20, 1848, (Ac. Rom. Mss. C. A. Rosetti).

early date. But they had no material strength. The militia, with its Russian-trained officers, was not reliable, and the new national guard was never really organized. Balcescu, versed in military history, yearned for battles and preached armed resistance against all enemies, but fate did not permit the Roumanian revolution to perish in martyrdom.[144] Morally, its back was broken when the conservatives, to please Suleiman, abandoned the original basis of the revolution to get Turkish recognition. The fire-eaters(Bălcescu, the Brătianus, Rosetti) wanted to fight both the Turks and the Russians then, and again in September, but they got no farther than fiery speeches in the clubs and on the Field of Liberty.[145]

The imported revolution from Paris, successful in June without fighting, went down in September without firing more than a couple of shots. Its unimpressive record in

---

144. Bălcescu, "Drepturile Românilor către Inalta Poartă," (Poporul Suveran, Aug. 2, 6, 1848 o.s., reprinted in Anul 1848, III, pp. 175-9).

145. Anul 1848, II, 642-3, 650, III, pp. 50-1, 96-7; IV, pp. 194-5; Maxim-Burdujanu, Demètre G. Golesco, pp. 72-3; Xenopol, Istoria Românilor, vol. XI, p. 91; Göllner, op.cit., pp. 197-8, 213-9; Report of Zablocki, in Panaitescu, Emigrația Polonă, p. 115; idem., Contribuții la o biografie a lui Bălcescu, pp. 79, 89; Ghica, Amintiri, pp. 36, 47-9; Hory to Foreign Ministry, Sept. 19, 1848, Aff. Etr., Corr. Pol., Bucarest, vol. 5; Colquhoun to Palmerston, Sept. 11, 1848, F.O. 78, vol. 743.

all fields, its attempt to leap over a century of development in one day, have left it with few defenders.[146] Recently there has been an attempt to interpret the revolution in the light of economic factors at home, minimizing the Parisian veneer. It was true that the petty bourgeoisie was solidly behind the revolution, but it produced no leaders.[147] Liberal reforms were demanded both because they were desired by this class at home and because the students brought them home ready-made from Paris, and it is not easy to strike the balance between the two. The record as a whole seems to justify the charge of importation; the speeches, writings, and official acts of practically every leader showed unmistakably the French inspiration. The Roumanian revolution was related to the other revolutions of 1848, but the similarity was more ideological than economic.[148]

---

146. Typical of the reaction of foreign observers was the acid comment of Czaika: "The Roumanian deputies, aside from Bălcescu and [Ștefan] Golescu, appeared more like students from the rue St. Jacques than deputies of the people." (Panaitescu, Emigrația Polonă, p. 68).

147. Only one member of the bourgeois class was taken into the Provisional Government.

148. Cf. E. Lovinescu, Istoria Civilizației Române, vol. I, pp. 46-7, 139-42, 145-72; C. T. Axente, Essai sur le régime représentatif en Roumanie, pp. 130-177; St. Zeletin, Burghezia Română. Origina și Rolul ei istoric, pp. 59-64; Ion, "Adevăratul 1848," (Viața Romînească, XXX, Mar. 1938, pp. 34-49).

CHAPTER V

THE FIRST YEARS OF EXILE, 1848-1853.

WAITING FOR THE WORLD REVOLUTION

1. Protests and propaganda, September 1848-May 1849

The inglorious collapse of September might have been a crushing blow to the faith and the hopes of the young revolutionaries who had so enthusiastically set out in June to lead the Roumanian people to a democratic Utopia. However, like the master revolutionary, Mazzini, they showed a remarkable resilience and immediately resumed activity as if there were not the slightest cause for discouragement. Unavoidable circumstances, the capture of some of the leaders by the Turks, the flight of others into Transylvania, prevented any immediate concerted action. Magheru and the others who had crossed the border into Transylvania had been disarmed and were closely watched by the Austrian police. Nevertheless troubled waters elsewhere on the Continent soon provided some of them with opportunities for fishing.

It was obvious that if salvation was to come, it would most likely be the result of a war in which some power would take upon itself the task of trying to check the advance of Russia: Austria, France, or England. Austria, completely disorganized and almost in dissolution because of the revolts of her many nationalities, gave no indication of being able to live up to the role of barrier to Russian expansion which British statesmen expected her to play The Liberals held only the city of Vienna and were soon to lose that; the Court party, far from blocking Russian expansion, was about to invite Russian troops into the heart of central Europe to help put down the Hungarians. Most of the Wallachian revolutionaries, schooled to regard Austria as a reactionary power, expected nothing from Vienna or Germany. The exception was Ioan Maiorescu, delegate of the Provisional Government to the German National Assembly at Frankfurt.

Completely out of touch with his government, so long as it still existed, and continuing to exercise his functions as "the representative of all Roumanians" long after the occupation of Wallachia by the Turks and the Russians, Maiorescu acted on his own initiative and in accordance with his own ideas. A Transylvanian with a German education, he had always been hostile to the exaggerated enthusiasm for everything French which characterized his colleagues of the national party. When at Frankfurt he wrote to A. G. Golescu:

> "I have never expected anything from France, nor will I in the future. I had no illusion that Europe would help us because of any principle of humanity. What people has France emancipated or helped? Greece would have perished but for

> Canning. What did Napoleon do for the Poles? What does France do for Italy today? If France will not help Italy, why will she help distant Roumania? I am no enemy of the French; I admire the virtues of the French people, their sympathy for the freedom of other peoples. But it is the masses who feel that way, not those who govern....Since the start of our revolution I have relied on the justice of our cause and on Turkey, waiting until the moment when Germany should be consolidated. In Germany is our hope, not because the Germans are more human than the French, but because the lower Danube is a vital question for Germany, as is the strengthening of all anti-Slav emements, such as the Magyars and the Roumanians. As far as interests go, England is more likely to help us than is France. But what is the use! Most of our youth believes in France!" 1

Maiorescu had never been to France, and he had little of the romanticism of his friends. His nationalism was derived not from the Collège de France but from his own experience with the realities of the struggle for existence in Transylvania. Although most of his career had been spent in Wallachia, he never lost sight of the importance of the Roumanians in the Austrian Empire, who had to depend on Vienna and the German element in order to hold their own against the Magyars.

Maiorescu watched with impatience the endless proceedings and debates of the Frankfurt Assembly. The sands of the revolution of 1848 were fast running out everywhere in Europe. He alternated between hope and despair as he waited for the Assembly to set up a central power, take a definite

---

1. Oct. 29, 1848, Bănescu & Mihăilescu, Ioan Maiorescu, pp. 230-1

decision on the Roumanian question, and send representatives to Constantinople and to the Principalities, with instructions to uphold the rights of the Porte and of the Roumanian nation. He saw Gagern, Schmerling, and Archduke Johann, who told him that the Ministry was unanimous in deciding not to let the Principalities fall a prey to Russia, and that Germany would soon intervene.[2] His conversations and memorandums brought the question before the Parliament, several interpellations were made, and one delegate announced that to Germany a Roumanian empire was more important than an independent Hungary.[3] Maiorescu first submitted a scheme whereby the Principalities would be joined to Transylvania and Bucovina, forming an independent state "under the suzerainty of Germany" and ruled by a Habsburg archduke. Austria could let Italy go in exchange for these gains in the east.[4] Later he substituted a milder plan: Germany was to induce the Porte to let the Principalities go, after which they would be united as a single state under German

---

2. Ibid., pp. 210-215.

3. Texts of Maiorescu's two memorandums and records of the debates on the Roumanian question in Ion Ghica, Amintiri din Pribegia, pp. 120-51, and in Anul 1848, IV, pp. 414-20, V, pp. 331-2, 361-9, 612-6. Maiorescu also made use of A. G. Golescu's brochure published in German at Vienna in August.

4. Maiorescu to A. G. Golescu, Sept. 26, 28, 1848, Convorbiri Literare, XXXII, 1898, pp. 159-62.

protection. The new German envoy had instructions to that effect.[5] All this depended on the "Germany" represented at Frankfurt, which had no army and no executive power. When the individual German states began to assert themselves, even its moral authority vanished, and along with it went Maiorescu's finely-spun plans.

The October rising in Vienna seemed to hold possibilities for all the peoples of eastern Europe. Maiorescu rejoiced in this victory of the "people," even considered going to Vienna himself but instead remained in Frankfurt to work with the democratic party there; he got one of his pro-Roumanian mémoires hitched to an address signed by 130 radical delegates and sent to Robert Blum in Vienna. Weary of Schmerling's unfulfilled promises, he began to think that perhaps more could be obtained from the radicals, who, he said, received with warmth his plan for a great Roumania and promised that if democracy triumphed, 100,000 Germans would march to the aid of the Principalities.[6] He even entered into negotiations with Europe's ubiquitous revolutionaries, the Poles, who promised to supply officers and volunteers; but the military alliance which they requested he felt unable to conclude.[6]

On december 8, 1848, Maiorescu left Frankfurt and went to Vienna.

---

5. Bănescu & Mihăilescu, op.cit., p. 232.

6. Ibid., pp. 217-9, 222, 226-7.

There he remained for ten years, devoting his energies to pleading for a constitutionally recognized unitary status for the Roumanians of the Empire. Their loyalty to the Emperor in the war against Hungary had been rewarded by incorporation into a centralized monarchy. No longer connected with the Principalities, he kept their problems in mind and kept in touch with the other emigrés. His relations with them were none too cordial, for he had to defend himself against accusations that he had been too pro-German and anti-Turk. More or less wrapped up in the affairs of the Transylvanians and limited in his activities because he held a minor position in the Austrian administration, he remained out of the general current of the emigration's activities.[7] While others tried to organize for the pursuance of an intensive campaign of propaganda and preparation for a new revolution, he remained a lone wolf at Vienna, compromised in the eyes of his compatriots in other capitals because of his connection with a reactionary government.

Maiorescu, the "realist," made no better showing than his colleagues with their faith in France and in democracy.

---

7. During his tenure of this position he continued writing articles for German newspapers (Allgemeine Zeitung, Augsburg, and Ostdeutsche Post, Wanderer, Vienna), some of them reproduced in J. F. Neigebaur, Die staatlichen Verhältnisse der Moldau und Walachei, (Breslau, 1856, Heft III of Die Donaufürstenthümern), pp. 24, 74-83, 94-103.

Rejecting the idea of collaboration with either Magyars or Slavs, rejecting the then popular idea of a Danubian alliance or federation, he was forced to fall back on Germanism. He proved in 1848 that he was no successful opportunist, for neither the new Germany nor the new Austria came into being; nor has time proved him a good prophet, for if the Roumanians' national ambitions have been achieved, it was not through the action of Germanism or the appearance of united Germany; in his case subsequent history has provided no compensatory vindication.

A. G. Golescu, still in Paris, kept in close communication with Maiorescu, with whose policy he agreed, and served as a link between Maiorescu and Ion Ghica, who still regarded Constantinople, not Vienna, as the logical point of diplomatic attack. These three, contemptuous of the ineptitude of the three former Lieutenants (Eliade, Tell, N. Golescu) and of the childish naiveté of Rosetti, proceeded to take into their own hands the direction of the "foreign policy" of the Roumanian emigration.

Ghica continued his attempts to convince the Turks of the error of their ways hoping for a clash between the Russian and Ottoman armies of occupation that would lead to war. No longer recognized as anything but a private citizen, he continued to see Aali Pasha and other Ottoman ministers, handing them petitions and protests which were never read.[8] Ghica's efforts had small chance of success. So long as British and French policy did not change, neither did the Turks, and the crowning blow came on May 1, 1849, with the conclusion of the Convention of Balta Liman between Russia and Turkey. This regulated the terms of the joint occupation of the Principalities, restored the Règlement Organique, shorn of its faintly liberal clauses, and buried the Roumanian revolution beyond hope of immediate resurrection.[9]

Ghica's task was certainly not lightened by the Turks' knowledge of Maiorescu's attempts to hand over the Principalities, Ottoman territory, to German "protection" and an

---

8 E.g., a protest against the conduct of Fuad, dated Sept. 29th and signed by D. Brătianu, Bălcescu, Kretzulescu, Rosetti, and 2,000 others, and a petition from the exiles in Paris, undated and signed by almost all the leaders, even by those who were not in Paris in the autumn of 1848. (Ghica, Amintiri, pp. 53-60). The first was brought from Wallachia by Ubicini, French publicist and a friend of the Serbs and the Roumanians. He had known Rosetti and others as students in Paris, and in 1848 he happened to be in Wallachia in search of promising youths to enroll in a school he was going to establish in France, when the revolution broke out. He served as secretary to the Lieutenance Princière. (Ubicini to A. Lévy, Nov. 27, 1847, Musée Mickiewicz Mss., 1035, fol. 41; G. Bengescu, Preface to Ubicini, Les Origines de l'histoire roumaine, Paris, 1885 pp. iii-iv; Boițoș, Bibliografiile româneşte ale lui Ubicini, pp. 7-8; Ubicini, "La Valachie en 1848," Le Siècle, Dec. 17, 1857-Apr. 1858, passim, Roumanian translation in Anul 1848, V, pp. 787-819).

9. D. A. Sturdza et al., Acte si Documente relative la Istoria Românilor, vol. I, (Bucharest, 1900), pp. 357ff.; cf. text of treaty in de Guichen, op.cit., vol. II, pp. 332-4, with modifications due to Anglo-French action.

Austrian prince. Roumanian professions of loyalty to their lawful suzerain were given less credence than ever.[10]

A. G. Golescu, meanwhile, helped by Czartoryski, was continuing his game of hide and seek with Bastide and Drouyn de Lhuys, asking not for guns but for a strong line at Constantinople, to force Russian evacuation of the Principalities.[11] Two mémoires, signed by himself and Maiorescu, and edited by Ubicini, were presented to the French deputies.[12] "In the name of liberty" they begged that "the noble and generous protection of the French Republic" be accorded to the Roumanian people, to guide their national emancipation. They pointed to the Roumanians'

---

10. "What Maiorescu is working on is a secret matter, and if it is discovered, we can disavow him." (A. G. Golescu to Ghica, Dec. 29, 1848, Ghica, Amintiri, pp. 85-6). Maiorescu maintained that his plans were consistent with loyalty to the Porte since Germany would act only through Constantinople and by persuasion. (Maiorescu to Magheru, Dec. 22, 1848, Ghica, Amintiri, pp. 159-60: Maiorescu to A. G. Golescu, Jan. 28, 1849, Convorbiri Literare, XXXII, 1898, pp. 432ff.). Golescu wrote to Ghica explaining how the Turks had nothing to fear, as the Roumanians were their most loyal subjects. This letter was written in French and intended for the eyes of the censor. An accompanying letter, in Roumanian, explained the ruse. (Dec. 26, 1848, Amintiri, pp. 94-102).

11. Handelsman, op.cit., p. 105.

12. Anul 1848, V, pp. 542-5, 551-2. To Bastide and Drouyn he gave a protest against Russian reprisals and a statistical memorandum. (Anul 1848, V, pp. 540-2, 548-50; Revista Istorică, XVII, 1931, pp. 187-9; Ubicini to Ghica, Nov. 11, 1848, Anul 1848, V, 377; Golescu to Ghica, undated, Ghica, Amintiri, pp. 102-5, 108-11).

legal rights, to France's interests, and to France's mission as "the angel of liberty." Golescu defended the sentimental tone of his petition as convenient:

> "While we still follow the more positive policy of interests, the policy of sentiment wins the sympathy of the demagogues, who may be in power tomorrow....The petitions for Frankfurt and London will doubtless be written in another way. To each nation, we must write its own language. It is not a bad idea to use the language of the heart to the French, because they make so much of it; or to throw the reproach of baseness and hypocricy in their faces....You know well the character of the French: they are just big children; we must wound them in their honor, their self esteem. That will certainly bring war next spring,...and you know that war alone can save us." 13

This cynical appraisal shows that his experience as a diplomat had pretty well cured Golescu of any romantic love for France left over from student days. Realism was more apt to obtain results than "those whose imagination is always soaring to the eternal absurd," D. Brătianu and Rosetti, who had just arrived in Paris to make life more complicated for Golescu. Brătianu had composed a "Protest of the Roumanian People," but Golescu was able to keep it out of print.[14] These internal divisions made no difference in the final outcome. France, wholly absorbed in a presidential election, was not to be goaded into action by either realistic or sentimental Roumanians.

---

13. Ghica, Amintiri, pp. 104-6.

14. Golescu to Ghica, Dec. 19, 1848, ibid., p. 90.

Toward the end of the year 1848, the other Roumanian exiles began to appear in Paris, drawn to the French capital as if by a magnet. Things had not been over-pleasant in Transylvania, where the Austrians, the Hungarians, and even the Roumanian "brothers" regarded them as suspect. Some had decided to go to Constantinople, but the majority of the leaders had chosen Paris. This gave the cause a score of diplomats in Paris in place of one, with no noticeable effect on the course of French policy. There was nothing to expect from the new President, Louis Napoleon.[15] All they could do was to keep up the production of official memorandums and try to initiate an effective campaign in the press.[16] Their old friends Lamartine, Michelet, and Quinet were not able to do much for them, though Quinet, supplied with data by Golescu, was anxious to have their cause brought up again in the National Assembly.[17] Ledru Rollin, a leader of what A. G. Golescu called "the demagogic party," had spoken warmly of them in his campaign addresses

---

15. An interview with Napoleon was requested by a group of Roumanians, probably without result. (Hurmuzaki, Documente, vol. XVIII, pp. 124-5).

16. Golescu and Vasile Alecsandri collaborated in the production of articles for Le National, La Réforme, Le Siècle, Le Courrier d'Orient, and Le Constitutionnel. (Bogdan-Duică, Vasile Alecsandri, p. 27).

17. Quinet to Golescu, Nov. 1, 1848, Anul 1848, V, p. 344.

advocating a holy alliance of democratic nationalities. At one banquet he mentioned his connections with the Roumanian revolutionaries, thus compromising those Roumanians who were leaning over backwards to prove the legitimate and non-demagogic nature of their movement.[18]

Ledru Rollin became the idol of the Roumanian "Reds." They attended meetings of the Montagne and "democratic and social banquets." At one meeting, at which Ledru was, in Rosetti's words, "sublime," he hailed Ion Brătianu, Rosetti, and Voinescu publicly as martyrs to democracy and promised that as soon as France was free, she would free Roumania.[19] Rosetti was convinced that Ledru would soon be victorious in France and that all Europe would thereupon experience a "holy explosion," a democratic and socialistic revolution.[20] Actually, Ledru's stock was going down all the time, especially after his defeat by Louis Napoleon, whose only crusade was to crush liberty and nationalism in Rome. Some of the Roumanians signed the protest, circulated by their friends of the Montagne, against this expedition.[21] The purge

---

18. A. R. Calman, Ledru Rollin and the Second French Republic, (New York, 1922, pp. 256, 322; Maiorescu to A. G. Golescu, Jan. 28, 1849, Convorbiri Literare, XXXII, 1898, p. 434).

19. C. A. Rosetti, Note intime, vol. II, pp. 23, 31-2.

20. Rosetti to Ghica, Apr. 20, May 10, Ghica, Amintiri, pp. 64, 74; Rosetti, Note intime, vol. II, p. 44.

21. F. Pulszky, Meine Zeit, mein Leben, vol. II, p. 344.

which followed removed from the political scene Ledru and their last remaining supporters.

The real help came not from well known figures but from lesser men who knew much more about the question: Ubicini, Bataillard, and Desprez. The result of Ubicini's collaboration was a Mémoire justificatif de la Révolution roumaine du 11 (23) juin 1848, addressed to the cabinets of all the great powers except Russia, and with a special letter to the Sultan, signed by "the members of the Wallachian Provisional Government and delegates of the emigration."[22] Opposition to Russia was pointed out as the sole purpose of their revolution; the idea of national unity and the borrowing of radical ideas from the West were said to be figments of the imagination of M. Nesselrode.

The eccentric Billecocq gave the Roumanians a certain amount of publicity, but his words carried no weight.[23] Desprez produced a long and competent article in the Revue

---

22. Paris, Impr. de Cosson, Feb., 1849. The letter to the Sultan, very similar to a previous letter sent by the three Lieutenants from Transylvania in October, is dated Feb. 9, and the mémoire to Drouyn de Lhuys, Feb. 26. (Cf. Hurmuzaki, Documente, vol. XVIII, pp. 123-4; Ghica, Amintiri, pp. 57-60; Ubicini, Provinces d'origine roumaine, p. 145, note 1; Anul 1848, V, pp. 326-31). A.G. Golescu's mémoire, "Histoire des derniers événements dans les Principautés," was presented previously, probably in Dec. 1848 (Anul 1848, IV, pp. 624-9; cf. Golescu to Ghica, Amintiri, pp. 109, 215).

23. Billecocq, Le nostre prigioni, vol. II, pp. 406-13, giving his letters to Bastide and Drouyn de Lhuys.

des Deux Mondes and published it also as a pamphlet.[24] He echoed the Mémoire Justificatif in showing that the revolution was not directed against Turkey, but did not hesitate to admit that it was intended to include Transylvania, Bucovina and Bessarabia.

The most effective publicity work was done by Bataillard, who was given free rein in a new journal, Le Temps, which appeared daily after March 1, 1849. His many articles pointed to the blindness, ignorance, and disregard of national interests which characterized French policy in the East, and called the Russian occupation of the Principalities a threat to Constantinople and to the whole European equilibrium. As for the Roumanian revolution, he said that of all the great insurrections produced by the revolution of February, it most merited the attention of republican France.[25]

These efforts of Bataillard gave the Roumanians the advertisement they felt they needed, but the French public did not learn easily, judging from the anecdotes, probably apocryphal, which were going the rounds in emigre circles. Ion Brătianu told one about an interview with Bastide, who

---

24. "La Révolution dans l'Europe orientale," (Revue des Deux Mondes, Nov. 15, Dec. 15, 1848, pp. 894-919); cf. Despres to A. G. Golescu, Dec. 31, 1848, Anul 1848, VI, p. 76.

25. Le Temps, Mar. 3, 1849, and later numbers. All of Bataillard's articles in this journal are analyzed and quoted at length in O. Boitos, Paul Bataillard et la révolution roumaine de 1848.

interrupted his exposition with the question: "What did you say was the capital of your country?--Bucharest, Excellency"--"Buchara! Ah, Buchara!! Pray continue."[26] Then there was the story of the young man who informed a questioner that he was a Roumanian, only to be met with "Roumanian? So young and already a Roumanian?"[27] Vasile Alecsandri wrote jestingly of the questions put to him. "Moldavian? What's that? The Moldo-Wallachian cause? Can one talk about that seriously and in good company without compromising oneself?" "In this beloved country of France," wrote Alecsandri, "people can be ignorant with so much esprit."[28]

Of the Roumanians the most active propagandist was Eliade Rădulescu, in Paris for the first time. Refused an audience at the Foreign Ministry and unable to establish contact with the better known journals, he turned out quantities of articles for the ephemeral sheets of the Left, which appeared only at irregular intervals and with frequent changes of name, thanks to financial difficulties and to the censorship.[29] Radical editors shared the antipathy of

---

26. Wladislaw Mickiewicz, Pamietniki, (Warsaw, 1926), vol. I, p. 129; cf. Eliade Rădulescu, A.M. Saint-Marc Girardin, (Constantinople, 1856, copy in Ac.Rom.Mss. 6, fol.140).

27. Mickiewicz, loc.cit.; cf. Ion Ghica, Scrisori, p. 154, placing the same conversation in Turin ten years later.

28. Alecsandri to "a member of my family," Oct. 14, 1848, Billecocq, Le nostre prigioni, vol. II, p. 413.

29. G. Oprescu, "L'activité de journaliste d'Eliade Rădulescou

the Roumanians for Russia and for the do-nothing policy of France, and felt that only among the nationalities was "the revolution" still alive. Eliade was thus able to write extensively, particularly in La Semaine and Le Peuple.[30]

Paradoxically, Eliade, the conservative of the Roumanian revolution, found himself consorting with and influenced by Proudhon, Pierre Levoux, Lamennais, Alphouse Esquiros, men who represented the advanced social thought of the time; they were much more radical than Lamartine, Quinet and the friends of the so-called "Reds" among the Roumanians. Eliade

---

pendant son exil à Paris," (Dacoromania, IV, 1924-6, pp. 67-76), p. 68. The Right journals (La Patrie, L'Assemblée Nationale, etc.), with whose editors Bataillard and the Roumanian refugees broke many a lance, got most of their information on the eastern question direct from the Russian embassy. Moderate papers (La Presse, Le Constitutionnel, etc.) depended on the German press, and Le National on Hungarian sources. This left little room for the Roumanians, but they made the most of the extreme Left journals and of Le Temps, with an occasional letter to La Presse or La Réforme. (Cf. Oprescu, "Contribution à la bibliografhie des événements de 1848-1850 en Transylvanie et dans les Principautés danubiennes," Rev. Hist. du Sud-Est Eur., III, 1926, pp. 27-37).

30. He himself states that he wrote or inspired articles in La Presse, La Semaine, Le Temps, Le Crédit, Le Positif, La Tribune des Peuples, La Ligue des Peuples, L'Europe Démocratique, La Démocratie Pacifique, La Republique, and La Voix du Peuple. This is an exaggeration. Some of these contain no trace of articles by him, others have but one or two. He did know some of the editors personally (Carpentier, Rhéal, Le Couturier, Pierre Leroux, and probably Proudhon). See Eliade Rădulescu, Scrisori din Exil, (Bucharest, 1891), pp. 6, 28, 734; Oprescu, Eliade Rădulescu şi Franţa, p. 58; idem, L'activité de journaliste d'Eliade Rădulescu, loc.cit.

did not like what he saw of official France, saw no virtues in "republicanism," and his temperament drew him toward Lamennais and a religious socialism, not Catholic or Jesuit, but that of his "proscribed and anathematized" friends; "Christianity," he wrote, "reappears today in France under the name of socialism or fraternization, and under the sovereignity of the People...."[31]

Eliade's disappointment in France was shared by the other Roumanians, not only the extreme Francophils, but moderates like Ştefan Golescu who wrote, in April 1849:

> "Far from making a close alliance with us the French Government today combats everywhere all republican movements....I am waiting to see what will be the result of the elections for the Legislative Assembly in France, and if it turns out to be as bad as the present Constituent Assembly, then I shall leave France and betake myself God knows where, but I will not stay here any longer, for I am completely disgusted with the French of today."[32]

What little hope remained gave way to black despair when news came of the Convention of Balta Liman. This put a sudden end to all talk of an imminent fight for Constantinople. An open letter to Le Temps from one of the emigrés, commenting on the remarkable zeal shown by Aupick and

---

31. Eliade Rădulescu, Mémoires, p. 212; N. B. Locusteanu, Amintiri din Trecut, (Craiova, 1896), p. 108; Oprescu, Eliade Rădulescu şi Franţa, pp. 68-73; D. Popovici, Ideologica Literară a lui I. Heliade Rădulescu, pp. 223-4.

32. Ştefan Golescu to D. Brătianu, April 8, 1849, Cretzianu, Din Arhiva lui Dumitru Brătianu, vol. I, pp. 207-9.

Canning in bludgeoning the Turks into accepting Russia's demands, expressed the bitterness which they felt at this betrayal by France and Turkey of "their own vital interests and most sacred duties." For the Turks he had only contempt and hinted that in the future the Roumanians would no longer be so blind as to protect with their own healthy chests the rotten body that was Turkey. His sharpest barbs he reserved for France, which had cast aside its revolutionary mission along with its obligations under the treaty of 1848.

> "Is it not one of the most singular stories of our time? The Romans of Tiber and their brothers in origin, the Roumanians of the Danube, trying to regain their political existence and to claim their sacred rights, are halted, the ones at Constantinople by the culpable abandonment of French diplomacy, the others at Rome by the very bayonets of France." 33

France, fountain-head of liberty and of the spirit of the immortal revolution, had sold out. Ion Ghica had the same reaction:

> "The result of all our efforts has been that one robber has replaced another in the principality. ...Everyone is happy, General Grabbe and Titov [Russian special emissary and ambassador respectively] included. The ambassadors of France and England sing of victory, peace is saved. Every day a banquet and every night a ball. I do not doubt the bourse of Paris has shown gains. I am nervous, tired, sick, and I can't continue although I started with the intention of telling you about many persons and many things." 34

---

33. Boitoș, op.cit., pp. 101-7.

34. Ghica to Rosetti, May 17, 1849, Musée Mickiewicz Mss. Dossier, 1109.

Parallel to what was going on in Frankfurt, Constantinople, and Paris, was the activity of Dumitru Brătianu in London. Preceded by A. G. Golescu, of whose visit we have no record, Brătianu arrived in the middle of November with credentials from the <u>Lieutenance Princière</u>, "a government recognized by Great Britain," as he said in his request to Palmerston for an audience. He was cordially received by Palmerston on December 8th, presented his case, but received no promise of diplomatic intervention.[35] Not willing to rest content with that, he proceeded to compose a long memorandum for the Foreign Secretary.[36] Calling attention to the "Wallach nation" as the shield of Christianity and civilization against barbarism, he castigated the depredations of Russia and the deplorable weakness of the Porte in violating treaties and the rights of humanity. For Britain's special benefit he brought in the route to India, prestige in the East, and the usual talk about raw materials, markets, and investments, calculated to appeal to the nation of shopkeepers. He pictured Wallachia as a martyred nation,

---

35. Cretzianu, <u>op.cit.</u>, vol. I, pp. 134-5.

36. Received at the Foreign Office in January, 1849. Later printed, together with an appeal to the members of Parliament, as <u>Documents concerning the question of the Danubian Principalities, dedicated to the English Parliament by D. Bratiano, intrusted with a special mission by the Princely Lieutenancy of Wallachia to the Government of Her Majesty the Queen of Great Britain</u>, (London, 1849).

subjected to the most barbarous invasion for the only crime of having followed the example of Great Britain, "the cradle of liberal institutions in the modern world."

Lord Dudley Stuart, perennial defender of the Poles, displayed great interest in Brătianu, put him in touch with several other Liberal M.P.'s, and encouraged him to publish his memorandum, which came out in February.[37] At about the same time appeared another pamphlet by W. L. Birkbeck, who seems to have used Brătianu's work as his main source.[38] Birkbeck listed the strategic, economic, and moral reasons for Britain to impose her will on Russia, with the aid of Turkey and "the nationalities: Moldavians, Wallachians, Tartars, Georgians, Cossacks, Poles, and Finns."

The circulation of these two pamphlets and the insertion of several articles in the press constituted Brătianu's preparation for the momentous session of Parliament in March 22nd., when Stuart raised the Principalities question in the House of Commons.[39] The debate found on the side of

---

37. Cretzianu, op.cit., vol. I, pp. 172-181. Through Stuart Brătianu made the acquaintance of Lord Beaumont, Sir Harry Verney, William Lloyd Birkbeck, and others.

38. Anon., The Russians in Moldavia and Wallachia, (London, 1849). This was published through the Literary Society of the Friends of Poland, of which Stuart was president.

39. Hansard, Parliamentary Debates, 3rd Series, vol. 103, pp. 1128-1161. Stuart's speech was reported almost in full by Bataillard in Le Temps, Mar, 24, 25, 1849, accompanied by some laudatory remarks on Stuart as a friend of the Roumanian nation.

the Roumanians a couple of Stuart's friends, and three Irish members who said that the British Government was "bound to...insist that every Calmuck and Russian be withdrawn from that soil which they polluted with their presence." On the other side was Palmerston who dismissed all criticism with a reference to the friendly relations existing between Britain and Russia. Brătianu, sitting in the public gallery, was disappointed in the thin attendance and in the results of the debate, but he mustered up courage to thank Palmerston for his speech (in which the Foreign Secretary had announced his faith in Russian promises and dashed all hope of support from Britain), saying:

> "[Your speech] filled my soul, and the souls of all the Roumanians, with happiness, since we are aware of...your generous efforts in favor of our nationality and our liberties. Soon, thanks to Your Lordship, the Roumanian nation will be able to express itself freely. Then it will speak and the whole world will be filled with the glory of our name." 40

This was putting a little better than the best face on a bad situation, but Brătianu was not given to pessimism. Palmerston transmitted his thanks for the letters and for the "very interesting album" (Billecocq's *Album moldo-valaque*), which Brătianu had sent, and continued his passive policy, disregarding Stratford Canning's prediction of aggression on Turkey and advocacy of an Anglo-French

---

40. Cretzianu, *op.cit.*, vol. I, pp. 174-6, 206-7.

naval demonstration and a defensive alliance with the Porte. His protests against the occupation of the Principalities were feeble. He was certain that the Russians would march not on Constantinople but northward into Transylvania, and in that he was prepared quietly to acquiesce. He counted on Austria balancing Russia in the Principalities and maintaining the Sultan's sovereignty there. The spectre of a war in which Turkey would have to face both Austria and Russia, with only the Hungarians and Roumanians revolutionary movements as allies, augured ill for Britain's whole position in the Near East, and the Convention of Balta Liman, which removed that danger, was given the blessing of the British Foreign Secretary.[41] There was no longer any reason for Brătianu to stay in London. In the middle of May he returned to his beloved Paris.

2. Efforts at co-operation with independent Hungary. The Transylvanian question in 1849.

The European governments were blind and deaf, but the Roumanians had another string to their bow. They could try

---

41. Puryear, England, Russia, and the Straits Question, p. 151; de Guichen, op.cit., vol. I, pp. 250-6, 318-35; C. Sproxton, Palmerston and the Hungarian Revolution, (Cambridge, Eng., 1919), pp. 80-4; S. Lane-Poole, Life of Stratford Canning, (London, 1888), vol. II, pp. 188-9; D. M. Greer, L'Angleterre, la France et la Révolution de 1848, (Paris, 1925), p. 298; H. W. V. Temperley, The Crimea, (London, 1936), p. 260; Palmerston to Ponsonby, Mar. 20, 1849, F.O. 7, vol. 363; Palmerston to Canning, Mar. 27, 1849, F.O. 78, vol. 768, cit. E. Horvath, "Origins of the Crimean War," (South Eastern Affairs, Budapest, VI, 1936), pp. 91,97.

to revive their own revolution by linking it with what remained of the national movements of other peoples. Out of this situation--none of the small nations being able to save itself from Austria and Russia by its own resources--grew a general demand for an alliance of nationalities and perhaps an eventual federation. The tragedy was that the leaders of no nation were willing to enter into such a grouping until they lost power at home and were driven into exile.

The Roumanian leaders, when in power, had scorned an alliance with Hungary. Now Hungary was the only part of Europe where the revolution was not knocked out or staggering. Kossuth was the champion of liberty; he might, with help, be able to win liberty for all the peoples of the Danubian basin. Ion Ghica, at Constantinople, saw the picture clearly. Though he had greater faith in diplomacy than in conspiracy, common action and a few brilliant victories by the embattled nationalities might banish the Porte's timidity and stir sluggish minds in London and Paris. He therefore put to advantage his relations with Polish, Italian, and Hungarian agents at Constantinople. Encouraged by Baron Tecco, Sardinian envoy, he and Ubicini, in the autumn of 1848, proposed that the Roumanian refugees organize, then get into communication with "the heads of the liberal parties of Hungary, Italy, Germany, and Poland."

At Constantinople, a newspaper to defend the interests of all nationalities and to propagate the idea of unity and fraternity among them, could be established.[42] No real organization was formed on the basis of these plans. They were merely a weathervane pointing to Roumanian willingness to join the revolutionary struggles of other nations and perhaps an eventual federation. The Italians and Poles, who had done much to spread this idea, were not sure Italy or Poland would enter such a federation, but they insisted on its desirability for the nations of the Danube and the Balkans. Anxious for allies against Russia and Austria, they tried to appease national conflicts and create a solid bloc of Magyars, Jugoslavs, and Roumanians.[43]

With the coming of 1849 and the intensification of the war in Hungary, possibilities for action increased. The most pressing question was Turkey's attitude in regard to Russia's use of the Principalities as a base of operations against Hungary. Turkey was nominally neutral but could not enforce her neutrality without provoking Russia to war. Ghica and the Roumanians hoped that the Turks, encouraged by the attitude of Stratford, would throw caution to the winds, join hands with the Hungarians and Roumanians, and

---

42. Ghica, Amintiri, pp. 60-61.

43. Al. Marcu, Conspiratori şi Conspiraţii în Epoca Renaşterii Politice a României, (Bucharest, 1930), pp. 9-17.

give England and France no choice but to come in. They were confident that they would then be able to revive their own revolution with ease. Reports received from friends at home stated that the people were on the point of a general rising against the Russian army and would be glad to co-operate with the Turks, whose exemplary conduct had effaced the ill will created by their entry into Bucharest in September.[44] After the failure of the first Russian incursion into Transylvania, Duhamel, the Russian commander in Bucharest, is said to have admitted to Fuad that "we are on a volcano."[45] The March victories of General Bem raised Roumanian hopes, for he was more in sympathy with them than was Kossuth. After his capture of Hermannstadt he let it be known that a Roumanian national government would be recognized by Hungary and suggested that Roumanian agents be sent to Hermannstadt (Sibiu) and Kronstadt (Braşov).[46] British agents made no secret of their

---

44. Cretzianu, op.cit., vol. I, p. 208; Boitoş, op.cit., pp. 94, 98, 128, 144-5; Bălcescu, Scrisori către Ion Ghica, pp. 33, 47; Anul 1848, VI, p. 75. General Lüders reported to St. Petersburg that agitations were going on in Bucharest, and that many people were in correspondence with the exiled revolutionaries. (Averbukh, Tsarskaya Interventsia v borbe s vengerskoi revolutsiei, p. 83).

45. Eugene Horvath, "Russia and the Hungarian Revolution," (Slavonic Review, XII, 1934, pp. 628-45), p. 639.

46. Bem to Ségur, Mar. 23, 1849, Hurmuzaki, Documente, vol. XVIII, p. 135; Bem to Boulay de la Meurthe, ibid., pp. 127-8; Timoni to Schwarzenberg, Apr. 4, 1849, Wiener Staatsarchiv, Walachei, No. 54, cit. Horvath, loc.cit.

sympathies. Colquhoun sent Effingham Grant to Hermannstadt, and he arrived just in time to witness the rout of the Austrians and Russians. After remaining in the city to greet and congratulate the conquering hero, he wrote exultantly to his brother-in-law, C. A. Rosetti, of his interview with "the defender of the cause of peoples."[47] A Hungarian-Turkish alliance, blessed by the British, seemed very possible.[48] Ghica tried to goad the Turks into action. In a note to the Porte he stressed the importance to the Ottoman Empire and to the Principalities of the Hungarian victories, which he said would bring into the war on Hungary's side all the populations of the Austrian Empire. He mentioned the prospect of the reconquest of Bessarabia and the Crimea, then suggested that arms be stored at Widin, "in preparation for any eventuality," and that agents be sent to Transylvania and the Banat to bring about an agreement between Magyars and Roumanians there.[49] This appeal of Ghica went unheeded, for the Russian representatives at Constantinople carried heavier guns than he. He then decided on a direct

---

47. Mar. 18, 1849, Cretzianu, op.cit., vol. I, pp. 197-200; cf. Timoni to Schwarzenberg, Mar. 20, 1849, in E. Horvath, "Origins of the Crimean War," (South Eastern Affairs, Budapest, VI, 1936), pp. 90-1.

48. D. M. Greer, op.cit., p. 301.

49. Ac. Rom., Mss. 5040 (Ion Ghica), dated only 1849 but obviously written shortly after Bem's capture of Hermannstadt.

approach to Kossuth and the formation of a Roumanian legion to fight in Hungary and in the Principalities. Bălcescu, in the company of Polish and Italian agents and two Roumanian aides, left Constantinople in the middle of April for Hungary and Transylvania, traveling by way of Belgrade, where they tried unsuccessfully to bring the Serbs into the grand alliance of peoples.[50]

Meanwhile in Paris, the haven for heroes of defeated revolutions, the idea of an alliance and federation of eastern European nations, with or without French support, was coming to the fore. Poles, Russians, Italians, and others formed a fraternity in exile, into which the Roumanians were welcomed. Many of them were in close relations with Czartoryski.[51] Rosetti, Ion Brătianu, A. G. Golescu, and Voinescu often went to the home of Mickiewicz where they met Count Teleki, envoy of the Hungarian Government, the Russians Golovin and Sazonov, the Italians Tommaseo and Ricciardi, the Chilean Bilbao, many German radicals, and countless Poles.[52] An inner circle of friends, chiefly

---

50. P. P. Panaitescu, <u>Contribuţii la o biografie a lui N. Bălcescu</u>, p. 107.

51. Handelsman, <u>op.cit</u>., p. 104, note 2.

52. W. Mickiewicz, <u>Pamietniki</u>, vol. I, pp. 17-18, 67; <u>idem</u>, <u>Zywot Adama Mickiewicza</u>, vol. IV, (Posznan, 1895), pp. 226, 262; <u>idem</u>, <u>La Tribune des Peuples</u>, p. 47; N. P. Smochină, "Sur les emigrés roumains à Paris de 1850 a 1856," (<u>Mélanges de l'Ecole Roumaine en France</u>, XI, 1933, pp. 155-203), p. 159, 165; Marya Kasteraska, "Mickiewicz şi Românii," (<u>Propilee Literare</u>, Bucharest, IV, 1929), No. 2-3, p. 22.

faithful devotees of the Collège de France, met often at the home of Alfred Dumesnil. These meetings, at which Rosetti was always present, kept alive the romantic idealism and faith in mankind which they had not lost despite the rude shocks of the previous twelve months.[53]

Mickiewicz became editor-in-chief of a new journal La Tribune des Peuples, founded in March, 1849, "to defend the liberty of nationalities, Italy, Poland, Germany, Denmark, Spain, the Slavic countries, Hungary, and the Danubian provinces." Ion Brătianu and A. G. Golescu were contributing editors. Solidarity of peoples was its watchword; now at last the international democratic movement had an organ worthy of its ideals.[54] At the very start unbridgeable differences appeared; Mickiewicz's faith in the Bonaparte family's mission was too much for Herzen and the other distinguished contributors.[55] Despite high hopes and a wealth of editorial talent, the paper "turned out poor

---

53. Smochină, op.cit., pp. 159-61.

54. La Tribune des Peuples, No. 1, Mar. 13, 1849. Cf. Ladislas Mickiewicz, Preface to La Tribune des Peuples, (Paris, 1907), the collected articles of Adam Mickiewicz, p. 7; J. Tanski, Cinquante années d'exil, (Paris, 1880), vol. II, pp. 4-5.

55. The opening banquet turned into a fiasco when Mickiewicz's speech praised Louis Napoleon and attacked the Russian people, and Herzen refused to propose an answering toast. (Alexander Herzen, My Past and Thoughts, London, 1924, vol. III, pp. 33ff.; Pulszky, op.cit., vol. II, pp. 308-9; L. Mickiewicz, La Tribune des Peuples, pp. 9-17.

and feeble,...existing after a fashion until the 13th of June, when its disappearance was as little noticed as its existence."[56]

The Roumanians did not figure very prominently in the *Tribune's* columns. One article, describing their revolution, made the mistake of hinting the Suleman Pasha's benevolence had been bought, a charge which provoked an indignant denial by Voinescu.[57] An editorial on the treaty of Balta Liman told the Roumanians not to despair, for the old Europe was crumbling and the despots and the treaties of 1815 would soon be swept into oblivion by the virile forces of "young Europe."[58]

La Tribune des Peuples did little to give concrete form to its ideal of the solidarity of peoples. More effective was Cyprien Robert's *La Pologne*, devoted solely to the nationality question in eastern Europe.[59] Robert's guiding conception was vast and vague, the creation of a huge non-

---

56. Herzen, *loc.cit*.

57. *La Tribune des Peuples*, Apr. 7, 12, 1849.

58. *Ibid*., May 21, 1849.

59. Despite its name it did not confine its sympathies to the Poles. The original subtitle was *Journal des Slaves confédérés, Lekhites, Tchekhs, Illyriens, Bulgaro-Serbes et Ruthéniens, publication de la Société Slave de Paris*. This was contracted and made more intelligible in the third issue, Nov. 1, 1848, to *Organe des intérêts fédéraux des Slaves de Pologne, de Bohême, de Hongrie et d'Orient*.

Russian Slavic confederation, with the surrounded and outnumbered non-Slavic nations (Magyars and Roumanians) as junior partners. Roumanian interests were not ignored; the few issues of the Journal in 1848 spoke of them as members of the future confederation of fifty million "Slavs and friends of Slavs" inhabiting Poland, Bohemia, Hungary, Moldo-Wallachia and Turkey."[60]

The early numbers of La Pologne were hostile to the Magyars, calling Hungary an "antique annex" of the rotting Habsburg Empire and denouncing their war against the Slavs, who, with the Roumanians as worthy allies, were trying to transform Austria into a federation of free peoples.[61] The events of the spring of 1849 changed this, for the new despotic and centralizing policy of the Vienna Cabinet seemed to leave the Slavs and Roumanians only one way out, a united defense of nationality with Turkey if possible, and even with the hated Magyars. News of the Magyar victories and the role of the Polish generals stimulated the belief that the Poles could act as mediators between the Magyars and the Slavs and Roumanians, so that all national forces

---

60. No Magyar or Roumanian was active on the paper at this time. In the lists of members of the society there are 121 Poles, 11 Frenchmen, 10 "Bohêmes," 9 Bulgarians, 5 Serbs, 1 Croat, 1 Ruthene, and 1 Italian. (La Pologne, Nos. 1, 2, June, July, 1848).

61. La Pologne, Nos. 3, 4, 5, Nov., 1848–Jan. 1849, esp. H. Desprez, "Les Valaques et leur alliance avec les Slaves du midi," (No. 4, p. 16).

might be united against the reaction. Czartoryski and his "diplomatic service" had been working for just such a reconciliation.[62] Robert took up the idea and repeated it again and again. "If Kossuth would only offer some guarantees, the Roumanians and Slavs would a hundred times rather be with the Magyars than with Austria." The war of race had become a war of principle.[63]

La Tribune des Peuples also favored a war of peoples against the reaction, and proposed a Hungarian-Turkish alliance as the best way to save the Principalities from Russia and Hungary from Austria.[64] It remained vague on Hungary's nationality policy and did not even mention the key problem of Transylvania. Bataillard's articles in Le Temps showed that his Roumanian friends in Paris shared the views of La Pologne. They wanted Hungary to win the war, but only if the Roumanians in Transylvania were given equality of status.

> "We sincerely desire the triumph of the Magyar nationality....But we seize upon this moment to remind the Magyars of their past mistakes; we advise them to be more conciliatory, more just toward

---

62. Handelsman, op.cit., pp. 112-4. Robert took up the idea and repeated it again and again (La Pologne, No. 7, Mar. 1- No. 14, May 13, 1849, pp. 25, 28, 34, 40, 43, 50, 53, 56-7). A brochure of Czartoryski on the same point published in Nov. 1848, mentioned on p. 27. Handelsman (p. 97) says that Czartoryski put up the money for La Pologne.

63. La Pologne, Nos. 10, 11, Apr. 15, 22, 1849)

64. La Tribune des Peuples, Apr. 7, 22, May 21, 1849.

> the nationalities which inhabit their country.... We demand that the Magyars recognize that these peoples have the same rights that they [the Magyars] are winning for themselves by their victories....Their triumph is at this price. Let us hope that Kossuth will understand that." 65

Emigré groups in Paris were thrilled at the news of Bem's capture of Hermannstadt. Bataillard, without naming his source, published long passages of a letter from Grant to Rosetti describing the victory.[66] Rumors said that Bem had dedicated himself to bringing the Transylvanian Roumanians into an "intimate alliance" with Hungary; that Magyars, Slavs, Saxons, and Roumanians had become totally reconciled and were all fighting, an army of free men opposing a Habsburg and Russian army of slaves.[67] An article in La Pologne suggested that the new Magyar-Roumanian understanding in Transylvania might be extended:

> "These Roumanians, whipped up by their leaders, do not want to limit themselves to defending their own territory; they dream of going to the aid of their Moldo-Wallachian brothers, to help the Turks to put an end to the Russian protectorate. These dispositions electrify all the Daco-Roumanian populations as far as Bessarabia and are appreciated by the Ottoman Cabinet...." 68

---

65. Le Temps, Apr. 12, 19, 1849. See also his articles in the issues of May 23, 24, June 2. (Boltoș, op.cit., pp. 82-3, 111-2, 118-9).

66. Le Temps, Apr. 13, 1849.

67. La Tribune des Peuples, Apr. 22, 1849; La Pologne, Apr. 22, May 6, June 24, 1849.

68. La Pologne, No. 13, May 6, 1849. See also Auguste S...., "De la diplomatie européenne dans les principautés

The main line of argument in this whole campaign, based on rumors of what was happening in Hungary, was that there should be a vast insurrection of peoples, of which Pest and Constantinople would be the centers, while Vienna and St. Petersburg would pay the bills. It did not seem to occur to these people that Turkish and Hungarian statesmen might hesitate, with some justification, to place themsleves at the head of any such holy war of nationalities for Pest and Constantinople might not come out of the mêlée without having to foot some of the largest bills themselves.

Ladislas Teleki, Kossuth's representative in Paris, was ready and willing to come to an agreement with the Serbs and Roumanians on the basis of mutual respect for nationality and a common front against Austria and Russia. He was devoted to Czartoryski, whose views on the nationality question he adopted, including the principle of national self-determination, application of which would threaten the existence of historic Hungary.[69]

---

du Danube," (*ibid*., No. 11, Apr. 22, 1849, first summarizing the arguments of the *Mémoire justificatif*, then charging the Turks and Magyars to gather round them all the nationalities in a great struggle for liberty. Cf. *Le Temps*, May 5, 1849.

69. Teleki's letters to Pulszky, Apr.-Sept., 1849, in Pulszky, *Meine Zeit, mein Leben*, vol. II, pp. 356-91, *passim*. Pulszky calls Teleki's ideas "höchst phantastisch" and says they were not shared by other leading Hungarians.

The official Hungarian theory about the civil war between Magyars and subject nationalities was that the responsibility lay not with the Magyars, who from the start had granted equal rights, nor with the subject nationalities, who were forced into opposition by the intrigues of the Vienna camarilla and by the interference of "Serbs and Wallachs from the other side of the frontiers, motivated by a blind jealousy."[70] Whether or not that was Teleki's personal opinion, he was willing to concede to the other nationalities the equality of status which they were demanding. He saw that, because of their numbers, the future lay with the Slavs, and that the Magyars were counting certain defeat by not conciliating them.[71]

When Rieger, the Czech leader, arrived in Paris, the stage was set for the negotiation of the great reconciliation and federation of nationalities. On May 18th at the Hotel

---

70. Teleki to Czartoryski, Mar. 7, 1849, published in Max Schlesinger, The War in Hungary, 1848-1849, (London, 1850), vol. II, pp. 329-34. The same letter, dated March 9th and signed by Szarvady, Teleki's subordinate, was sent to Count Zamoyski at Constantinople as "the official opinion of the Hungarian Government and particularly of the Magyars." (Ghica, Amintiri, pp. 179-85). Kossuth and other leaders in Hungary shared the idea that the Wallachian revolutionaries, working for a Daco-Roumanian kingdom, had stirred up the Transylvanian Roumanians against the Magyars. (Bălcescu, Scrisori către Ion Ghica, pp. 45,55).

71. Pulszky, op.cit., vol. II, p. 330.

Lambert there was a long conference between the representatives of the Hungarian Government (Teleki, Pulszky, Szarvady) on the one hand, and Czartoryski and Rieger, representing the nationalities of the Austrian Empire, on the other. Reports of what actually took place at this meeting are conflicting. Pulszky and Rieger later denied that any agreement was made,[72] but a copy of the procès-verbal was preserved by Ion Ghica and published in his memoirs. The agreement recognized the deposition of the House of Habsburg and demanded that Austria be replaced by

---

72. Pulszky (pp. 330-1), writing thirty years later and trying to show that he disapproved negotiating with the Roumanians over Transylvania, tells only of a heated argument with Rieger over Slovakia, and calls the whole meeting a comedy, for, after all, "Teleki and I were not the Kingdom of Hungary and Rieger was not Bohemia." Rieger, in a letter later in 1849, denied that he had entered into any agreement, and says that he argued in favor of a Habsburg-ruled Austria based on equality of nationalities, opposing the Hungarian plan. But in the meantime Austrian police had intercepted a copy of the agreement intended for Kossuth, and Rieger, to avoid arrest on his return, was going out of his way to prove his loyalty to Austria. However, in another letter he mentioned the document and blamed Teleki for signing it without authority from his government. "Teleki and Pulszky to not come out of the affair with clean hands." (Jan Heidler, ed., Přispěvsky k listářy Dra Frant. Lad. Riegra, Prague, 1924, pp. 54-67). Cf. the copy published in Die Presse, Vienna, Sept. 6, 1849, and Journal des Débats, Paris, Sept. 13, 1849; Hübner to Schwarzenberg, Sept. 13, cit. E. Horvath, "Törekvesek Magyarorszag federalizalasara, 1848-49," (A Haborus Felelösseg, Budapest, I, 1928-9, pp. 234-52), pp. 243-6; idem, "A magyar kormany nemzetisegi politikaja 1848-49ban," (ibid., II, 1930-1, pp. 15-38), p. 26, indicating that one of the Golescus was present at the meeting.

a strong federal state made up of the Czechs and Jugoslavs from the hereditary lands,[73] and of the peoples of a federalized Hungary which would maintain the Crown of St. Stephen as the only link between its national units. "Nationalities well defined by the limits of the territory they occupy and by their traditions of separate existence, Croatia, the Voivodina and the Roumanians," would be given complete autonomy. It was agreed that the Hungarian Diet should formulate these declarations in a solemn and official act, and that the non-Magyar peoples of Hungary should accept them and immediately turn their efforts and their arms against the common enemy, the Austrian-Russian coalition.[74]

The editors of La Pölogne took cognizance of the agreement by putting out a new journal, L'Orient Européen, "devoted to the cause of the emancipation, progress, and confederation of all the Slavic and non-Slavic peoples of eastern Europe." The second number prescribed federalism

---

73. "The Bohemians, Moravians, Silesians, and Illyrians," leaving the Poles to a future Poland, the Italians to Italy, and the Germans to a Greater Germany.

74. Ghica, Amintiri, pp. 396-402. Ghica's copy probably reached him through Czaika or Zamoyski. E. Horvath states (Slavonic Review, XII, 1934, p. 631) that a copy reached Hungary and that the Diet voted the Law of Nationalities of July 21 (sic) on the basis of it. But the Law did not admit the principle of federalism, allowed only cultural and limited administrative autonomy. It was based on a draught project of Bälcescu and Murgu, accepted by Kossuth.

for Hungary in the exact words of the agreement of May 18th.[75] *La Pologne* itself began to talk less of Slavism and more of the Magyar-Slav-Roumanian problem. The articles in *L'Orient Européen* were for the most part abridgements of longer articles in *La Pologne*.[76]

Treaties and editorials written in Paris did not change the actual situation in Hungary. Teleki did not speak for Kossuth, and Czartoryski, though he was probably authorized to speak for the Roumanian emigrés in Paris, did not represent Avram Iancu, the leader of the Transylvanians, who, far from being ready to join a crusade against the Russians, was grimly intent on carrying on the war of mutual extermination with the Hungarians.[77]

If reconciliation and common action were ever to be realized, the agreement would have to be negotiated not in Paris, but directly between Kossuth and the nationalities. That was the job assumed by Bălcescu, who was sincerely anxious for a Roumanian-Hungarian alliance. He thought it "a great misfortune" that his Transylvanian brothers had been giving aid and comfort to the reaction. "The sentiment of nationality," he had noted on his previous

---

75. *L'Orient Européen*, Paris, Nos. 1, 2, June 1, July 1, 1849.

76. *La Pologne*, 2e. année, Nos. 1-5, May 27-June 24, 1849.

77. I. Lupaş, "Avram Iancu," (*Anuarul Institutului de Istoria Naţională*, III, 1924-5, pp. 1-62), p. 25.

visit in December 1848, "has had for the cause of liberty very unfortunate effects."[78] He hoped to correct this by persuading Iancu to adopt at least a neutral attitude toward the Hungarians. To do that he would have to get real guarantees from Kossuth. He wanted also to create a Roumanian legion which should fight alongside the Magyars or invade Wallachia.[79] In this way he hoped to give "a better and higher direction to the movement of the Transylvanian Roumanians which until then had been "not at all national."[80] It broke his heart when he saw the "brave Hungarians and their enthusiasm" and thought of the sorry ("prost") role which the Roumanians had played.[81]

On May 19th he had a talk with General Bem, who,

---

78. Bălcescu to Ghica, Dec. 28, 1848, Scrisori, p. 10.

79. The earlier plans, concocted by Bălcescu and Ghica and entertained by Magheru and others, of a combined force of Transylvanians and Wallachian refugees invading the Principalities, with Hungary's blessing, had fallen through. The refugees had been considered by the Austrians as "dangerous republicans" and were kept under observation in Saxon cities and towns. (Lupaş, Avram Iancu, p. 41). As a matter of fact, they were, according to Bălcescu, "making republican and anti-Russian propaganda." (Scrisori, p. 15; cf. the report of Zablocki, in Panaitescu, Emigraţia Polonă, pp. 81-3; Ghica, Amintiri, pp. 62, 187-8, 211-2, Magheru to Kossuth, Mar. 29, 1849, in Regnault, Histoire politique et sociale des Principautés, pp. 486-8).

80. Bălcescu to A. G. Golescu, May 13, 1849, cit. Panaitescu, Contribuţii la o biografie a lui Bălcescu, p. 107.

81. Bălcescu to Ghica, May 12, 1849, Scrisori, p. 35.

although well disposed, said that he was but a soldier and could not take the responsibility of political decisions; yet he did promise to go ahead with the creation of a legion, saying that within ten days he could get together two thousand Roumanians.[82] As for officers, Bălcescu hoped to find them among the refugees from Wallachia, but Bem was sceptical. Ghica tried to solve this problem by contracting with Czaika for the services of three Polish officers.[83]

Bălcescu found Kossuth at Debreczin, the temporary seat of the Hungarian Government, on the 28th of May. He was quite satisfied with his welcome, characterizing the Hungarian leader as enlightened, distinguished, and an "homme de bien." Kossuth, he wrote to Ghica, accepted wholeheartedly the idea of a confederation and promised to form a Roumanian legion.[84] That Kossuth took the legion

---

82. Ibid., pp. 38-9.

83. Ghica, Amintiri, p. 403. A. G. Golescu suggested Magheru, who remained in Trieste and did nothing. (Ibid., pp. 207-15). Bălcescu hoped some of the boys from Paris would come to fight: "Ecrivez à tous ceux (sic) Mess. de Paris. Expliquez leur la politique que nous voulons soutenir ici et dites que ostaşii se vie în Ungaria." (Bălcescu to Ghica, May 9, 1849, Scrisori, p. 28). Rosetti, Ion Brătianu, and A. G. Golescu thought seriously of going but then discovered better reasons for staying in Paris. (Rosetti, Note intime, vol. II, p. 45-55; Cretzianu, op.cit., vol. II, p. 211; Ghica, Amintiri, pp. 233-4).

84. Bălcescu to Ghica, May 29, 1849, Scrisori, pp. 42-6.

idea seriously is shown in a letter to Bem, whom he apprised of his agreement with Bălcescu and assigned to work out the details. He said it was "a very important matter," because in case of an invasion of Wallachia, the Roumanian battalion could be the advance guard to prove that the Hungarians came as friends and liberators.[85] The "confederation" which Kossuth accepted was an alliance of Danubian states (Hungary, Moldavia, Wallachia, Serbia), and not of peoples, for Kossuth and Batthyanyi insisted, and Bălcescu agreed, that the integrity of Hungary should be maintained. Diplomatic wheels were immediately set in motion to create this alliance and to secure Turkish and British consent to it. Bălcescu offered to Kossuth the services of the Roumanian emigrés in Constantinople and in Paris, and his suggestion that Andrassy, Hungarian envoy

---

85. "Jetzt etwas sehr wichtiges, Herr Feldmarschalleutnant! Die Herren Golesco (sic) und Bolliak, Emigranten aus der Walachie, tragen mir an, eine walachische Legion zu ...formieren. Ich nahm es in Prinzip an....Ich empfehle sie, die Sache ist sehr wichtig, sollten Sie in die Walachei vorrücken (was mir erwünscht wäre), da sollte dieser Bataillon die Avantgarde bilden, der Erfolg wäre unberechenbar....In der Proclamation erachte ich fur sehr nötig, dass gesagt werde, wir kommen als Freunde der Türken und Walachen, um sie vom Drucke der Russen zu befreien. Die Turken befolgen eine zweideutige Politik. Il faut le compromettre!" (Kossuth to Bem, July 9, 1849, Lupaş, Avram Iancu, pp. 51-2; also quoted in Die magyarische Revolution, Kurzgefasste Schilderung der jüngsten Zeitereignisse in Ungarn und Siebenbürgen, von einem Augenzeugen, 2nd. ed., Pest, 1850, pp. 230-4, giving the names as "Herren Bolexes und Bolliak." "Bolexes" was Bălcescu.

in Constantinople, communicate with the Porte through Ghica, was accepted, since Andrassy was having trouble getting into even unofficial contact with the Turks; Kossuth also asked him to instruct the Roumanian agents in London and Paris to defend the Hungarian cause. Bălcescu, in turn, sent his messages to Ghica by way of Andrassy, with the co-operation of Hungarian officials.[86]

Andrassy's instructions were to win over the Ottoman Government to active support, and "to appeal both to governments and to the peoples."[87] On his way to Constantinople Andrassy had negotiated with Garašanin at Belgrade, for Kossuth for military reasons, considered an agreement with the Serbs more important than one with the Roumanian exiles, who controlled no territory and no army. Nothing definite was signed, but Andrassy reported that Garašanin sincerely favored an alliance with Hungary.[88] Bălcescu, for his part, hoped for little from the Serbs. Their movement, he thought, had "disappeared," because of their fighting with and for Austria.[89] He wrote to Golescu in

---

86. Bălcescu, Scrisori, pp. 47, 50-51; S. Dragomir, "N. Bălcescu în Ardeal," (Anuarul Institutului de Istoria Natională, V, 1928-30, pp. 1-34), p. 21.

87. Eduard Wertheimer, Graf Julius Andrassy, Sein Leben und seine Zeit, (Stuttgart, 1910-13), vol. I, pp. 20, 26.

88. Andrassy to Batthyanyi, June 11, 1849, Horvath, "Origins of the Crimean War," South Eastern Affairs, VII, pp. 193-4; Wertheimer, op.cit., vol. I, pp. 24-6.

89. Bălcescu to Ghica, May 8, 1849, Scrisori, p. 23.

Paris:

> "I sympathized with the Slavs last year, when their struggle had no other character than to emancipate them from Magyar domination, remaining with them in a confederation. But from the moment when, betraying their national movement, they became satellites of despotism...and were ready to call in Russian help, I had no further sympathy with them." 90

We have no record of negotiations between Andrassy and Ghica or of their attempt to persuade the Turks to favor the proposed federation.[91] The Turks were sympathetic and might have been persuaded, but Palmerston strongly pressed neutrality upon them and said that in case of war Turkey would not get British support.[92]

In London were Pulszky and D. Brătianu, each trying to blow his own nation's horn in the press and in official circles. Brătianu seems to have done nothing to push the idea of a federation of Danubian states; Pulszky, on the other hand, used it as a talking point in favor of British support for Hungary, for such a federation would be a unit of great-power strength and a substitute for Austria in the

---

90. Bălcescu to A. G. Golescu, May 13, 1849, cit. Panaitescu, *Contribuţii la o biografie a lui N. Bălcescu*, p. 107. Bălcescu had a real fear of Panslavism, which made the Magyar alliance seem all the more necessary. (*Ibid.*, p. 96).

91. Ghica, usually a better judge of men, considered Andrassy "a man of little capacity," and probably relations between them were not very close. (Ghica, *Amintiri*, p. 334).

92. Palmerston to Canning, June 26, July 2, 7, 26, F.O. 78, vols. 771, 772.

European equilibrium. The British Government, early in June, knew about Kossuth's plan of "a federated republic upon the plan of the United States of America," including Hungary and "some of the Turkish provinces."[93] Palmerston was inclined to favor the idea of a strong federation of virile nations replacing the "European China," whose future was problematical and whose methods he detested. The plan was too nebulous, however, and Kossuth's régime was by that time on its last legs.[94]

There is nothing to show that Brătianu co-operated with Pulszky in London, although both traveled in the same circles and were guided by Dudley Stuart. The Hungarian Propaganda

---

93. D. J. Vipan to Pulszky, June 7, 1849, South Eastern Affairs, VII, pp. 186-7. Horvath ("Kossuth and Palmerston," Slavonic Review, IX, 1931, p. 622) says the British must have heard of the May 18th Paris agreement, since Kossuth made no federation proposals before his exile. But he did agree with Bălcescu on the desirability of a federation, and a circular letter of Batthyanyi in June shows that he was aiming at an alliance with neighboring states, and Batthyanyi's letter to Pulszky, dated July 14th, tells the latter to suggest to the British Government a scheme whereby "Turkey, the Turkish protectorates and Hungary" might be formed into a union of states (Staatsverband), of which the Sultan should be the nominal chief. (Pulszky, op.cit., vol. II, pp. 396-410).

94. Vipan to Pulszky, June 7, 8, 1849, South Eastern Affairs, VII, pp. 186-8; Palmerston to Magenis, July 2, 1849, F.O. 7, vol. 364, publ. ibid., p. 209; Pulszky to Batthyanyi, July 16, 1949, cit. D. A. Janossy, "Great Britain and Kossuth," (Archivum Europae centro-orientalis Budapest, III, 1937, pp. 53-190), p. 75; Sproxton, op.cit., pp. 581-63; Greer, op.cit., p. 302; Horvath, Kossuth and Palmerston, pp. 623-5; idem, Russia and the Hungarian Revolution, p. 642.

Committee, of which Stuart and Birkbeck were members, discussed at length the federation question and publicized it in the press.[95] Pulszky was neither pro-Roumanian nor enthusiastic over planning dream-worlds with the exiles of other nationalities, especially as he represented an existing government and they nothing but their own hopes.[96] Brătianu, for his part, was not partial to Hungarians even in time of need.

Bălcescu noted in Hungarian circles and particularly among the Polish volunteers, a fairly widespread opinion that the Magyars could win the war only by granting full equality to the Slavs and Roumanians.[97] Dembinski, with

---

95. Horvath, Kossuth and Palmerston, p. 624; idem, South Eastern Affairs, VII, pp. 190-6.

96. Pulszky, op.cit., vol. II, pp. 307, 331, 335. He does mention the presence of Roumanian emigrés in London, and speaks of having met "the Golescos and the Bratianos" in Paris in March, though only Ion was there then. Both Dumitru and Ion were in London in May.
 Roumanians and Hungarians had been propagating the Danubian federation idea in the Paris press, but hurling insults at each other in the process. See the article by "Un Hongrois" in La Réforme, Feb. 24, 1849, and the reply by "Un Roumain," ibid., Mar. 3, comparing the "feeble and aristocratic" Hungarian revolution with the glorious democratic revolution of Bucharest. Also Pulszky's article in Le Constitutionnel, Feb. 25, advocating an "Austrian" confederation including Serbia and the Principalities. Pulszky was displeased at the pro-Roumanian articles in the French press, especially those of Desprez in the Revue des Deux Mondes. (W. Sandford to Pulszky, Mar. 8, 1849, and Vipan to Pulszky, June 18, 1849, South Eastern Affairs, pp. 77-8, 196).

97. Bălcescu to Ghica, June 3, 1849, Scrisori, p. 47.

whom Bălcescu was very friendly, was trying unsuccessfully to make Kossuth see things in that light, and Bem who posed as dictator of Transylvania was eager to be rid of the opposition of Iancu's men, whom he could not subdue and who immobilized many of his troops needed elsewhere.[98] This was exactly what Kossuth did not propose to grant. If the Paris agreement of May 18th ever reached him, he paid no attention to it. Ghica sent word of it to Bălcescu in June, saying that he thought the Magyars were not obligated to grant at the very least the concessions provided by it. Ghica meanwhile used it as a basis for a confederation plan of his own, to include Hungary, Transylvania, the Banat, and Wallachia.[99] Kossuth explained his position to Bălcescu, and even more clearly in a letter to Iancu:

---

98. For the military aspects, see Radu Rosetti, "Un episod din anii 1848-49 în Transilvania: Apararea Munților Apuseni în primăvară și vară anului 1849," (<u>Anuarul Institutului de Istoria Națională</u>, IV, 1926-7, pp. 81-118. For Bem's attitude and projects, see S. Wedkiewicz, "General Bem a ruchy wolnosciowe Rumunow," (<u>Przeględ Wspolczeeny</u>, Cracow, 1928, pp. 143-7); A. Lewak, <u>Dzieje emigracji polskiej w Turcji</u>, (Warsaw, 1935), p. 60. Bălcescu wrote to Iancu suggesting he come to terms with Bem and encourage him to place himself at the head of a movement "more Roumanian, or purely Transylvanian without reference to nationality," in case of the defeat of the Hungarian Government. (Balcescu to Ghica, July 1, 1849, <u>Scrisori</u>, p. 90). Boliac promised Bem a more brilliant career, perhaps even a crown, if he would come over to the Roumanians and chase the Russians out of Wallachia. (<u>Ibid</u>., p. 105; Lukasik, <u>Pologne et Roumanie</u>, p. 89).

99. Ghica, <u>Amintiri</u>, pp. 333-4.

> "Political nationality can be understood only on the basis of a delimited territory, a country can have only the territory, on which there may be any number of languages and religions, and if we want liberty, every one of us, without regard to language or religion, must be equal in right, in law, and in liberty; but to divide a country according to the languages spoken in it and to accord to each part a distinct political nationality on a distinct territory means to destroy that country, to dissolve it....But perhaps the Roumanians have in view, although not clearly, the idea of a federation. Hungary might federate with Wallachia, Serbia, etc. However, within itself, that is to say with the citizen inhabitants of its own body, it cannot enter into a federation. That would be an absurdity."[100]

A sincere entente, or even a working agreement was impossible, in view of the irreconcilable differences over Transylvania. While he would not admit it to Kossuth, Bălcescu regarded that province as destined eventually to be part of a greater Roumania, even though as a practical expedient, he felt it necessary to tell the Transylvanians to remain for the present within Hungary, "even in a position of slight inferiority," otherwise the only one to profit would be the Tsar." "Sacrifices would be imposed in the present in order to gain advantages in the future....The Roumanians...should realize that they cannot rise from slavery to be the masters in one jump."[101] Kossuth was naturally reluctant to make concessions which he knew would lead only to more demands. He said that he could

---

100. Kossuth to Iancu, July 5, 1849, Dragomir, op.cit.,p. 26.

101. Bălcescu to Ghica, June 6, 1849, Scrisori, pp. 57-8.

understand the desire to incorporate Transylvania in a Roumania, but that of course he could not allow it. The claims to "recognition of nationality" he said he could neither understand nor take seriously.

> "They suffered in the past from Magyar nobility and from the Germans, but now when we liberal Magyars give them freedom from that oppression, they rise in arms against us and ally with the Germans and the Russians, who are your enemies as well as ours." 102

Kossuth had on his side all the best arguments of mid-century liberalism. But the fact was that those principles had not obliterated national lines in eastern Europe, and it was absurd to claim that all citizens of the Hungarian state were equal in practice as well as in theory.

Batthyanyi, the Foreign Minister, was even more stiff-necked than Kossuth. To Bălcescu's proposals for recognition of the Roumanian nationality, use of the Roumanian language in petitions and laws, bi-lingual schools, etc., he replied that they were not in consonance with two fundamental principles on which there could be no compromise: the unity of the Hungarian state and the supremacy of the Magyar element. He even said that he favored a Magyarization of the other

---

102. Ibid., p. 45. Iancu, like Kossuth, based his argument on liberty, equality, and fraternity, "which have penetrated our soul as deeply as those of other nations which up to now have seen more of the light of liberty." (Iancu to the Hungarians, July 15, 1849, Lupas, Avram Iancu, pp. 52-5).

nationalities.[103]

No common love of "liberty" could bridge this gap. At times Bălcescu was almost ready to give up:

> "I myself despair, and I no longer believe there is any way of reconciling these two nations. You cannot reason with the hate, revenge, fanaticism, national pride, and bitterness of them both. The greatest guilt of the Hungarians. Now it is late. Fate has run its course. Both nations have dragged each other into the grave."[104]

The spectacle of seeing two nationalities, one of them his own at each other's throats, and with no apparent way to blame it on the intrigues of the Tsar, was enough to break the heart of this romantic revolutionary who had believed in a new era of brotherhood of free peoples.

It was the desperate military situation which finally forced Kossuth into an agreement. Iancu was a thorn in the Hungarian side that would have to be removed if there was to be any real defence against the Austrians and Russians.[105] On July 14th Batthyanyi issued a decree giving the nationalities the concessions they wanted. After ratification by

103. Bălcescu to Ghica, June 27, 1849, Scrisori, p. 76; Ghica, Amintiri, pp. 293-8.

104. Bălcescu to Ghica, June 31, 1849, Scrisori, p. 86; cf. ibid., pp. 10, 55, 83.

105. The Russian general Lüders, later paid tribute to the help he got from the Transylvanian Roumanians: "Their union with the Hungarians would probably have put a different face on the insurrection....Without Yanco, I could not have succeeded." (Eugène Poujade, Chrétiens et Turcs, Paris, 1862, p. 305).

the Diet, the nationalities were to have a recognized status, use of their own language in communes and districts where they formed a majority, full freedom of religious organization, and other less important concessions. This was accompanied by official acceptance of the "Project of Pacification" which Bălcescu had submitted and the order for the formation of a Roumanian legion at Cluj.[106]

Bălcescu's joy was so great that he forgot how critical was the military situation which he had not hesitated, a short while before, to call very bad indeed. He waxed lyrical in describing the new turn of events:

> "Ghica, dear Ghica, kneel and give thanks to God, our country will be saved. I come from seeing Kossuth. That which I scarcely dared to dream will be fulfilled. Bem has beaten the Muscovites at Bistrița and has chased them out; now he has gone to Brașov and next it will be into Wallachia. I have seen his dispatches. Omer Pasha will be won over with money; and so it will happen. Imagine my joy when Kossuth proposed to me that Iancu and his whole army be sent into Great Wallachia. It is necessary, he said, that all the Roumanians of Transylvania and the Banat go to save the Principalities, where lies the foundation of Roumanian nationality. Thus, in a short while, together with

---

106. These measures were all drawn up previously by Balcescu, used as a model for the Serb demands, and taken over by Kossuth. See Ghica, Amintiri, pp. 371-84; Bălcescu, Scrisori, pp. 68-70; Bystrzanowski to Czaika, June 23, 1849, in Panaitescu, Emigrația Polonă, p. 117. See also D. Iranyi et C.L. Chassin, Histoire politique de la Révolution de Hongrie, (Paris, 1859), vol. I, pp. 357-60; E. Horvath, Modern Hungary, (Budapest, 1922), p. 125; O. Jaszi, Dissolution of the Habsburg Monarchy, (Chicago, 1929), pp. 310-11, and the Hungarian references cited in those works.

> Bem, I shall enter Great Wallachia with a great force, and eight million Roumanians will have risen against the Muscovites....Kossuth is in truth a great man. Now I believe that the cause of liberty will conquer. Never have I been so happy as at this moment." 107

Needless to say, his happiness was not of long duration. He left immediately for the mountains of Transylvania to present the proposals to Iancu, who was not easily persuaded that the Russians were his real enemies. After three days of talking he agreed to remain neutral unless attacked and was induced to make a friendly reference to the "Hungarian brothers." The Roumanian legion would have been too much for him to swallow, and Bălcescu discreetly made no mention of it.[108]

Meanwhile Bem made his long-heralded invasion of the Principalities, crossing the mountains into Moldavia. Though he had no Roumanian legion, he came as a "friend and liberator." His proclamation called upon the people to rise against the Russians, assuring them of support from Hungary and Turkey.[109] A Russian functionary at Jassy

---

107. Bălcescu to Ghica, July 14, 1849, Scrisori, pp. 106-8.

108. Dragomir, N. Bălcescu în Ardeal, pp. 27-9.

109. Text of his first proclamation in Ghica, Amintiri, pp. 392-3, and Anon., Die magyarische Revolution, kurzgefasste Schilderung, pp. 234-5. Second proclamation, same text, but issued five days later (July 24th) published in Lupaş, Avram Iancu, p. 52; cf. J. Czetz, Bems Feldzug in Siebenbürgen, (Hamburg, 1850), p. 338; P. Korn, Neueste Chronik der Magyaren, (Hamburg, 1852), vol. II, pp. 94-5.

reported "incredible alarm" in the city, since there were "thousands of rascals just waiting to turn on us if Bem triumphs."[110] This event aroused the greatest enthusiasm in Paris, as had Bem's victories in March. It was predicted that the Roumanians would proclaim a revolutionary government and spread a vast insurrection over all provinces where the Roumanian language was spoken. If the Turks shirked their duty and failed to help, the Roumanians would declare their independence, following the example of Hungary.[111] This was misplaced optimism. The Moldavians failed to revolt, and the Turks told the Hungarians to go back where they came from.[112]

Bălcescu hurried back to Kossuth with Iancu's answer. By this time it was early August, the enemy armies were closing in, and both knew that the game was up. Bălcescu's dream was shattered. He tried, in true romantic style, to end his life on the battlefield in a blaze of glory fighting with the remnants of the Hungarian army, but even that was denied him. Sought by the Austrian police as a collaborator of Kossuth, and by the Hungarians as a friend of Iancu, he had to flee to the mountains, where he spent

---

110. Averbukh, op.cit., p. 152.

111. La Pologne, 2e. année, No. 12, Aug. 12, 1849; Le Temps, Aug. 6, 1849, Boltoş, op.cit., p. 127.

112. M. Popescu, Documente inedite privitoare la Istoria Transilvaniei, (Bucharest, 1929), pp. 90-3.

a month in hiding with Iancu's soldiers, then made his way to Paris.

3. Problems of organization and doctrine

Probably a psychologist could make a truer estimate of the activities of a group of political exiles than a specialist in any other field. Many otherwise unaccountable facts might take on meaning to one who could really penetrate the state of mind and spirit of his subjects. Certainly the sharp changes of principle, the pursuit of impossible ends, the chronic inability to get along with others, can be partially attributed to a mental state unknown to those who have not personally experienced a period of exile. Living in the past, with its shattered ideals and its failures, and in the future, with its uncertainties and ever-receding hopes, and rarely in the present, which nevertheless thrust itself roughly upon them, the Roumanian emigrés left a mottled record of courage and meanness, of accomplishment and failure.

Ion Ghica hesitated before publishing in his memoirs a rich collection of letters dating from the period of exile, so filled were they with the mutual suspicious, accusations, and invective of the revered national heroes toward one another. Wisely, he decided to let history profit and reputations suffer.

> "The exile, far from his native land, separated from his family and all the affectionate associations of his childhood, lives in want and privation, scarcely tolerated in the land where he has been able to find a melancholy refuge, his spirit embittered and his heart hardened; he believes himself persecuted, betrayed, spied upon; he becomes suspicious, rancorous and unjust." 1

Behind all their quarrels, there was a re-examination of the national question. Theorizing and political thinking accompanied factionalism. Eliade, mouthpiece of the emigration's right wing and self-styled personification of the "legitimate" Wallachian revolution, contributed little. He was deserted by all except one follower in Paris, Grădișteanu, and a handful of adherents in Brusa, where the refugees who had fled to Turkey were interned. His two principles, raised from the level of tactics to dogma, were loyalty to the Sultan and insistence on the autonomy of Wallachia. Roumanian unity, he said, was an ultimate ideal, but since put forth by Russia, it was impracticable and poisonous.[2] These views were intolerably narrow to those who had in the year of revolution seen wider perspectives opening up before them.

At the other extreme were the Reds, the Brătianu

---

1. Ion Ghica, Amintiri din Pribegia după 1848, p. 5.

2. Letters to the refugees at Brusa, in Ghica, Amintiri pp. 674-707; Eliade Rădulescu, Epistole și Acte ale Oamenilor mișcării române din 1848, (Paris, 1851), pp. 27-41; idem, Mémoires sur l'histoire de la régénération roumaine, pp. 242, 403-4.

brothers and C. A. Rosetti, supported by Boliac and a group of younger students. They stuck to faith in democracy and the revolution, as they had learned it at the Collège de France and tried to practise it at Bucharest. They accepted the current simplified interpretation of all political developments as phases of the conflict between the revolution (good) and the reaction (evil), with an optimistic belief in the imminence of the triumph of the former. The struggle being European, the initiative lay with France; they therefore associated closely with the representatives of the revolution in France (the Montagne) and with the exiles of other nations who were gathered in Paris and London waiting for the general revolution to break out. They were members of a masonic lodge, Fraternité des Peuples, composed of Poles, Hungarians, Greeks, and others.[3]

France remained their guiding star, even though their "true France" of Michelet's lectures and of February, 1848, was hidden behind the figure of Louis Napoleon. The faith in the Montagne was not uncritical. D. Brătianu bitterly denounced its betrayal of its own child, the harmonious revolution of 1848.[4] The coup d'état was of course a

---

3. N.P. Smochină, Sur les émigrés roumains à Paris, p. 193, note.

4. A fragment of it published in Cretzianu, Din Arhiva lui Dumitru Brătianu, vol. I, pp. 193-7. Brătianu included the entire text in a letter to Michelet, Apr. 28, 1850, Bibliothèque de la Ville de Paris, Papiers Michelet, K. 2. 11, No. 12, published by I. Breazu, Michelet si Românii, pp. 143-57.

blow to them, though not unexpected. "Before December 2nd. the world was full of hope and the monarchs trembled; after it the latter were revived."[5]

Their relations with Quinet and Michelet became closer. The faith was still strong; failure had not brought disillusionment.[6] D. Brătianu, while in London in 1850, wrote to Michelet some incredibly long letters, in which he poured out his love for France, (his "religion," "the soul of the world"), his anguish at her sufferings, shared by the Roumanians; he sang the glories of the revolution of 1848, and praised France for not coming to the aid of the rest of Europe, for the nationalities were thus forced to rely on their own resources and to learn union and brotherhood by bitter experience; he wrote also at great length about Roumania, of the customs and spirit of the people, the "ancient democratic institutions," the "intense patriotism," and the "treasures in the hearts of the Roumanian peasants," about whom he knew little, as he had spent but a few months in Roumania since he first came to Paris at the age of sixteen.[7] Michelet made good use of these

---

5. C. A. Rosetti, Note intime, vol. II, pp. 82, 93-4.

6. "Your words give us faith in the future and the power to hope, to have the certainty that we will create an independent and free country,...Roumania." (Maria Rosetti to Michelet, Jan. 23, 1850, Bibl. Ville de Paris, Papiers Michelet, K. 2. 11.

7. D. Brătianu to Michelet, Mar. 10, Apr. 28, Oct. 25, 1850, Bibl. Ville de Paris, Papiers Michelet, K. 2, 11.., Nos.

letters, lifting certain passages word for word for his brochure Principautés Danubiennes, Madame Rosetti, 1848, a romantic treatment of one of the episodes of the Wallachian revolution.[8] Rosetti and Ion Brătianu also were intimate friends of Michelet, and communicated to him information on the Roumanians, and Michelet's works and ideas served as models for their literary efforts.[9]

Quinet, also remained an idol, including among his admirers many of the Roumanians, especially after his marriage to the daughter of Gheorghe Asachi, Hermione, at Brussels in 1851. But his closest connections were with his former students at the Collège de France.[10]

The solution of the nationality question caused the Reds no deep concern. The triumph of the European revolution

---

11-13; the first two published by I. Breazu, Michelet și Românii, pp. 130-157; the third, from an undated copy kept by Brătianu, in Cretzianu, op.cit., vol. I, pp. 234-260. See also Michelet to D. Brătianu, Aug. 27, 1852, Cretzianu, vol. I, pp. 279-82.

8. Published first in 1851 in L'Événement, then in 1853 in Le Siècle and separately, then in Michelet, Légendes démocratiques du Nord, (Paris, 1854), pp. 277-366.

9. Breazu, Michelet și Românii, pp. 75-8, 81ff., 96-8; idem, "Jules Michelet și folklorul românesc," (Anuarul Arhivei de Folklor, Bucharest, II, 1933, pp. 181-93); Rosetti to Michelet, May 31, June 27, Dec. 12, 1850, Nov. 8, 1851, Papiers Michelet, K. 2. 11.

10. Breazu, Edgar Quinet et les Roumains, pp. 326-9. D. Brătianu to Ledru Rollin, June 10, 1849, Cretzianu, op. cit., vol. I, p. 212, mentioning Quinet as the deputy who presented to the Legislative Assembly the Roumanians' protest against Balta Liman.

would see an uprising of nationalities. The universal social and democratic republic would bring in its train the Roumanian Republic, the representative of democracy in Eastern Europe, and the spring of 1848 would be repeated.[11] It would of course include all the Roumanian lands, for Europe would be organized by nationalities. There was the matter of Transylvania; this, while the "brave Hungarians" were fighting in 1849, they were willing to overlook, but when the "Day" arrived, it would of course become part of the Roumanian Republic through the will of the majority of its inhabitants.[12]

There was no need to spare the feelings of those decadent barbarians, the Turks. Turkey and Austria, which had betrayed the Roumanians again and again, were both

---

11. I. C. Brătianu, "România," (Republica Română, No. 1, Paris, 1851, republished in Din scrierile și cuvîntările lui Ion C. Brătianu, Pt. I, 1821-1868, (Bucharest, 1903), pp. 24-35; Dan Simonescu, Din Istoria presei românești: Republica Română, (Bucharest, 1931), pp. 34, 47-61; C. A. Rosetti, Note intime, vol. II, pp. 34, 44-5, 70, 74.

12. I. C. Brătianu, "Naționalitate," (Republica Română, No. 2, Brussels, 1853, republished in Din scrierile și cuvîntările, pp. 39-61); cf. Rosetti's article, "Rusia," (Republica Română, No. 2, republ. in Scrierile lui C. A. Rosetti, Bucharest, 1887, vol. I), in which he quotes copiously from Herder (Quinet's translation), adducing historical and moral justification for the theory that in the future "no nation will ever be able to subjugate another, and Russia, Austria, and Turkey will inevitably be dismembered and give way to freely constituted united nations, according to the law of nature and the guiding genius of each." (pp. 8-9).

doomed. Ion Brătianu, writing the leading article for the first number of Republica Română, clearly expressed this refusal to compromise:

> "We want the Roumanian to re-establish himself in his own eyes as a man, to enter into his rights so that he may develop and perfect himself according to the law of nature, and fulfil his mission in society....
>
> "We want a free and independent fatherland of ten million Roumanians, who will have equal rights and equal duties....
>
> "Young Roumanians! You who in your young hearts can feel the power of the Roumanian people and by your instruction are destined to be the advance guard of its victories. Prove to those who still doubt that, if in '48 the Roumanians..., instead of losing time in diplomacy and crying 'Long live the Sultan,' in Wallachia, and 'Long life the Emperor,' in Transylvania..., had risen in all parts of Roumania under the standard of the Roumanian Republic, one and indivisible, and ten million voices had cried 'unity and freedom, or death,' no power would have dared to attack us or to deny us our sacred rights!".... 13

This had not happened in 1848, as the Roumanians did not know their own strength, and the surrounding peoples had not been penetrated with the spirit of democracy. Now, the nations had learned that they must stand together against

---

13. Din scrierile si cuvîntările lui Ion C. Brătianu, pp. 14-24; cf. C. A. Rosetti, "Cronica politică," (Republica Română, No. 1, publ. Simonescu, op.cit., pp. 47-61; Vintilă C. A. Rosetti, Amintiri istorice, pp. 129-138. Cf. also the article of Dumitru Brătianu, "Cronica politică," (România Viitoare, Paris, 1850, pp. 65-75), in which he preceded his brother in condemning the "Long life the Sultan, Long live the Emperor" division of 1848, and predicted a united rising "from the Theiss to the Black Sea," when the hour of revolution should strike, "for the Roumanian people are the most revolutionary in the world."

the alliance of monarchs; that alliance of peoples would bring greater Roumania into being.

A younger group, made up of students and not of exiles, put out a paper called "Roumanian Youth," which expressed the same sentiments as Republica Românǎ. Their program was: 1) the independence and union of all Roumanians; 2) war on oppressors, (Austria, Russia, and Turkey), solidarity with the oppressed, ("the Poles, the Hungarians, and the Italians"); 3) the organization of true democracy. Salvation, they held, would never come from crowned heads, nor from abroad, but from the inner strength of Roumanian nationality, and from the natural rights of insurrection and national sovereignty. The aim of the paper was to interest all in the national renascence and to treat literature, art, history, and politics from one point of view: Patria.[14]

In contrast to the Reds, who stuck to the indestructible alliance between nationalism and political democracy, a

---

14. Junimea Românǎ, Paris, No. 1, May 1851, pp. 1-2. A student society of the same name met weekly to discuss these patriotic issues. Its leaders were Gheorghe Crețeanu and Al. Odobescu. The titles of the articles give an idea of the scope of the society and of the periodical: "Faith and Union," "The Roumanian Worker," "The Awakening of Transylvania," in No. 1; "Moral Reform," "Roumanian Revolutions," "The Idea of our National Unity," in No. 2. (Only these two numbers were published. For the activities of the society, see Al. Odobescu, "Junimea românǎ din Paris pe la 1852," Opere Complete, vol. II, (Bucharest, 1908), pp. 241-8; Cretzianu, op.cit., vol. I, p. 229.

center group began to think almost exclusively in terms of nationalism. They were, in theory at least, the Cavours of the generation of 1848; they aimed at creating greater Roumania not overnight, but piece by piece, taking into account the nature of the problem in each province and the actual political forces involved. Maiorescu, for example, felt that the Transylvanian Roumanians were the nation's most virile branch, and that guarantees for their existence must be secured, even if it were necessary to deal with reactionary Austria. He would hear of no alliance with the Slavs, "bought by Moscow," but only with the Germans, whether they appear to represent reaction or liberty. "All else is but opportunism, a thing of the moment, and we must create an edifice for the future."[15]

A. G. Golescu placed similar emphasis on Transylvania; he tried to look beyond the ideological conflicts of the day and came also to the conclusion that if the Roumanians could become masters of the territory they inhabited within the Austrian Empire, the Principalities would fall into line later:

> "I am convinced that if Roumanism is reborn in Austria, it can never perish in the Principalities, even if the Muscovites remain there forever; therefore I consider the question of Roumanism in Austria a question of life and death for us."

---

15. Bănescu & Mihăilescu, <u>Ioan Maiorescu</u>, pp. 194, 207; Maiorescu to Magheru, Dec. 22, 1848, <u>Anul 1848</u>, V. pp. 615-6.

He had no great faith in Turkey but thought it necessary to try to win the Turks' favor, for just as by alliance with Vienna the Transylvanians could escape from Magyarism, so by alliance with the Sultan the Roumanians of the Principalities could escape from Slavism. If Turkey became strong and liberal, it would draw to it the Roumanians of Austria; if not the process would work the other way round, and the Principalities would be drawn to Austria.[16]

Golescu wished that the Roumanians had fought like the Croats and made themselves known to the world:

> "The Wallachs, like the Croats, should have been for those who promised them a national existence. We should have been respected, as the Croats are, even though instruments of reaction....When there is a question of nationality, the question of democracy counts for nothing." 17

Ion Ghica agreed substantially with Golescu's way of attacking the problem, though his main concern was with the Principalities, union of which he kept pressing on the Turks. Ghica was an intimate friend of Stratford Canning and was inclined to look to diplomacy as the only sensible means of reaching the desired goals. Contemptuous of those who predicted an immediate general revolution which would break into bits the Habsburg and Ottoman Empires, warning

---

16. A. G. Golescu to Ghica, Dec. 17, 1848, Ghica, Amintiri, pp. 82-92.

17. A. G. Golescu to Ghica, Apr. 27, 1849, ibid., p. 210.

his friend Bălcescu that the real power in Europe lay with the governments of the great powers, who would shy away from any such "anarchistic" scheme, he proposed organizing two autonomous Roumanias, one Ottoman and the other Austrian, and leaving the ultimate unity to the distant future, though, in contrast to Maiorescu and A. G. Golescu, he thought it "far better that the suzerainty of the Porte should absorb the Roumanians of Austria and Russia than that they should absorb us."[18] At the same time he favored having "men who could put their hands on the revolutionary movement, if it breaks out and is serious," and he negotiated with Kossuth over the results of a possible break-up of Austria, but always acting with the Turks, not against them.[19]

In 1853, taking stock of the diplomatic situation, he publicly announced his disbelief in the possibility of the "Daco-Roumanian dream." It would require dispossessing three empires, "historical realities," of their provinces, and

---

18. Ghica to Bălcescu, Aug. 4, Sept. 24, 1850, in N. Cartojan, N. Bălcescu și Ion Ghica, Scrisori inedite, (Bucharest, 1913), pp. 14, 45-7; Ghica to Alexandrescu, July 20, 1850, in N. Georgescu-Tistu, Ion Ghica Scriitorul, pp. 129-30.

19. Ghica to A. G. Golescu, Oct. 7, 1848, Anul 1848, V, p. 51; Ghica to Ion Filipescu, Dec. 30, 1849, in C. D. Aricescu, Corespondența secretă și acte inedite ale capilor revoluțiunii române de la 1848, vol. I, (Bucharest, 1873), pp. 12-15; Ghica to E. Poujade, Dec. 15, 1850, Ac. Rom. Mss., 5040, fol. 319-321; Cartojan, op.cit., pp. 24-5, 47.

for that he could find no example in history. To talk of Roumanian independence was to play Russia's game. The Mazzinian confederation of nations he called a mirage; it could only be a war of nations, as in 1848-49. The wisest course was to stick to the integrity of Turkey and the autonomy of the Principalities. On the eve of the Crimean War, Ghica retreated from Daco-Roumanism altogether and would go no further than the union of the Principalities under Ottoman suzerainty and a foreign prince.[20]

Occupying a position half-way between the realists and the Rosetti group was Bălcescu. This hardy social reformer, the only real "Red" of the revolution of 1848, though he maintained he had been but a moderator between the Eliade party and the Brătianu party,[21] also came to the conclusion that the national question was more crucial than that of liberal and democratic government, whereas before he had thought the social and democratic revolution should precede that of national unity. Much impressed by what he saw in in Transylvania, he wrote:

> "For me the question of nationality is more important than that of liberty. Until a people exists as a

---

20. Ghica to Cor, [1853], *Ac. Rom. Mss.*, 5040, publ. Tistu, *op.cit.*, pp. 143-8; G. Chainoi, *Dernière Occupation des Principautés Danubiennes*, pp. 4-9.

21. Bălcescu to A. G. Golescu, Mar. 8, 1849, cit. Panaitescu, *Contributii la o biografie a lui N. Bălcescu*, p. 85; cf. *idem*, Introduction to Bălcescu, *Patru Studii Istorice*, (Bucharest, 1928), p. 11.

> nation it can't do anything with liberty. Liberty can easily be reconquered, when it is lost, but nationality, no." 22

In a manifesto to the emigration urging unity of action, he wrote:

> "The Roumanians in 1848 cried 'We want liberty,' when before anything else they should have cried 'We want our national unity!'....National unity is the sole principle of life, our only salvation. ...There can be no happiness without liberty, but there can be no liberty without strength, and we Roumanians cannot be strong until we are all united in the same body politic." 23

This new insistence on nationality was perhaps the result of the month spent with Iancu's men, which gave him a new appreciation of the Transylvanian Roumanians. In a speech in Paris on the third anniversary of the Blaj meeting, he paid tribute to them, asserted that they wanted union with Wallachia in 1848, and again stressed national unity as the supreme desire in the heart of every Roumanian.[24]

Bălcescu at first thought the Principalities to be the heart of the nationality question, and his attempts at agreement with Kossuth in 1849 were aimed at freeing them from the Russians.[25] But he had always counted heavily on the

---

22. Bălcescu to Ghica, Jan. 21, 1849, Scrisori, pp. 16-17.

23. Panaitescu, Contribuţii la o biografie a lui Bălcescu, p. 102.

24. "Mişcarea Românilor din Ardeal la 1848," (Junimea Română, No. 2, June 1851, pp. 10-14, republ. in Bălcescu, Scrieri istorice, (ed. Panaitescu, Craiova, n.d.), pp. 193-201.

25. Bălcescu, Scrisori către Ion Ghica, pp. 97-8.

Transylvanian Roumanians, hoping to use them as soldiers to liberate the Principalities; later he came to regard Transylvania as a link with the European revolutionary movement. The mere attainment of the union of the Principalities, he thought, would be an isolated and fleeting gain. Ghica's plan for two Roumanias be condemned. "Your mistake is that you believe stupid diplomats and are easily deceived." The end, the foundation of a kingdom of Dacia, should be openly proclaimed. Only the means demanded secrecy.[26] The means he intended to use were not those of Ghica but those of the Reds, the international revolutionary movements directed by Mazzini. Bălcescu had none of Ghica's hopes of getting anything out of the Turks. "The Turks have betrayed us every time," he said, "and will continue to do so in the future."[27]

Bălcescu, though he had no great confidence in Rosetti and the Brătianus, considering Rosetti and Dumitru sentimental phrase-makers and Ion a man of agitation but not of constructive thought or action, was nevertheless very close to them in his ideas. <u>România Viitoare</u>, intended as the mouthpiece of the emigration was put out largely through his efforts, and the opening address to the Roumanian people,

---

26. Bălcescu to Ghica, Dec. 6, 1850, <u>ibid</u>., pp. 224-5.

27. Bălcescu to Ghica, May 20, 1849, <u>ibid</u>., p. 39; cf. same to same, Oct. 16, 1850, <u>ibid</u>., pp. 212-4.

written by him and signed by the committee,[28] embodied the republican-democratic-unity program of the Brătianus, damning the Turks and proclaiming that the triumph of democracy, the hour of deliverance, was near. In the battle against tyranny the Roumanian was said to be the advance-guard, and his would be a glorious future; Roumania would become one and indivisible.[29] In an article on "the progress of the revolution in the history of the Roumanians," he stressed national unity as the immediate aim:

> "We want to be a free and strong nation. It is our right and our duty,...and we have a mission to humanity to fulfill,...This union into a single nation, through nationality, through the same language, religion, customs, sentiments, through our geographical position and our history, and through the need to save and preserve ourselves, is absolutely necessary....Since 1848 the words unity and nationality are in every mouth in Europe, the sentiment is in every heart, every man has taken up arms and shed blood for them, blood which will continue to flow until the map of Europe is changed,

---

28. Signed by N. Bălcescu, C. Bălcescu, N. Golescu, S. Golescu, D. Brătianu, C. A. Rosetti, Magheru, Voinescu, Mălinescu, C. Florescu, and A. Paleologu.

29. România Viitoare, (Paris, Biblioteca Română, 3 Piata Sorbona, Impr. E. de Soye, rue de Seine 36, Nov., 1850). de Soye had a préss with Cyrillic characters and published most of the writings of the émigrés.
Almost a year before, Bălcescu had notified Ghica of his intention to found a paper "to defend our revolution and to prepare a new one," giving an outline of the program substantially as it appeared in the leading article. The national, social, and political aims were given in that order of importance . Ghica, in reply, warned against making the journal too radical. (Bălcescu to Ghica, Dec. 15, 1849, Scrisori, pp. 132-3; Ghica to Bălcescu, Sept. 24, 1850, Cartojan, op.cit., p. 45).

> until states based on conquest and denial of the rights of nations are smashed, and nations are reestablished in full freedom, and the holy alliance of peoples is founded." 30

Despite the failure of every one of his projects, and his grief at seeing France under a tyrant's heel Bălcescu refused to abandon this faith that ultimately Roumania would be united and free and that its principles, Justice and Brotherhood, would rule the whole world. Aware that his own death could not be long postponed, he knew he would never see the great day, but it must come, "the day when no man and no nation would be a slave, when no man and no nation would be the oppressor of another."[31]

On social issues, which the exiles subordinated to nationalism, there was much confusion of thought. Eliade hobnobbed with Leroux and Proudhon and spoke of "a new Christianity, socialism," but denounced anarchists who

---

30. Bălcescu, "Mersul Revoluţiei în Istoria Românilor," (<u>România Viitoare</u>, pp. 7-15), In this periodical was also published for the first time the famous <u>Cântarea României</u>, an epic of the Roumanian past, of great significance for the mythology of Roumanian nationalism. Alleged to be "discovered in an old monastery," its authorship was long attributed to Bălcescu, but it was actually written by Al. Russo, originally in French. It shows a strong influence of Lamennais and Mickiewicz. (P. V. Haneş, <u>Alexandru Russo</u>, pp. 660-70; Panaitescu, <u>Contribuţii la o biografie a lui N. Bălcescu</u>, pp. 129-138.

31. Note written at Hyères, Dec. 17, 1851, quoted in Al. Odobescu, Preface to 1877 edition of Bălcescu's <u>Istoria Românilor sub Mihai Vodă Viteazul</u>, in <u>Opere Complete</u>, vol. II, p. 197. Odobescu gives 1850 as the year, but Bălcescu did not go to Hyères until 1851.

would dare tamper with the rights of property. A. G. Golescu, the man who favored "terror" in 1848 longed for "the democratic and social republic", but abhorred the materialistic doctrine of socialism.[32] "Long live the democratic and social revolution," he wrote to Ghica,"but death to all these socialist republicans who are not worth a tinker's damn; may God preserve our country from that plague!!!"[33] Bălcescu remained an adherent of the principle of land reform, and published a study of it in 1850,[34] but he now subordinated that and all other reforms to the one great question of national unity and independence. The Reds continued to talk generally about equal rights for all, absolute democracy, and even "abolition of private property à la Proudhon," but they hardly merited the appellation of socialists bestowed upon them by Ion Ghica and others.[35]

---

32. A. G. Golescu to Madame Quinet, Jan. 6, 1852, I, Breazu, Edgar Quinet et les Roumains, pp. 370-2.

33. A. G. Golescu to Ghica, Feb. 24, 1849, Ghica, Amintiri, p. 207.

34. Question économique des Principautés Danubiennes, (Paris, 1850), repeating his views of 1848 and blaming the government of 1848 for its hesitations. Ion Ghica (Dernière Occupation des Principautés Danubiennes, Paris, 1853), and A. G. Golescu (De l'abolition du servage dans les Principautés Danubiennes, Paris, 1856) also spoke out for land reform, at the same time defending it against charges of socialism and communism.

35. Bălcescu to Ghica, Oct. 26, 1850, Scrisori, p. 260. Note Rosetti's remarks, written in 1852, on property as "the fruit of labor"..."property, like right, is in

The France of the early 1850's, a Napoleonic dictatorship on the one hand and a "socialistic" revolutionary movement on the other, with the ideal France of the Roumanians squeezed out of the picture, presented few attractions except for those who felt at home in the revolutionary ranks. Others experienced a disillusionment with France. A. G. Golescu discovered that the "seconde patrie" of the Roumanians, the France of Quinet, just did not exist and probably would not for another generation. He hated the stifling dictatorship, but he hated also the socialists, and the mass of people he found to be ignorant, servile, and politically indifferent.[36] Ion Ghica was another who was far from being an uncritical enthusiast for France and for democracy. This is what the former president of the Society of Students wrote in 1853, referring to his associates:

> "No one is so allergic to eccentric ideas as political refugees...such as the great number of young Wallachians who, thrown on to the streets of Paris or London, with the Polish, Italian, German, Magyar, and French crowd of revolutionaries, become adherents of the theories of the Mazzinis, the Ledru Rollins,

---

the conscience of every man." (Scrierile lui C. A. Rosetti, vol. I, Rusia, p. 13). Cf. Bălcescu's remark: "Our communists [Rosetti, etc.] are dissatisfied that we did not demand the abolition of property. We who attacked privilege and monopoly will one day have to fight to defend property against communism." (Balcescu to Ghica, June 6, 1850, Scrisori, p. 188).

36. A. G. Golescu to Mme. Quinet, Jan. 6, May 7, 1852, Breazu, op.cit., pp. 370-5.

> the Louis Blancs. Some of them dream of a confederation of national republics"..."Too ardent not to be seized with exaltation and enthusiasm at the words of Michelet and Quinet, not mature enough to get anything from them but a passionate admiration for revolutionary ideas,...they entered into relations with only the agitators of society, they all imbibed the most dangerous doctrines...." 37

These sharp differences of opinion, buttressed by personal dislikes, made impossible any united émigré organization to work for "the cause," which they all claimed to have at heart.

Eliade, attempted to perpetuate his authority, had himself and the other two Lieutenants (Tell and N. Golescu) elected as chiefs of the emigration by a group of hand-picked followers on October 1848 at Brasov shortly after the flight from Wallachia.[38] This was logical since the Lieutenance Princière had been the recognized government of Wallachia and could pretend to the right to speak on equal terms with the other governments of Europe. It was not, however, acceptable to the other leaders, who had distrusted

---

37. Chainoi, op.cit., pp. 3, 78-9; cf. Ghica to Cor, [1851 or 1852] Ac. Rom. Mss., 5040, fol. 361-4, admitting that the indifference shown to the Roumanians by Turkey and by Europe gave them every reason to throw themselves into subversive schemes, to desire a general bouleversement and a new social order.

38. Eliade Rădulescu, Epistole si acte ale oamenilor miscării din 1848, p. 20; Ghica, Amintiri, p. 49, says about 30 participated in the election; Locusteanu, Amintiri din Trecut, p. 98, says there were 250; cf. Ghica to A. G. Golescu, July 14, 1849, Georgescu-Tistu, op.cit., p. 110; A. G. Golescu to Ghica, June 27, 1849, Ghica, Amintiri, pp. 218-9.

and opposed Eliade during the revolution and were not disposed to bow down to him now that there was nothing to lose.

Those who had reached Paris held a meeting in December 1848, a banquet in memory of a national hero, Stephen the Great. "What do we need to become a strong nation? Union, only union! Long live the union of the Roumanians!" Such was the toast proposed by Costache Negri, a Moldavian.[39] The Wallachian émigrés drank solemnly to union, but all indications were that unity among themselves was an unattainable ideal. They all agreed, after much argument, to sign the memorandum to the French Assembly and the Mémoire justificatif, in which loyalty to Turkey and the non-demagogic character of the revolution were stressed.[40] That was the last document which could make any pretence of representing a unamimity of opinion. Even before it appeared, Rosetti bluntly challenged the authority assumed by the Lieutenants on the basis of their election at Braşov, but at a meeting he was supported only by N. Kretzulescu and was voted down.[41]

---

39. C. Negri, Versuri, Proză, Scrisori, (Bucharest, 1909), pp. 1-3.

40. C. A. Rosetti to Ghica, Apr. 20, May 11, 1849, Ghica, Amintiri, pp. 66-7, 71-7; A. G. Golescu to Ghica, Apr. 27, June 27, 1849, ibid., pp. 214, 218-9; Rosetti, Note intime, vol. II, pp. 31-9. Final text of the petition in Ghica, Amintiri, pp. 114-7.

41. Cretzianu, op.cit., vol. I, pp. 178-79; C. A. Rosetti, Note intime, p. 37; Eliade Rădulescu, Scrisori din Exil, pp. 629-30.

Eliade attempted to stabilize his authority by telling D. Brătianu in London and Ion Ghica in Constantinople that they were henceforth the representatives of the <u>Lieutenance</u> and were to follow instructions. Brătianu was told that a deviation from the path assigned, (<u>i.e.</u> "to renew our old connections with the Porte, and in all matters to convince it of our sincerity and our faith"), would be disavowed and would have to be answered for before all Roumanians."[42] It was not long before a flareup over some uncomplimentary remarks about the Turks in Brătianu's brochure of March 1849, which Eliade condemned as "childish unseemliness" (<u>o necuviință copilărească</u>). To avoid a storm Brătianu wrote a pro-Turkish article in the <u>Morning Herald</u> but made no retractions. The outcome of the whole affair, in which Brătianu was strongly defended by Rosetti, was that no pretense of a united emigration was any longer maintained. Brătianu said that no one could rob him of his right to speak for the Roumanians, and Eliade continued to insist upon "our indivisible union with Turkey, our faith as vassals in our legitimate sovereign."[43] Neither Brătianu nor Ion Ghica considered

---

42. Circular letter from Eliade, Tell, N. Golescu, to D. Brătianu et al., Feb. 20, 1849, Cretzianu, <u>op.cit</u>., vol. I, pp. 178-80; Ghica, <u>Amintiri</u>, pp. 647-50.

43. Cretzianu, <u>op.cit</u>., vol. I, pp. 180-6, 201-5; Eliade Rădulescu, <u>Epistole și acte</u>, p. 22; C. A. Rosetti, <u>Scrieri din junețe și din esiliu</u>, pp. 60-2; Ghica, <u>Amintiri</u>, pp. 213-4, 790, 803. Eliade (<u>Scrisori din Exil</u>, p. 2), says that he had a counter-brochure published in London and distributed many thousand copies in the chief cities of England. Of this I have found no trace.

himself a delegate responsible to anyone but himself and his own ideas of Roumanian interests, certainly not to Eliade. Between Eliade and Ghica there arose a bitter hatred, not so much on policy but because each suspected the other of being pro-Turkish for the purpose of gaining the throne of Wallachia. Ghica considered the Lieutenants as quite incompetent and wanted the whole emigration to be put under the authority of a single head, proposing Costache Negri, or former prince Alexander Ghica, or Nicolae Golescu, who, of "the three men of equal political incapacity," had the most prestige.[44] Bălcescu wanted none of the Lieutenants; "Golescu would be the best precisely because he is the most nil. Tell is a second edition of Eliade, and Eliade is a wretch (blestemat)."[45] Eliade meanwhile was denouncing Ghica, Bălescu, Brătianu, Rosetti, etc. as agents of Russia and traitors who were selling the country to the Magyars; both sides were making accusations that the public funds had been misused. The quarrels were carried to the Ottoman Government and to its embassy in Paris and into the columns of the press, until "the cause had very little left in the

44. Ghica, Amintiri, pp. 51-2, 60; A. G. Golescu to Ghica, June 27, 1849, ibid., pp. 215-29; Ghica to A. G. Golescu, July 14, 1849, Georgescu-Tistu, op.cit., p. 108; Ghica to A. C. Golescu, Nov. 4, 1849, ibid., pp. 120-1.

45. Bălcescu to Ghica, Jan. 21, 1849, Scrisori, pp. 18-19.

way of prestige.[46]

The Centre and Left, which might have ignored Eliade and formed a strong organization of their own, were soon at each other's throats over the question of a single chief. That, said Rosetti, would be dictatorship and quite unacceptable to good democrats. Besides, Negri, Ghica's choice, lacked "the faith of a revolutionary."[47] The dictator idea was, for purposes of efficiency and prestige, accepted by Bălcescu, A. G. Golescu and a few others, and the twenty-odd Wallachian exiles at Brusa, acting on a proposition of Ghica and others at Constantinople, cast fifteen votes for Negri as chief, five for N. Golescu, and for the supporting committee they cast most votes for Alecsandri, A. G. Golescu, and Eliade.[48] But the exiles in Paris did not approve the

---

46. Georgescu-Tistu, op.cit., pp. 107-27; Ghica, Amintiri, pp. 62, 763-8; A. G. Golescu to Ghica, Aug. 17, Nov. 7, 1849, ibid., pp. 748-55, 849-51; Ghica to A. G. Golescu, Oct. 5, 1849, Ac. Rom. Mss., 5040, fol. 15-16; Ghica to Sefels, 1849, ibid., fol. 7; Eliade's letters to the emigrés in Brusa, 1849, publ. in Ghica, Amintiri, pp. 674-710, 714-20, 722-39, 769-75; Eliade's five manifestoes to the Roumanian people, separate copies in Ac. Rom. Mss., 6, and collected in Eliade Rădulescu, Epistole și acte, pp. 3-75; N. Rousso [Locusteanu], Suite ou supplément à l'histoire politique et sociale des Principautés Danubiennes, (Brussels, 1855), pp. 13-16, 80-96, 104.

47. C. A. Rosetti to Ghica, Apr. 20, May 11, 1849, Ghica, Amintiri, pp. 67-73.

48. Iorga, "Note despre Unirea românească," (Revista Istorică, VI, 1920, pp. 1-11), pp. 9-10; cf. Ghica, Amintiri, pp. 709-14. The election was held May 14, 1849.

election, Negri decided to decline anyway, and the matter went no further.[49]

From widely scattered points came new proposals, none of which were acted upon. Maiorescu and Magheru suggested that all emigrés come to Trieste for a great meeting to elect a national committee and agents for the European capitals.[50] Ghica had proposed Constantinople as the central point, with a single direction for Moldavians and Wallachians working for union of the Principalities under the suzerainity of the Porte.[51] At Paris the three-cornered battle continued. A. G. Golescu, while carrying on his feud with Eliade, was at swords points with the Reds, with whom he had "a quarrel of uncommon violence." "In less than a month I have had disputes with Tell, Eliade, Rosetti, Bratiano, Voinesco, C. Balcesco, and a few others."[52] The same was true of the others. They could not agree on the text of a protest against the treaty of Balta Liman, as their views on what language to use toward the Turks differed widely. Finally they split openly, and one protest, referring to the Principalities as an "integral part" of the Ottoman Empire, actually was drawn

---

49. Ghica, Amintiri, pp. 234-, 340.

50. Magheru to Ghica, Feb. 5, 1849, ibid., pp. 156-7.

51. Ghica, Amintiri, p. 61; Ghica to A. G. Golescu, Nov. 4, 1849, Georgescu-Tistu, op.cit., p. 118; Revista Istorică, VI, 1920, p. 9.

52. A. G. Golescu to Ghica, June 27, 1849, Ghica, Amintiri, p. 221.

up by an Ottoman diplomatic official; it was signed by the Lieutenants. It was aimed at the radicals as much as at Russia, saying that "despotism and demagogy have in our opinion the same tendencies and present the same dangers: to govern by terrorism, to excite the poor against the rich, to trample on the sacred rights of property and of the family."[53] Rosetti, D. Brătianu, Voinescu, Mălinescu, and G. Marghiloman, as the "Roumanian Democratic Committee," put out their own protest and also had it printed in La Tribune des Peuples on June 8th. Invoking the natural and impre-scriptable rights of peoples, scorning treaties, it cried out against "the crime committed by two absolutist powers." These two protests were poles apart, and the united organization was farther away than ever.

When Bălcescu arrived in Paris in the autumn of 1849, he had every intention of taking matters in hand and bringing order out of chaos. He was a link between the moderate group and the radicals, and the prospects seemed good. But the air was soon filled with accusations about what had happened to the public funds, and each one had to give an accounting before a committee.[54] By that time tempers were

53. Paris, June 28, 1849. See Rosetti, Note intime, vol. II, pp. 47-9, for the disputes over the drawing up of the protest.

54. Money matters were highly important to them, for lack of funds was one of the reasons for their failure to accomplish more. The mutual accusations were for the

very much on edge, a couple of duels were fought, and the atmosphere was generally cloudy. Pessimism and doubt soured tempers, as the expected revolution failed to come, and the inferiority complex, helped along by the obvious comparison between their own revolution and those of the Italians and Hungarians, who had gone down in a blaze of glory, fixed itself more firmly on them through their own impotence. On the 28th of November, a guiding committee of five was chosen, leaving the Lieutenants out in the cold, and a few days later the statutes of the <u>Asociaţie Română</u>, an attempted revival of the old 1848 revolutionary organization, were adopted,[55] but in January Bălcescu resigned "because of the

---

most part unfounded, though the money they got away with in 1848 was spend haphazardly by those who happened to be in possession of it, and it was all mixed up with private funds. It must be admitted that the meanness of spirit displayed by all on this question was balanced by the generosity of some, like the Golescus and the Brătianus, who liquidated large properties at home in order to keep the exiles going. The wealthier Moldavians like Negri and Alecsandri, also contributed heavily. Eliade and Tell, with no private income, were supported by sums sent by their followers in Brusa, who gave what they did not use of their monthly pensions from the Ottoman Government. On these matters see Ghica, <u>Amintiri</u> pp. 650-66, 776-86, 852-8; Resolution of the Paris group, Nov. 28, 1849, <u>Ac. Rom. Mss.</u>, 82 (Bălcescu), fol. 446; Reports of A. G. Golescu and Bălcescu, copies in <u>Ac. Rom., C. A. Rosetti Mss.</u>, II, 2, 14; Bălcescu, <u>Scrisori către Ion Ghica</u>, pp. 13-4, 127, 137; Aricescu, <u>op.cit.</u>, vol. I, pp. 60, 63, vol. II, pp. 58-75; Locusteanu, <u>Amintiri din Trecut</u>, pp. 102-7; Eliade Rădulescu, <u>Scrisori din Exil</u>, pp. 5-129, <u>passim</u>, and 647-8.

55. Members of the committee were to be D. Brătianu, Rosetti, Bălcescu, Ion Ghica, and Magheru. (Resolution of 14

dissension over matters of principle as well as of personality," and because Ghica and Magheru had refused to join.[56] Yet he continued to work with the others and later took an active part on the "Commission of Propaganda," which was to be a link in the chain of national revolutionary bodies co-ordinated by Mazzini in London,[57] but the "mediocrity" of his colleagues decided him to retire to a quieter spot and write his history before tuberculosis finished him.[58] After his departure things got no better. A. C. Golescu, spokesman

---

Paris émigrés, Nov. 28, 1849, Ac. Rom. Mss., loc.cit.; cf. Bălcescu to Ghica, Dec. 6, 1849, Scrisori, p. 126; Ghica, Amintiri, pp. 795-801, giving Dec. 2 as the date of the founding of the association, the text of the statutes, and a slightly different list of signatures; cf. Ariceseu, op.cit., vol. I, pp. 47-51; A. C. Golescu to the committee, Nov. 29, 1849, Ac. Rom., C.A. Rosetti Mss., II, 14.

56. Bălcescu to Ghica, Jan. 26, Feb. 6, 16, 1850, Scrisori, pp. 156, 159-61, 165; letter of émigrés in Constantinople and Brusa to those in Paris, Jan. 31, 1850, Cretzianu, op.cit., pp. 222-6.

57. Bălcescu to Ghica, Sept. 6, Nov. 26, 1850, Scrisori, pp. 205, 222-3. "A commission of propaganda, to strengthen the revolutionary faith, after which organization will follow," was composed of D. Brătianu, Bălcescu, and Voinescu. (Voinescu to the emigrés at Constantinople and Brusa, Sept. 28, 1850, Ghica, Amintiri, pp. 866-7).

58. "Je ne connais pas dans tout l'ordre animal de bête plus féroce, plus affreux, qu'un compatriote-patriote. Le séjour de Paris m'a été toujours et de tout temps désagréable [à cau]se de ces animaux-là. ...Il est donc [désira]ble que je quitte Paris [pou]r chercher loin des Patriotes un peu de tranquillité ." (Bălcescu to Mme. Ghica, Feb. 2, 1850, Cartojan, op.cit., pp. 9-10). He retired to Ville d'Avray, then to Hyères, then to Italy. He died at Palermo in November, 1852.

for the Brusa group, made desperate attempts to secure a single chief, or a committee of three, or five, or nine, anything to secure a permanent organization, and asked each exile to contribute one half of his wealth, but Reds and Whites and Pinks in Paris could not agree among themselves and always raised objections to proposals from Brusa.[59] Rosetti, in his answer attributed their failure to egoism, "the capricious Roumanian character," and "lack of faith in the Revolution." "The trouble with us," wrote Rosetti, "is that our education is incomplete, we don't believe in the triumph of democracy and are not willing to sacrifice everything in order to conspire."[60]

A banquet held in 1851 to commemorate the revolution illustrated the pass to which matters had come. After years of exhortation to unity, organization, action, they added up their accomplishments and got a negative total. The banquet, at which several of the young patriots got drunk, ended in loud argument and bedlam, with Ion Brătianu, raising

59. Emigrés in Brusa to those in Paris, Dec. 17, 1849, Ghica, Amintiri, pp. 776-83; same to same, Dec. 20, 1849, Cretzianu, op.cit., vol. I, pp. 219-22; Bălcescu to Ghica, Feb. 6, 1850, Scrisori, pp. 159-60; D. Brătianu to A. C. Golescu, Feb. 7, 1850, Cretzianu, op.cit., vol. I, pp. 226-9; A. C. Golescu to emigrés in Paris, June 25, 1850, Ghica, Amintiri, pp. 861-6; A. C. Golescu to Zane, Ac. Rom. Mss., 235 (Bolintineanu), fol. 7-9.

60. Rosetti to Zane, Apr. 15, 1850, Ac. Rom. Mss., 235. Cf. Rosetti, Note intime, vol. II, p. 76: "apart from Ion Brătianu, not one of us has the qualities of a revolutionary."

his voice above the din to propose the following toast: "May God grant that Roumania never again be represented by men like us."[61]

The propagation of the faith remained a matter for each individual or faction according to its own tastes. Eliade produced three books of memoirs, first published in French, then in Roumanian. These, together with his five manifestoes to the Roumanian people and with copies of newspapers containing his articles, he sent in large quantities to Constantinople and Brusa, and from there some were sent secretly into Wallachia. Even after Eliade retired to Chios in 1851, he had Grădişteanu in Paris, and Russo-Locusteanu and others in Constantinople and Brusa working for him in this propaganda traffic.[62]

Ghica at Constantinople was in a much better position to act diplomatically and to keep in contact with Bucharest, for, thanks to his friendship with French and British consuls and diplomats, he was able to use their couriers. In correspondence with Grigore Alexandrescu in Bucharest, he had authoritative information as to the state of the revolutionary movement, and a means of distribution for propaganda

---

61. Rosetti, _op.cit._, vol. II, pp. 77-8.

62. E. Vîrtosu, I. _Heliade Rădulescu. Scrisori si Acte adnotate si publicate_, pp. 60-66; Eliade Rădulescu, _Scrisori din Exil_, _passim_.

sent to him by the exiles in Paris.[63]

The propaganda efforts of Bălcescu and of the Red party were more intensive and more successful. The making of appeals and protests to governments, which had occupied their attention in 1849, was now replaced by real incitement to revolution, after Bălcescu's interview with Palmerston in January, 1850, a last attempt to bring about diplomatic intervention.[64] Their propaganda was directed toward counteracting that of Eliade and toward preparing spirits in the Roumanian provinces of Austria and in the Principalities for the great day of revolution, and they wanted to be in touch with popular leaders, so that when the button was pushed in Paris, the ten million Roumanians would rise in arms. That was a necessary corollary of their participation in the revolutionary plots of Mazzini and other leaders in London.

4. Negotiations for a Danubian confederation

The end of the Hungarian war of independence inaugurated a new phase of the federation question, for now Kossuth,

---

63. E. Lovinescu, Grigore Alexandrescu. Viața și opera lui, și Corespondența lui cu Ion Ghica, (3rd. ed., Bucharest, 1928), pp. 255, 267; Bălcescu, Scrisori, pp. 185-7, 190-1.

64. Bălcescu to Ghica, Jan. 26, 1850, Scrisori, pp. 153-8. On this London visit he became acquainted with Dudley Stuart, Cobden, and others, and established connections with several newspapers. Later in the year he sent Stuart a copy of his brochure on the social question, with the request that it be given to Palmerston. (Ac. Rom. Mss., 82, fol. 462).

chastened by defeat, for the first time took the matter seriously, and Bălcescu was still willing to work for a common front against the enemies of God and of mankind, the Muscovites and the "Schwarzgelbi." Kossuth did not invent the idea of an eastern confederation, as is often said, but his active promotion gave it greater significance than before.[1] Late in October, 1849, at Widin, acting on suggestions from Polish sources, he proposed the following reorganization, to be effected after the defeat of Austria and Russia: an alliance and customs union between Hungary and Serbia, with Croatia joining Serbia or remaining separate, "the whole to be as Serbia now is under the protectorate of the Porte...." "Poland, Dalmatia, Wallachia, Moldavia, etc. might not be indisposed to enter this confederation under Turkish protectorate."[2] Count Zamoyski thereupon wrote a long memorandum which was agreed to by Kossuth and Batthyanyi (for the Magyars), Monti (for the Italians), Zamoyski and Bystrzonowski (for the Czartoryski party), and General Wysocki (for the democratic Polish party). Kossuth's aims were said to be "a vast confederation of states (Danda

---

1. Cf. O. Jaszi, Dissolution of the Habsburg Monarchy, pp. 312-3.

2 F. Henningsen (British journalist, agent of Kossuth) to Zamoyski, Nov. 2, 1849, Hajnal Istvan, A Kossuth-Emigracio Törökorszagban, (Budapest, 1927), pp. 527-8; cf. T. Lengyel, "The Hungarian Exiles and the Danubian Confederation," (Hungarian Quarterly, V. Autumn 1939, pp. 450-61), p. 451.

orientale) including Hungary, Poland, Croatia, Serbia, and the Roumanian countries." On the nationality question within Hungary Kossuth was vague, and the point was not pressed; nothing was said about territorial concessions to the Roumanians, although the Poles were under the impression Kossuth was ready to cede territory to Serbia and "Roumania."[3]

Kossuth favored tying his cause to that of Turkey, and consequently to that of England, so that all possible forces would be united against Panslavism. He proposed to the Ottoman Government, which was on the brink of war over the question of the extradition of these very refugees, that a union of states, including Hungary, be formed under the Sultan's suzerainty. He maintained that the Hungarians still had plenty of fight and that the Roumanians were "in full insurrection." Later he repeated the request and stated that the moment for squaring accounts with Russia had never been so favorable.[4] The key to the matter was federation:

> "Against the idea of Panslavism only the idea of Federalism can be successfully opposed. Federalization of several small peoples, with a guarantee of their nationality, secures them against foreign domination. This idea of Federalism must conquer, in Germany, in Italy, and above all in eastern Europe. For with Federalism there is freedom, with Panslavism slavery and the absorption of every nationality." 5

---

3. Hajnal, op.cit., pp. 173, 283, 529-39.

4. Nov. 22, Dec. 30, 1849, ibid., pp. 542-6, 616-25.

5. Kossuth to Boekh (Prussian diplomatic agent), Dec. 30, 1849, ibid., pp. 625-6. Cf. Otto Zarek, Kossuth, (Zürich, 1935), p. 533.

He was convinced, influenced by news from Serbia and by information from Boliac, Racoviţa, and other Roumanians, that a basis for federation already existed. He predicted great things for the coming spring.[6]

With the Serbs he immediately began negotiations; he regarded them as a vital link in the alliance and wanted to organize the war in Serbia, with Hungarian and Roumanian legions co-operating with the Serbian and Turkish armies. He offered equality for the Serbs within Hungary, and, besides Croatia, would consent to small territorial cessions of purely Serb districts, but not the Voivodina.[7] His agents reported that Garašanin was ready to act with the Magyars when the time came, but no agreement was concluded.[8] The Serb leader was anti-Austrian but would have made Kossuth pay a high price, the autonomy of the Voivodina.[9]

Kossuth also set much store by an agreement with the Roumanians, for he knew that England would be more likely to go to war over the Principalities than over Poland or Hungary.[10] Ion Ghica, probably informed of Kossuth's plans

---

6. Ibid., pp. 171, 262, 281, 354, 377, 647.

7. Kossuth to Carosini, Jan. 19, 1850, ibid., pp. 671-7.

8. Carosini to Kossuth, Feb. 15, 1850, Eugenio Kastner, Mazzini e Kossuth. Lettere e Documenti inediti, (Florence, 1929), pp. 102-3.

9. Hajnal, op.cit., pp. 174, 281, 376; Lengyel, op.cit., pp. 452-3.

10. Hajnal, op.cit., pp. 389, 573-4, 591.

by Boliac, was ready to open negotiations. He also felt that the interests of the Porte and of the Hungarians, Poles and Roumanians could be best served by common action against Russia and the creation of a Danubian federation. He explained his position in a letter to Sefels, a Pole in Ottoman service:

> ...The political existence of all the Roumanians in general, and of the...Principalities in particular, is closely bound up with the existence of a powerful Turkey and with the regeneration of Poland and Hungary.
>
> "The Magyars will realize sooner or later, if they do not already, that their own existence depends on federation with the surrounding populations on the basis of equality, as was agreed on in principle in the protocol of the conference in Paris, between Czartoryski and the Hungarian and Czech representatives...." 11

Ghica favored at this time the creation of a "great and strong Roumania, either under Ottoman suzerainty or federated with Hungary," or both. He wanted the Serbs to take part in any federation because of their similar political position. He instructed Ion Filipescu, who was at Belgrade, to negotiate with the Serbs, using the good offices of Czartoryski's agents.[12] Pleased that Polish and Hungarian leaders found his arguments good, and notified that Kossuth and Batthyanyi wanted to come to an understanding

---

11. Ghica to Sefels, 1849, Ac. Rom. Mss., 5040, fol. 8-9.

12. Ghica to Filipescu, Nov. 9, Dec. 30, 1849, Jan. 6, Mar. 31, 1850, C. D. Aricescu, Corespondința secretă ale capilor revoluțiunii române, vol. I, pp. 9-10, 16, 21-3, 30-1.

with the Transylvanians "on a wider and more liberal basis," Ghica, on February 1st, transmitted to Wysocki a federation scheme "to serve as the basis of an entente with M. Kossuth in respect to the matter of Transylvania."[13] The memorandum pointed to the United States of America as a model on which could be based a federation of Croats, Serbs, Magyars, and Roumanians. He proposed taking the Paris agreement of May, 1849, providing for a federalization of Hungary, as a starting point. Then the whole of Hungary was to come under the suzerainty of the Porte, and, presumably, a Greater Serbia and a Greater Roumania would come into existence as component parts of the federation. Ghica was quite vague about this point, as well he might if the proposal was to have any chance of acceptance by Kossuth, for it involved the partition of Hungary and its reduction to a purely Magyar unit as a junior member in the federation. Ghica therefore tried to make the plan a little more palatable by leaving the questions of language and religion to the future, recommending, again pointing to the American example and stating a thesis known to be favored by

---

13. <u>Ac. Rom. Mss.</u>, 5040, fol. 74-79. I have reproduced this letter in full in an appendix. See pp. 430-39.
Ghica later wrote directly to Kossuth at Kutahia, asking permission to transmit, from time to time, "ideas on the Magyar-Roumanian differences,...and thus add another stone to the great political edifice...of which you will be the architect." (Ghica to Kossuth, 1850, Georgescu-Tistu, <u>op.cit.</u>, pp. 127-8).

Kossuth, a large measure of decentralization, leaving minor questions concerning both nationality and religion to the communes. As for the Poles, they were to help in the fight for freedom, but after that they were to be allowed to go their own way; being strong enough to stand on their own feet and not being a Danubian nation, there would be no reason to include them in the new confederation. The essential thing was for the Danubian peoples, and especially the non-Slavic Magyars and Roumanians, to stand shoulder to shoulder as a barrier against Panslavism.

Bălcescu meanwhile, uninformed of the details of these negotiations, was working on plans of his own.[14] In Paris he had several meetings with the Hungarian representatives, and on the 4th of January, 1850, he went to London in the company of Andrassy and Teleki. There they met Henningsen, sent by Kossuth, and conferred on the federation question; they agreed on starting a publicity campaign and on approaching Palmerston. No great success was achieved in either direction. Palmerston thought it an interesting idea, but impossible of realization without a general war, which he did not want.

Bălcescu, according to his own report, founded at this time a committee of eastern European representatives.

---

14. Writing to Ghica, Jan. 26, 1850, he expressed his agreement with "your idea of an eastern confederation, in which I am happy to have anticipated you." (<u>Scrisori către Ion Ghica</u>, p. 157).

"...There will be three representatives of each of the following six nations: Roumanians, Hungarians, Poles, Russians, Bohemians and Turks; Southern Slavs. The end is a democratic confederation of all, the means revolution, and agreement, unity, and solidarity in action. This committee is secret. At present the members are: for the first nation, myself, and I have recommended you [Ion Ghica] and Arapilă [A. G. Golescu]. If you find a good Moldavian, then one of us can give way to him; for the second nation, General Klapka, Teleki, and Pulszky; for the third, Prince Lubomirski and Count Branicki (both are very rich and have promised money); for the fourth, Golovin. No definite decision can be taken unless all the nations are represented. You must not speak of this to anyone on earth not even Czaika. If Kossuth, when he escapes, falls in with our idea, one of his men will make a place for him." 15

This "committee" of Bălcescu's never did anything, though there were several meetings. The stumbling block seems to have been, despite the rich Poles, lack of money for a newspaper.[16]

Bălcescu got on very well with Teleki and Klapka, and wrote to Ghica of having won them over completely to his views. Klapka he characterized as "a man of very broad ideas" and in favor of the federal organization of eastern Europe, with a central diet in which the French and German

---

15. Bălcescu to Ghica, Jan. 26, 1850, loc.cit. Golovin was about to launch a newspaper, Le Fédéral, and asked Bălcescu to contribute articles. (Ibid., pp. 158,170).

16. Pulszky, op.cit., vol. III, pp. 30-31. Pulszky gives no dates, and it is not clear whether the "secret society for the liberation of Eastern Europe" which he mentions is the same as Bălcescu's. He says Golovin,Klapka, Teleki, himself, Lubomirski, "Bratiano and Golesco" attended the meetings.

languages would be used. Bălcescu proposed Latin, since it was extensively known in Poland and Hungary and much favored, though unknown, among the Roumanians. Teleki was also favorable to federalism, as in 1849, and would have agreed to a plebiscite for Transylvania.[17]

Bălcescu, pleased with the plan submitted by Ghica to Kossuth, drew up one of his own in greater detail, to serve as a basis of negotiations. He knew he could not hope for much from Kossuth, who, he said, was "very _entêté_ in his ideas."[18] He planned on working with Teleki and Klapka, letting Kossuth rest peacefully in his political grave.

> "It seems to me wrong that you and [A.G.] Golescu should disturb the dead in their cemeteries. Kossuth is dead and can be of no further use to us; leave him in peace. I did all that possibly could have been done with him. I forced him to deny his life and his principles by granting those incomplete concessions to the Roumanians. That was an act of suicide. He can go no further than that. We must turn to the Hungary of the future...." 19

Kossuth was, however, the recognized chief of the Hungarian emigration and could not be ignored. As a basis of negotiation between Ghica and Kossuth, and for himself in the West, Bălcescu drew up a constitution for a federal state to include the Magyars, the Roumanians, and the

---

17. Pulszky, _op.cit._, vol. II, p. 313; D. A. Janossy, _Great Britain and Kossuth_, p. 106; Bălcescu to Ghica, Jan. 26, Feb. 6, 1850, _Scrisori_, pp. 158, 161.

18. Bălcescu to Ghica, Apr. 6, 1850, _Scrisori_, p. 175.

19. Bălcescu to Ghica, May 6, 1850, _ibid._, p. 182.

Jugoslavs, divided according to the desires of the majority in each district. The new state, "The United States of the Danube," would take in the territory of Hungary, Serbia, Moldavia, Wallachia, Bucovina, and Bessarabia "when it is won." A central assembly of one hundred and fifty deputies, fifty from each nationality, would meet annually, the three national capitals playing host to it in turn. Its debates would be in French or German. The federal government would have only three ministers, for war, for foreign affairs, and for commerce and communications. All in all, the scheme was not unlike the Ausgleich of 1867, except that its trialistic mechanism might have been more difficult to work than a simple dualism. Also, Bălcescu made no mention of a common sovereign. Perhaps that place would be filled by the Sultan; Bălcescu himself would prefer his United States a republic.[20]

The Hungarians in London, headed by Andrassy and Teleki, thought they might perhaps be able to appease the nationalities by granting wide autonomy, but the resolute desire of the latter in favor of union with their brothers across the frontier made them despair of even that. They knew that Kossuth's scheme, a mere alliance of states, would never be accepted.[21] Teleki, willing to give provincial

---

20. Bălcescu to Ghica, Apr. 6, 1850, ibid., pp. 175-6.

21. Szarvady to Kossuth, Jan. 27, 1850, cit. Janossy, op.cit., p. 106.

autonomy to the nationalities, was ready to negotiate with Bălcescu, but he was not willing to consign Kossuth to the graveyard. He tried persuasion, writing several letters urging his chief to make a public declaration to the non-Magyar nationalities of full recognition of federalism on the basis of nationality. Kossuth's replies left no doubt that his position had not changed basically since his talks with Bălcescu in 1849. Hungary must remain historic Hungary:

> "Count Teleki should be kind enough to write me clearly what he understands by 'internal federation' ...The Wallachians know very well what they understand by it: they mean that we should detach Transylvania and the counties of Krassó, three fourths of Bihar, Szathmár, and Mármaros from Hungary and make of them a Roumania which would kindly promise to confederate with us, preserving the right to coalesce with Wallachia and Moldavia, their natural relatives...Thank you! This I could never, never accept, because the natural consequence of this action would be that in the north we should give fifteen counties to the Slovaks, in the south the counties of Torontal, Bács, Baranya, and half of Zala to the Serbs, a northern strip to the Russians, a western to the Germans...that is, we should kill the Magyars. Even Austria does not do more than this. Never, for such a result, shall I spill my nation's blood."[22]

Kossuth had been to Brusa and talked to the Roumanians there. He was incensed at their arrogance:

> "They even found fault with our not having erased the name of Hungary (Magyarország) as the title of our Fatherland, since it is inhabited by several

---

22. Kossuth to Teleki, June 15, 1850, quoted in Jaszi, "Kossuth and the Treaty of Trianon," (Foreign Affairs, New York, XII, Oct. 1933, pp. 86-97), pp. 88-90; Janossy, op.cit., pp. 104-5.

> nations---that is, they wish me to consent to Transylvania becoming Roumania...--against this I shall fight as eternally as I have fought and shall fight against the plans of Austria, which are not a bit more deadly than these." 23

In vain Teleki begged Kossuth to be less stubborn, and argued that giving the Roumanians and Serbs "the collective national existence for which they have been longing" would not necessarily break Hungary into national units; if there were only a recognition of the principle, the details could be left to a constituent assembly.[24] Kossuth replied:

> "I wish to see Hungary federated with Serbia, Croatia, Moldo-Wallachia, Poland, and other countries, but...not...divided into federated provinces....It would be an error to think of the example of North America [here he was replying to the arguments of Ghica]...They did not divide their country into provinces along lines of nationality, they made a federation of independent states. That is exactly what I wish.... If the Serbs and Roumanians...are not satisfied ...[we cannot] commit suicide out of courtesy to them." 25

---

23. Jaszi, loc.cit. T. Lengyel (op.cit., p.453, source not cited) says that the "Golescu brothers" came to Kossuth at Shumla in August, 1850, and proposed a confederation in which Roumania would have Transylvania, and that Kossuth indignantly refused. These were probably not Nicolae and Ştefan Golescu. They may have been Radu and A. C. Golescu, who were at Brusa.

24. Teleki to Kossuth, July or August, 1850, Jaszi, op.cit., p. 93.

25. Kossuth to Teleki, Aug. 22, 1850, Jaszi, op.cit., pp. 94-5, and Janossy, op.cit., p. 106. The originals of the Kossuth-Teleki correspondence are in the Hungarian National Museum, Budapest.
    Kossuth's idea that a common foreign policy with the surrounding provinces would take the edge off the nationality conflict in Hungary was ingenious, but it was hardly a "scrupulous and thoroughgoing satisfaction of the claims of the nationalities." (cf. Jaszi, Dissolution of the Habsburg Monarchy, pp. 312-3).

This left Teleki little room for negotiation, in view of the known Roumanian attitude. Bălcescu, in his answer to the original Kossuth-Zamoyski proposal of November 1849, defined that attitude in unmistakable terms. He accepted fully the idea that a federation of oppressed nations (Poland, Hungary, Croatia, Serbia, the Roumanian countries, and perhaps Italy) was essential, but he wanted a few points cleared up, especially Kossuth's interpretation of the term "Roumanian countries."

> "Does this mean the Principalities alone, or the Principalities plus the districts in Hungary peopled exclusively or in the majority by Roumanians?... I insist on this point, first because I am a Roumanian...; and even were I a stranger to this particular question, I should insist just the same.... Men of liberty, let us not shun the light, and let us have the case of each one known and understood before the battle, so that we will not be at each other's throats after having won freedom for our nationalities.
>
> "The idea of the Bande orientale originated a long time ago. It had been taken up because it is a matter of general aspiration. The difficulty is in giving it a material existence, in putting it into effect, and this difficulty is raised by the country which has the greatest interest in it, by Hungary. M. Kossuth says, 'that he is above all a Magyar, and that it is to Magyar Hungary that he is devoted; that he insists on all that he believes to be indispensable for the existence of the Hungarian state; that outside of certain indispensable conditions he will concede to the different races and language groups in Hungary complete equality of civil and political rights and even full national development....' This profession of faith deeply perplexes me; for it seems to me to be descriptive of the unfortunate system practised in 1848 and 1849....
>
> "In our view, the political unity of Hungary, a Magyar state with a Magyar administration and the Magyar language, is an impossibility, and this

impossibility, Monsieur la Comte, springs from the numbers, the geography, the history, the customs, the opposing traditions, and the habits of the different races. The Magyars, as Magyars, will have a distinguished place in the Bande orientale, but the Magyars, a political body absorbing and directing Roumanian and Slavic individuality, can only resuscitate the conflict of races and perpetuate the civil war...this would violate the fundamental principle of the general association, respect and recognition of nationalities....

"Serious study and the knowledge of the profound antagonism of the various races of Hungary have convinced me of the impossibility of a Hungarian state as the political and historic unity that M. Kossuth sees it. I should not be a Roumanian if I thought otherwise; to join to the league of peoples Hungary in this form, based on the Magyar principle, is to prepare the way for incalculable evils....I think that historical right is an improper right to invoke, for it is the right of force, of invasion, of conquest, and we seek to liberate ourselves by the immutable right: justice. Now what is just for the Magyar, for the Pole, for the Italian, should also be just for the Slav and the Roumanian; there cannot be a double standard of justice....

"The Roumanians and the Slavs also have their historical rights, rights which antedate that of the Magyars. There you have two historical rights confronting one another; which is the more just? Would it not be better if the nationalities in Hungary, instead of eternally slaughtering each other in the name of history, made their appeal to natural law, the sole imprescriptible right, and tried to live as brothers in a common fatherland? ...Providence...has taken care to facilitate the solution of the nationality question by grouping each one apart from the others and marking each land with the indelible character of the people inhabiting it; the Hungarians living among the Roumanians, the Slavs among the Hungarians and vice versa, are but individual cases or scattered colonies which will rapidly become denationalized.

"Hungary, then, cannot enter the league as a Magyar state without undergoing an internal transformation. This transformation, according to us Roumanians, will not lessen the rank, the force, or the influence which Hungary will have in the league, and will even increase its territorial extent by attracting to it the Roumanians of the Principalities; the transformation will consist in a demarcation of races according to well-established majorities; each nationality will organize itself in accordance with its own needs and aptitudes, and between them there will be a federal tie, as in Switzerland....Such are the general ideas of the Roumanians on the subject....If M. Kossuth wants to assure the existence and the development of the Magyar nation and to collaborate in the liberation of the subjugated nations, he can count on the ten millions of Roumanians, and probably on the Slavs also, but only if they are considered as allies, as partners, as brothers. Our political principle is simple: respect, recognition, equality, and solidarity of nationalities...." 26

This lengthy exposé of the Roumanian point of view laid down the line of argument which they were to follow throughout the rest of the period of exile. It is worth noting that the case was thus stated by Bălcescu the most conciliatory of the Pasoptisti, the man who less than a year before had gone into transports of joy when Kossuth had agreed to grant exactly what he was proposing now, and who had sought death in the field fighting for the Magyars. He now felt the Roumanians to be in a good bargaining position and that they could afford to wait. He was convinced that Transylvania could never again become a mere district of Hungary. It must be given its character of a Roumanian land.

This completely deadlocked the negotiations, and Kossuth gave them the coup de grâce by a belated negative reply to Ghica's proposal of February. Henningsen told

---

26. Bălcescu to Zamoyski, July 1, 1850, Ghica, Amintiri din Pribegia după 1848, pp. 515-532.

Ghica that co-operation would be possible if all emigrés would place themselves under one head (*i.e.*, Kossuth). This was absurd. The Roumanians would not even accept one of their own number as dictator, much less Kossuth.[27]

It soon became evident that the European revolutionary movement of Mazzini offered great opportunities to both sides and might be a means of bringing them together. In February, 1850, Bălcescu was talking of the need of working with Mazzini and with their old friend Ledru Rollin; he envisaged a great revolutionary solidarity in all of Europe.[28] He got into contact with Manin, then in Paris, whom he hoped would be a member of the new European revolutionary committee. He looked forward to the time when there would be a hierarchy of committees; his own for eastern Europe and Mazzini's new one would be at the top, with various national committees below them, including a central Roumanian organization in Paris and others in each of the five Roumanian lands.[29]

In July Mazzini formed the Central European Democratic Committee, with members representing Italy (Mazzini), France (Ledru Rollin), Germany (Arnold Ruge), and Poland (Albert

---

27. Ghica to Bălcescu, Sept. 24, 1850, in N. Cartojan, *N. Bălcescu și Ion Ghica, Scrisori inedite*, p. 46.

28. Bălcescu to Ghica, Feb. 16, 1850, *Scrisori*, p. 164.

29. Bălcescu to Ghica, Mar. 6, 1850, *ibid.*, pp. 170-1.

Darasz).[30] No Roumanian was included, as none were in London at the time. In September the active Roumanians in Paris met to decide who should go, and Bălcescu was chosen, but because of his health and his desire to finish his history of Michael the Brave, he declined.[31] None of the others volunteered, and Roumania remained unrepresented until the following year.[32]

Mazzini appealed to Kossuth, personally and in the name of the Central Committee, to help give the alliance of peoples the unity of action it needed to break the power of the alliance of kings. He pointed to the victory which would result from a junction of "our two revolutions," and

---

30. Giuseppe Mazzini, Scritti, (edit. nazionale), vol. XLIII, pp. 191ff.; A. R. Calman, Ledru Rollin et les proscrits français en Angleterre, (Paris, 1921),p.95.

31. Bălcescu to Ghica, Sept. 6, 1850, Scrisori, p. 205. At the meeting were Nicolae and Ştefan Golescu, D. Brătianu, Rosetti, Voinescu, Mălinescu, Nicolae and Constantin Bălcescu.

32. Mazzini passed through Paris in September, and wrote to Emilie Hawkes of having seen "three or four persons there, a Wallachian among others, whom you will probably see in London before long." (Mazzini, Scritti, vol. XLIV, p. 57). The editors of Mazzini's writings (loc.cit., note 1) say that this was Nicolae Golescu, and that he promised Mazzini that he would represent the Roumanians on the Central Committee. In a letter to a friend in New York (Sept. 21, 1850, Scritti, XLIV, p. 62) Mazzini wrote that "The Central European Committee, composed of Ledru Rollin for France, myself for Italy, Darasz for Poland, Ruge for Germany, Gonesco (sic) for the Moldo-Wallachians, Klapka for the Hungarians, and others who will join, meets in London." See also ibid., XLV, p. 320, note, where the editors again mention Mazzini's negotiations with "one of the two Golescu brothers."

set forth as his ultimate aim a free confederation of Italians, Slavs, and Magyars. He wanted to know Kossuth's ideas on a pact of fraternization among the Magyars, the Jugoslavs, and the Roumanians, with whom he was in contact.[33] Kossuth left these letters unanswered, because he did not want to compromise his relations with the Piedmontese Government and other moderate elements, and he was no doctrinaire republican; he thought first and foremost of Hungary's interests and cared little about Mazzini's idea of a new Europe based on the revolution of all nations against their oppressors, and he feared Mazzini's organization might be too friendly to Serb and Roumanian claims on Hungary.[34] Also he was still counting on Turkey and on British policy, whereas Mazzini shunned alliances with existing governments and put Turkey in the same category as Austria, fit only to be torn asunder by its nationalities.[35]

---

33. Mazzini to Kossuth, Aug. 7, 15, Nov. 23, 1850, Mazzini, Scritti, XLIV, pp. 9-10, 315-9; Kastner, op.cit., pp. 3-6.

34. Kastner, op.cit., p. 116; M. Menghini, Luigi Kossuth nel suo carteggio con Giuseppe Mazzini, (Aquila, 1921), p. 25; A. Marcu, Conspiratori si Conspiratii, p. 22.

35. Mazzini included the Greeks, Roumanians, Serbs and Croats, and even the Bulgarians in his scheme of break-up the Ottoman Empire. See C. Kerofilas, La Grecia e l'Italia nel Risorgimento italiano, (Florence, 1919), pp. 59-64; D. Spadoni, "La Grecia e l'Oriente in un carteggio inedito di G. Mazzini," (Rivista d'Italia, XVIII, 1915, 621-6); F. Momigliano, "I popoli slavi nell'apostolato di G. Mazzini," (Nuova Antologia, June 1, 1915, pp. 434ff.).

Mazzini's "international" was as unsuccessful as that of Czartoryski in mediating the Magyar-Roumanian differences. Likewise was the less forceful attempt of certain circles in Paris to secure an agreement on federation. As the French radical leaders were in exile, the discussions were rather academic. Czartoryski had had about enough of emigré quarrels and he detested Kossuth, though he still kept in touch with the Roumanians.[36] Robert's La Pologne strongly advocated federation of nationalities, after an agreement with Bălcescu whereby the paper was to be made less Slavic in tone and more generally in favor of all nationalities.[37]

Michelet, whose friends and pupils had fought against each other in the valley of the Danube in 1848 and 1849, took a lively interest in the federation question. He knew little of the facts of the Transylvanian dispute but deplored the animosity which it engendered, and he was convinced, as were so many others, that the small nations must

---

36. Handelsman, op.cit., p. 122; Czartoryski to Zamoyski, Jan. 7, 1850, Hajnal, op.cit., pp. 638-9.

37. Bălcescu to Ghica, Dec. 15, 27, 1849, Scrisori, pp. 140, 143. For the results, see La Pologne, 2e. année, No. 29, Dec. 9, 1849, and following numbers, esp. the articles "Du fédéralisme en Turquie, chances d'attirer par ce système, vers l'empire d'orient, les nationalités opprimés d'Autriche," (3e. année, No. 5, Feb. 3, 1850, pp. 17-8), and "Les gouvernements et les nationalités," (No. 7, Feb. 17, 1850, pp. 25-7). La Pologne had a very restricted circulation and died in 1850 for lack of funds.

federate or perish.[38] A letter from Rosetti to Michelet shows that even some of the "internationalists" among the Roumanians felt so strongly against the Magyars that agreement was impossible. Denying that the Roumanians were blinded by hate he said their attitude was due to the whole past of the Magyars being nothing but iniquity toward the Slavs and the Roumanians, and that when the world praised them for their eighty battles for democracy and fraternity, it merely confirmed them in their absolutistic ideas. He said that while he favored an alliance of peoples, any attempt to create an America or a Switzerland would have no other result that a war of extermination.[39]

Bălcescu did what he could to make his colleagues see the necessity of the attempt at agreement with the Slavs

---

38. "Sans elle [fédération] ni la Hongrie, ni la Roumanie, ni la Slavie ne résisteront." (Michelet to D. or I. Brătianu, July 7, 1851, Bibl. Ville de Paris, Papiers Michelet, K. 1. 2); Breazu, Michelet și Românii, pp. 40-1, 55. For the similar attitude of Quinet, Ulbach, Chassin, etc., see Bela Tóth, "Edgar Quinet et la Hongrie," (Revue des études hongroises, VI, 1928, pp. 356-372), pp. 368-70.

39. Rosetti to Michelet, Nov. 8, 1850, Papiers Michelet, K. 2. 11; cf. D. Brătianu to Michelet, Oct. 25, 1850, Cretzianu, op.cit., vol. I, p. 255. Michelet inclined toward the Roumanian viewpoint. In a letter to Brătianu he wrote that he feared the Hungarians' attachment to the past was no good omen for the future federation. (July 7, 1851, cit. supra). In 1854 he felt that "the Wallachian revolution, the most radical of the time, was the indispensable keystone of the Danubian confederation that would check Russia." (Note in Michelet's handwriting, dated Feb. 4, 1854, Musée Adam Mickiewicz Mss., 1035, fol. 61).

and Magyars. The latter did not accept the principles laid down in the letter to Zamoyski, but it was wise to keep trying to convince them. Since there was not a moment to lose in preparing for the explosion which Mazzini said was just around the corner, Bălcescu undertook to establish real bonds between the emigrés and the revolutionary movement in the Roumanian provinces, otherwise all decisions taken in Paris and London would be pointless. Reports from home indicated that a revolt was brewing in Wallachia, and they wanted to be able to direct it and spread it to other provinces. There was to be a network of wires carrying the electric current of revolution from the exiles in the West to the hearts of the eight million Roumanians. It was agreed that certain of them should move nearer to the scene of action. A. G. Golescu was sent to Vienna and Transylvania, to concert with Iancu and other leaders and to found an association including all Roumanians. Bălcescu wrote to Laurian at Sibiu telling him to secure many subscriptions to the new review published in Paris. Ion Brătianu also set out for Transylvania, where Kossuth's agents were already active, and where a rising of Magyars and Roumanians against Austrian centralism and absolutism was talked of. Bălcescu sent Marghiloman, a young student, to agitate in Wallachia, told Magheru to go to the Banat, and Bolliac to Bulgaria, where they could cross the Wallachian frontier at a moment's notice. He also had high hopes of Moldavia.[40]

Prince Ştirbei in Bucharest was well aware of the movements of these subversive agents gathering on the frontier. He complained to the Austrian Government of the presence of Magheru at Sibiu and of N. Golescu and others in the Banat, "organizing their clubs and secret societies," and to the Turks that Ion Ghica was in correspondence, through the British consulate, with "Hetairists" in Wallachia. Schwarzenberg obliged by setting his police on those in Austria. A watchful eye was also kept on Rustchuk, on the Bulgarian side of the Danube, where Boliac was operating. Ştirbei was also troubled by revolutionary brochures of Rosetti, which were circulating among his subjects.[41]

Ion Brătianu's activities in Transylvania were the most daring and effective, though without immediate result. He established himself at Sibiu in August, 1850, where he could easily communicate with Wallachia. His sisters crossed the frontier to visit him and returned with quantities of revolutionary publications. Brătianu was aided by a Roumanian who held an official post as distributor

---

40. Bălcescu, Scrisori, pp. 167-225, passim.

41. N. Iorga, Corespondenţa lui Ştirbei-Vodă, (Bucharest, 1904-5), vol. I, pp. 106-11, 371-2, vol. II, (Mărturii Istorice), p. 325; Hurmuzaki, Documente, vol. XVIII, pp. 274-5; Aricescu, op.cit., vol. II, p. 98. Eliade denounced all these preparations as a Russian plot. (Scrisori din Exil, p. 41).

of the laws and ordinances of the monarchy; he spread Brătianu's secretly published propaganda in official packages which were never disturbed by the authorities. However, this could not last long, for the police of several countries were on his trail, and he took a hurried departure through a back window when the gendarmes came to arrest him, escaped to Cluj, and somehow got back to Paris without being apprehended. His mission had drawn closer the links between the Wallachian emigrés and the Transylvanian leaders. He reported that the spirit among the Roumanians of Transylvania, "even the peasants," was good, and that in Wallachia "every one is for us."[42]

And so the year 1850 came to an end, with no European revolution and no Roumanian revolution, no Roumanian-Hungarian entente, and no effective action by Mazzini's committee, which had issued a few proclamations, put out a newspaper, and nothing more. The following year saw no turn in the tide of reaction, but in the hearts of exiles in Paris and London hope did not die. Mazzini intensified his preparations for revolution in Italy and spoke of the future in glowing terms. As the eastern European wing of his organization was woefully weak, he redoubled his

---

42. Ion I. C. Brătianu, "Din Amintirile altora şi ale mele," (Cugetul Românesc, I, 1922, pp. 513-23); I. Fruma, Ion C. Brătianu la Sibiiu, 1850-1851, (Bucharest, 1938), pp. 8-11; Bălcescu, Scrisori, pp. 200, 206, 216-7, 220, 233.

efforts to bring in Kossuth, the Jugoslavs, and the Roumanians. Kossuth was still disdainful of committees and bombastic proclamations, but hinted that he would co-operate on the basis of action, not words.[43] He had become disgusted with the weakness shown by the Turks and by Palmerston, and was turning to the idea of an Italian-Hungarian revolutionary alliance, which would be a match for Austria, "if only these central committees would cease making so much noise....Damn your committees."[44] He was, however, hostile to the idea of a revolutionary crusade against all established governments, and he was not disposed to modify his attitude on the nationality question in order to please Mazzini. He made his own position clear on that in a definitive statement which he completed in April. It purported to lay down the bases of the future organization of Hungary, and was intended for Mazzini and also for Teleki and Klapka, who were at that very time continuing the negotiations with Bălcescu.

Bălcescu's memorandum of February 1851, drawn up at the request of the Hungarian committee headed by Teleki and Klapka, repeated his earlier claim for "Liberty,

---

43. Kossuth to Mazzini, Mar. 19, 1851, Menghini, op.cit., pp. 21-29.

44. Kossuth to Mazzini, Apr. 23, 1851, ibid., pp. 28-30. The last three words are in English. The rest of the letter is in French.

Equality, Fraternity for nationalities." A federation on that basis was the only possible way to plant the flag of liberty on the banks of the Danube. He considered only two nationalities qualified by geographical position and national development to be federated with the Magyars as equals, the Croats, united with the Slavonians, Dalmatians, and Serbs, and secondly the Roumanians. Boundaries between the three national states could be settled by plebiscite in the border districts. The trialistic federal government was to be on the same lines of his proposal of the previous year. The federation, including all Ottoman territory inhabited by Jugoslavs and Roumanians, would be a great state of over twenty-two million people, with sea coast on the Black Sea and the Adriatic. The immense power and advantages for all three peoples, "destined to have but one political existence, on the example of Switzerland and the United States of America," would certainly make up for what the Hungarians wrongly called the partition of their state. The Turks would have no reason to lament their loss of territory, for the new federation would protect them from Russia. As for questions of detail, Bălcescu, like Teleki, left them to the future federal diet. What was essential was an agreement in principle.[45]

---

45. Full text of the memorandum in Marcu, op.cit., pp. 30-5, from a copy made by Teleki. The original, sent by Teleki to Mazzini and by the latter to Kossuth, is in

Teleki, speaking for himself and Klapka, replied that he shared the fraternal sentiments expressed by Bălcescu and grasped with pleasure the hand extended to them. They accepted the "sublime principle of the brotherhood of peoples" and favored an entente, but professed their inability to discuss details without first consulting "several influential members of our emmigration now living outside of France."[46] That put the matter up to Kossuth, whose reply was embodied in his famous Exposé.[47] The crucial part of this document was its treatment of the nationality question. To allow autonomy was impossible as it would expose the state to dissolution. Language, he held, was not the sole criterion of a nation; unity of language did not suffice to make national unity, nor did linguistic differences prevent it, and here he turned the tables on the Roumanians by citing

---

the National Museum, Budapest. Bălcescu sent another copy to Ghica, along with Teleki's answer, with instructions to forward them, after perusal, to A. C. Golescu at Brusa. (Bălcescu to Ghica, Mar. 26, 1851, Scrisori, p. 236).

46. Teleki to Bălcescu, Mar. 22, 1851, Marcu, op.cit., pp. 29-30.

47. Exposé des principes de la future organisation publique de la Hongrie, dated Apr. 25, 1851, at Kutahia. Full text in Kastner, op.cit., pp. 120-40, and in Iranyi & Chassin, Histoire politique de la Révolution de Hongrie, vol. I, pp. 365-92. The texts are not identical. That given by Iranyi and Chassin is probably a translation back into French of a Hungarian translation of the original. I have taken my quotations from the text in Kastner.

as examples the United States and Switzerland. No nation had the right to exist as a state within a state; that would mean death for the state as a whole.

Kossuth refused to countenance the political nationalism of any group except the Magyars. Demands of other nationalities for self-expression he proposed to meet by recognizing nationality as a cultural and social phenomenon, similar to religion, which need not be connected with politics and still less with territorial questions, which are determined by legal and historical factors and not by accidents of language. Free association for this purpose would be allowed locally and also into state-wide national groups, under chief, voivoda, or hospodar. These organizations would control the schools, churches, etc., of the various nationalities. This statesmanlike plan of Kossuth's was an adaptation of the Ottoman millet system and in its main lines was the same solution later proposed by Viennese Socialist thinkers for the Austrian problem. It may, in the future, prove to be the only possible way out for the Danubian peoples, reduced to impotence and poverty by the extremes of political nationalism. It would be feasible, however, only in a Europe which had not yet reached, or had outgrown, the stage where territorial nationalism had become the religion of the leaders and was beginning to penetrate to the masses. In 1851 it seemed very much like the old Magyar intransigence dressed up to look like something else. That was the way the Roumanians interpreted it.

Kossuth was willing to let Croatia have autonomy, but not the "mixed" provinces of Voivodina or Transylvania, "which is but a part of Hungary."

> "...I know the proposal, or rather the scheme, of those Roumanians of Moldo-Wallachia. They say: 'Let us establish a great Danubian confederation... There will be no frontiers, but for internal administration the boundaries will be drawn according to nationality'....Let's be frank. These Roumanian gentlemen want Transylvania. They want it annexed to Moldo-Wallachia and governed...from Bucharest....They want us to make them a gift of such a province. That's modesty for you. What they want is that we should sacrifice the Szeklers, that glory of our race, that steel wall of our security. But that would be worse than suicide, it would be shame, cowardice, treason. Never!
>
> "And they want more. They want the Hungarian nation to rise and shed blood in the fight against Austria and the Tsar...and, as a reward of victory...be torn into shreds by Wallachia, Serbs, Slovaks, Ruthenes, and Germans--the Magyars of Transylvania transformed into subjects of Daco-Roumania, and the rest of the Hungarian nation shut up in its central plain,...stifled and expiring....
>
> "And they call that a solution! Thank you."

Kossuth did not spare MM. les Moldo-Valaques in his private letter to Mazzini. He accused them of causing the war in Transylvania in 1848 and said that if they were really friends of liberty they would mind their own business and forget about Daco-Roumania. Mazzini could hardly be encouraged by this stand which revealed not only Kossuth's refusal to negotiate about Transylvania, but also his deep mistrust of the Roumanian leaders and his contempt for the Roumanians in general.[48] Yet he did not give up; he continued to urge a truce which would leave the final settlement until after the victory. Bălcescu was very much discouraged and took a less active part in the negotiations. He did not go to London because he had "neithe the money, nor the health, nor the invitation."[49] Dumitru Brătianu went in his place. He announced his presence by a letter to the Central Committee, saying that the Roumanians saw in it the image of the great brotherhood that would soon unite all free peoples. The Committee's principles, he wrote, were those of ten million Roumanians who in 1848 inscribed on their flag "Justice, Brotherhood," and who were ready to fight for European democracy.[50] He immediately began to work with Mazzini and Ledru Rollin, and the first

---

48. "Ils n'étaient pas des guerriers formidables, mais des cannibales qui s'enfuyant dans leurs montagnes à notre approche ne descendirent que pour indendier et piller les villages sans défense, et pour égorger les femmes et les enfants. (Kossuth to Mazzini, June 19, 1851, Menghini, op.cit., pp. 31-7).

49. Bălcescu to Ghica, May 26, 1851, Scrisori, p. 235.

50. May 10, 1851, Cretzianu, op.cit., vol. I, pp. 265-6. Sept. 11, 1851 is the date generally given for Brătianu's joining the committee. But Mazzini wrote to a friend on July 14th, "It is true, Bratiano is a member of the European Committee. He is the delegate of all the members of the revolutionary committee of 1848 and of the members of the ministry of that time. He also mentioned having Brătianu's written adherence "To our address which called his fellow citizens to

tangible result was a lengthy address to "the Roumanian populations," signed by the four original members in the name of the committee.[51]

The address gives the impression of having been composed by Mazzini after a few talks with Brătianu, the latter supplying the minimum of information about the Roumanians' history and mission in eastern Europe. The Roumanians are exhorted to live up to their sacred and historic role of advance guard of the "Greco-Latin race" in the East, by planting there those great principles which the other Latin peoples have created in the West, namely individual liberty and collective progress. Great stress is laid on the

---

the crusade against Russia. (Mazzini, Scritti, XLV, pp. 320-1). Brătianu's signature appeared on the Committee's manifesto of July 20 to the Poles. He was thus definitely a full-fledged member before that date. (Scritti, XLVI, p. 96). On May 31, 1851, the "Revolutionary Committee of 1848" voted to send Brătianu credentials as representative of Roumania. (Rosetti, Note intime, vol. II, p. 74).

51. The original text was in French and dated June 26, 1851. (Mazzini, Scritti, XLVI, pp. 81-7). Italian versions appeared in the papers Italia e Popolo, Genoa, July 2, and La Voce del Deserto, Turin, July 3. Professor Marcu, after a careful comparison of Italian and Roumanian texts, concludes that the latter version was a translation from the Italian and that the translator was Bălcescu. (Conspiratori şi Conspiraţii, pp. 44-50). It seems more likely that it was a translation from the French, with which they were more familiar. Rosetti's diary says: "I translated Mazzini's proclamation to the Roumanians." The entry is July 9, but it refers to all the days since June 29, and the day on which Rosetti noted the appearance of the proclamation in the French press. (Note intime, vol. II, pp. 78-9).

necessity of the Roumanians' acting as a cohesive force uniting with themselves the Slavic and Magyar races. "The consciousness of this mission will constitute and will guarantee your nationality! In the name of the peoples who today are subscribing to the preliminaries of a European federative pact, we state this to be your duty and your right." Following a careful explanation of the meaning of nationality as the instinct of peoples to win their liberty, without egotism, without jealousy and hatred of other peoples, the address points out to the Roumanians their real enemies, the forces of evil represented by the Tsar and the Austrian Emperor, and their real friends, "the Slav, the Magyar, the Italian, and the Greek, your brothers whose enemies are also yours." The concluding appeal voices Mazzini's hope and conviction that a federation of free peoples would soon arise in the valley of the Danube:

> "The great confederation of the Danube will be a reality in our time. This thought will guide you in all your efforts. The bridge of Trajan is now nothing more than a pillar on each side of the Danube; it is the symbol of the situation today. Your hands must construct the new spans; that is your duty for the future." 52

The references to Danubian co-operation were an appeal to the emigrés to come to an agreement. After receiving Brătianu's "full and entire adherence in the name of the Roumanian people," Mazzini wrote:

---

52. Marcu, op.cit., pp. 44-50.

"You agreed with Ledru Rollin to write an address in answer to ours. You must do so. In it you must speak some words of peace to the Hungarians. The principles which we have put forward: pacific solution; universal suffrage guaranteed, consequently free expression of the desires of the populations; adjournment of disputes until after the victory and the formation of a democratic European congress--have been accepted by the Hungarians. The Roumanians must do the same. We are rapidly approaching the great battle, and we must prove to all, friends and enemies, that we are strong, organized, and united." 53

"The Hungarians" who had given their consent were probably Teleki and Klapka. Kossuth's resolute attitude certainly gave Mazzini no basis for such a conclusion.

Brătianu, then in Paris, did not reply immediately with words of peace. He was in fact, at this very time, engaged in a polemic with Daniel Iranyi, a loyal disciple of Kossuth, in the columns of La Presse.[54] Iranyi's first letter and Bratianu's reply were replete with invitations to fraternization and references to the approaching struggle against despotism. The Danubian confederation, wrote Brătianu, quoting Mazzini's address, "will be the great work of our

---

53. Mazzini to D. Brătianu, undated, Cretzianu, op.cit., vol. I, pp. 268-9.

54. The series of letters, beginning in the issue of June 18, 1851, two by Iranyi and two by Brătianu, was published in October of the same year as Lettres hongro-roumaines, edited by Henri Valleton, a French liberal republican and friend of Brătianu. The preface refrains from taking sides and speaks of the need of reconciling all democratic groups for the struggle for the universal republic.
Rosetti's diary says, "We published the Iranyi-Brătianu debate in a brochure." (Note intime, vol. II, p. 81).

epoch." This was counterbalanced by a sharp debate over the events of 1848. In the later letters the question of title to Transylvania was brought out into the open, and the general lines of the Kossuth-Bălcescu debate were followed. Iranyi affirmed the necessity of maintaining Hungary intact and poured scorn on the conception of a united Roumania:

> "You want to sacrifice the most valiant defender of the freedom of peoples. What guarantees for humanity will you furnish for the success of the experiment? A thousand-year-old state cannot be broken up in that way. What divine law, what law of democracy demands that peoples, united for centuries, should be separated, to be joined to other groups merely because of identity of language? According to that reasoning, Alsace should go to Germany."

Brătianu's rebuttal, in which he claimed to speak for all Roumanians, including those in the Habsburg Empire, insisted that freedom and equality could come only with national self-determination:

> "Is a Roumanian equal in a Hungarian national state, with a Hungarian government, a Hungarian army, the Hungarian language, etc.? Would the Hungarians consider themselves equal in an Austrian republic where everything was Austrian?... You say you want democracy, and at the same time you want the thousand-year-old Hungarian state. But the two are incompatible....
>
> "You mention the case of Alsace, but how can you compare that with Transylvania? The Alsatians want to be French, are French, and will fight against those who wish to detach them from France. But the Roumanians do not want to be Hungarian, are not Hungarian, and will fight against those who wish to attach them to Hungary. ...Out of respect for democracy,...let us speak no longer of bastard states composed of heterogeneous elements...; let us be of our own time, and understand that for free peoples there can only be

> free associations....The Transylvanian Roumanians cannot contribute to the great idea of a Danubian confederation of free peoples if united to Hungary, but only if joined to the Roumanians of the Principalities. To be sure there are other nationalities in Transylvania, but a very small number. They can go to join their own national families; and the Roumanians not in the new Roumania can come to it....You will....not be astounded at the Roumanians wanting to be united in a single national body, even if they have to pay the price of their own blood to attain that goal."

The Hungarians, by force of circumstances, had to deny both racial or linguistic national determinism and the doctrine of self-determination by plebiscite. As that could not be counterbalanced by a superficial liberalism, they had to swim against the general trend of the 19th century. Brătianu made the most of their inconsistencies. He could afford to stand squarely on national self-determination, anticipating Renan's classic argument on the question of Alsace, and to accept all the logical consequences of that liberal nationalism of which Mazzini was the prophet.

Mazzini himself, wanting the co-operation of both parties, and particularly that of Kossuth, refrained from taking sides in the controversy. He was vexed with Brătianu and wrote that he counted on him not to let any more "irritating polemics" jeopardize the chances for a "Truce of God" between the Hungarians and the Roumanians "for the supreme crisis which is months--not years--away."[55] Brătianu,

---

55. Mazzini to D. Brătianu, Aug. 21, 1851, enclosed in a letter to Michelet, Cretzianu, <u>op.cit</u>., vol. I, p. 270.

after considerable delay, complied with the request and prepared an address from the new Roumanian National Committee.[56] It repeated and amplified the reference made to the Roumanian nation as the advance guard in the East of the "Greco-Latin race" and of the immortal principles of individual liberty and collective progress. The promised words of peace for the Hungarians were embodied in a general declaration of "united action with Hungarians, Slavs, and Greeks in the holy crusade of democracy..., one for all and all for one." Delimitation of territories could be left to a future congress of European democracy. Mazzini had promised justice, and all would submit to its decisions.

> "The great Confederation of the Danube will be a fact of our epoch,...yes, as will the freedom of the Danubian peoples....Our neighbors need not worry....Each will retain individuality and independence of action....
> "The Roumanian will not deceive the hopes which democracy has placed in him; we have sunk into the earth the new piers of the bridge of Trajan, and this...bridge of the holy alliance of peoples will ...be a symbol of the great European fraternization." 57

---

56. This was the new name given to what had been the Revolutionary Committee of 1848. On June 1 this committee had issued an anti-Russian manifesto "To the Roumanian People," written by Rosetti and signed by Bălcescu, N. Golescu, and Rosetti. (Cf. Rosetti, Note intime, vol. II, pp. 73-4; Panaitescu, Contribuţii la o biografie a lui N. Bălcescu, p. 117, note 7, 145, note 8; Marcu, op.cit., p. 44, note 2; Bălcescu, Scrisori, pp. 247, 253).

57. The French text, dated Sept. 11, 1851, appeared in Le National, Oct. 14, 1841, and in other French papers.

Everything was being prepared for the great European insurrection. Kossuth, informed by his many agents that it was imminent, had finally decided to collaborate with the Central Democratic Committee in London. He gave Mazzini his word of honor that an Italian revolution would be followed by the revolt of Hungary.[58] Details were to be arranged on Kossuth's arrival in England. Mazzini urged all the national committees to prepare the revolution among their own peoples. The Roumanians in exile had rather neglected their contacts with their country and certainly had no ready-fashioned revolt which would break out at a signal from them. Bălcescu felt that the whole policy of acting with the London committee rested on their strengthening their grip on the national movement in all the Roumanian provinces, otherwise they would only be deceiving Mazzini and themselves.[59] In 1851, therefore, they intensified their propaganda.

It is given by Smochină, *Sur les émigrés roumains á Paris*, pp. 187-93. The Roumanian text was published in *Republica Română*, No. 1, Paris, 1851, reproduced in *Lui C. A. Rosetti*, pp. 255-8. Marcu (*op.cit.*, pp. 54-9) gives a Roumanian translation of an Italian version. Marcu believes Bălcescu was the author of the address; others think D. Brătianu wrote it. (Cf. Marcu, *op.cit.*, p. 60; Breazu, *Michelet şi Românii*, p. 63).

58. Kossuth to Mazzini, June 16, 1851, Menghini, *op.cit.*, p. 31. Reports of Kossuth's agents, *ibid.*, p. 42; Kastner, *op.cit.*, pp. 102-3, 140-63.

59. Bălcescu to Ghica, Nov. 26, 1850, *Scrisori*, p. 223.

Subversive literature printed in Paris began to appear in greater quantity in the Austrian provinces and in the Principalities, notably Rosetti's "Appeal to all Parties" and the issues of Junimea Română, with its advocacy of the Roumanian Republic and of "the principle of insurrection, the primary right of an oppressed nation," and its request to readers to copy the articles and pass them around, and to national leaders in Transylvania, Bucovina, and the Banat to get in touch with the editors in Paris. This propaganda, printed on tissue paper, made its way over the frontiers through the regular mails. Sometimes the authorities were able to detect and confiscate some of it, but most of it got through. It was sent to trusted friends, including the Golescus' mother and other women, who saw that it was distributed. The authorities blamed everything on "the revolutionary Society of Roumanian Students" in Paris.[60]

When Mazzini's "Proclamation to the Roumanian Populations" was issued, the Revolutionary Committee of 1848, formed as one of the national committees of the Mazzinian hierarchy, undertook to give it wide publicity. Ion

---

60. S. Reli, C. A. Rosetti si N. Bălcescu în lumina cenzurei austriace, (Cernăuţi, 1930), pp. 7-10; Iorga, Corespondenţa lui Ştirbei-Vodă, vol. I, p. 480, vol. II, pp. 325-7, giving a report supplied to Ştirbei by the French police, naming "Dimitri Bratiano et son frère Eugène" as the leading plotters and erroneously stating them to be in Moldavia.

Brătianu took it around to the leading Paris dailies, and it appeared on June 29th in L'Evénement, Le Siècle, Le National, and even the conservative Journal des Débats. The next day it came out in several other papers, including La Presse. Copies of these papers were then shipped to Bucharest, Jassy, Brașov, and other central points. The proclamation was translated into Roumanian, under the auspices of the Roumanian Revolutionary Committee for 1848, and printed on thin paper. Then the committee set out to inundate Transylvania and the Principalities with copies.[61] Rosetti's friend Daniel Rosenthal was sent to Sibiu and to Bucharest to act as distributor, but he got no further than Budapest, where his cargo of proclamations was discovered. He was arrested and thrown into prison, where he hung himself.[62] The Wallachian police was also on the qui vive and intercepted Rosetti's letters to his friend Winterhalder in Bucharest, with whom Rosenthal was to work. Intercepted letters from the Golescus and other exiles, addressed to

---

61. Rosetti, Note intime, vol. II, p. 78. The French police notified Știrbei that Boliac had had 1500 copies printed. (Iorga, Corespondența lui Știrbei-Vodă, vol. II, p. 327). Alexandrescu in Bucharest wrote to Ghica that he had received many copies of the address. (Aug. 8, 1851, Lovinescu, Grigore Alexandrescu, p. 267).

62. Rosetti to Rosenthal, July 14, 1851, Iorga, op.cit., vol. II, p. 329; Rosetti, Note intime, vol. II, pp. 79-80; Barbu Lazareanu, "Mărturii despre Daniel Constantin Rosenthal, (Adevărul Literar și Artistic, IV, July 15, 22, 1923).

Colquhoun and to Grant, were full of information about the events of 1848 and allusions to the approaching revolution.[63] Alexandru Manu, one of the few who had been allowed to return, took a hand in the underground revolutionary movement. He was probably acting under the direction of the Paris committee, and was a link between the Roumanian and Hungarian and Polish revolutionaries, who were at this time gathering at Constantinople, at Rustchuk, and moving about in the Principalities.[64]

Much of the revolutionary literature which arrived at Bucharest made its way northward across the mountains into Transylvania. Some, destined for Wallachia, was caught by the Austrian authorities even before it reached the frontier. The military governor at Sibiu noted the arrival of "many envelopes from Paris, addressed to persons in Wallachia" and containing manifestoes of Eliade and of Bolintineanu. Mazzini's proclamation to the Roumanians, with its bitter attack on Austria and Russia, was immediately noticed by the Austrian police. The matter was considered serious enough to call for a warning to the Wallachian Government not to be so lax in letting this propaganda arrive in Bucharest, and Stirbey in turn requested the Austrians not

---

63. Iorga, op.cit., vol. I, pp. 257-8, 479, vol. II, pp. 215, 327-35.

64. Ibid., vol. I, pp. 259, 478-9, 586, vol. II, pp. 329-33; Lukasik, Pologne et Roumanie, p. 90.

to let Roumanian exiles establish themselves in Austrian cities near the Wallachian frontier. The solidarity of thrones was considered necessary in order to stamp out these troublesome manifestations of the alliance of revolutionaries.[65]

The word was passed around everywhere in democratic Europe that the spring of 1852 would see the awaited explosion. Kossuth, on his visit to London, found time amid his speeches and banquets to talk with Mazzini and to put the finishing touches on their plans. They agreed to synchronize their two revolutions. The agreement was not extended to include leaders of other nations; either Kossuth refused to make an entente with the Roumanians or else the matter was not brought up at all. Mazzini sized up Kossuth as ultra-Magyar, "the incarnation of Hungary," and had no illusions about his republicanism or his devotion to the brotherhood of nations. There is no record of any interview between Kossuth and Brătianu at this time; the latter lived in Brighton and may have purposely avoided going to London while Kossuth was there.

Louis Napoleon's <u>coup d'état</u> was a blow to those who

---

65. Reli, <u>op.cit</u>., pp. 11-15. It was reported also that subtler methods of smuggling were being used; the incitement to revolution might be on sheets hidden in boxes of cigars, or written indelibly on a colored handkerchief that could be read only after the dye was washed out.

hoped France would take the lead in the revolutionary movement, but neither Mazzini nor Kossuth had ever had much faith in France. Mazzini always stressed the solidarity of nations and the inspiration of Italy as against the French initiative. He continued to work for the Italian revolution, whose outbreak would, he thought, be followed by ten other movements. One of these would be that of the Roumanians. He retained close ties with Brătianu, who in November 1851, in the name of the Roumanian committee, handed over fifteen hundred francs to Mazzini "to be used according to the needs of democratic propaganda."[66]

The spring of 1852 went by without revolution, but Mazzini kept up his hopeful preparations. Brătianu shared the hopes and collaborated in the preparations. He was in communication with his friends and colleagues on the Continent who continued to send him reports. Nicolae Golescu was in Athens trying to establish relations with revolutionary groups there.[67] Ştefan Golescu, in a long report on the

66. Cretzianu, <u>op.cit</u>., vol. I, p. 275.

67. N. Golescu to D. Brătianu, Mar. 6, May 26, Sept. 27, 1852, <u>ibid</u>., pp. 277-8, 309-10; cf. Alexandrescu to Ghica, May 3, 1852, Lovinescu, <u>op.cit</u>., p. 281. At this time the Mazzinian and friend of some of the <u>Paşoptişti</u>, Canini, was also in Greece promoting a project of "simultaneous and synchronized revolution of all the subjugated peoples of the Orient." (Iorga, "Un prevestitor al confederaţie balcanice, Marc Antonio Canini," <u>Ac. Rom., Mem. Sect. Ist</u>., Ser. II, vol. XXXV, 1912-13, pp. 107-10).

prospects of revolution in Germany and Austria, said that only a change in Paris would provide the necessary spark. In Vienna he saw Maiorescu and Magheru, who were in touch with Czech leaders. Their plans called for the proclamation of a "provisional government of the united states of Austria" when revolution should break out; they would announce the unity of Roumania and of the Serbs, for if democracy were victorious, they expected Turkey to collapse. Czechs, Roumanians, and Jugoslavs were said to be ready to fight together against the Habsburgs and also against the Magyars, "whom they consider the enemies of all the other nationalities which today make up the Austrian Empire."[68] This report, which reached Brătianu in London while Kossuth was still there, can hardly have encouraged Mazzini's hope of a Hungarian-Slav-Roumanian entente. Kossuth, dazzled by the great reception given him by the English, began to count more on England and America than on Hungary's neighbors.

During 1852 Brătianu continued to work with the Central Committee. He signed proclamations and attended meetings. At the funeral of Darasz in August, he marched with Ledru and Mazzini at the head of a great procession.[69] He was on good terms with Hungarian exiles in London, and this

---

68. S. Golescu to D. Brătianu, Nov. 5, 1851, Cretzianu, op. cit., vol. I, pp. 271-5.

69. A. R. Calman, op.cit., p. 164; Kastner, op.cit., p. 81, note; W. J. Linton, European Republicans, (London, 1893), p. 319.

spirit of co-operation was extended to Italy, where Manu worked with a Mazzini-inspired "Italo-Danubian Union," which was engaged in encouraging desertions from the Austrian army.[70]

Brătianu put out an "Appeal to the Transylvanian Roumanians in the Austrian army," telling they no longer had to shed blood in other people's battles but could fight under their own flag for their own country, Roumania, with the Hungarian, the Pole, and the Serb for allies. The Hungarian was said to have repented of his past errors.[71] Another appeal was addressed "To the inhabitants of the Principalities," and told them to prepare for the war in which Roumanians of all lands would fight shoulder to shoulder against the Tsar. It would be not a local but a European fight, in which the immortal Revolution of 1848 and the collective forces of European democracy were certain to overcome the powers of darkness. Roumanians must join hands with the Slavs and Magyars and fulfil their mission to humanity. The new Roumanian Republic would be a citadel of democracy in the East.[72]

All these preparations led the Roumanians exactly

---

70. Marcu, op.cit., p. 65.

71. Cretzianu, op.cit., vol. I, pp. 283-9. It was undated, printed in Brussels, on thin paper.

72. Signed "Dumitru Brătianu, for the Roumanian Revolutionary Committee," Sept. 10, 1852, (ibid., pp. 289-301).

nowhere. The crowning disillusionment came with Mazzini's failure at Milan in February 1853. Thereafter the movements and organizations he represented were in full retreat. Brătianu had less and less to do with the Central Committee. The diplomatic crisis in the East brought a new situation and new opportunities However, since there was a possibility that the Holy Places dispute might turn into a war of nationalities, he was willing to heed Mazzini's final desperate plea for an agreement with Kossuth.

Late in the autumn of 1853, Mazzini invited Kossuth and Brătianu, to his lodgings in London.[73] The only account of the meeting was written twenty years later by Brătianu in a necrological article on Mazzini in a Bucharest newspaper.[74] He describes it as follows:

> "I did not want to see Kossuth in England any more than I had wanted to seehim in Hungary in '48, for he had been too unjust, too violent with the Roumanians. At the beginning of the Crimean War, on the eve of my departure for Turkey, Mazzini said to me: 'Kossuth wants to see you; you must see him. I have made an appointment with him at my house, be sure to come. The evil which Kossuth has done to the Roumanians in the past does not release you

---

73. Invitation to Brătianu, undated: "Mon cher Bratiano, Voulezvous vous trouver chez moi Samedi entre onze heures et midi? Kossuth y sera." (Cretzianu, <u>op.cit</u>., vol. I, p. 358) Kossuth's reply to his invitation, also undated: "Je serai charmé de voir Bratiano chez vous Samedi." (Menghini, <u>op.cit</u>., pp. 158-9).

74. <u>Românul</u>, (ed. C. A. Rosetti), 1872, reprinted in <u>Românul</u>, June 26, 27, 1892, and in Cretzianu,, <u>op.cit</u>., vol. II, pp. 282-9.

from your duty; and your duty is to try to come to an understanding with him, to come to a decision before your departure, for we do not know how far this war may spread, as it has a European character.' Mazzini met us at his house, and with his persistence and help we agreed that, if the Hungarians and the Roumanians in the Austrian Empire should have occasion to take up arms, we would address them in a manifesto written in Hungarian and Roumanian and signed by Kossuth and myself, calling upon them to act in common; each nation was to fight under its own flag, and after the victory, the Transylvanians were to decide, by a free plebiscite in which all should vote, whether or not they wanted their country to be united to Hungary." 75

Teleki and Klapka, who had for several years been willing to agree to a plebiscite,[76] were going ahead with their own negotiations with the Roumanian emigrés, and with the Serbian and Turkish governments, with a view t a common war against Austria and Russia, and a confederation to follow it. Klapka went to Constantinople in November and reached an

---

75. In C. A. Rosetti's papers (Ac. Rom. Mss., 4777, fol. 113) there is a manuscript copy of this passage, but it is in the handwriting of neither D. Brătianu nor Rosetti. It is apparently a draught, or more likely a copy, of this portion of Brătianu's article, and not a contemporary document, as Constantin V. Rosetti, who published it in 1923 as a record of a meeting between Kossuth and Rosetti, believed. (Cf. C.V. Rosetti, "Din hârtiile lui C. A. Rosetti, Adevĕrul, Bucharest, May 3, 1923, pp. 1-2).

76. Ion Brătianu's son mentions a meeting of a mixed commission of Ion Brătianu, A. G. Golescu, Bălcescu, Andrassy, Teleki, and another Hungarian, at which it was decided that the fate of Transylvania should be settled by plebiscite. (I. I. C. Brătianu, Din Amintirile altora şi ale mele, p. 515). These men were all in Paris in 1850 and 1851, but there is no evidence that the Magyars in Paris then defied Kossuth by making such an agreement. Brătianu's statement may refer vaguely to the agreement of 1853 in London or Constantinople.

agreement with the Roumanians there.[77] He consented to the "independence" of Croatia and Transylvania.[78] As Kossuth was at that time consenting to practically the same thing with Brătianu, probably the Klapka negotiations had his consent.

If Kossuth actually agreed to such terms, he had come a long way from the stand he took in 1851, when the very idea of a plebiscite in Transylvania was anathema to him. The change can be attributed to the new diplomatic situation in Europe, which was more favorable to the aspirations of the Roumanians than to those of the Hungarians; an entente with the Roumanians therefore became sufficiently desirable in his eyes to warrant concessions on the Transylvanian question. Apparently as a consequence of the bargain with Brătianu, Kossuth signed an address to the "brave Roumanian patriots of Moldo-Wallachia," dated December 6, 1853, and signed "Louis Kossuth, Gouverneur élu de Hongrie." In this

---

77. Klapka in his memoirs speaks of traveling to Constantinople on the same boat as Nicolae and Ştefan Golescu, and of discussing with them the need of a confederation including also Serbia. He does not mention any agreement on Transylvania. (G. Klapka, Aus meinen Erinnerungen, Zürich, 1887, pp. 315-6).

78. T. Lengyel, The Hungarian Exiles and the Danubian Confederation, pp. 455-6, is the only authority I have for the Constantinople negotiations. No references are given, but the information most probably comes from Hungarian sources. From the Roumanian side we have no confirmation of this agreement, but there is no doubt that they would have been glad to negotiate on those terms, which represented a Hungarian acceptance of their position.

address he announced that he was sending an emissary to assure his "worthy and estimable neighbors of Moldo-Wallachia of the friendship, esteem, and fraternal sentiments of the Hungarian nation," and to make known his desire to "cultivate a fraternal entente and perfect accord with their brave nation for the future and particularly for the present crisis." As for Hungarian intentions towards the Roumanians in Transylvania, he spoke vaguely of "full national autonomy for their political and social position," adding that the justice and sincerity of these intentions could not fail to be appreciated.[79]

This "settlement" of the Transylvanian issue brought no concrete results, because the powers did not allow either the Hungarians or the Roumanians to enter the war. The crusade of nationalities was indefinitely postponed, and Transylvania, which Magyars and Roumanians had been so unwilling to assign to each other, remained in the hands of Habsburgs.

5. The trial and imprisonment of Ion Brătianu

Mazzini may have thought that the initiative for the universal revolution must come from Italy; the Roumanians were convinced it could come only from France. It was for that reason that the coup d'état of 1851 was such a blow

---

79. Copy in Ac. Rom. Mss., 4635, fol. 3, reprod. by Marcu, op.cit., pp. 66-67.

to them. It even affected Bălcescu's physical condition and hastened his death, so broken was his spirit.[80] The Roumanian radicals, who had been waiting for the presidential election of 1852 and the victory of Ledru Rollin, and instead saw the Republic itself disappear before their very eyes, naturally hated the author of the coup d'état with a deadly loathing. In answer to a letter of Michelet, who condemned France for believing in "the shadow of a shadow," D. Brătianu declared his own opinion of the new Caesar in strong terms:

> "...The man who pillages and oppresses France is no Frenchman. Nor is he an Italian; Italy repudiates him. He is a bastard, a miserable wretch, without country and without family; born in debauchery, raised in crime, he has been sent to you expressly to drown in mud and in blood the baneful prestige which, still in 1849, was associated with the name of Napoleon." 81

One day in Paris, one of Rosetti's small children ran home breathless with the announcement: "Lulu saw him! He has a nose and mouth and ears like a man!" From the conversation of Rosetti and Ion Brătianu around the house the child had been given the impression that Napoleon was a monster of some sub-human species.[82]

Even before December the French police had begun to

---

80. Panaitescu, Contribuţii la o biografie a lui N. Bălcescu, p. 147.

81. D. Brătianu to Michelet, Apr. 10, 1852, Cretzianu, op. cit., vol. I, pp. 307-8.

82. W. Mickiewicz, Pamietniki, vol. I, p. 130.

treat the Roumanians as "undesirable aliens." Their rooms had been searched and their papers confiscated. Dumitru Brătianu had been told to leave the country, and the others expected the same. "Political conditions" forced Rosetti to leave Paris in December, and later in the year he followed Michelet to Nantes. He remained in correspondence with D. Brătianu and their letters often mentioned "business affairs" as being good or bad, lively or quiet; these were references to the state of the revolutionary movement in France. Brătianu and his friends in Paris may have served as a channel of communication between Ledru Rollin in London and his followers in France, although of this there is no definite proof.

Ion Brătianu was the only one bold enough to take a direct part in the plots of his former student friends who were ready to employ such methods as political assassination and a call to the barricades in order to bring to life the democratic and social republic. When arrests were made of the conspirators in the plot against Napoleon's life frustrated in June, 1853, one of those detained was Ion Brătianu.[83] The police had discovered in his rooms a large wooden chest containing a printing press and sheaves of revolutionary proclamations "all of great violence, abominable provocations against the Emperor and appeals to insurrection and massacre."

---

83. For information that another Roumanian was implicated in the plot, and got away to London, see Pulszky, op.cit., vol. III, pp. 31-2.

Brătianu refused to say to whom the press belonged and was hustled off to Sainte-Pélagie, where the other prisoners baptized him "the Ottoman."[84] His friends, Michelet, and Armand Lévy, tried to intercede with the authorities to have him released,[85] but he remained, and on November 7th he was brought before the Cour d'Assises de la Seine, along with a host of others rounded up by the police for participation in the plots against Napoleon. They formed roughly two groups, one of idealistic republicans of the salons and of Michelet's courses, the other of socialist workingmen; the two had had very little connection with each other. Brătianu, ninth on the list of accused, was charged with having been a party to the plot.[86]

Unable to prove his participation in meetings where the plot was hatched, the prosecution made the most of his brother's connection with the revolutionary committees in London. He was said to be "as supple as he is violent,

---

84. A. Darimon, Histoire d'un Parti, Cinq sous l'Empire, (Paris, 1885), p. 196.

85. Smochină, Sur les émigrés roumains à Paris de 1850 à 1856, p. 176; Breazu, Michelet și Românii, p. 96.

86. J. Tchernoff, Le parti républicain au coup d'état et sous le second empire, (Paris, 1906), pp. 170-1, 216-9; idem, Dans le Creuset des Civilisations, (Paris, 1937), vol. III, pp. 137-8: Cours d'Assises de la Seine, Attentat contre la vie de l'Empereur et contre la securité du Gouvernement. Acte d'Accusation, (Paris, 1853), p. 2; Cour d'Assises de la Seine, Complots dits de l'Hippodrome et de l'Opéra-Comique, (Paris, 1853), pp. 3-4; Smochină, op.cit., pp. 175-6.

and, all in all, extremely dangerous." The accusation described him thus:

> "Bratiano, proprietor, residing at rue Mézières 4, Paris. His the brother of Dimitrix (sic) Bratiano, Wallachian refugee in London and member of the European central democratic committee. Affiliated with the Wallachian committee in Paris, he is very active in secretly printing a revolutionary catechism destined to demoralize the soldiers and peasants of Wallachia. He meddles also, in spite of what he says, in the political affairs of France. His opinions, his connections place him close to the most influential men of the demagogic party, so that if a real link exists between the secret societiès in Paris and those in London, none is better placed than Bratiano to serve as intermediary." 87

There was no question as to the revolutionary activity of the French refugees in London and their hand in the instigation of this and other plots. The French police had ample evidence of that, and had since 1851 been trying to get the British Government to take measures against them.[88] There was, however, no evidence to fasten on Bratianu the role of intermediary for which he was so well placed. As for the chest he stuck to his story that he knew nothing of its contents. Mere possession of it did not constitute being

---

87. Albert Fermé, Les Conspirations sous le Second Empire. Complot de l'Hippodrome et de l'Opéra-Comique, (Paris, 1869), pp. 35-8.

88. G. Bourgin, "Mazzini et le Comité Central Démocratique en 1851," (Il Risorgimento italiano, VI, 1913, pp. 353-71; Alexandre Zévaès, "Les proscrits français en 1848 à Londres," (La Révolution de 1848, XX, 1923-4, pp. 345-75, and XXI, 1924-5, pp. 94-114), pp. 104-6; Tchernoff, Le Parti républicain, p. 231.

party to the conspiracy.

The deficiencies in his unlikely story were glossed over by the eloquence of his lawyer, Jules Favre, who here had much of the same role he was to have five years later at the trial of Orsini. Favre maintained that Brătianu had no connections with the other accused. "What would my client be doing among this mob?", he shouted.[89] Favre gave a sketch of his client's career, with a good deal thrown in about "the misfortunes and aspirations of Roumania,...which has fought against Turkey, against Russia, against Austria, which is of Latin origin, which has always had with France a community of interests and of sentiments...." He told of Brătianu's role in 1848, as "a member of the provisional government elected by the vote of all the people," of his fighting for three months against foreign invasion, etc. Brătianu was a conspirator, said Favre, but only for the independence of his country. As for plotting against France, that was impossible, for France was his "second homeland." All he wanted was that it should give a hand to the first; the Foreign Minister

89. "Mon client, que serait-il allé faire du mileu de cette cohue? (mouvement sur le banc des prévenus)." Fermé, op.cit., p. 161. On p. 215 Fermé quotes a letter from Rano, a student among the accused, who told of their surprise at this insult. He said that Brătianu was much wounded by the incident and later made explanations in clear terms. (Cf. statements of Rano to Tchernoff, in Tchernoff, Dans le Creuset des Civilisations, vol. III, p. 138).

(Drouyn de Lhuys) could confirm that. He should be acquitted, said Favre, so that he could return to lead the "Roumaniotes" in battle against the Russians. He read a letter from Michelet which said that Brătianu's incarceration would be of service only to the Tsar. Rouland, the prosecutor, was not impressed by Favre's arguments. The talk about the noble Wallachian awaited as leader by his countrymen he attributed to the fertile imagination of M. Favre. "For his brother Arthur (sic) Bratiano, who is quite free and can fly to Wallachia, prefers to remain in London and to write programs for a socialistic republic with Kossuth and Ledru Rollin. Thus I am not convinced that the Roumaniotes are awaiting any liberating messiah from the Brătianu family."[90]

On November 16, 1853, the jury brought in a verdict of "not guilty" for Brătianu and five others. The rest were sentenced. But those acquitted were immediately ordered to appear before the <u>Tribunal Correctionnel de la Seine</u>, where they were tried again, this time for belonging to secret societies, and Brătianu also for possession of a secret printing press. This time Favre's arguments were of no avail; the court found Brătianu guilty of being "chief or founder" of a secret society and sentenced him, on January

---

90. Fermé, <u>op.cit</u>., pp. 141, 157-64, 184, 196; <u>Complots dits de l'Hippodrome et de l'Opéra-Comique</u>, pp. 8-9, 13-14, 21-22; Maurice Reclus, <u>Jules Favre</u>, (Paris, 2nd. ed., 1913), pp. 193-4; Smochină, <u>op.cit</u>., pp. 177-80.

16, 1854, to a fine of five hundred francs and three years in prison.[91] The intervention of his friends, Michelet, Dumesnil, and Lévy in high places, even with Prince Napoleon, could not save him, but they did secure his removal, on the ground of his poor health, from the prison to the sanitarium of a certain Doctor Blanche at Passy.[92] There he remained for two years.

---

91. Reclus, op.cit., pp. 194-5; Fermé, op.cit., pp. 2-7-10.

92. Smochină, op.cit., pp. 180-2, 196-7.

CHAPTER VI

THE LATER YEARS OF EXILE, 1853-1857. WAR. PEACE, AND PROPAGANDA

1. The monster becomes a benefactor

The year 1853 brought momentous changes in the European outlook, as the Tsar marched his armies across the Pruth, and the British and French fleets moved nearer to Constantinople. It brought changes also in the policies of the Roumanian emigrés in the West. In one of history's most striking examples of opportunism, they were able to drop their burning faith in the general democratic revolution of peoples, as a snake sloughs off its old skin, and to hitch their chariot to the star of Louis Napoleon, the butcher of December 4th, for whose destruction they had previously been so anxious. That this could happen as it did, with a minimum of hesitation and soul-searching, shows how lightly the Mazzinian doctrines rested on Roumanian shoulders. It is explained by the fact that their nationalism was stronger than their republicanism and their hatred of the reaction. If Napoleon showed signs of being better able than Mazzini's world revolution to free the Principalities, well and good; they would court Napoleon. Some of the exiles, Ion Ghica for example, had always preferred the policy of trying to interest the powers in fighting to save the Ottoman Empire, and in the process the Principalities also, from destruction at the hands of Russia. In 1853 he publicly proclaimed his faith in the diplomacy and military strength of the western powers and Turkey as the only means of salvation for the Principalities.[1]

For the Golescus, who were moderates by nature and never comfortable in the role of revolutionaries, the transition was not difficult. For Dumitru Brătianu and Rosetti, it was no overnight change of heart, but a gradual abandonment of a policy which had failed in favor of one which promised them a more certain, though partial, attainment of national aims. It was the same evolution of policy which took place with Manin and other Italian nationalists. Besides, they had all along been pursuing a double line of attack, and the collaboration with international revolutionaries had been the result of the complete failure of the efforts to make any impression on Palmerston and on the ministers of the French Republic. Naturally, they looked on the advent of Napoleon's dictatorship as making the situation worse by providing Tsar Nicholas with an ally in the Tuileries. Then in 1853 it seemed to them that Palmerston was beginning to wake up, and that the new Napoleon, by scorning the timid foreign policies of preceding French governments, might be preparing to challenge not only the Tsar but all the treaty settlements upon which the territorial division of Europe

---

1. G. Chainoi, Dernière Occupation des Principautés Danubiennes, p. 18.

was based. Mickiewicz had seen long before that the coming of a Bonaparte to power was a better sign for the nationalities than any attempted return to February. It would be interesting to know if any of his Roumanian friends shared his views in 1849. Only blindness could have kept them from trying to take advantage of the new situation in 1853. They did not intend to become mere sycophants, fawning upon the Emperor and hoping for crumbs from his table, but they did want to influence him if they could, and to turn the eastern crisis to their own advantage.

The modification of aims involved, on the political side, the abandonment of republicanism for France and for Roumania, and on the national side, a return to the idea of co-operation with Turkey and a limitation of demands to the union of the Principalities, plus Bessarabia if possible. If the war should turn into a war of nationalities against Austria, the Daco-Roumanian idea might be trotted out again, but as it became clear that the western powers' war aims did not go beyond clipping Russia's wings and preserving Turkey, Transylvania was left out of the picture.

Advantages of the modification of aims were patent. Besides having a better chance of acceptance by the powers, the new program, union and a foreign prince, was certain to take hold in the Principalities, where even before 1848 it was accepted by people who would not flirt with political radicalism or a too ambitious program of territorial expansion. The ranks of the exiles themselves were more nearly closed and their authority strengthened. After being continually at odds over how to win national unity and what attitude to take toward Turkey, they could now finally agree on the union of the two most closely connected Roumanian provinces, leaving the others out of consideration. This was not easy to do, but years of continued failure had begun to temper optimism and doctrinaire attitudes.

The first to accept Napoleon as more likely than the Republic to aid the Roumanians was Cesar Boliac. In April, 1852, at a time when his colleagues were still suffering from the blow of the coup d'état, he asked for a private audience with the Prince President, and though that was not granted, he was informed that his letter had been read with interest. The letter expressed "the faith which the Roumanians have in the name which you bear," and the hope that the feeble policies of the July Monarchy would be replaced by the great traditions of Louis XIV and Napoleon I. It then explained the position of the Roumanians, "twelve million souls of a warlike Gallo-Latin nation," situated on a strategically important territory and having their own language, literature, and national genius. This nation desires, said Boliac's letter, the union of the Principalities, a foreign Prince of Latin blood, respect for treaties, recognition of nationality, institutions in harmony with the needs of the country, development of the welfare of all classes, and abolition of serfdom and slavery.[2] Although Boliac was never accepted by the others as spokesman, the program set forth here may be considered as laying down the line which was followed during the next seven years.

There may have been other attempts in 1852, besides that of Boliac, to penetrate to officialdom with protests and mémoires but the real campaign began in 1853. In London the new policy was in the hands of D. Brătianu, who tried to rouse Parliament, press, and public to a consciousness of their own interests and Roumania's desires. In 1849 he had played the "Wallachian nobleman" in London society, then become a man of the people and colleague of Mazzini; now he returned to his former role. In a letter to Dudley Stuart, he announced his change of policy:

> "My Lord, Since my return to England, the line of conduct I believed it necessary to adopt forced me to break off all relations with the political men of this country....Now I change my resolve because of an almost imperative mandate addressed to me by a large number of the notable inhabitants of the Danubian Principalities, telling me to call the attention of the Government and the Parliament to the new misfortunes which menace those unhappy countries." 3

---

2. C. Boliac, Choix de Lettres et de Mémoires, (Paris, 1856, lithographed), pp. 3-4. I have not seen the original of this or of Boliac's other letters, and have taken his word on the text and date. This collection was put out in 1856 for propaganda purposes.

3. D. Brătianu to Stuart, Mar. 20, 1853. This and several

Stuart and Austen Layard tried to help him out in Parliament, but the Government would not be questioned.[4] His publicity campaign also fell flat when his English friends advised against holding the public meetings he and Nicolae Golescu had planned for the big cities of the Midlands.[5] It was fairly evident that the English were getting ready to go to war to defend Turkey. Brătianu wanted to make them realize that in fighting to eject Russia from the "two Turkish provinces" she had invaded, they would also be fighting for the Roumanian nation, which could furnish an army of 100,000 men to the cause of civilization. While at Manchester he took the opportunity of writing some articles for the press and of publishing his correspondence with Stuart, which made these points clear.

At this time he began to change his opinion of the "bastard born in debauchery and raised in crime, whom both

---

other letters between Brătianu and Stuart were published by the latter, with Stuart's permission, (Manchester, 1853), and also as an appendix to the brochure of A. Lévy, La Russie sur le Danube, (Paris, 1853), pp. 27-43. Those of Stuart appear also in Cretzianu, op.cit., vol. I, pp. 323-55, passim.

4. Cretzianu, op.cit., vol. I, pp. 333, 354-5; Hansard, Parliamentary Debates, 3rd Series, vol. 129, pp. 1161-64. On Aug.16, Layard spoke of the eventual union of the Principalities and Bessarabia in an independent state.(Ibid.,pp.1769-80).

5. Layard to Brătianu, July 14, 15, 1853, Cretzianu, op.cit., vol. I, pp. 151-3; N. Golescu to S. Golescu, July 7, 14, 1853, George Fotino, Din Vremea Renașterii Naționale a Țării Românești, Boierii Golești, (Bucharest, 1939), vol. IV, pp. 32-3.

France and Italy repudiated." He was later willing to claim him for Roumania. "In modern times," he wrote, "the men to whom Roumania owes most are Tudor [Vladimirescu], who freed us from foreign rule, Lazăr, who reawakened us to national life, and Napoleon III, who laid the bases of the Roumanian state."[6]

In Paris the new policy was confirmed by a meeting at which all present gave their word not to do anything which would compromise the cause with the European cabinets or the Porte.[7] The old game of writing protests was resumed; as before, Russia's conduct provided ample occasion for protest. On receipt of the news of the occupation of the Principalities, what remained of the Roumanian National Committee, with a new member in the revolutionary cleric, Josaphat Snagoveanu, produced a moving plea for assistance, with the usual additions concerning Latin origins, fighting the barbarians, etc. It concluded that if no help were granted, the Roumanians were prepared to help themselves. This protest was submitted to the Ministry of Foreign Affairs, and it was also published.[8]

---

6. D. Brătianu, Napoleon III, (Bucharest, 1873), pp. 8-9.

7. N. Iorga, "Documente nouă de istorie românească," (Revista Istorică, VIII, 1922, pp. 81-95), p. 94. A. G. Golescu, who tells of this meeting, does not mention the exact date or who was present.

8. Aff. Etr., Mémoires et Documents, Turquie, vol. 54, cit. N. Corivan, Din Activitatea Emigranților Români în Apus,

Ion Brătianu's signature was missing from this protest; he was at the time languishing in jail. His conviction and confinement, however, did not prevent him from taking part in the further production of memorandums and articles for the press. The terms of his imprisonment were extraordinarily lenient. He was allowed to go daily to the Bibliothèque Nationale, and no obstacles were put in the way of his disposing of his time as he liked. His connections with Drouyn de Lhuys and other influential persons were helpful, and Napoleon did not regard him as a dangerous political enemy. The house of Dr. Blanche was a pleasant place to stay, and it was also a favorite meeting place for many of the prominent political and literary figures of the time. It was there that, probably through his friends Lévy and Mickiewicz, he met Prince Jerome Napoleon.[9] That connection is said to have brought him an audience with the Emperor. However, Prince Napoleon was notoriously a friend of many radicals and foreign refugees, and their having access to the Palais-Royal did not necessarily open to them the doors of

---

(Bucharest, 1931), p. 30. Published in La Presse, July 14, 1853, and in Lévy, op.cit., pp. 3-5.
The protest is signed: "Au nom de nos compatriotes, 12 juillet 1853, Bolliac, maire de la ville de Bucarest,
Stéphan Golescu et C. A. Rosetti, membres du gouvernement provisoire en 1848,
J. E. Voinesco, ministre, secrétaire d'état,
Josaphat, archimandrite."

9. Smochină, op.cit., p. 183; Lui Ion C. Brătianu, pp. 68-9.

the Elysée. It is not probable that Napoleon ever gave Brătianu an interview while the latter was still serving his sentence. It is, however, probable that he read the mémoires on the Roumanian question which Brătianu wrote.

Brătianu remained in effect the director of the propaganda efforts of the Roumanians in Paris.[10] In 1853 Armand, Lévy published a pamphlet, La Russie sur le Danube, in the composition of which he probably had a hand, though he was still in Ste.-Pélagie at the time of its publication.[11] It repeated the old refrain about the Principalities being the key to Constantinople and to the European equilibrium, also the usual references to the Latin brothers, and a Napoleonic version of the liberty against autocracy theory. Then came a violent denunciation of the treaties of 1815, an entreaty to France to remember the Grande Armée and the tradition of the first Napoleon, who had unfurled the flag of the liberation of nations, and finally a call for a war of principle against Russia and a redrawing of the map of Europe on lines of nationality. Among other new states would be a reborn Poland, a new Bohemia, a South Slav state,

---

10. See the letter in La Presse, June 18, two days after his arrest, signed: "Pour mes compatriotes, Jean Bratiano." It stressed the Roumanians' glorious past and their present willigness to fight the barbarian if given one word of encouragement from France.

11. Smochină, op.cit., p. 183.

and a Roumania extending from the Theiss to the Dniester. This was applying the principle of nationalities with a vengeance; indeed it was the Mazzinian program in Napoleonic dress. The solicitude for Turkey and Austria, which D. Brătianu was required to show in order to make any headway with his propaganda in England, was not necessary with Napoleon, who had little faith in Turkey's ability to survive and hated Austria as the incarnation of 1815.

A memorandum which Brătianu sent to Napoleon in 1854 offered the actual aid of the Roumanian nation, which he said could contribute 100,000 soldiers, who would fight under their own flag. By thus making use of Roumanian nationality, said Brătianu, France and England could solve the eastern question. All they need do was to create a Roumanian state out of Bessarabia and the Principalities; this would be a barrier for Turkey and for Europe against Asiatic invaders and would give the Roumanians a chance to serve civilization as their ancestors did. The new state would be a French colony, economically and morally, without costing France a sou; for France always would remain the Roumanians' ideal. This was followed by a more urgent appeal. Allow us to fight, Brătianu begged, so that Europe will see we do not lack patriotism or courage.[12]

---

12. Din scrierile şi cuvîntările lui Ion C. Brătianu, pp. 35-9. That Brătianu presented this mémoire to the

Brătianu's most notable production in this period was his long Mémoire sur l'empire d'Autriche dans la question d'Orient. This was in many ways a restatement of the points made by Lévy brought up to date. France he characterized as the incarnation of the principle of nationalities and therefore the implacable enemy of Austria. He condemned the western powers for handing over the Principalities to Austria and Turkey, instead of making use of the national movements of the Poles and the Roumanians. The reconstitution of the East on the basis of nationalities he held to be the only solution to the eastern question. It was France's destiny to triumph with these new ideas, or to fall by opposing them. One of these nations, the Roumanian, he stated occupied the territory between the Theiss, the Dniester, the Danube, and the Black Sea. By leaning on that nation France could transform the East and establish French influence there on a solid basis. The means would eventually present themselves. For the present, France should force Austria to evacuate the Principalities, allow them to unite on a purely national

---

Emperor at a personal interview seems unlikely, (cf. Lui Ion C. Brătianu, pp. 68-9), as does the date usually given for it (1853). Ladislas Mickiewicz's memoirs say that the Emperor would not receive Bratianu, and until January, 1854, the latter was in Ste.-Pélagie or in the courtroom and hardly in a position to request an audience to discuss the Roumanian question. (Cf. W. Michiewicz, Pamietniki, vol. I, p. 129).

13. Paris, Oct., 1855.

basis and to enter the war immediately with that same hypothetical army of 100,000 men he had mentioned before. So great was the faith of the Roumanians, Brătianu concluded, that, whether noticed or not, they would knock at the doors of France to be accepted as France's own representatives and advance guard in the East

Of the other Roumanians in Paris, Boliac was the most active at this stage. He attempted to influence the course of French policy by direct appeals to the Emperor and indirectly through Prince Napoleon, with whom he had an interview and who displayed a certain interest in the Roumanians. Boliac sent maps, documents, and pleas for the application of the principle of nationalities. Roumanian unity, in the limits of ancient Dacia, he argued, would cut Panslavism permanently in two and would represent Latin civilization. Complete unity, depending on the solution of the Austrian question, could be left to time. All the Roumanians demanded for the present was the union of Moldavia and Wallachia with Bessarabia, into a single autonomous state, which might be willing to recognize the suzerainty of the Porte, and which would have as prince a foreigner, elected by universal suffrage. In his appeals to Napoleon, Boliac begged that France take over the Principalities as a protectorate, and above all send arms so they could fight. "It is in France alone that we place our hopes....A great future is opened up for France on the Danube. It is the dream of the return of Napoleon." The principle of nationalities required the existence of a sovereign and independent Roumania, based on liberty and equality.[14] A. G. Golescu made the same demands, less lyrically, in a memorandum submitted to the Foreign Ministry, and another, written in the name of the Roumanian national committee by Ubicini, who stood in well with Napoleon's closest advisers, was conveyed to the Emperor.[15]

Inasmuch as Napoleon's adoption of the idea of the union of the Principalities was largely responsible for its realization, it would be interesting to know whether these writings submitted by the Roumanian exiles had any part in determining his policy. No one has succeeded in turning up conclusive evidence to prove Napoleon's exact motives, and that very fact tends to indicate that he had no clearly defined reasons and was acting on the basis of a vague sympathy with small nationalities and with the Roumanians in particular, who would be a center of French cultural influence and perhaps a diplomatic asset. This seems all the more probable, since other alleged motives, (the creation

---

14. Letter to Napoleon, Feb. 5, 1854, Boliac, Choix de Lettres et de Mémoires, pp. 6-30; letters to Prince Napoleon, Feb. 10, Mar. 29, 1854, and Mar. 10, 1855, ibid., pp. 31-40, 73-80. Boliac had an interview with Prince Napoleon, Mar. 10, 1854.

15. Bengescu, Les Golesco, p. 244; Ubicini, Les Origines de l'histoire roumaine, pp. xv-xvi.

of a barrier to protect Turkey, the weakening of Austria, etc.) are definitely known to have been comparatively unimportant in determining his policy.[16] Once adopted, of course, in the face of opposition by several European powers, the Roumanian cause became a question of prestige and could not be dropped. The important period was, therefore, 1853 and 1854, when Napoleon was making up his mind on the matter. It seems very probable that his attitude was determined by a combination of desires to break up the system of 1815, to aid small nationalities, and to make Paris the diplomatic capital of Europe. It is unlikely that the idea that Roumanian nationalism could be used as a part of such a program reached him through his ministers who were not enamored of his Roumanian policy, and it is unlikely that the reports of the French consuls, most of them contradictory, had any influence on his judgment. It seems more likely that the propaganda of the Roumanian exiles provided him with the idea that the experiment was worth trying. Even the "Latin sister-nation" talk may not have been without its

---

16. See on this point East, The Union of Moldavia and Wallachia, pp. 54-65; Riker, The Making of Roumania, pp. 28-9; Iorga, Partea lui Napoleon III în Unirea Principatelor, (Bucharest, 1915), pp. 14-21; N. Corivan, "La politica orientale di Napoleone III e l'unione dei principati romeni," (Cercetări Istorice, Jassy, X, 1934, pp. 225ff.); Marcu, op.cit., pp. 85-7; J. Dontenville, "Les idees napoléoniennes. La politique extérieure de Napoléon III," (Revue des Etudes Napoléoniennes, XXI, 1923, pp. 190-217), pp. 196-7.

effects. As later events showed, Napoleon was not so sincere and disinterested as to be above diplomatic horse-trading which would sacrifice the Principalities in return for changes in Italy, a question nearer his heart and his frontiers, but he did take a personal interest in the Roumanians, and that must have been the result of the noise made by the emigrés.

Dumitru Brătianu, who had several talks with the Emperor, wrote later he had always been received with exceptional good will and even with pleasure.

> "He was so sympathetic that I said to myself it was a good thing I did not see him at the time I was conspiring against him, for I should have been seduced, conquered. The Roumanian question had without doubt a great attraction for him....Usually inscrutable and unsmiling, when he talked about Roumania his face became expressive, his eyes shone, a smile came to his lips....He was very ill-informed on the Roumanian question....One day he said to me, 'Just what do you Roumanians want?' I told him all I had in my heart, and he listened attentively....
>
> ...'We shall succeed,' he said, 'if we go slowly and take each point by assault, leaving the rest to the future, but do not rush me; content yourselves with a limited solution for the present.' He told me to write it all down, so that he could have a memorandum on which to proceed diplomatically." 17

This is no impeccable authority, and no date is given for this particular interview, but it shows that Brătianu was definitely given the impression that Napoleon's favor was a policy of sentiment rather than interest, and that he viewed the problem from the point of view of the Roumanian nationalists in Paris.

---

17. D. Brătianu, Napoleon III, pp. 4-6.

2. <u>The exiles and the Crimean War</u>

Before war was declared by the Turks in October 1853, some of the Roumanian exiles had conceived the idea of returning to raise the nation in revolt, or perhaps of creating a Roumanian legion to fight with the Turks, under the Roumanian flag, against the Russians. Here at last was the chance to prove the nation's vitality, to win independence by fighting for it. To fight side by side with the Turks meant swallowing much that they had said and written about Turkey in the last couple of years. D. Brătianu and others were of the opinion that it would lower them in the eyes of the European democrats with whom they had been associating.[18] That was true enough, but the new opportunism overcame any scruples. The prospect of a Russian military defeat and a termination of the Russian protectorate was too inviting. "No one has criticised the Turks more severely than I," said D. Brătianu, "but the Porte, often left in the lurch by England and France, had some excuse for its mistakes, and now we must take what allies we can get in order to combat Russian influence in the East." Turkey is decadent all right, he said, "but <u>Austria will dissolve first</u>."[19] This was a hint that a Roumanian legion which started out as an

---

18. Fotino, *op.cit.*, vol. IV, p. 25.

19. D. Brătianu to Stuart, Mar. 20, May 27, 1853, Lévy, *La Russie sur le Danube*, pp. 31, 37-43.

auxiliary corps of the Turkish army might become an army of liberation for the Roumanians in all provinces. Rosetti had not changed his feelings toward the Turks and hoped for nothing from them, but felt that it was desirable to go nearer the scene of action. "The only path open to us is to raise our country in revolt and make ourselves a power," he wrote on the day he left Paris with D. Brătianu, and Ştefan and A. C. Golescu.[20] He was sure the country would revolt, but both arms and money were lacking. Military leadership they expected would be taken care of by Magheru and Tell.[21] Arrived at Malta, they did not yet know whether to try to go through Austria without passports, or go to Constantinople. Finally they took the only available boat, landed at Gallipoli, and sent A. C. Golescu up to Constantinople to sound out the situation.[22]

The situation was complicated by the lack of agreement in Turkish circles as to the advisability of making use of the exiles, the interference of Lord Stratford in the question, and the factionalism that reappeared in the ranks of

---

20. Nov. 21, 1853. C. A. Rosetti, Amintiri istorice adunate şi anotate, (Bucharest, 1889), p. 11; cf. Rosetti to D. Brătianu, Nov. 3, 1853, Cretzianu, op.cit., vol. I, p. 360; A. C. Golescu to S. Golescu, undated, Fotino, op.cit., vol. IV, pp. 41-4.

21. D. Brătianu to Magheru, June 16, 1853, Cretzianu, op. cit., vol. I, pp. 335-8.

22. Rosetti, Amintiri istorice, pp. 12-18.

of the Roumanians. Ion Ghica was negotiating with the Turks regarding a proclamation of the autonomy of the Principalities, another for the creation of a legion and an amnesty for the exiles, and the arrival of Brătianu and Rosetti compromised his negotiations.[23] A. G. Golescu wrote them to say they were crazy to come and told them to go back to London and Paris.[24] Rosetti was despondent. The sacred cause of the nation was once again getting tangled up in diplomacy, which would strangle it. He cursed the Turks and was bitter at the rebuff from Golescu and Ghica. The only thing they could think of to do was to move northward through Sofia and Belgrade to Widin, where they could look across the river to their native land.[25]

Ghica's negotiations at first promised success. Reshid Pasha was favorable, and in Stratford's presence, the proclamations were signed and sent to Omer Pasha, commander of the army.[26] There was to be a Roumanian legion of 10,000 men. Magheru was called from Vienna to serve as a commander

---

23. Ion Ghica, Scrisori către Vasile Alecsandri, pp. 372-3.

24. Fotino, op.cit., vol. IV, pp. 53-7, 61.

25. Rosetti, op.cit., pp. 19-30; D. Brătianu to I. Brătianu, Jan. 20, 1854, Democrația, Bucharest, I, 1913, p. 115.

26. Ghica, Scrisori, pp. 371-2; A. Melik, L'Orient devant l'Occident, (Paris, 1856), p. 170; Regnault, Histoire politique et sociale des Principautés Danubiennes, p. 516.

in Oltenia and Tell also was commissioned to form a division.[27] Both were military men and the Turks considered them safe. Tell immediately went to Omer Pasha's camp at Shumla and with the help of some Polish officers, set about making an army of the Roumanians who had fled from Wallachia to Turkish territory.[28] As the months passed, the Roumanians received nothing but empty promises. The Turks were held back by Stratford and by the Austrian internuncio, with whom they were negotiating in regard to an Austrian occupation of the Principalities. This would eliminate the Roumanians altogether from military considerations, and from the political viewpoint the Turks had never been over-sympathetic towards the exiles.[29] Hearing of the arrival on Turkish soil of a member of Mazzini's committee, they closed their official doors to all the Roumanian exiles. Whatever pressure was necessary to keep the Porte from consenting to the formation of a Roumanian legion was supplied by the British and Austrian diplomats. Austrian neutrality was made

---

27. C. V. Obedeanu, O pagină asupra evenimentilor de la 1854, (Bucharest, 1923), p. 10.

28. Tell to Col. Bernarzyk, Jan. 26, 1854, mentioning "the army of Wallachia which His Majesty the Sultan has charged me to organize and to command." (Ac. Rom. Mss., 5287); A. Lewak, "La politique polonaise en Orient," (La Pologne au VIIe. Congrès des sciences historiques, Warsaw, 1933, III, pp. 15-48), p. 27.

29. A. G. Golescu to S. Golescu et al., Dec. 1853, Fotino, op.cit., vol. IV, p. 60.

conditional on the Turks' not making use of "revolutionary elements," Poles, Hungarians, and Roumanians.[30]

Omer Pasha was at first very friendly to the Roumanians, and those whom Tell had gathered at Shumla counted on being sent across the Danube into Wallachia. They began to dream of seeing the newspapers of Paris and London filled with news of great Roumanian victories.[31] These hopes were not fulfilled, primarily because the Turks were hesitant about accepting the Roumanians as partners in the war, secondly because the divisions between the emigré factions projected themselves into the picture and nullified whatever real chance the legion idea might have had. The arrival at Shumal of Eliade and of three of the Golescus greatly complicated the affair. Nicolae and A. C. Golescu came from Constantinople, Ştefan from Widin where D. Brătianu and Rosetti were still waiting for the chance to enter Wallachia and vainly begging the local pasha for arms to distribute to the Oltenian peasants.[32] Eliade had

---

30. S. Golescu to Radu Golescu, Mar. 25, 1854, Fotino, op. cit., vol. IV, pp. 86-91; Ghica, op.cit., pp. 375-6; Regnault, op.cit., pp. 516-7.

31. A. C. Golescu to D. Brătianu, Jan. 31, 1854, Fotino, op.cit., vol. IV, p. 72. According to Czaika, Omer was friendly to the Roumanians because he had the idea of becoming ruler of a Roumanian state. (G. Duzinchevici, "Contribuţii la istoria Românilor în timpul razboiului Crimeii," Revista Istorică Română, III, 1933, p. 249).

32. Rosetti, Amintiri istorice, pp. 31-2.

arrived from Constantinople. At this time he was on the best of terms with the Turks, agreeing with them in everything. He even sported a fez and was known as Eliad Bey or Vlach Bey. Omer treated him as chief of the Roumanians, and Eliade took advantage of the situation to strike back at his opponents. He called them tools of Russia and renegades, who had deserted the principles of 1848 by turning against the Turks and were now, without sincerity, trying to get back into their good graces. They, for their part, accused Eliade of intriguing with Omer to turn the Principalities into a pashalik, or else to have himself named prince.[33]

Omer told the Roumanians they would have to agree among themselves before anything could be done. At Constantinople an attempt was made to establish a truce, and a pledge was drawn up, signatories of which would agree to put aside their personal views and think only of energetic and patriotic co-operation with the Porte in order to free their unfortunate country.[34] The effort failed. The Golescus and Tell had swallowed their pride and made peace with Eliade, but

---

33. Eliade Rădulescu, Scrisori din Exil, pp. 229-30, 252-9, 313-5; N. Rousso, Suite ou supplément à l'histoire politique et sociale, pp. 180ff.; Melik, op.cit., pp. 171-2; Aricescu, Corespondenţa secretă, vol. II, p. 34; Rosetti, Amintiri istorice, pp. 32-3; Regnault, op.cit., pp. 517-8; Tell to Melik, Feb. 2, 1854, Revista Istorică, VII, p. 92; N. Golescu to Melik, ibid., p. 93.

34. Mar. 25, 1854. (Revista Istorică, VII, pp. 93-4).

when Omer lectured them on their anti-Turkish and anti-Austrian attitude and called for a public recantation of their "Daco-Roumanian utterances," they firmly refused.[35] Tell made peace with Eliade but got no permission to leave with his legion. In March all the Roumanians at Shumla, except Eliade, were told to go back to Constantinople.

Desperate attempts were made to interest the French and English ambassadors and the commanders of the armies.[36] In May a note was presented to Prince Napoleon, then in Constantinople, explaining the Eliade affair, complaining of Omer's hostility to the Roumanians, and asking that France supply arms for a legion and bring the Turks to reason.[37] This was no more successful than the similar appeals being made in London and Paris by Ion Brătianu and Cesar Boliac.[38] Until the Roumanians could prove they were a military factor of some weight, Turkey and Turkey's allies

---

35. S. Golescu to Omer Pasha, Mar. 8, 1854, Fotino, op.cit., vol. IV, pp. 92-7; S. Golescu to Radu Golescu, Mar. 30, 1854, ibid., pp. 81-5.

36. Edmond Texier, Appel au Congrès en faveur des Roumains, (Paris, 1856), p. 36.

37. "Note presentée par des Roumains au Prince Napoleon au mois de mai 1854," (Revue Historique du Sud-Est Européen, V, 1928, pp. 355-6), probably written by Rosetti and presented by Rosetti and N. Golescu. (Rosetti, Amintiri istorice, pp. 34-5).

38. Din scrierile și cuvîntările lui Ion C. Brătianu, pp. 61-6; Boliac, Choix de Lettres et Mémoires, 29, 57-62, 64-72.

were not going to listen to them or to alienate Austria just for sentiment's sake.

Prince Napoleon handed over the note presented to him to General Wysocki, a leader of the Polish democratic party, apparently with the idea that the Roumanian legion could be combined with the Polish legion then being formed. As a matter of fact the Roumanians were already in contact with both wings of the Polish emigration. Ghica had acted in close co-operation with Zamoyski and Czaika in his negotiations with Turkey, and agents of the Polish democrats, supported by Prince Napoleon, were working on a plan of common action with the Hungarians, Roumanians, and Serbs.[39] Dumitru Brătianu, who had crossed over to Oltenia from Widin and was working with Milkowski, Polish democrat, called on Magheru to come and head an army of volunteers, regardless of the Porte's attitude.[40] The Roumanians gained nothing through these connections with their former revolutionary friends. As for their relations with the Czartoryski group, friendship turned to hostility when it became known that Zamoyski and others were trying to make a deal whereby Austria would give up Gallicia to a new Poland and take the

---

39. Ghica to Zamoyski, Feb. 27, 1854, Musée Adam Michiewicz Mss., 1044; Lewak, La politique polonaise en Orient, p. 31; Lukasik, Relațiunile lui Mihail Czajkowski-Sadyk Pașa cu Românii, p. 248; W. Klapowska, note in Rev. Hist. du Sud-Est, V, p. 372.

40. Lukasik, Rumunja a Polska w XIX wieku, p. 39.

Principalities in compensation. Although some may have welcomed this as a way to win Daco-Roumanian unity, it raised such a storm in Roumanian circles that Czartoryski and Czaika repudiated the project.[41] The failure of the legion plan, closely followed by the Austrian-Turkish treaty of June 14th and the Austrian occupation of the Principalities, led to the complete disruption to what little unity remained among the Roumanian exiles. Eliade, victorious over his rivals, remained with Omer's army and made a triumphal entry into Bucharest, after the Russians had left. Ion Ghica, discouraged that the Roumanians had been sacrificed to "an excess of precaution" but realizing that Austria and Turkey did not want to risk a revolutionary war that would bring Kossuth and Mazzini into the picture, washed his hands of Roumanian affairs and took a post in Ottoman service as Bey of Samos.[42] Already in possession of a reputation as a man of intrigues and a puppet of Stratford, this step disgusted most of his compatriots and turned them against him. Thus another huge rent appeared in the

---

41. W. Knaplowska, Kandidaci do tronu polskiego czasie wojny krymskij, (Posznan, 1927), p. 21, cit. Iorga in Rev. Hist. du Sud-Est, VI, 1929, p. 100; Duzinchevici, op.cit., p. 254; Lewak, op.cit., p. 32; Klapka, Aus meinen Erinnerungen, pp. 368-9.

42. Ghica to his wife, July 30, 1854, Ac. Rom. Mss., 2910, fol. 54-6; Memorandum of Ghica, undated, Ac. Rom. Mss., 5040, fol. 124-30.

fabric of unity of purpose and action. At the beginning of the year Ghica had written to Rosetti of his acceptance of the unity decided upon at Paris, his desire to follow all who raised the Roumanian flag, and his willingness to retract the unkind words he had written in his recent brochure.[43] Rosetti replied to these words of peace with doubts as to Ghica's integrity and patriotism and demanded an explanation of the rumors of his personal ambitions.[44] He got no answer. The Golescus also turned against Ghica, blaming him for the legion debacle, and in the note submitted to Prince Napoleon by Rosetti and Nicolae Golescu, he was called an intriguer an aspirant to the Wallachian throne, and classed with Eliade as an enemy of the national party.[45]

Feeling also ran high between A. G. Golescu and the Reds. Golescu accused D. Brătianu of sending to Constantinople three hundred revolutionary manifestoes signed by Mazzini's committee one month _after_ the general agreement on moderation and unity. "What can you do with that sort of man? Nothing, nothing, nothing."[46]

---

43. Ghica to Rosetti, Jan. 31, 1854, _Ac. Rom. Mss._, C. A. Rosetti Papers, II, 12.

44. Rosetti to Ghica, Mar., 1854, _Amintiri istorice_, pp. 57-62.

45. Fotino, _op.cit._, vol. IV, pp. 90, 106, 120; _Rev. Hist. du Sud-Est,_ V, p. 356; Boliac, _op.cit._, p. 60.

46. A. G. Golescu to Melik, Feb. 26, 1854, _Revista Istorică_, VII, pp. 94-5.

There was nothing further to be done as a group. Some of the Roumanians volunteered to serve as individuals in the Turkish army, others entered the legion of "Ottoman Cossacks" led by Czaika. When the Turks entered Wallachia, these Roumanians aided Czaika in trying to enroll some of the inhabitants in his regiment. But these activities were frowned upon by the Austrian military authorities, and Czaika's legion was removed from Wallachia at their request.[47]

In the confusion resulting from the Russian evacuation of the Principalities and the entry of the Austrian and Ottoman armies, a few of the exiles slipped over the frontier to have a look at old haunts and to see if some last desperate measure might be undertaken. According to the Austrian documents, Rosetti, Nicolae Golescu, and others were functioning as a national committee, with headquarters at Cotroceni, on the edge of Bucharest, associated with Hungarian and Polish refugees; all of them, deserted by the Turks and the powers, were said to be plotting to overthrow Austria by revolution.[48] The Austrians were worried by the

---

47. I. Nistor, Corespondenţa lui Coronini din Principate, (Cernăuţi, 1938), pp. 79-83; Lukasik, Pologne et Roumanie, p. 90; Obedeanu, op.cit., pp. 11-13; Handelsman, "La guerre de Crimée et les origines du problème bulgare," (Revue historique, Paris, CLXIX, 1932, pp. 271-315), p. 278. Czaika's force indluded Hungarians, Roumanians, Bulgarians, Italians, and Jews, under Polish officers.

48. Alfons Wimpffen, Erinnerungen aus der Walachei während

activities of "two Wallachians, Rosetti and Golescu, who lately appeared in Wallachia and were spreading socialistic doctrines, and now may be spreading them among Austrian troops." Eliade they placed in the same category. The Turkish Government, to whom a complaint was made, directed Omer to send these individuals back to Constantinople. Omer notified the Austrian authorities that all the "undesirable and suspicious individuals, of Wallachian as well as other nationality," would be ejected, Eliade included.[49]

Perseouted by the Austrians and the Turks, ignored by the French and English, the Roumanians could do little but retrace their steps and go back to Paris, weary of the

---

<u>der Besetzung durch Österreichischen Truppen in den Jahren 1854-1856</u>, (Vienna, 1878), pp. 70, 94; N. Popescu, <u>Documente inedite din preajma Unirea Principatelôr</u>, (Bucharest, 1928), pp. 4-5.

49. Grand Vizir to Omer Pasha, Aug. 27, 1854, Nistor, <u>op. cit.</u>, pp. 66-7; Ludolf to Buol, Sept. 7, 1854, <u>ibid.</u>, pp. 79-83.
An Austrian protest also reached Colquhoun through Clarendon. He was told to look into the matter of these revolutionaries, Rosetti and Golescu. The strange part about all this was that the two men, as Colquhoun reported, had not even been in Wallachia and had returned to Paris in July. Ştefan was the only Golescu who came near the Wallachian frontier, and the Turks arrested and imprisoned him at Rustchuk. Colquhoun was incensed at this, and told Clarendon that if "<u>respectable</u> refugees" like the Golescus were so treated and kept out of the country, he "could not sanction the entrance of such men as Eliade." He requested Stratford to secure Eliade's removal. (Clarendon to Colquhoun, Sept. 9, 1854, F.O. 78, vol. 1010; Colquhoun to Clarendon, Oct. 13, 1854, <u>ibid.</u>; cf. Ariceseu, <u>Corespondenţa secretă</u>, vol. II, pp. 34-41).

world and its injustices.

On his return Rosetti wrote to his friend Bataillard:

> "Twice within six years I have seen my country almost rise from its grave and amaze the whole world with its acts and its victories, and twice I have seen it fall back again into slavery and ignominy, unknown, deserted, even despised by the world, and this because of the faults of those who love her, and I even include myself." 50

3. The propaganda offensive, 1855-1857

It was too early to call the war the colossal failure it seemed from the Roumanian point of view. If the western powers should win, they would have to face the problem of what to do with the Principalities, for the abolition of the Russian protectorate was listed as the first of their war aims.

During 1855 there was still hope of convincing ministers in Paris and London that the war was being fought on the wrong terrain, that Russia should be attacked in Bessarabia, and that in such an operation the Roumanians could contribute their hundred thousand soldiers. D. Brătianu submitted a proposition to Palmerston and to the Minister of War asking that the Roumanians be armed and given officers. He volunteered to find the officers himself, in Belgium, France and Spain. There would, he said, be no language difficulties. The Roumanian soldiers would be

---

50. Rosetti to Bataillard, Sept. 17, 1854, Lui C. A. Rosetti, p. 372.

able to understand commands in any Latin language. And no need to worry about discipline, as was the case with the Turks, since the Roumanians were "an occidental people who feel and think like the French and English." Lord Panmure "duly considered the proposition but was not now prepared to adopt it."[51]

The obstacle to this, as to the exiles' plans for the reorganization of the Principalities, was the Austrian occupying army, which was beginning to make even the Russians regretted. Every means was used to depict to western statesmen the baneful effect of the presence of the Austrians, but until the war was over it was plain that there was no chance that anything would be done about it. Meanwhile, the biggest question of all remained that of the future status of the Principalities. The task which nationalists set themselves was to prepare the ground, at home and in the West, for a solution which would in effect revive their revolution of 1848, with the consent and guarantee of Europe to insure its survival. As in 1848, they stood for national independence, liberal constitutional government, and social reform. If they were to have any success, they could not put the case to the world as the revival of a revolution. They had to find a simple formula which would enable them to unite among themselves and to

---

51. Cretzianu, op.cit., vol. II, pp. 27-37.

win the support of those in whose hands lay the determination of the future. The formula they hit upon was "Union and a Foreign Prince." Union was the essence of the problem. Its attainment would amount to European recognition of the Roumanians' right to a national state; it would be a permanent, though partial, victory of the principle of nationality, and, by bringing the generation of 1848 to a position of influence, would permit the introduction of all the national political and social reforms necessary for the development of the nation. The foreign prince idea, with its obvious advantage of stabilizing the new state and holding off interference by neighbors, was at first a matter of expediency and in fact a contradiction of nationalistic theories in being an admission that the great Roumanian nation could not produce another Michael the Brave, but through constant repetition it became, like union, a matter of dogma. The adherence of the republican fringe was vital because of their ability, their connections in European capitals, and their popularity at home, and it was not an easy dogma for them to accept, but they allowed themselves to be persuaded. Ion Brătianu later congratulated himself on his statesmanlike action in renouncing his republican convictions.[52]

After 1855 there was no valid distinction between

---

52. G. Bengescu, Bibliographie franco-roumaine, p. xxiv.

moderates and radicals, and it was the former Reds who took the lead in working for the realization of the moderate program. D. Brătianu remained a member of the Central Democratic Committee, which now included Kossuth, and he was on the best of terms with Mazzini, Ledru, and Ruge, but he remained voluntarily inactive. His energies, and those of Rosetti in Paris, were now devoted to winning the favor of official Europe for union. The nominal head of the movement was Nicolae Golescu, whose qualities as a figurehead were always recognized, but the real work was done by Brătianu, Rosetti, Ştefan and A. G. Golescu. For once there was an appearance of harmony, though Ghica and of course Eliade, living on islands in the Aegean, were left out of the harmonious picture.[53]

Their efforts were now for the first time ably seconded by a party in the Principalities, particularly in Moldavia, where the mild régime of Gregorie Ghica allowed a measure of freedom of expression not tolerated by Stirbei in Wallachia. The Moldavian Forty-eighters, with the one exception of Mălinescu, had not shared the vicissitudes of fortune of the Wallachian exiles, preferring the tranquillity of government posts and literary activity in Moldavia, where

---

53. Ghica nevertheless continued working for exactly the same program as the others, for it was what he had advocated for several years. See Ghica to Thouvenel, 1855, Georgescu-Tistu, Ion Ghica Scriitorul, pp. 153-6.

they had been allowed to return in 1849 by Ghica, Sturdza's well-intentioned successor. The abrupt changes brought about by the Crimean War opened up new prospects and stirred them to action. Negri and others proposed a military offensive against the Russians in Bessarabia; even Prince Ghica favored this idea, obviously impossible so long as the Austrians remained in occupation.[54]

The essential thing for the Roumanians in the Principalities as in the West was not fighting, which could be left to the powers, but to make a lot of noise, to demonstrate to the world that the Roumanians had legitimate desires for national unity and were capable of making good use of it if granted. One of the biggest obstacles which the Roumanians in the West had to overcome was the scepticism, particularly noticeable in England, with which their claims to nationhood were regarded. It was important that the national movement show signs of life in the Principalities, and that action there be co-ordinated with that of the Wallachian exiles. The action took the form of demonstrations in favor of the western allies and petitions in favor of union. The co-ordination was obtained through the correspondence of D. Brătianu and Rosetti with Kogălniceanu, who now emerged as leader of the national or union

---

54. Duzinchevici, Contribuţii la istoria Românilor in timpul războiului Crimeii, p. 257; V. I. Ghica, Spicuiri Istorice, (Jassy, 1935), pp. 75-7.

party in the Principalities.[55] His new journal, Steóa Dunării, founded in October, 1855, became a rallying point for unionists in both principalities and in the West. Its clear-cut program of union, maintenance of the legal tie with the Porte,[56] and "peaceful assimilation of the institutions of civilized Europe with our own institutions," was the same toned-down program of 1848 upon which the exiles had united.[57]

Kogălniceanu and his colleagues worked well in preparing the people to pronounce in favor of union if ever they should have a chance to express themselves. That depended on decisions to be made in Constantinople and elsewhere. The Roumanians soon discovered that the elimination of the Russians had opened the gates to the Austrians and the Turks, against whom the national movement had to fight for its

---

55. N. Bănescu, "Scrisorile politice ale lui Dumitru Brătianu," (Viața Românească, XI, 1908, pp. 166-76, 337-46), giving Brătianu's letters to Kogălniceanu; Cretzianu, op.cit., vol. II, passim, giving letters of Rosetti and Kogălniceanu to Brătianu; Vintilă C. A. Rosetti, Pagini din Trecut, Corespondința, (Bucharest, 1902), pp. 47-62.

56. This point was often left vague. When the situation demanded, they consented to the maintenance of Ottoman suzerainty. In many appeals they expressed the desire for complete independence, attainable by paying off in a lump sum the tribute to the Porte. "The Roumanians want union," wrote D. Brătianu to Layard in 1855, "but they want independence even more, also the restitution of Bessarabia." (May 22, 1855, British Museum, Add. Mss., 39065, Layard Papers, vol. CXXXV).

57. Steóa Dunării, Jassy, No. 1, Oct. 1, 1855, pp. 1-2.

life. They had to lean all the harder on France and on Britain. Napoleon was already converted. In March 1855 his representative at the Vienna conference put France on the record as favoring union. At the same time Benedetti in Constantinople was trying to convince the Ottoman ministers of its advantages. Both, acting in accordance with instructions, put forward the argument, so often advanced by the Roumanian exiles, that the united Principalities would serve as a barrier to protect the Ottoman Empire. Bourqueney at Vienna even suggested a foreign prince.[58]

In the case of England, whose policy was uncertain, much remained to be done. Dumitru Brătianu did what he could to influence Palmerston and Clarendon, apparently with no great success,[59] although the arguments used by Clarendon in his instructions to Stratford to work against the project of a collective protectorate decided upon at the Vienna conference, were the same as those which appeared in an address, signed by the Roumanians in Paris and submitted to him by Brătianu, namely that such a protectorate

58. East, The Union of Moldavia and Wallachia, pp. 37-8; Benedetti to Drouyn de Lhuys, Aff. Etr., Mem. et Doc., Turquie, vol. 55, fol. 83.

59. D. Brătianu to Clarendon, June 30, July 27, 1855, Layard Papers, vol. CXXXV, fol. 156-69. Brătianu complains of the British policy at Vienna, recommends union of the Principalities, the return of Bessarabia, independence, and the return of the émigrés.

would be nothing but an excuse for interference by Russia and Austria, the nearest "protectors."[60]

At any rate Brătianu convinced Clarendon that union and independence under a foreign prince "would be the most agreeable arrangement to the people." In November Clarendon wrote to Cowley that he had long thought independence to be the best settlement, even though counter to the Ottoman integrity principle.[61] All that, however, was still a matter for the future, and British statesmen, especially Palmerston, would never have been willing to go ahead in this matter without the approval of the Turks. Brătianu's idea of having N. Golescu immediately proclaimed Lieutenant or temporary ruler of one or both principalities was not taken seriously, nor were his proposals that the Austrians be forced out of the Principalities and the exiles of 1848 be allowed to return.[62] Palmerston and Clarendon were nevertheless very cordial to him, and his notes submitted to

---

60. Cretzianu, <u>op.cit</u>., vol. II, pp. 15-18; Clarendon to Stratford, Sept. 15, 1855, cit. East, <u>op.cit</u>., p. 39; cf. Riker, <u>The Making of Roumania</u>, p. 32.

61. Clarendon to Palmerston, Oct. 17, 1955; Clarendon to Cowley, Nov. 16, 1855, (H. Temperley, "The Union of Roumania in the private letters of Palmerston, Clarendon, and Cowley," (<u>Rev. Hist. du Sud-Est</u>., XIV, 1937, pp. 218-32), pp. 220-1.

62. Brătianu to Palmerston, Aug. 26, 1855, Cretzianu, <u>op. cit</u>., vol. II, pp. 28-37. Another of his wild proposals was that the Duke of Cambridge be made King of a united Roumania (<u>ibid</u>., p. 49).

the Foreign Office were read and acknowledged.

In his attempt to focus the attention of public opinion on his nation Brătianu relied principally on the Daily News, a paper traditionally friendly to oppressed peoples. He had an agreement with its editor, William Weir, who promised "to obtain publicity for the cause of your country... if you furnish me with the means."[63] As the means were not always forthcoming, and the paper published the material only when there was a scarcity of other news, and since Bratianu had the annoying habit of sending in his articles written in French, the agreement did not work out any too well. The cause was better served by a long article of Layard's in the Quarterly Review, in which he condemned the British Government for not knowing for what it was fighting, and for letting the Austrians occupy the Principalities; he repeated Brătianu's statements almost word for word in recommending the union of the Principalities with the addition of Bessarabia.[64] Brătianu placed great hopes in Layard, especially after a speech the latter delivered in Liverpool in May, 1855, warning England against Austria's attempt to make permanent her hold on the Principalities.[65]

---

63. Weir to Brătianu, July 10, 1855, ibid., p. 20.

64. "Objects of the War." (Quarterly Review, XCVII, June 1855, pp. 245-290).

65. D. Brătianu to Layard, May 22, 1855, Layard Papers, vol. CXXXV, enclosing an address to Layard from the Roumanians of Paris (Rosetti, N. and S. Golescu, Voinescu, Ion Brătianu, etc.).

Brătianu and Layard were both of the opinion that much more could be done to interest the British public, especially by putting the greatest emphasis on Roumania's resources and prospects as a future market.[66] Trade had increased tremendously between Britain and the Danubian ports within the last few years, but hardly enough to influence policy in a direction inimical to Turkey.

The termination of the war and the commencement of serious negotiations on the Roumanian question opened a period of feverish activity on the part of the nationalists. They were kept busy trying to influence the decisions of international conferences, then in protesting loudly when those decisions failed to come up to their expectations or were considered to be a violation of their rights. During the conference at Constantinople in January, 1856, Negri, Rallet, Eliade, and Ion Ghica were all in the Ottoman capital, but had no influence on the course of the negotiations, which ended in a protocol most distasteful to Roumanian nationalists.[67] The conference settled nothing, omitted

---

66. Brătianu to Layard, May 20, 1855, Layard Papers, vol. LII

67. Eliade accused the others of having prepared a memorandum which was, through Stratford, directly taken over and put into the protocols. Eliade Rădulescu, Scrisori din Exil, pp. 503-4; Regnault, Mystères diplomatiques aux bords du Danube, (Paris, 1858), p. 19, repeats the accusation against Ghica, "espèce de pseudo-patriote." Cf. Negri to Alecsandri, Jan. 31, 1856, M. Bogdan, Autrefois et Aujourd'hui, (Bucharest, 1929), pp. 203-4.

to take up the question of union, and purported to give the Turks rights in the Principalities they had not had before the war. The result was an outcry, in Moldavia and in Paris, and a flood of petitions and protests, insisting that the congress about to meet in Paris disregard these decisions. It did.

At Paris the Roumanians were much more successful in making their views known. Shortly after the congress opened, mémoires signed by Nicolae Golescu in the name of all his compatriots were placed in the hands of the representatives of France, England, and Sardinia. D. Brătianu had an inside track from the start, for he traveled to Paris with Lord Clarendon, who obtained for him interviews with Cowley, Walewski, and others, so that he would have the best possible chance to present his case. Brătianu supplied Walewski with all the data he needed to back up his proposal in favor of union as desirable for and desired by the inhabitants of the Principalities. The emigrés saw to it that one memorandum after another was given the delegates.[68] Some were from the Roumanian exiles in Paris,

---

68. See esp. Roumanians in Paris to Walewski, Feb. 24, 1856, Aff. Etr., Mem. et Doc., Turquie, vol. 54, fol. 99-102; Roumanians in Paris to representatives of Great Britain, France, & Sardinia, Mar. 3, signed by N. Golescu as head of emigration, ibid., vol. 55, fol. 182-9; N. Golescu to Aali Pasha, undated, (copy to Walewski), ibid., vol. 55, fol. 190-6; (copy to Clarendon), Cretzianu, op.cit., vol. II, pp. 52-4; Roumanians in Paris to Clarendon, Mar. 10, Mem. et Doc., Turquie,

some from the Roumanian students in Paris, some from individuals, others from groups in Moldavia, where the prince had become an ardent unionist. One petition which Kogălniceanu sent, covered with thousands of signatures, was discovered by the police at Cernăuţi and never got any further, as the Austrian Government was taking every possible means to prevent any decision in favor of union.[69]

Following Brătianu's belief that the diplomats had to be told a thing ten times before it registered, the refrain was always the same: union; an hereditary prince, preferably from one of the ruling houses of Europe, but if a native prince, then he must be elected by universal suffrage; and thirdly, although sometimes a willingness to accept the Sultan's suzerainty was expressed, there was generally a demand for independence and the formation of a neutral state made up of Wallachia, Moldavia, and Bessarabia. The new state of Roumania, with a strong frontier on the Dniester, would be a formidable barrier against Russian invasion. Other arguments were calculated to win sympathy or interest. Those addressed to French

---

vol. 54, fol. 140-2; Grădişteanu to Walewski, Mar. 16, *ibid.*, vol. 54, fol. 161-9; N. Golescu et al. to Napoleon III, Mar. 15, cit. Corivan, *op.cit.*, pp. 101-4; D. Brătianu to Walewski, Mar. 21, Apr. 5, *Mem. et Doc., Turquie*, vol. 54, fol. 170, 177-84.

69. Kogălniceanu to Rosetti, telegram, Corivan, *op.cit.*, p. 106; D. Brătianu to Layard, Mar. 26, 1856, *Layard Papers*, vol. LIV.

statesmen contained the now familiar theory that Roumania would be a second France in the East, an anchor of French influence and prestige, and that the Roumanians wanted nothing more than to have a French prince rule over them. To the English they mentioned rich natural resources, trade possibilities, fields for capital investment, etc.

These arguments of the Roumanians were seconded by the official French press, which was naturally following the orders of the Emperor, and also by loyal or paid friends, who produced a goodly number of articles and pamphlets. Paul Bataillard, who served as secretary on the official committee dealing with the Principalities, wrote a pamphlet which gave legal, moral, and military reasons for Roumanian national independence.[70] Edmond Texier wrote an _Appel au Congrès en faveur des Roumains_, which parrotted all their arguments about the little Latin brothers, the representatives of western civilization in the Orient, and stressed also the advantages to French trade and French diplomacy to be gained from the creation of a new state on the lower

---

70. Bataillard, _Premier point de la question d'Orient. Les principautés de Moldavie et de Valachie devant le Congrès_, (Paris, 1856). Bataillard followed this with _La Moldo-Valachie dans la manifestation de ses efforts et de ses voeux_, (Paris, 1856, and also in _Revue de Paris_, July 1, 1856); _La Moldo-Valachie_, (Paris, 1856, and also in _Revue de Paris_, Oct. 15, 1856; _De la situation regulière de la Moldo-Valachie vis à vis de la Porte_, (Brussels, 1857, and also in _La Libre Recherche_, Brussels, VII, 1857).

Danube, an eastern Belgium.[71] The most appreciated defence of Roumanian claims came from the pen of the illustrious exile, Edgar Quinet, who since 1853 had been intending to write a book to fulfil his duty to the Roumanian nation. Using Ion Brătianu's brochure on Austria and other material supplied to him by Rosetti, he produced a historical work, Les Roumains, which appeared in the Revue des Deux Mondes at the time when the congress was meeting.[72]

The Roumanians had no chance of influencing any other delegation but the British. All others definitely had their minds already made up. Clarendon's attitude was wavering and undecided. The British policy, as laid down by Stratford in December, 1855, was against union, and in an interview with Napoleon, Clarendon made certain strong objections to the Emperor's desire to satisfy the Roumanians on the union question.[73] The strong opposition to union was, however, Palmerston's policy rather than Clarendon's, for

---

71. See Bibliography, Part VII, for a list of these brochures and books directly inspired by the Roumanian emigrés.

72. Quinet, "Les Roumains," (Revue des Deux Mondes, Jan. 15, Mar. 1, 1856, and separately, Paris, 1857); cf. Breazu, Edgar Quinet et les Roumains, pp. 376-94, with texts of letters to Quinet from the Roumanians in Paris regarding the work; Quinet to Rosetti, Mar. 3, Aug. 20, 1856, Ac. Rom., C.A. Rosetti, Mss., II, 26; T. G. Djuvara, Edgar Quinet, Philo-roumain, pp. 49-53.

73. Memorandum on British policy, submitted to Walewski by Cowley, Aff. Etr., Mem. et Doc., Turquie, vol. 55, fol. 127-9; East, op.cit., pp. 40-1, 47; Temperley, op.cit., p. 221.

we have seen that throughout 1855 Clarendon personally favored it. In the session of March 8th he supported Walewski's motion "to admit and proclaim union," and mentioned the necessity of consulting the will of the people. The stand he took, and which he later repudiated, he said was due to his conviction that union would create a bulwark against Russia, (Brătianu's argument), and he believed that "opinion was in favor of the arrangement."[74]

The reason for Clarendon's public espousal of union remains obscure, but since even before then he had thought it "might be best for the Principalities," it would not be illogical to stress his contacts with Brătianu as contributing greatly to the formation of that opinion.[75] This victory turned out a hollow one, for British policy became definitely anti-unionist after Clarendon's return to London. Even before the congress was over, Brătianu wrote to Layard of an unsatisfactory interview with Cowley and complained that the English representatives, on whom he had felt justified in relying, had refused, "for frivolous reasons," to join with those powers which wish to satisfy the wishes of the Roumanians. He felt that he would have to fall back on Parliament and the press in order to force the Government's

74. Riker, op.cit., pp. 41-2; East, op.cit., p. 48.

75. Cf. Temperley, op.cit., pp. 219-21; Riker, op.cit., pp. 42-44.

hand.[76]

The Treaty of Paris, signed March 30th, left the Roumanian question in the air and created a host of new troubles for the Roumanians. It did recognize the autonomy of the Principalities, on the basis of the capitulations (actually forgeries) which they had quoted so much in their propaganda that the powers accepted them. It recognized also that the desires of the populations should be consulted and ascertained by a European commission. Postponement of a final decision put the intitiative in the hands of those who had some degree of control over the actual situation, the Austrians, whose army occupied the country, and the Turks, who were using their authority as suzerain to extend their own influence in the Principalities. The change of policy on the part of England also contributed to making the picture very black for the Roumanians, and even the rapid-fire production of mémoires and brochures, the citing of ancient treaties and the appeals on the ground of interest and sentiment had very little real effect on the development of the diplomatic situation in which the Roumanians themselves were almost hidden behind the issues of prestige and prejudice which had turned the Principalities into the center of an

---

76. Brătianu to Layard, Mar. 26, 1856, Layard Papers, vol. LIV.

international quarrel.[77]

It was to be over a year before the exiles were allowed to return, a year in which the wrangling of the powers and the intrigues fostered by Austrian and Turkish agents went to unparalleled lengths. They had little to cheer about. Even the departure of Stirbey from the throne did not bring them an amnesty. Meanwhile they busied themselves with the latest of their chronic committees. This committee, formed to work "for union," adopted the common program already agreed upon, and attracted to it a large number of Roumanians in Paris. Its purpose was to maintain contact with "the country" through sub-committees in Jassy and Bucharest, each capital sending 3 members to become part of the other's committee. This was intended as a practical means of preparing for the elections and of creating a spirit of unity which was considered absolutely necessary. "The aim of the committee is to rally all parties under the same flag, to arrive, by regular means, at fulfilling the wish of all true Roumanians."[78] At the head of the committee was Gregorie Ghica, former prince, now devoted to union. This committee,

---

77. It would be a tedious business to mention and analyze here the pamphlets turned out by the Roumanian exiles and students in 1856 and 1857. None showed any great originality, and their arguments have already been touched upon. I have listed them in the Bibliography, Part VI.

78. Plan d'organisation d'un comité roumain à Paris en vue de l'Union des Principautés, (Paris, 1856).

like its predecessors, probably did not advance beyond the plan stage. In actual fact, however, there were connections between London, Paris, Bucharest, and Jassy, as a means of preparing for the elections and the union which would surely follow. There was certainly a world of difference between the committees of 1850 and 1851, with their revolutionary programs, and this "Committee for Union." So was there a difference in the atmosphere in Roumanian circles in Paris. Saint-Marc Girardin, not Michelet or Quinet, was now the professorial hero of the Roumanian students, who gathered at the Café Voltaire to drink toasts to him and to talk politics.[79] The new papers, Buciumul and Opiniunea had as their triple slogan, "Autonomy, union, a foreign prince," which was a far cry from the liberty and universal revolution of Republica Română.[80]

Not long after the end of the congress, D. Brătianu returned to London to try to set right the course of British policy, so far had it strayed toward the Turkish camp since the signing of the treaty. His brother Ion, in June 1856, finally received an imperial pardon and was liberated. Because of his exemplary conduct, the consolidation of the

---

79. [Leon Grenier], Le Quartier Latin, (Paris, 1861), pp.68,115

80. Buciumul, Paris, Nos. 1-5, Mar. 22-Apr. 23, 1857; Opiniunea, Paris, Nos. 1-8, Mar. 30-May 14, 1857. Kogălniceanu's paper, suppressed in Jassy, appeared in Brussels, beginning Dec. 4, 1856, as L'Etoile du Danube, ed. N. Ionescu. It was devoted solely to unionist propaganda.

Empire, and the unexpected developments in the eastern question and the changed official attitude toward the Roumanian exiles, steps were taken for his release. The report on his conduct said his misdeeds had been the result of the exploitation of his Wallachian patriotism by demagogues. "He has repented and offered to serve the Government of France in his own country, and he has received a severe enough lesson...." On July 1, 1856, the pardon was granted.[81] There was now no cause to be resentful toward Napoleon. In point of fact the Brătianus had made their peace with him long before this.

The Emperor's services were appreciated but there was no certainty that he would remain a steadfast friend. A more certain guarantee, thought D. Brătianu, would be the public opinion of a great free nation. With this in view he tried his luck once again with the London press. He established relations with several journals, including the Morning Post, known as Palmerston's paper.[82] "We now have the Morning Post at our disposition," wrote Rosetti, "but until we have about 2000 galbens in our treasury, we cannot do much

---

81. Archives Nationales, Paris, BB[24] Min. de la Justice, Dossier 474-9, No. 3676. These documents are published in Smochină, op.cit., pp. 198-203.

82. N. Browne to D. Brătianu, Aug. 30, 1856, Jan. 14, 1857, Cretzianu, op.cit., vol. II, pp. 137, 187. There were periods when the Post, on orders from Palmerston, turned against the Roumanians.

against our powerful adversaries."[83] That was the main drawback, lack of money, for Bratianu had to pay high for the privilege of telling the British public about the rights of descendants of Trajan's legionaries and the misdeeds of the Russians, Austrians, and Turks. Eyre Crowe, who put Brătianu's material into the Post, the Examiner and other papers, received forty pounds a month for his services, and Brătianu, questioned by Rosetti and Kogălniceanu, estimated at sixty pounds the monthly cost of the campaign.[84]

Reference to the London press of the years 1856 and 1857 shows that Brătianu was very active in putting his case before the public, though not all the papers which consented to print his articles gave him editorial support. Most of them were favorable to the Roumanians, but never became really indignant about their plight and refrained from harrying the Government on the issue. The Times remained firm as a rock for the integrity of Turkey and against the Roumanian pretensions. The Morning Herald strongly opposed all attempts to convert "an integral part of the Ottoman Empire" into any kind of a Roumanian state,

83. Rosetti to I. Filipescu, May 27, 1856, Aricescu, Corespondenţa secretă, vol. II, p. 39.

84. Brătianu to Kogălniceanu, Feb. 26, 1857, N. Banescu, Scrisorile politice ale lui D. Brătianu, p. 344; Crowe to Brătianu, undated, Cretzianu, op.cit., vol. II, p. 199.

but it printed a long and spirited exchange of letters between Brătianu and one of Urquhart's committees.[85] A similar controversy appeared in the Morning Advertiser, with letters by "Justitia," "A Friend of Roumania," and Arnold Ruge upholding the Roumanian point of view.[86] The Morning Chronicle with which Brătianu had connections, was indifferent to the question, though its frequent quotations from the Etoile du Danube may have been supplied by him. The Star was wholly in favor of letting the Roumanians have whatever they wanted, and looked forward to the day when "Moldo-Wallachia" would be joined with Serbia, Bulgaria, and Greece in a great southeastern confederation.[87] The Daily News was in 1856 hostile to any change which might weaken Turkey and called the idea of a "Moldo-Wallachian kingdom" merely the vision of "some few natives of the Principalities, of whose judgment and integrity we entertain a high opinion" but by 1857 it was defending union, whether the Porte liked it or not, as the opinion of nine tenths of the Roumanian

---

85. See esp. Morning Herald, Sept. 6, 1856, p. 4; Oct. 11, p. 4; Oct. 17, p. 6; Oct. 24, p. 3; Nov. 12, p. 3; Nov. 22, p. 4.

86. Morning Advertiser, Oct. 4, 1856, p. 4; Oct. 6, p. 4; Oct. 9, p. 2; Oct. 11, p. 3; Oct. 14, p. 2; Oct. 17, p. 6; Oct. 27, p. 3; Nov. 3, p. 4; Nov. 11, p. 3.

87. Evening Star, July 14, 1856, p. 3; July 28, p. 2; Oct. 3, p. 2; Oct. 16, p. 2; Nov. 5, p. 2; Nov. 7, p. 2.

population.[88] John Bull and Britannia was violently anti-Palmerston for his subservience to Austria and for "playing false to the Roumans" after the promises given at Paris; the Principalities, in John Bull's editorial opinion, must inevitably unite to form an independent kingdom, "most favorably placed for occupying the position which must soon be vacated by the effete Ottoman Empire."[89]

"The zealous exertions of Mr. Bratiano," wrote a correspondent of the Daily News, "...have not succeeded in persuading the British public of the necessity of the union. ..."[90] That was quite true. The public could not easily see why Britain, which had just fought a war to preserve the integrity of the Ottoman Empire, should now proceed to partition it at the conference table. Was not Russia in favor of union? That made it a Russian scheme. None of Brătianu's

---

88. Brătianu was able to get many long articles in the News. See esp. his letters to the editor in the numbers of Oct. 10, 18, Nov. 10, 1856. One or more of these long letters appeared also in the Examiner, the Herald, and also in the conservative Times and Evening Mail, which took issue with Bratianu editorially.
   J. G. Dodson, a friend of Brătianu's wrote in the Daily News: "There is a strong feeling of nationality in the breasts of all Roumanians....An independent Roumanian state would be a thorn in the side of both Austria and Russia. The cry of Pan-Roumanism would in large measure silence that of Pan-Slavism. (Sept. 27, 1856, p. 5).

89. John Bull and Britannia, Nov. 10, 1856, p. 712.

90. Daily News, Nov. 4, 1856, p. 5.

arguments, (the right of nationalities to unite, the commercial importance of the Principalities, the theory that Pan-Slavism would be cut in two, or that of an eastern Belgium, with an army of free men and an international guarantee), could overcome this one objection.

Brătianu planned to organize a committee of influential Englishmen, who would take under their patronage the interests of Roumania.[91] He intended that it should include "all the men of good will in the country," and that it should have in London a centre, a combination office, library and club. The library was to contain "all that had been written on the Roumanian nation."[92] Early in August the committee was formed, with several M.P.'s among the members, but in action the scheme did not turn out according to the original plans. It boiled down to a central office, where those interested in the question could gather, and where Brătianu carried on his business of writing articles and letters, and

---

91. Brătianu to Kogălniceanu, July 3, 1856, Bănescu, op.cit., pp. 174-6; Crowe to Brătianu, July 14, 1856, Cretzianu, op.cit., vol. II, p. 116.

92. Cretzianu, op.cit., vol. II, pp. 122-3. He intended that the organization should send English people to the Principalities; after their return they could go on lecture tours in England. In 1856 both Crowe and Layard visited the Principalities, though not sent by any committee. Crowe's avowed purpose was to write back pro-Roumanian articles to the Morning Post. Layard, on a tour of observation, went armed with a letter of introduction from Brătianu to Kogălniceanu. (N. Browne, of the Post, to Brătianu, Aug. 30, 1856, ibid., p. 173; Brătianu to Layard, June 12, 1856, Bănescu, op.cit., p. 137).

sending and receiving bundles of newspapers.[93]

In October, 1856, Brătianu planned the biggest publicity event of his stay in England, a public meeting at Brighton, to be the first of a series held in Manchester, Birmingham, Sheffield, and elsewhere. Arnold Ruge, his former colleague on the Central Committee, helped him in the preparation, sending invitations to "all men of distinction."[94] The meeting was held on October 6th at the City Hall, which was illuminated in the Roumanian colors, and a large Roumanian flag was crossed with the Union Jack. The Mayor of Brighton presided; on the platform were a Member of Parliament, some of Brighton's respected citizens, Ruge, and Brătianu. Speakers referred to the Roumanians' right to become a "free self-governing nation, (loud cheering)." Ruge spoke a few words on behalf of Brătianu "who unfortunately did not speak English well enough to enable him properly to address the meeting." Finally a petition to the Queen was

---

93. Brătianu to Kogălniceanu and Mălinescu, Aug. 8, 1856, Cretzianu, op.cit., vol. II, p. 133; Brătianu to Walewski, Dec. 6, 1856, Corivan, op.cit., p.142; Brătianu to Rosetti, Feb. 11, 1857, Cretzianu, op.cit., p. 201.

94. Brătianu to Ruge, Sept. 30, 1856, Arnold Ruge, Briefwechsel und Tagebuchblätter aus den Jahren 1825-1880, (Berlin, 1886), pp. 170-1. Ruge wrote an article for the Herald to arouse enthusiasm for the meeting, and Brătianu urged him to have several thousand copies of it printed and distributed. He told Ruge to have the posters speak of the eastern war and the Anglo-French alliance, since "the English public does not yet get very excited about the Principalities alone."

adopted by acclamation. It begged that union be "insisted upon by Your Majesty's Government,...and the Rouman people be erected into a free, powerful, and self-governing nation, in conformity with the treaties with the Sublime Porte." The ceremonies closed with three cheers for the union of the Principalities.[95]

The meeting was a success, most of the newspapers were friendly to the Roumanians, but the desired results, in the form of a change of heart on the part of the Cabinet, were not forthcoming. Rosetti was ready to give up. "Why not save our money and leave the English in peace?", he asked. Brătianu said no. England, he felt, was the key to success or failure of the campaign for union, and the situation was not hopeless.[96] It would, however, have taken more than a few letters to the editor, questions in the House of Commons, and the submission of memorandums to the Foreign Office, to

---

95. The meeting was reported at great length in the London press, most of the papers copying those of Brighton. See Evening Star, Oct. 8, 1856, p. 3; Morning Herald, Oct. 8, p. 6; Morning Advertiser, Oct. 8, p. 3; Daily News, Oct. 8, p. 3.

96. Brătianu to Rosetti, Feb. 11, 1857, Cretzianu, op.cit., pp. 200-1. Brătianu even wrote to Walewski, telling him of his success and that opinion in England was becoming pro-union; and that members of the Government admitted that if France insisted on union, England would have to give in and support it also. (Brătianu to Walewski, Dec. 6, 1856, Corivan, op.cit., pp. 141-3).

budge Palmerston.[97] He made no concessions in favor of union until faced with the real possibility of war with France, in July and August of 1857, and then only when Napoleon abandoned his own uncompromising position. By that time Brătianu had left London for Bucharest.

In Paris there was no need for such desperate efforts to educate public opinion. With governmental approval, the most respectable journals advocated the union of the Principalities as the only desirable solution. The two papers closest to the Roumanian exiles were the <u>Journal des Débats</u>, which published the articles of Saint-Marc Girardin, and <u>Le Siècle</u>, where union was warmly defended by Leon Plée.[98]

4. The return of the exiles

The men who had disturbed the established order in Wallachia in 1848 were exiles by virtue of an Ottoman firman, promulgated at the request of Russia, and it was Russian influence which until the Crimean War kept the Porte from

---

97. The most important of Brătianu's letters to ministers were: to Clarendon, May 27, 1856, Temperley, "Four documents on the future of Roumania," (<u>Rev. Hist. du Sud-Est</u>, XIV, 1937, pp. 232-42), pp. 237-40; to Palmerston, Dec. 5, 1856, Corivan, <u>op.cit</u>., pp. 128-41; to Clarendon, Feb. 11, 1857, Cretzianu, <u>op.cit</u>., vol. II, pp. 197-9.

98. Plée was not only for union and complete independence, but would have liked to see "united under a single government the whole ancient Roumanian race." But since the time for that was not quite ripe, he pressed for the union of the Principalities as a partial victory. (<u>Le Siècle</u>, Apr. 6, 1857).

allowing their return. The émigrés themselves always maintained that the Turks were friendly to them and had acted against them only under pressure from Russia. That was confirmed by the conduct of the Turkish Government. It allowed Ion Ghica to remain in Constantinople, then made him an Ottoman functionary. It permitted Eliade to settle at Chios. It was very lenient in its treatment of those who were interned at Brusa. In foreign capitals, Paris and London, the émigrés were often in friendly contact with the Turkish diplomats, who encouraged them so long as they professed complete loyalty to the Sultan. However, the anti-Turkish pronouncements of Bălcescu, Rosetti, and the Brătianus made a very bad impression in Constantinople, and the wrangling over the legion question in 1854 did not make the Turks any more benevolent. The émigrés soon learned that others beside the Tsar wanted to keep them out of their native land. The Austrians were firm on that point. The presence of such restless spirits, notorious friends of Kossuth, in the occupied territories would be very bad for the morale of the troops and of the inhabitants and a danger to Transylvania. While the Austrian occupation lasted, until the spring of 1857, Austrian pressure at Constantinople was sufficient to maintain the ban on the émigrés, even had the Turks desired to lift it. They showed no desire to do so, for since the disappearance of the power of Russia, the common enemy of the Turks and the Roumanians, the whole basis for loyal co-operation between them had broken down. The Roumanians brought up the question of union and agitated for independence, while the Turks for their part tried to use the victorious war and the support of the great powers to extend their control over the Principalities. The new theories of the Tanzimat encouraged these centralizing tendencies. This produced a strange situation. The émigrés who had for years been advertising their hatred of Russia and their loyalty to Turkey, now, in their agitation for union, had to direct their fire against Turkey, and the proposal for union was being supported by Russia. It was no wonder that the English were sceptical of the Roumanians' best argument, that the united Principalities would serve as a barrier to protect Turkey from Russia. It was also no wonder that the Turks were not anxious to have the Forty-eighters back in Bucharest agitating for Roumanian independence.

At the time of the Congress of Paris, and in the following months, the exiles placed before the powers complaints of the injustice of continuing their exile, for their only crime had been their realization of Russia's aims five years before the western powers awoke to the situation. Brătianu told Walewski and Clarendon that it was absolutely essential that these men, "the most enlightened of their nation," be allowed to participate in the elections to the divans ad hoc provided for by the treaty of Paris.[99]

The pleas made in London and Paris were received sympathetically. Both the French and British Governments were of the opinion that justice required the return of the emigrés, and they recommended at Constantinople a revocation of the firman of exile.[100] The Porte postponed the matter and did nothing. Stratford told A. G. Golescu that he had several times requested that the ban be lifted, but that the Turks showed no signs of changing their attitude. Golescu got the impression that Stratford, annoyed at the agitation for union, was opposed to their return.[101] Crowe wrote that only the combined action of France and England

---

99. Brătianu to Walewski, Feb. 6, Mar. 4, 1857, Corivan, op.cit., pp. 145-50.

100. Brătianu to Clarendon, Feb. 6, 1857; cf. Foreign Office to Brătianu, Cretzianu, op.cit., vol. II, p. 196; Brătianu to Clarendon, Feb. 11, 1857, ibid., pp. 197-9.
   In July, 1856, Colquhoun had recommended an amnesty for the exiles, and Clarendon wrote in the margin of the dispatch: "To Stratf. recom. amnesty to Porte." (F.O. 78, vol. 1200. Date of dispatch is July 17th).
   Otway, a friend of Brătianu's, brought the matter up in the House of Commons on July 18, 1856, asking the Government to enable these "gentlemen of high character, banished without trial or condemnation, ...whose only crime was opposition to the Russian protectorate," to return to their country. The reply was that the Government hoped an arrangement could be made. (Hansard, Parliamentary Debates, vol. 143, p. 1040).

101. A. G. Golescu to Ştefan Golescu, Sept. 4, 1856, Cretzianu, op.cit., vol. II, pp. 139-42.

could make the Porte yield on the matter, and that Stratford would never act with Thouvenel.[102]

In April 1857, the Brătianus and the Golescus heard from Bucharest that permission had been granted for their return to Wallachia. Their passports were all in order, visas for the Principalities were granted by the Ottoman Embassy in Paris, and the British Government secured the Vienna Government's permission for them to travel across Austria. The Turks had finally given in, having no legitimate reason to refuse, and Austria, in the process of evacuating the Principalities, no longer insisted, but when Rosetti, D. Brătianu, Ştefan and Nicolae Golescu arrived at Turnu Severin, they found that the Wallachian frontier authorities would not let them in. Alexander Ghica, former prince now serving as temporary ruler, said he was forbidden by Constantinople to act in the matter.

---

102. Crowe to Brătianu, Sept. 8, 1856, ibid., pp. 145-6. Crowe and Golescu met in Constantinople and did what they could to bring about the desired changes by interceding with the ambassadors, with the newly arrived European commissioners (Bulwer for England, Talleyrand for France), and even with the Turkish ministers. (Crowe to Brătianu, Sept. 8, 10, 11, Oct. 5, 1856, ibid., pp. 146-50, 173; Crowe to N. Golescu, Sept. 18, 1856, ibid., p. 163). At the same time Armand Lévy was in Constantinople, also trying to influence the Turks in favor of leniency. (Lévy to C. A. Rosetti, Sept. 18, Dec. 20, 1856, Ac. Rom., C. A. Rosetti, Mss., II, 64). Bulwer was a friend of the exiles and anxious to secure permission for them to return. (Ştefan Golescu to A. G. Golescu, Aug. 22, 1856, Fotino, Boierii Goleşti, vol. IV, pp. 167-8).

At the same time the Turkish ministers were saying it was a matter for the Wallachian Government, not for the Sublime Porte. The exiles went down the Danube to Rustchuk and there they waited for two months, while nationalists demonstrated at Bucharest and demanded their return for both Ghica and the Porte wanted to keep them out until the elections were over.[103] But the matter could not be put off forever, and new appeals to France and England, particularly Brătianu's letter to Bulwer, whom he much preferred to Stratford, brought new representations at Constantinople. There was difficulty over Rosetti and over Brătianu, former Mazzinian revolutionaries, and the Golescus would not enter without them. At the end of June, the long-awaited permission to enter their native land was given.[104] They were received in Bucharest by cheering crowds, a triumphal parade, and a mass meeting on the Field of Liberty. 1848 had come to life again.

---

103. Brătianu et al. to Alexander Ghica, May 2, 1857, Cretzianu, op.cit., p. 206; Lui C. A. Rosetti, pp. 278-81; L'Etoile du Danube, No. 41, June 2, 1857.

104. D. Brătianu to Bulwer, May 29, 1857, Cretzianu, op. cit., pp. 207-12; N. Golescu to Mocquard, June 15, 1857, Corivan, op.cit., pp. 150-3; Brătianu to Kogălniceanu and Alecsandri, June 12, 19, 1857, Bănescu, op.cit., pp. 345-6; Fotino, op.cit., vol. IV, pp. 198-9, 203, 205; L'Etoile du Danube, July 16, 1857; Rosetti, Amintiri istorice, pp. 38-55; Stratford to Clarendon, July 6, 1857, cit. East, op.cit., pp. 144-5.

The events of the year 1857 were on the surface merely steps in the development which began with the Russian invasion of the Principalities in 1853 and ended with the double election of Alexander Cuza in 1859. Actually, because of the return of the exiles and the decisions of the divans ad hoc, 1857 marked the beginning of a new era. The return of the Forty-eighters put the national movement into the hands of men who, with their knowledge both of Roumania and of European diplomacy, could bring the union campaign to a successful close. Because of the moral authority which, in revolution and in exile, they had gained over the nation, and because of their electioneering skill, they dominated the divans ad hoc in Bucharest and Jassy, where the "desires of the populations" were expressed in four-point program: autonomy, union, representative government, and a foreign prince. Kogălniceanu in the Moldavian divan spoke out for agrarian reform as well. After this victory for nationalism came others: the limited union agreed on by the powers at Paris in 1858, the election of Cuza, the European recognition of union, the final establishment of a constitutional monarchy with a foreign prince, and the attainment of complete independence. These were the accomplishments of the men of 1848, serving as the ministers and diplomats of the new Roumania.

As for the French influence, which had molded these

men, it remained strong in the field of culture, though not without competition from the critical school of the German-trained philosopher, Titu Maiorescu. In politics and diplomacy the influence has not been so overwhelming as was expected when the "second France," the "<u>point d'appui</u>" of France in the East, was being created. Roumania's constitutional development represented an attempt to evolve a limited monarchy like that of England or Belgium, and her constitution of 1866 was a copy of that of Belgium. Internationally, Roumania had to determine policy on the basis of her position between great powers, her desire for independence of Turkey, and her national aspirations in the direction of Transylvania and Bessarabia. There was, nevertheless, a permanent French influence, founded on the cultural connections and on the whole history of the growth of Roumanian nationalism, and also on France's traditional role as the defender of small nations in eastern Europe, resting on geography and on what is left of the spirit of February 1848. These permanent influences had their origins in the activities of the men of 1848 as students, as literary innovators, as revolutionaries, and as exiles.

The record shows us plainly enough that they were no legendary heroes. They were typical representatives of a naive and romantic generation, pushed about by events, not directing them. They were unsuccessful in 1848, and the years of exile formed a long and dreary chapter of ineffective action and disappointed hopes. They could not agree among themselves on what to do and how to do it; they could not agree, even in principle, with the Hungarians, though both groups recognized the need for co-operation. Their attempts to stir up a national revolution and to fight in the Crimean War failed. Their efforts to persuade the British Government and public opinion to support Roumanian nationalism were futile. The one decisive element in their favor was the strong diplomatic support given by Napoleon III, and their part in determining his attitude is uncertain. Nevertheless, without their well-advertised revolution and their propaganda, diplomatic support from this or any other source would have been highly improbable, and there would have been no Roumanian national state as early as 1859. The Hungarians brought themselves to the attention of Europe by fighting, the Bulgarians by being massacred, the Roumanians by talking and writing.

Their many failures were counterbalanced by the fact that, unlike Mazzini, Kossuth, and the men of 1848 in Germany, they regained positions of political power and stamped the impression of their liberal nationalism on the public life of the Roumanian people. As statesmen, however, with the exception of Kogălniceanu and Ion Brătianu, they were not outstanding. Politics in Bucharest still required unscrupulousness and a measure of those "Phanariot" methods, which did not vanish with the elimination of foreign interference and the breaking of the power of the big boyar clique, and for this the Pasoptisti were not suited by temperament or by training. To the social problem, the crucial importance of which they had recognized, they were, as in 1848 but now with years instead of weeks at their disposal, unable to find a satisfactory solution.

Their real contribution to Roumanian history lay not in practical accomplishment or in the solution of any of these problems, but in the permanent establishment of the two lines of development which have since dominated the politics and the culture of Roumania as of the other nations of the Near East, "Europeanization" and nationalism.

APPENDIX

Ion Ghica's proposal for a Danubian confederation, intended to serve as the basis of an entente between Kossuth and the Roumanian émigrés. This memorandum is contained in a letter to General Wysocki, Constantinople, Feb. 1, 1850. The Original is in <u>Academia Română</u>, <u>Mss. fondului român</u>, vol. 5040.

Le mouvement de 1848, tout démocratique et social dans son origine, devait se transformer au fur et à mesure qu'il pénétrait chez des peuples placés dans des conditions differentes.

A mesure que la révolution se propageait dans des états composés d'éléments héterogènes, le mouvement, de social qu'il était d'abord, devait nécessairement devenir politique et national. En Lombardie, dans le duché de Posen, il ne pouvait pas manquer de prendre ce caractère. Les peuples de races différentes devaient avoir des tendances différentes, par cela même qu'il y avait domination. Dans le duché de Posen, le sentiment national était dans tous les esprits; on voulait être d'abord Polonais, avant de devenir citoyen. Plusieurs considérations nouraissaient cette idée: d'abord l'action incessante de la préponderance allemande; un grand peuple se sentaient constamment blessé dans son amour-propre national et religieux; il opposait à l'action de la Prusse un travail religieux et littéraire qui maintenait les esprits dans les idées de nationalité et d'inimitié contre la race allemande; ce travail [était] fortement aidé par l'action de l'émigration de 1831 qui était en devoir de conserver religieusement son drapeau et d'allier successivement tous ses frères autour de ce drapeau et de se préparer à reconquérir tot ou tard leur patrie, la Pologne. La question nationale se compliquait devantage à mesure que la révolution avancait vers le Danube; là, se trouvait la vieille Autriche; là, la haine courait depuis des siècles entre les différentes nationalités, superposées les unes aux autres, de manière que la compression était d'autant plus forte, que l'on descendait le Danube vers les Carpathes. Les Allemands honnis par les Madjares qui à leur tour pesaient sur les Croates, les Serbes et les Roumans, domination sur domination, haine politique, haine nationale, haine religieuse, toutes devaient éclater à la fois; le mouvement révolutionnaire s'est trouvé tout d'un coup enveloppé dans des prétentions et des susceptibilités pouseées quelquefois jusqu'à l'absurde par les instigations habiles des Camarilla; défiance d'une part, tenacité obstinée de l'autre, le tout devait se résoudre en luttes et déchirements entre les peuples, tandis qu'au fond, ils avaient les mêmes ennemis, un seul et même intérêt, un seul et même but; ils voulaient tous secouer le joug, de quelque nature qu'il fût, et vivre libres et heureux pour le suprême bonheur du genre humain.

C'est malheureux que les peuples n'avaient pu oublier pour un instant leur haine de race, et combiner leurs efforts pour combattre les systèmes corrupteurs et tryanniques, par une fraternisation générale; plus tard, ils se seraient plus facilement entendus entre eux, pour se grouper selon leurs tendances et de la manière la plus convenable pour l'Equilibre Européen.

Dans mon esprit il n'y a de blâme pour personne; c'était la force des circonstances; aucune action ne pouvait empêcher cette lutte, il fallait que la société se purifie en passant par ce tourbillon.

Le sentiment national a divisé les peuples et compromis le bonheur et la tranquillité de l'Europe pour longtemps, et qui plus est, le monde se trouve aujourd'hui presque à la discretion d'une personne absolue qui a su exploiter ces haines et les tourner à son profit; les peuples également malheureux, également opprimés, doivent s'entendre et agir de concert; c'est à ceux qui ont pris l'initiative et qui ont dirigé les mouvements partiels, de s'entendre entre eux et d'arriver à lui donner la généralisation qu'exige le succès, quelque long, quelque pénible, quelque difficile qui soit ce travail, il faut l'entreprendre. Qu'est-ce que quelques années dans la vie d'un peuple? Peuvent-elles compter plus qu'une seconde dans la vie d'un homme?

La liberté eut été trop à bon compte, trop facile à

conquérir si on n'avait eu à la disputer qu'à l'etranger; chèrement achetée, après des souffrances et des martyres, elle sera mieux scellée dans la pierre fondamentale qui servira de base au nouveau système, et dans l'histoire, les peuples veilleront mieux et plus attentivement, quand ils sauront ce qu'elle a coûté de sang et de lutte.

Aujourd'hui que l'on se trouve avoir terminé la première campagne, à la veille peut-être d'en commencer une seconde, il faut rallier les esprits et les préparer de nouveau à la lutte. Un coup d'oeil rétrospectif nous fera peut-être bien pénétrer des erreurs qui ont amené la première catastrophe pour réparer les torts autant que faire ce peut, afin que dans la lutte qui va s'engager, on puisse avoir toutes les chances de succès.

En 1848 le soulèvement a été général et spontané, parceque la souffrance et l'oppression étaient partout; mais il faut l'avouer, le mot d'ordre a manqué: l'idée d'union, l'idée qui eût pu cimenter et agglomérer les différentes parties ensemble, n'existait pas; il n'y avait partout que défiance et dissension. Ce mot d'ordre doit être puisé dans un sentiment supérieur à toute idée individuelle et égoiste, au dessus de toute susceptibilité. A l'heure qu'il est, dans un moment où les Etats-Unis d'Amérique vont descendre peut-être dans l'arène, on pourrait bien demander à l'histoire de cette Union, l'idée qui nous a manqué. On se demanderait tout d'abord comment dans un pays, ou il y a des Etats séparés, dont les populations sont bien différentes les unes des autres, les uns habités exclusivement par des Anglais, ce sont à la verité les plus nombreux, a côté d'Etats composés exclusivement d'Allemands ou de Français, différents sous le rapport des races, de la langue et du rite; là, pourtant, point de disputes religieuses, point de querelles de langue, point de haine nationale; tout l'amour-propre d'un état se concentre à surpasser l'état voisin en bien-être, en culture, en industrie. Là, donc le problème qui nous divise et qui a coûté la vie à un si grand nombre de frères, qui nous a plongé dans le deuil, qui a empêché le succès, se trouve résolu. A quelle combinaison, à quel miracle l'Amérique du Nord doit-elle cet admirable résultat? C'est à la liberté, au respect individuel appliqué aux groupes comme aux individus. Chaque état s'administre à sa manière et comme il l'entend, sans s'inquiéter des institutions qui régissent le monde des états voisins. Il est indifférent pour un état si dans l'état voisin le noir est libre ou esclave, de quelle manière on adore Dieu, quelle langue l'on parle; ce qui leur importe à tous, c'est d'être toujours uni pour la sécurité commune et pour l'intérêt general. On ne peut manquer de remarquer une tendance pour la généralisation de la langue anglaise, mais on remarque aussi, que personne ne l'impose, elle s'impose d'elle-même....D'ailleurs la langue anglaise n'est le symbole d'aucune oppression, bien au contraire, la liberté a été apportés aux diverses populations de l'Amefique du Nord dans cette langue. Elle a été en quelque sort l'étendard de la liberté; personne ne s'en défie comme d'un instrument de domination ou d'oppression. On s'en sent volontiers, et insensiblement peut-être, les autres ne tarderont pas à être oubliées. Chaque commune est libre d'entretenir telles écoles qu'elle juge nécessaires; elle y fait enseigner la langue qui lui plait, paye l'église dont elle a besoin, sans que personne ait à se mêler ou à faire la moindre observation. Dans l'administration, comme dans la justice, c'est toujours la langue de la commune; personne ne questionnera les Madjares qui s'établissent en Amérique, ni sur la langue qu'ils désirent parler, ni sur la religion qu'ils comptent professer. On ne leur imposera qu'une entière liberté, c'est à dire le droit de se dével-opper et de se perfectionner moralement, intellectuellement, et matériellement, de toute la force de leur intelligence et de leurs muscles.

En Suisse à peu pres le meme système a donné des résultats presqu' analogues. Allemands et Francais vivent en très bonne intelligence, unis par les intérêts communs.

Le moyen donc pour sortir du pas difficile dans lequel nous nous trouvons, est tout résolu, si nous voulons suivre l'example des Etats-Unis. Je n'entends pas parler ici de la forme de gouvernement; elle est indépendante de ces questions. En laissant de côté ce qui concerne les querelles des Madjares avec les Croates et les Serbes, en n'exigeant que le différend Madjare-Rouman, je dirai, la main sur la conscience et la persuasion dans l'âme, qu'il y a eu des erreurs et des exagérations de part et d'autre. Si les uns ont commis la faute d'exiger trop, des garanties nationales et religieuses, les autres à leur tour ont commis la faute non moins grande, de ne pas leur accorder tout ce qu'ils demandaient et même devantage, si on avait de demander plus. Les Roumans seraient arrivés plus facilement au but desirè par eux en ne mettant pas en doute qu'il y a un droit ou une liberté au monde dont il ne leur sera pas permis de jouir. Les Madjares à leur tour ne se seraient pas aliénés les Roumans s'ils ne leur avaient pas laissé le droit de se défier par le refus d'accéder à quelques unes de leurs demandes. Dans le siècle ou nous vivons, à moins que le monde ne retombe encore une fois dans la barbarie, la domination d'une race sur une autre ne pourra plus être que l'effet d'une superiorité morale. On dominera par les arts, les sciences, les lettres et l'industrie.

Dans le protocole de la conference tenue a Paris entre le Prince Adam Czartorinski (sic) et les envoyés Madjares, Comte Teleki et Mr. Pulszky, la question se trouve bien placée, bien résolue. La Pologne a des tendances à former un état à part exclusivement Polonais avec telle ou telle autre forme de gouvernement. Les Madjares, les Roumans n'ont rien à y voir, n'ont pas le droit de la gêner le moins du monde dans ses tendances et dans ses désirs une fois que Polonais, Madjares et Roumans se seront entr'aidés pour secouer le joug qui pèse également sur tous et qui arrête le développement et le bien-être de toutes ces nationalités. Tous devaient être libres de suivre leurs tendances. La Pologne peut être assez fort pour vivre à part. Il n'en est pas de même des trois ou quatre autres nationalités, Croates, Serbes, Madjares et Roumans; aucune d'entre elles ne pourrait exister individuellement à l'exemple de la Belgique. L'esprit de conservation les pousse et les poussera davantage vers l'Union; cette liaison est surtout indispensable entre les Madjares et les Roumans, destinés peut-être par leur situation providentielle a se parer et a empêcher à tout jamais la réalisation du Panslavisme; digue infranchissable s'ils sons unis, dénationalisation et slavisation avant peu, s'ils sont divisés. L'existence des Madjares et des Roumans est au prix seul d'une union intime fortement cimentée, et s'il le faut, ils sauveront la civilisation.

La tendance de domination amenera toujours la lutte et la défiance par là, le triomphe le l'ennemi commun; la confédération, sous le principe d'une liberté absolue, peut seule unir les races; il faut laisser au temps de résoudre les questions de langue et de religion.

Une confédération entre les Croates, les Serbes, les Madjares et les Roumans, voilà ce qui peut garantir toutes ces nationalités individuellement et arrêter le danger qui menace l'Europe.

Se place ici une difficulté qui n'en est une que par les susceptibilités auxquelles elle peut toucher, mais qui deviendra peut-etre cause d'une transaction dont le résultat serait une garantie de plus pour l'existence de cet état et pour l'équilibre Européen. Cette difficulté vient des tendances des Serbes et des Roumans de l'Autriche pour leurs frères des Principautés Turques.

Les Roumans ne rêvent pas indépendance. L'Autriche et la Russie ne demanderait pas mieux que de donner cette tendance aux idées et d'en aider la reussite afin d'en faire plus tard une nouvelle Crimée, ou une autre Cracovie. Une entente entre la Turquie et la Hongrie pour que l'une abandonne quelque chose à l'autre, serait impossible, ou du moins très difficile; elle affaiblirait l'état féderatif, si on lui retirait un de ces elements, et ce serait toucher à la dignite Musulmane que de passer à une renonciation de ses droits sur l'une de ses principautés. Or, quelle est la domination ou la suprématie de la Porte? quelle est la position des Principautés vis-à-vis de la Turquie? Non pas leur position telle qu'elle leur a ete faite par la Russie, mais telle qu'elle résulterait de ses droits. Je ne saurai mieux faire que dicter ici ces capitulations.

Si l'on compare cet état de choses à la position qu'avait la Hongrie vis-à-vis de l'Autriche avant 1848 on la trouverait infiniment meilleure. Les Madjares n'ont jamais joui d'autant de droits de nationalité séparée sous la famille des Habsbourg.

Si l'on pouvait mettre de ce côté la susceptibilité mal comprise de quelques Madjares exclusifs, la suzeraineté de la Porte sur une confédération du Danube comprenant les Madjares, les Croates, les Serbes et les Roumans, serait peut-être tout ce qu'il pourrait en devenir de plus heureux pour l'Europe.

BIBLIOGRAPHY*

I Documents and Bibliography

In the realm of unpublished sources, there is much material on Roumania in the diplomatic and consular reports in the archives of the various European foreign ministries. I consulted only those of London and Paris. At the Roumanian Academy there are many manuscripts of the men of 1848; most of them have been published. The papers of Ion Brătianu for this period are not available to any but a chosen few. At the Academy and in the State Archives at Bucharest there are documents on the revolution of 1848. In the libraries of Paris (*Bibliothèque Nationale, Bibliothèque de la Ville de Paris, Bibliothèque Polonaise*, there is a certain amount of manuscript material on the Roumanians, especially in the correspondence of Michelet and Quinet. The Layard Papers in the British Museum also contain unpublished correspondence concerning the Roumanian question.

As for published documents, two great collections supply a tremendous fund of source material, most of it diplomatic correspondence. These are:

Hurmuzaki, Eudoxiu: *Documente privitoare la Istoria Românilor.* 30 vols. Bucharest, 1876-1922.

For the nineteenth century, vols. X, XVII, XVIII, and Suppl. I, vols. 1-6.

---

*I regret very much not having been able to consult two recent studies which cover approximately the same period as this thesis; they would probably have added much interesting detail, and might even have altered some of the main lines. George Fotino's *Din Vremea Renasterii Nationale a Tării-Românesti, Boerii Golești*, (Bucharest, 1939), is a collection of the correspondence of the Golescu family, three volumes of letters and one volume of commentary. *Raporturile Pasoptistilor cu Ledru Rollin si partizanii săi*, by Olimpiu Boitoș, was, according to the author, to have been published late in 1939. Fotino's work reached me in the last week of March, 1940; that of Boitoș has not yet arrived in America.

Sturdza, D. A., et al: Acte si Documente relative la Istoria Renascere României. 10 vols. Bucharest, 1900-10.

General bibliographical information is scattered. Practically nothing worthwhile was done in that line before the World War.

Querard, J. M.: La Roumanie. Moldavie, Valachie et Transylvanie; Serbie, Monténégro et Bosnie. Essai de bibliothèque (sic) française historique de ces Principautés. Paris, 1857.

Juvara, T. G.: Bibliografia Cestiunei Nationale. Bucharest, 1895.

These two bibliographies are scanty and inaccurate.

Popp, Alexandru: Bibliografia Publicătiunilor Românesti. Bucharest, 1888.

Useful bibliography of newspapers and periodicals. Arranged chronologically.

Hodoş, Nerva, and Sadi Ionescu, Al.: Publicătiile Periodice Româneşti. Bucharest, 1913.

More complete than the work of Popp. Arranged alphabetically.

Since 1920 bibliographical work has been done more methodically. The best bibliographies are in the periodicals Dacoromania (Cluj, 1920 ff.), Anuarul Institutului de Istoria Natională. (Cluj, 1922 ff.), and Revista Istorică Română, (Bucharest 1930 ff.).

The following are also important:

Adamescu, Gheorghe: Contributiune la bibliografia romănească. 3 vols. Bucharest, 1921-28.

Deals chiefly with literature. Arranged by authors.

Georgescu-Tistu, N.: "Pubblicazioni storiche rumene dalla guerra in poi" (Archivio Storico Italiano, Ser. VII, vol.13, 1930, pp. 115-136).

Competent and scholarly.

Teodorescu, Barbu: Bibliografia Iorga. Bucharest, 1937.

Lists Iorga's thousands of books and articles.

Crăciun, Ioachim: Bibliographie de Transylvanie. Cluj, 1937.

A special supplement to the Revue de Transylvanie. vol. IV.

Michoff, Nicolas: Bibliographie des articles de périodiques allemands, anglais, français, et italiens sur la Turquie et la Bulgarie. Sofia, 1938.

This unique and informative work includes notice of articles on the Principalities.

II General Works on Roumanian History

1. Xenopol, A. D.: Istoria Românilor din Dacia Traiană. 6 vols. Jassy, 1888-94. (3rd edition, 14 vols. Bucharest, 1925-30).

The first standard history on a "scientific" basis. On many questions it is unreliable or out of date, but it is quite useful for reference purposes. The Pasoptisti are given laudatory treatment.

2. Iorga, Nicolae: Geschichte des rumänischen Volkes in Rahmen seiner Staatsbildungen. 2 vols. Gotha, 1905.

3. Iorga, N.: Histoire des Roumains et de leur civilisation. Paris, 1920. 2nd. edition, Paris, 1922. English edition, London, 1925. Roumanian edition, enlarged, Bucharest, 1930.

4. Iorga, N.: Istoria Românilor. 9 vols. Bucharest, 1937-1938.

Of these three great "syntheses" by Roumania's best known historian, the first is still in many respects the most satisfactory. The second is very sketchy. The last, his "definitive" history, is the fullest, but gives evidence of having been hastily assembled. It has a good chapter on the period of exile. Volume 9 deals with the period 1834-1859.

5. Seton-Watson, R. W.: A History of the Roumanians. London, 1934.

The best history in English, but unbalanced chronologically and in other ways. It states, but does little to fill, the need for more authoritative information on the work of the men of 1848.

6. Iorga, N.: La Place des Roumains dans l'histoire universelle. 3 vols. Bucharest, 1935-36.

Repeats much of what he says in his other works. Iorga is not infallible, but he is about the only European historian with the requisite knowledge of Roumanian history, and the only Roumanian historian with a broad enough approach to fit Roumania into European history. The work of Constantin Giurescu (Istoria Românilor, 2 vols. to date, 1935-37), which promises to supersede that of Iorga, has been carried only to the beginning of the eighteenth century.

7. Schmidt, Ernst: Die verfassungsrechtliche und politische Struktur des rumänischen Staates in ihrer historischen Entwicklung. Munich, 1932.

A straightforward history from 1812 to history from 1812 to 1832, too brief to be of much value.

III <u>Works on the French Influence, on Roumanian Nationalism, and on the Question of a National Culture</u>.

1. Bengesco, Georges: <u>Bibliographie franco-roumaine</u>. Paris, 1895. 2nd. edition, Brussels, 1907.

   Only volume I of this work appeared. It is a careful work by an experienced bibliographer, far from complete but with many illuminating notes. Periodical articles are not included.

2. Rally, Alexandre et Getta-Helène: <u>Bibliographie franco-roumaine</u>. Vol. I, Parts 1 and 2, Paris, 1930.

   This work is much richer than that of Bengesco in number of titles. It is valuable for reference. It is uncritical and not logically arranged. The authors promise a second volume on periodical articles.

3. Eliade, Pompliu: <u>De l'influence française sur l'esprit publique en Roumanie</u>, 1750-1848. Compiegne, 1897.

   Outline of a project which was completed only up to 1834.

4. Eliade, P.: <u>De l'influence française sur l'esprit publique en Roumanie</u>. Paris, 1898.

5. Eliade, P.: <u>Histoire de l'esprit publique en Roumanie au XUX^e siècle</u>. Vol. I, <u>L'occupation turque et les premiers princes indigènes, 1821-1828</u>. Paris, 1905.

6. Eliade, P.: <u>La Roumanie au XIXe siècle</u>. Vol. II. <u>Les Trois Présidents plénipotentiares, 1828-1834</u>. Paris, 1914.

   These works are of fundamental importance, though their faults are legion. The documentation is bulky but not always well chosen. The author's imagination is fertile and his love of France great.

7. Demetrescu, Alexandre: L'influence de la langue et de la littérature françaises en Roumanie. Lausanne, 1888.

8. Iorga, N.: Histoire des relations entre la France et les Roumains. Paris, 1918.

A convenient outline. The year of publication gives an indication of its tone.

9. Iorga, N.: Etudes Roumaines. I. Influences étrangères sur la nation roumaine. II. Idées et formes littéraires françaises dans le Sud-Est de l'Europe. Paris, 1923-24.

10. Maneș, Vasile V.: Formarea Opiniunii franceze asupra României în secolul al XIX-lea. 2 vols. Craiova, 1929.

The author falls short of his purpose of creating a great synthesis of Franco-Roumanian relations, but he has done a useful service of compilation. The projected later volumes, covering the 1848-1866 period, have never appeared.

11. Defeuilles, Paul, et Lassaigne, Jacques: Les Français et la Roumanie. Bucharest, 1937.

Excerpts from many French works on Roumania.

12. Sturdza, A. A. C.: Le nationalisme roumain au XIXe siècle, 1821-1866. Paris, 1914.

A series of lectures delivered at the Sorbonne.

13. Iorga, N.: Desvoltarea ideii unității politice a Românilor. Valenii de Munte, 1915.

14. Lupaș, Ioan: Istoria Unirii Românilor. Bucharest, 1937.

A popular survey, with emphasis on the tendency toward union through the centuries.

15. Seişanu, Romulus: *Principiul Naţionalităţilor*. Bucharest, 1935.

An historical study with particular emphasis on the Roumanians and the treaty settlements of 1918-20.

16. Roşu, Nicolae: *Dialectica Naţionalismului*. Bucharest, 1935.

Treats the evolution of Roumanian nationalism, the foreign influences, the most eminent representatives.

17. Rădulescu-Motru, C.: *Ideologia Statului Român*. Bucharest, 1934.

18. Rădulescu-Motru, C.: *Românismul*, 2nd. edition, Bucharest, 1939.

These are stimulating works by an eminent Roumanian student of philosophy. Conservative and anti-materialist.

19. Lovinescu, Eugen: *Istoria Civilizaţiei Române*. 3 vols.

Presents the westernizing case and inclines toward an economic interpretation wherever possible.

IV The Revolution of 1848

1. Göllner, Carol: *Anul revoluţionar în principatele române. O contribuţie bibliografică*. Cluj, 1934.

The latest and best bibliography.

2. *Anul 1848 în Principatele Române*, 6 vols. Bucharest 1902-1910.

Although this is not, and could not be, all-inclusive, it is an extraordinarily rich collection of official documents, private correspondence, and excerpts from the contemporary press. Bibliography in Vol. 6, pp. 309-325.

3. Iorga, N.: "Despre Revoluția de la 1848 în Moldova," Acad. Rom., Mem. Sect. Ist., Ser. III, vol. 20, 1938, Mem. 2.

Documents from the district of Fălciiu, supplementing those in Anul 1848.

4. Georgescu, Elvire: "Documents concernant les Principautés Danubiennes au XIXe siècle," Revue Historique du Sud-Est Européen, vol. VIII, 1931, pp.6-30, and vol. XIV, 1937, pp. 125-50.

Documents from the French Foreign Office Archives.

5. Hurmuzaki, Eudoxiu: Documente privitoare la Istoria Românilor, vol. XVIII. Bucharest, 1916.

The above collections give us a wealth of documentary material on the revolution. They may be supplemented by unpublished documents in the archives of the British Foreign Office, the French Foreign Office, and the Roumanian Academy.

The memoir material, including historical accounts and polemics written by contemporaries, is rather extensive. The anti-pașoptist point of view is well represented in the first three accounts listed below.

6. Crutzescu, Radu, (ed.): Amintirile Coloneluui Lăcusteanu, Bucharest, 1935.

7. Voinescu, Ion: Amintirile, (Acad. Rom., Ms. 3828, published in part in Revista Carpatilor, vol. 1, Part 2, Bucharest, 1860, pp. 131 ff.).

8. Iorga, N.: "Un cugetător politic moldovean," Ac. Rom., Mem. Sect. Ist., Ser III, vol. 23, 1932.

Memoirs of Ștefan Dăscălescu, covering the whole period from 1821 to 1860.

9. Ubicini, J. H. A.: "La Valachie en 1848," Le Siècle, Paris, 1857-8, translated into Roumanian, in Anul 1848, V, pp. 787-819.

The author served as secretary to the Provisional Government.

10. Iorga, N.: "Memoriile unui vechiu dascăl," Ac. Rom., Mem. Sect. Ist., Ser. III, vol.15, 1934.

11. Kinezu, Emanuil: Revoluţia din anul 1848 de la Dunare sau misterele politicei în Principate. Bucharest, 1859.

12. Cernătescu, P. I.: Istoria Contimpurană de la anul 1815 până la în zilele noastre. Bucharest, 1871.

Contains some original material on 1848.

The secondary accounts of the events of 1848 are of uneven quality; the most useful ones were written in 1898 on the occasion of the semi-centennial of the revolution.

13. Bibesco, Georges: Règne de Bibesco. Vol. II, pp. 353-457. Paris, 1894.

14. Bibesco, Georges: A propos de l'insurrection de 1848 en Valachie. Réponse a M. A. D. Xénopol. Geneva, 1895.

A scathing denunciation of the Forty-eighters, written in defence of Prince Bibescu by his son.

15. Colescu-Vartic, C.: 1848.Zile revoluţionare.Bucharest, 1898.

Quite competent, considering its appearance before the publication of Anul 1848.

16. [Bibicescu, I. G.]: 1848 în România. Bucharest, 1898.

17. Albini, S.: "Introducere", written to accompany the documents of Anul 1848, published in Vol. 6, pp. I-CXXXVIII.

18. Thenen, Meier: Die Wirren des Jahres 1848 in Rumänien. Berlin, 1911.

A doctoral dissertation, University of Bern. Based entirely on Anul 1848.

19. Göllner, Carol: Revoluția anului 1848 în Principatele Române și ecoul ei în presa săsească. Ms. Diss., University of Cluj, 1933, partially summarized in Revista Istorică, vol. 22, 1936, pp. 105-111.

Göllner adds material found in the Transylvanian Saxon press.

20. Xenopol, A. D.: "Partidele Politice in Revoluția din 1848 în Principatele Române," Ac. Rom., Mem. Sect. Ist, Ser. II, vol.32, 1909.

Really a brief history of the national-liberal movement from 1804 through 1848.

21. Ion, I. C.: "Adevăratul 1848", Viața Românească, Bucharest, XXX, 1938, pp. 7-19 (Feb.), pp. 34-49 (Mar.).

A Marxist interpretation.

Of the pamphlets published in 1848, the following are the most important:

22. [Golescu, A. G.]: Die politische Stellung der Roumainen Moldo-Walachen) gegenüber der Türkei, nach den franz von A. G. Golesco, Mitglied der provisorichen Regierung der Walachei, deutsch bearbeitet von Edward Wolf. Vienna, 1848.

23. [Ghica, N.]: Bemerkungen über die russische Note vom 1931 Juli d. J. in Betreff der Intervention in den romanischen Donaufürstenthümern. Von einem Moldauer. Vienna, 1848.

24. Kogălniceanu, M.: Dorințele partidei naționale în Moldova. Cernăuți, 1848.

The revolutionary press of Bucharest in 1848 is very informative on the question of interpretation of the aims and motives of the Paşoptişti. Monitorul Român, Poporul Suveran (eds, D. Bolintineanu and N. Bălcescu), and Pruncul Român (ed. C. A. Rosetti) were the most important. The Roumanian papers outside the Principalities, namely, Bucovina (ed. Hurmuzachi, Cernăuţi), and Gazeta Transilvaniei (ed. Bariţ, Braşov), are valuable. Of the foreign press, the Allegemeine Zeitung of Augsburg, and the National and Journal des Débats of Paris carried the most extensive news of Roumania. Many of the contemporary newspaper articles have been reproduced in Anul 1848.

V Letters, Memoirs, Biography

1. Iorga, N., et al.: Figuri Revoluţionare Române. Bucharest, 1937.

   Short biographies of Vladimirescu, Câmpineanu, Iancu, and the Brătianu brothers.

2. Arîţescu, C. D.: Corespondenţa secretă şi acte inedite ale capilor revoluţiunii române de la 1848. 3 vols. Bucharest, 1873-74.

   The first valuable collection of the letters of the emigrés.

3. Tăuşan, G., and Lazăr, G.: Ion C. Brătianu, 1821-1891. Bucharest, 1937.

   Very brief and sketchy. Brătianu's biography is yet to be written.

4. Din Scrierile si cuvântările lui Ion C. Brătianu. Part I, 1821-1868. Bucharest, 1903.

5. Lui Ion C. Brătianu, 1821-1891. Bucharest, 1921.

   These two very similar volumes publish the writings and speeches of Brătianu's early career.

6. Fruma, J.: Ion C. Brătianu la Sibiu. Bucharest, 1938.

7. Cantacuzino, Sabina: Din Viața familiei lui I. C. Brătianu. Bucharest, 1933.

Brătianu's family life, written by his daughter.

8. Cretzianu, Al.: Din Arhiva lui Dumitru Brătianu. Bucharest, 1933-34.

A very full and revealing correspondence covering the period 1840-1870, preceded by a biographical sketch.

9. Ulbach, Louis: C. A. Rosetti. Paris, 1885.

A short, laudatory biography.

10. Lui C. A. Rosetti, la o sută de ani de la nașterea lui. Bucharest, 1916.

A commemorative volume, containing selections from his writings, some not previously published, and a 50-page biographical study by A. Ștefanescu-Galați.

11. Rosetti, C. A.: Scrieri din Junețe și Exiliu. 2 vols. 2nd. ed., Bucharest, 1885.

The second volume contains his political writings of the period of exile.

12. Rosetti, C. A.: Note intime, scrise zilnic. 2 vols. Bucharest, 1902, 1916.

Rosetti's personal diary for the years 1844-1859. Factually uninformative but very revealing of the thoughts of a troubled and romantic spirit.

13. Rosetti, C. A.: Amintiri Istorice (ed. Vintilă Rosetti). Bucharest, 1889.

14. Rosetti, C. A.: <u>Pagini din Trecut. Corespondinta.</u> (ed. Vintilă Rosetti). Bucharest, 1902.

These two volumes contain a few of the letters of Rosetti not destroyed by fire. Others are at the Roumanian Academy, still unpublished.

15. Bengescu, George: <u>Une famille de boyards lettrés roumains au XIXe siècle. Les Golesco</u>. Paris, 1922.

A sympathetic treatment, giving most attention to the literary members of the family.

16. Fotino, George: <u>Din Vremea renasterii nationale a Țării-Românesti. Boerii Golesti</u>. 4 vols.

See footnote at beginning of bibliography.

17. Panaitescu, P.P.: <u>Contributii la o biografie a lui N. Bălcescu</u>. Bucharest, 1924.

A very careful and scholarly biography.

18. Bălcescu, N.: <u>Patru Studii istorice</u>. Bucharest,

Some of Bălcescu's short historical works edited with a biographical introduction by P. P. Panaitescu.

19. Bălcescu, N.: <u>Scrisori către Ion Ghica</u>. Bucharest, 1911.

A popular edition in convenient form of Bălcescu's letters taken from Ghica's memoirs.

20. Cartojan, N.: <u>N. Bălcescu si Ion Ghica. Scrisori inedite</u>. Bucharest, 1913.

A small number of Bălcescu and Ghica letters not previously published.

21. Georgescu-Tistu, N.: <u>Ion Ghica. Scriitorul</u>. Bucharest, 1935.

A short, scholarly work of biography and literary criticism. Some of Ghica's letters are published in an appendix.

22. Ghica, Ion: Scrisori către Vasile Alecsandri. 2nd ed., Bucharest, 1887.

Ghica's memoirs, in the form of letters. Written long after the events they describe and not wholly reliable.

23. Ghica, Ion: Amintiri din Pribegia după 1848. Bucharest, 1889.

This is indispensable because of the great number of letters and documents it contains.

24. Alecsandri, Vasile: La France Jugée à l'étranger, 1855-1885. Lettres inédites du poète roumain à Edouard Grenier. Paris, 1911.

25. Zotta, Sever: La Centenarîul lui Vasile Alecsandri, 1821-1921. Jassy, 1921.

26. Petrașcu, N.: Vasile Alecsandri. 2nd ed., Bucharest, nid.

These two studies are more concerned with Alecsandri's poetry than with his politics.

27. Bogdan-Duică, G.: Vasile Alecsandri. Povestirea unei vieți. Bucharest, 1926.

The best biography of Alecsandri, adding much hitherto unpublished material.

28. Marcu, Alexandru: V. Alecsandri și Italia. Bucharest, 1927.

In the process of recounting Alecsandri's connections with Italy, the author writes a good biography.

29. Russo, Alexandru: Scrieri (ed. P. V. Haneș). Bucharest, 1934.

Contains his memoirs, reflections, and the Cântarea României.

30. Haneș, Petru V.: Alexandru Russo. O pagină ignorată din literatura română. Bucharest, 1902. (2nd. ed., 1930).

31. Kogălniceanu, Mihail: Scrisori, 1834-1849. Bucharest, 1913.

A very important source. The only complete series of letters we have describing the period of study in the West.

32. Iorga, N.: Mihail Kogălniceanu. Scriitorul, Omul politic și Românul. Bucharest, 1921.

33. Dragnea, Radu: Mihail Kogălniceanu. 2nd ed., Bucharest, 1927.

Analysis and comment overshadow the factual narrative. This may be considered the best biography of Kogălniceanu until the work of N. Cartojan appears.

34. Negri, Costache: Versuri, Proză, Scrisori. Bucharest, 1909.

Contains letters important for diplomatic history.

35. Papadopol-Calimach, A.: "Amintiri despre Costache Negri", Revista Nouă, Bucharest, Vol. 2, 1889, pp. 321-34, 385-93, 441-5.

36. Lovinescu, Eugen: Grigore Alexandrescu.

Contains many letters from Alexandrescu to Ion Ghica.

37. Bolintineanu, Dimitrie: Călătorii pe Dunare și în Bulgaria. Bucharest, 1858.

38. Cartojan, N.: "Scrisori ale lui D. Bolintineanu", Neamul Românesc Literar, I, 1909, No. 6; III, 1911, No. 3,4,5.

39. Petrașcu, N.: Dimitrie Bolintineanu. Bucharest, 1932.

A sketchy biography which passes over many points of interest.

40. Kretzulescu, Nicolae: Amintiri istorice. Bucharest,

Throws some light on the activities of the students in Paris.

41. Xenopol, A. D.: Nicolae Kretzulescu. Viața și faptele lui, 1812-1900. Bucharest, 1915.

A solid biography. The emphasis is on his later career as a statesman.

42. Eliade Rădulescu, Ioan: Mémoires sur l'histoire de la régénération roumaine. Paris, 1851.

A highly colored personal account, in which the author's opponents come out second best.

43. Eliade Rădulescu, Ioan: Echilibru între antiteze. 2 vols. Bucharest, 1859, 1869.

A mass of half-formed theories mixed with autobiography.

44. Eliade Rădulescu, Ioan: Scrisori din Exil. Bucharest, 1894.

These letters, edited by N. B. Locusteanu, give us information on Eliade's life in Paris, in Constantinople, and at Chios.

45. Vîrtosu, Emil: I. Heliade Rădulescu. Acte și scrisori adnotate și publicate. Bucharest, 1928.

Scattered letters from all periods of Eliade's career, the bulk of them forming a supplement to the letters from exile already published.

46. Locusteanu, N.B.: Ioan Heliade și detractorii săi. Craiova, 1898.

Eliade is defended by a loyal disciple.

47. Scraba, G.: Ion Heliade Rădulescu. Inceputurile filosofie și sociologiei romîne. Bucharest, 1921.

48. Oprescu, Gheorghe: Eliade Rădulescu și Franța. Cluj, 1923.

A detailed study of the influence on Eliade of French thought and French literature, and of his own direct contacts with France.

49. Popovici, D.: <u>Ideologia Literară a lui I.Heliade Rădulescu</u>. Bucharest, 1935.

A brilliant and carefully documented monograph.

50. Crețu, I.: <u>Viața lui Eliade</u>. Bucharest, 1939.

51. Lovinescu, Eugen: <u>Gheorghe Asachi</u>. <u>Viața și opera lui</u>. Bucharest, 1921.

An authoritative work.

52. Bănescu, N., and Mihăilescu, V.: <u>Ioan Maiorescu. Scriere comemorativă cu prilejul centenariului lui, 1811-1911</u>. Bucharest, 1912.

A laudatory biography with several documents annexed.

53. Sion, Gheorghe: <u>Suvenire contimpurane</u>. Bucharest, 1888.

Interesting material on the Moldavian exiles in 1848-9.

54. Bogdan-Duică, G.: <u>Viața și Opera întâiului țărănist român</u>. Craiova, 1922.

Analyzes and summarizes Ionescu's theories, treating him as a forerunner of the peasant party.

VI <u>Writings of the Exiles and Students, 1849-1858</u>.

<u>1849</u>

1. Eliade et al.: <u>Mémoire justificatif de la révolution roumaine du 11/23 juin 1848</u>. Paris.

2. Eliade et al.: <u>Lettre au Ministre des Affaires Etrangères de France sur l'occupation des principautés danubiennes par la Russie</u>. Paris.

3. Brătianu, D. et al.: A l'assemblée législative de la République française. Paris.

4. Brătianu, D.: Documents concerning the Danubian Principalities. London.

5. Eliade Rădulescu: Souvenirs et Impressions d'un Proscrit. Paris.

1850

6. Eliade Rădulescu: Le Protectorat du Czar, ou la Roumanie et la Russie. Paris.

7. Eliade Rădulescu: Résurrection des Peuples. La Roumanie renaissante. Paris.

8. Bălcescu, Nicolae: Question économique des Principautés Danubiennes. Paris.

9. Bălcescu, N., et al.: România Viitoare. Paris.

10. Rosetti, C. A.: Apel la oamenii cei liberi. Paris.

11. Idem: Domnilor Eliade și Tell. Paris.

12. Idem: Apel la toate partidele, urmat de Încrederea în sine. Paris.

13. Idem: Epistolă domnului Barbu Stirbei. Paris.

14. Idem: A doua epistolă domnului Barbu Stirbei. Paris.

15. Golescu, Ştefan: Un mot sur le manifeste de M.Stirbey, prince régnant de Valachie. Paris.

16. Golescu, Ştefan: Lettre à MM. les rédacteurs de tous les journaux de la presse parisienne. Paris.

1851

17. Eliade Rădulescu: Epistole și acte alle ómenilor mișcării române din 1848. Paris.

18. Eliade Rădulescu: Mémoires sur l'histoire de la régénération roumaine. Paris.

19. Rosetti, C. A.: *A treia epistolă domnului Barbu Stirbei*. Paris.

20. Brătianu, I. C., et al.: *Republica Română*. No. 1. Paris.

21. Florescu, D., et al.: *Junimea Română*. Paris.

22. Bolintineanu, D., et al.: *Albumul Pelerinilor*. Paris.

23. Bolintineanu, D.: *Proclamation aux Roumains au sujet du retrait des troupes russes des Principautés Danubiennes*. Paris.

24. Brătianu, D., & Iranyi, D.: *Lettres hongro-roumaines*. Paris.

1853

25. Chainoi, G. (Ion Ghèca): *Dernière Occupation des Principautés Danubiennes*. Paris.

26. *Republica Română*. No. 2. Brussels.

27. *Letters of D. Bratiano and Lord Dudley Stuart*. Manchester.

1854

28. [Filipescu, Constantin]: *Mémoire sur les conditions d'existence des Principautés Danubiennes*. Paris.

29. Bolintineanu, D.: *Les Principautés roumaines*. Paris.

30. Eliade Rădulescu: *Une Dacie cosaque et une Roumanie turcophile*. Constantinople.

1855

31. Grădișteanu, G.: *Mémoire relatif à la solution de la question moldo-valaque dans l'intérêt de l'équilibre européen.* Paris.

32. Brătianu, I. C.: Mémoire sur l'empire d'Autriche dans la question d'Orient. Paris.

33. Rousso, N.: Suite ou supplément à l'histoire politique et sociale des Principautés Danubiennes de M. Elias Regnault. Brussels.

1856

34. Golescu, A. G.: De l'abolition du servage dans les Principautés Danubiennes. Paris.

35. B[olintineanu, D.]: L'Autriche, la Turquie et les Moldo-Valaques. Paris.

36. Boerescu, Vasile: Mémoire relatif à la question politique et économique de la Moldo-Valaquie. Paris.

37. Boerescu, Vasile: La Roumanie après le traité de Paris. Précédé d'une introduction par M. Royer-Collard. Paris.

38. Kogălniceanu, M., and Ionescu, N.: L'Etoile du Danube. Brussels (1856-58).

39. Eliade Rădulescu (ed.): Conservatorul. Constantinople (1856-57).

40. Boliac, C.: Memoires pour servir à l'histoire de la Roumanie. I. Topographie de la Roumanie. Paris.

41. Boliac, C.: Choix de Lettres et Mémoires sur la Question Roumaine, 1852-1856. Paris.

42. Golescu, N.: Mémoire adressé à l'Empereur Napoléon III. Paris.

43. Magheru, G.: Reponse à la circulaire de la Porte Ottomane.

44. Snagoveanu, Iosaphat: Discours prononcé dans l'Eglise roumaine de Paris. Paris.

1857

45. Boliac, C. (ed.): Buciumul. Paris.

46. Urechia, V. A. (ed.): Opiniunea. Paris.

47. [Brătianu, D. ?] Documents pour servir à l'histoire de l'Artièle 24 du traité de Paris en Moldavie. London.

48. Brătianu, D. Lettres sur la circulaire de la Porte du 31 juillet 1856, relative à la réorganisation des Principautés. Berlin.

49. Brătianu, I. C.: Mémoire sur la situation de la Moldo-Valachie depuis le Traité de Paris. Paris.

50. Boerescu, V.: Le Firman turc pour la convocation des Divans ad hoc des Principautés du Danube. Paris.

51. [Eliade Rădulescu]: A. M. Saint-Marc Girardin. Constantinople.

52. Maiorescu, I., & Hurmuzachi, C.: Desvoltarea Drepturilor Principatelor Moldo-Române în urmă tratatului de la Paris. Brussels.

1858.

53. [Bălăceanu, I.]: Lettres sur les Principautés à M. le Chevalier Vegezzi Ruscalla. Geneva.

54. Brătianu, D. & Golescu, N.: Documents concerning the Danubian Principalities. London.

55. Strat, J.: Un coup d'oeil sur la question roumaine. Paris.

56. Boerescu, Constantin: Les Principautés devant le second congrès de Paris. Paris.

57. Boerescu, V.: Examen de la convention du 19 aout, relative à l'organisation des Principautés danubiennes. Paris.

VII <u>Works directly inspired by the Roumanian Exiles</u>

1. Desprez, Hippolyte: <u>La Révolution dans l'Europe orientale</u>. Paris, 1848.

2. [Birkbeck, W. L.]: <u>The Russians in Moldavia and Wallachia</u>. London, 1849.

3. Desprez, H.: <u>Les peuples de l'Autriche et de la Turquie</u>. (chaptersoon the Roumanians) Paris, 1850.

4. Lévy, Armand: <u>La Russie sur le Danube</u>. Paris, 1853.

5. Michelet, Jules: <u>Principautés Danubiennes. Madame Rosetti, 1848</u>. Paris, 1853.

6. Regnault, Elias: <u>Histoire politique et sociale des Principautés Danubiennes</u>. Paris, 1855.

7. Ubicini, J. H. A.: <u>Provinces d'origine roumaine</u>. Paris, 1856. (<u>Univers pittoresque</u>, vol.39).

8. Bataillard, Paul: <u>Premier point de la question d'Orient. Les principautés de Moldavie et de Valachie devant le Congrès</u>. Paris, 1856.

9. Bataillard, Paul: <u>La Moldo-Valachie dans la manifestation de ses efforts et de ses voeux</u>. Paris, 1856.

10. Texier, Edmond: <u>Appel au congrès en faveur des Roumains</u>. Paris, 1856.

11. Quinet, Edgar: <u>Les Roumains</u>. Paris, 1856.

12. Melik, A.: <u>L'Orient devant l'Occident</u>. Paris, 1856.

13. Bataillard, Paul: <u>De la situation regulière de la Moldo-Valachée vis-à-vis de la Porte</u>. Brussels, 1857.

14. Ubicini, J. H. A.: <u>La question des principautés devant l'Europe</u>. Paris, 1858.

15. [Lévy, Armand]: L'Empereur Napoléon III et les principautés roumaines. Paris, 1858.

16. Regnault, Elias: Mystères diplomatiques aux bords du Danube. Paris, 1858.

VIII Monographs of special importance for this subject

1. Filitti, Ioan, C.: Domniile Române sub Regulamental Organic, 1834-1848. Bucharest, 1915.

A badly organized but rich mass of material on the Règlement period.

2. Panaitescu, P.P.: Planurile lui Ioan Câmpineanu pentru Unitatea Natională a Romănilor. Cluj, 1924.

3. Idem: Emigrația Polona și Revoluția Română de la 1848.

These two works are based principally on material in the Czartoryski archives dealing with the Roumanian national movement in its European setting, particularly in relation to the Polish emigration.

4. Breazu, Ion: "Edgar Quinet et les Roumains", Mélanges de l'Ecole Roumaine en France. Paris, pp. 213-401.

5. Breazu, Ion: Michelet și Romănii. Cluj, 1935.

Two careful studies of the relations between the Roumanian students and their "dear masters". The work on Michelet deals more extensively with his literary influence.

6. Boitoș, Olimpiu: "Paul Bataillard et la Révolution roumaine de 1848," Mélanges de l'Ecole Roumaine en France, 1929, pt. 2, pp. 1-158.

7. Boitoș, Olimpiu: Raporturile Pașoptiștilor cu Ledru Rollin și partizanii săi. Bucharest, 1940.

See note on first page of this bibliography.

8. Smochină, N. P.: "Sur les emigrés roumains à Paris de 1850 à 1856", Mélanges de l'Ecole Roumaine en France, 1933, pp. 155-203.

Deals only with a few specific incidents, notably the trial of Ion Brătianu.

9. Corivan, N.: Din Activitatea Emigranților Români în Apus 1853-1857. Bucharest, 1931.

Publishes several documents from the archives of the Ministère des Affaires Etrangères, Paris, chiefly mémoires submitted by Roumanians in 1855 and 1856.

10. Marcu, Alexandru: Conspiratori și Conspirații în Epoca Renașterii Politice a României, 1848-1877. Bucharest, 1930.

An informative work, based almost wholly on Italian sources. "Mazzini, Cavour, and the Roumanian question" would be a title more descriptive of the contents of the book.